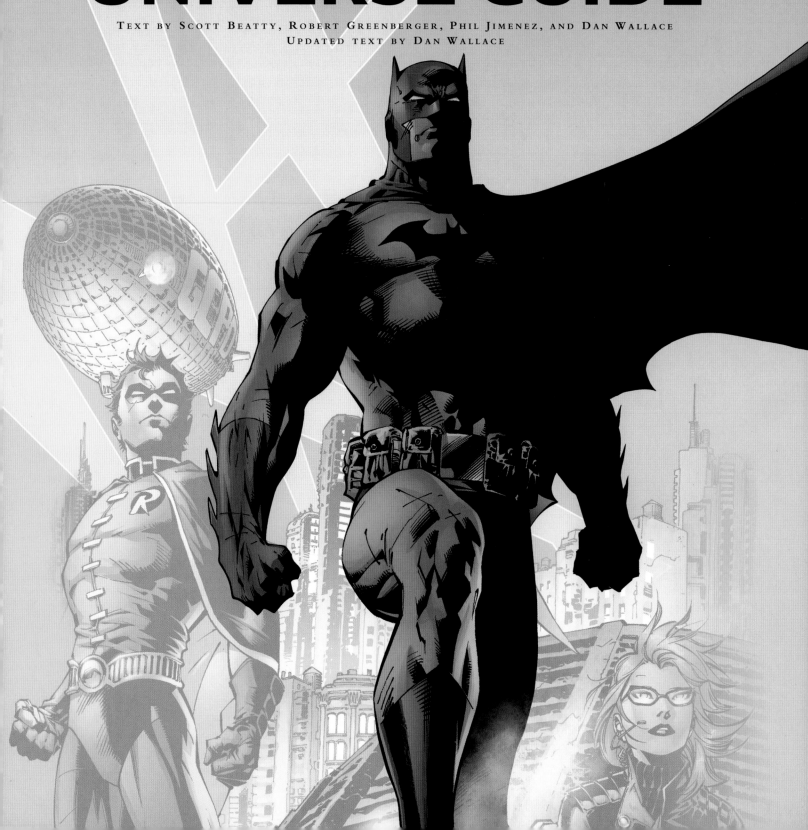

DC COMICS
UNIVERSE GUIDE

Text by Scott Beatty, Robert Greenberger, Phil Jimenez, and Dan Wallace
Updated text by Dan Wallace

CONTENTS

AUTHORS' INTRODUCTION

DC COMICS TRACES its publishing history back to 1935; however, the mythology that links literally thousands of comics and characters together now stretches from the Big Bang to the end of time itself!

Of course, it was not the original intention for there to be a continuity that linked Batman to the Seven Soldiers of Victory or Adam Strange to Angel & The Ape; this process began gradually. In 1940, during comics' Golden Age (which ran from the 1930s to the mid-1950s), All American Comics—then a sister company of DC—gathered its greatest heroes together to swap stories at the monthly meeting of the Justice Society of America. That story, in *All Star Comics #3*, was the first time DC's main characters had spoken to one another. By the next issue, they had banded together; however, each mission required them to work on their own in chapters usually drawn by the series artist. And since there was little in the way of character development or recurring plot lines, the stories were fairly static.

Stan Lee changed all that. In 1961, when he started writing the adventures of the Fantastic Four, Spider-Man, Thor and others at Marvel Comics, he allowed his characters to refer to each other. Crossovers between characters, all operating out of New York City at the same period in time, offered rich story possibilities. And so the Marvel Universe was born.

By the late 1960s, DC editors began linking events from one book to another. This process accelerated rapidly as plots became more complex and characters more rounded; suddenly it was not unusual to have explanatory footnotes, which might refer a reader to the previous month, or as far back as 1945! As DC acquired properties from other companies (Captain Marvel and Blue Beetle among others), their characters and backstories were added to the expanding DC Universe, providing fresh grist for the mill.

However, after a while, the interrelatedness of stories and characters from one book to another threatened to become so complex that readers couldn't tell the players and their worlds without a scorecard! Occasional "reboots" of characters by new creative teams wanting to put their own stamp on their favorite heroes only added to the confusion.

By the mid-1980s, DC felt the situation was getting out of hand and a new storyline was introduced, the *Crisis on Infinite Earths*, to limit characters and action

to one earth and one timeline. DC also reintroduced its top characters to a new generation. Frank Miller and David Mazzucchelli's *Batman: Year One*, George Perez & Greg Potter's *Wonder Woman*, and John Byrne's *Superman* loudly told readers to forget the past; new legends were about to begin. Since then, some of those reinvention have been modified again as seen in the Superman: Birthright series. And the entire Universe received a sprucing up in a 2004 mini-series *Identity Crisis*.

The *DC Comics Encyclopedia* spans the timeline of the DC Universe. The facts about characters' pasts, powers and personalities are current, as of early 2004 and, since DC continues to publish monthly, some facts may change over the next few years. We've worked closely with the editors to make sure we're reflecting the right information, so if you remember an incident differently than as reported here, it probably means circumstances were retrofitted to work within the current framework of the DC Universe.

We would have loved to include every DC character of any significance, but, sadly, this was impossible. However we have selected well over one thousand of DC's finest heroes villains, and team-ups, every one illustrated by great DC artists past and present. The *DC Comics Encyclopedia* is devised to run chronologically from A to Z, with a comprehensive index. The most important characters, such as Superman, Batman, the JLA, have their own double-page features; each major character has an entire page, and each supporting character has a panel or entry. Each character also has his or her own data box detailing key facts and special powers. In addition there are several themed double-page features on topics such as vehicles, battles, bases, team-ups, and romances.

So, if you can't find a favorite weird little character from way back when, we hope these packed pages will offer you plenty in the way of compensation, celebrating, as they do, more than 70 years of fun, excitement and comic-book history.

Scott Beatty
Robert Greenberger
Phil Jimenez
Dan Wallace

ALL-STAR SQUADRON

FIRST APPEARANCE JUSTICE LEAGUE OF AMERICA #193 (All-Star Squadron) (August 1981); YOUNG ALL-STARS #1 (Young All-Stars) (June 1987)

STATUS Hero team (disbanded) **BASE** New York City

NOTABLE MEMBERS AND POWERS

Amazing Man I (Will Everett) Able to transform himself into any material he touched.

Commander Steel (Hank Heywood) Injured body repaired with steel alloy frame and micro-motor muscles.

Firebrand II (Danette Reilly) Possessed power of flight and the ability to create and control flames.

Hawkgirl I (Sheira Sanders Hall) Flew with artificial wings and "Ninth metal" anti-gravity belt.

Johnny Quick (Johnny Chambers) Speed and flight enabled by speaking speed formula "3X2(9YZ)4A."

Liberty Belle (Libby Belle Lawrence) Superstrength, agility, and ability to project sonic pulses.

Plastic Man (Eel O'Brian) Superpliable and rubbery resilient body.

Robotman I (Dr. Robert Crane, a.k.a. Paul Dennis) Powerful robotic frame housed human brain.

Shining Knight (Sir Justin/Justin Arthur) Rode winged steed Victory while wielding enchanted armor and sword.

Tarantula I (Jonathan Law) Masked vigilante armed with web-line emitting web-gun.

Following Imperial Japan's sneak attack on Pearl Harbor in 1941, U.S. President Franklin D. Roosevelt called upon all active "Mystery Men"—the costumed heroes and heroines of America, including the entire membership of the Justice Society of America—to band together as a unified fighting force to combat the Axis powers bent upon dominating the world. Both on the home front and in top-secret missions on the battlefields and behind enemy lines, the Squadron—which included more than fifty members at its most powerful—answered only to F.D.R. and the War Department. Many of its greatest adventures are still classified decades later.

THE PERISPHERE

During its tour of duty, the All-Star Squadron was based in New York City and held court in the Perisphere, a hollow sphere 200 feet in diameter built for the 1939-1940 New York World's Fair. The Perisphere included living quarters for all active members of the Squadron. The 610-foot Trylon, a spire erected next to the Perisphere, served to house the team's All-Star Special, a modified Curtiss XP-55 Ascender aircraft outfitted with a Star-Rocket Racer motor courtesy of Pat Dugan (Stripesy), adult sidekick of Squadron member the Star-Spangled-Kid.

EARLY DAYS Dr. Mid-Nite, Hawkman, and Atom pore over pictures of potential recruits.

THE YOUNG ALL-STARS

In 1942, the All-Star Squadron found its ranks bolstered by an influx of younger heroes, a splinter group of "Young All-Stars" whose primary focus was thwarting the superpowered group of German, Italian, and Japanese soldiers dubbed "Axis Amerika." Among the Young All-Stars ranks were the atomic-punching Dyna-Mite, the furry-winged Flying Fox, the powerhouse Fury, the nigh-indestructible "Iron" Munro, the aquatic avenger Neptune Perkins, and the Japanese-American tidal wave-wielding Tsunami. Together, these young heroes did their part to protect the home front from Axis aggression. Both the adult All-Star Squadron and its youthful counterpart disbanded following the conclusion of hostilities. SB

FIENDISH FOES Among the Squadron's numerous nemeses were Night and Fog, Nazi siblings who served as Hitler's superpowered assassins.

1) The Atom 2) Amazing Man 3) Johnny Thunder 4) Dr. Fate 5) Green Lantern 6) Plastic Man 7) Robotman 8) Liberty Belle 9) Firebrand 10) Steel 11) Guardian 12) Hourman 13) Tarantula 14) Hawkgirl 15) Hawkman 16) Shining Knight

KEY STORYLINES
• ALL-STAR SQUADRON #4 (DECEMBER 1981) The Squadron first battles the Dragon King.
• JUSTICE LEAGUE OF AMERICA #207-209, ALL-STAR SQUADRON #14-15 (OCT.-DEC. 1982) The Squadron teams with the modern-day JLA and JSA to prevent Per Degaton from unleashing a nuclear nightmare and altering the course of history.

AMAZO

FIRST APPEARANCE THE BRAVE AND THE BOLD #30 (June 1960)
STATUS Villain **REAL NAME** None
OCCUPATION Adventurer **BASE** Mobile
HEIGHT 8ft **WEIGHT** 485 lbs **EYES** Red **HAIR** None
SPECIAL POWERS/ABILITIES Absorption cells throughout Amazo's synthetic body permit the android to replicate the special abilities of any super-beings in his immediate proximity. With every hero or heroine encountered, Amazo becomes even more powerful and virtually unstoppable.

The android dubbed "Amazo" was built by rogue scientist Professor Ivo in his quest to achieve immortality. Powered by Ivo's patented absorption cells, Amazo first set out to fulfill his maker's prime directive by duplicating the superpowers belonging to the founding membership of the Justice League of America, energies Ivo hoped would grant him eternal life. Despite facing a single foe as mighty as the team in its entirety, the JLA defeated Amazo and lulled him into an electronic slumber. Over the years since his creation, Amazo has emerged from this digital dormancy on various occasions, upgrading himself with new abilities depending on the JLA's ever-changing roster, and continuing to do Professor Ivo's preprogrammed bidding by attempting to destroy the world's greatest super heroes. In a recent battle with the JLA, Amazo faced the League's entire roll call, including reservists and part-time members, thus tripling the amount of powers he absorbed. Professor Ivo failed to combine Amazo with Red Tornado II's body to make an indestructible shell for Solomon Grundy. Ivo also created Amazo's cyborg "son," who lived as a college student before embracing his identity of Kid Amazo. **SB**

LIKE FATHER Amazo's son meets the JLA.

AMAZONS

FIRST APPEARANCE (historical) ALL-STAR COMICS #8 (Winter 1941); (current) Wonder Woman (2nd series) #1 (February, 1987)
STATUS Heroes **BASE** Themyscira
CURRENT MEMBERS AND POWERS (See key)

The Amazons were created in 1,200 bc by a collection of five Olympian goddesses to teach mankind equality, justice, and peaceful harmony. Three thousand in number, the Amazons built the city of Themyscira and established a powerful nation-state in ancient Greece. The Amazons were led by Queen Hippolyta and her sister Antiope.

Heracles and his men, under the influence of the evil war god Ares, seduced the Amazons and ransacked Themyscira. Craving vengeance, Antiope, along with a bloodthirsty faction of Amazons, pursued Heracles to Attica. Hippolyta and her Amazons, following the decree of their goddesses, instead settled on a remote island. Hippolyta's Amazons rebuilt Themyscira (see Amazing Bases, pp. 72–3), and, granted immortality by their goddesses, were charged with guarding the gate to Pandora's Box, housed beneath their new home.

3,000 years later, as Ares plotted to destroy the world in a nuclear war, Hippolyta's daughter Diana became Themyscira's champion, known to "Patriarch's World" as Wonder Woman. After Wonder Woman ended Ares's threat to the world, and also destroyed the hellish creatures within Pandora's Box, the Amazons opened their shores to the outside world for the first time in 3,000 years.

After several attempts at cultural exchange with Patriarch's World, Antiope's descendants, a warrior tribe of Amazon assassins nestled in Egypt, were transported to Themyscira by Circe. Soon after, Darkseid invaded Paradise Island, killing half the Amazons. The two tribes of Amazons forged an uneasy peace to help defend Earth from the threat of Imperiex (see Great Battles, pp. 186–7), and joined forces when several goddesses remade Themyscira, transforming it into an interdimensional university devoted to the exchange of knowledge, where the Amazons continued to promote their peaceful ideals. The Amazons invaded Washington DC under the orders of a resurrected Hippolyta, earning the wrath of Athena (Granny Goodness in disguise), who banished many to live lives as mortal women. **PJ**

NOTABLE AMAZONS PAST AND PRESENT
1) Cydippe (handmaiden) 2) Myrrha (deceased)
3) Pallas (artisan) 4) Mala (friend to Diana)
5) Clio (scribe) 6) Timandra (architect)
7) Mnemosyne (historian) 8) Aella (warrior)
9) Niobe (priestess) 10) Oenone (botanist)
11) Epione (physician) 12) Pythia (philosopher)
13) Euboea (warrior) 14) Penelope (priestess)
15) Ipthime (deceased) 16) Archon Phillipus
17) Menalippe (deceased)

AMBUSH BUG

FIRST APPEARANCE DC COMICS PRESENTS #52 (July 1983)
STATUS Would-be hero **REAL NAME** Irwin Schwab
OCCUPATION Adventurer **BASE** Metropolis
HEIGHT 5ft 10in **WEIGHT** 145 lbs **EYES** Green **HAIR** None
SPECIAL POWERS/ABILITIES Can teleport anywhere on Earth (exact limits are not defined); green suit provides some protection against attack.

Irwin Schwab somehow came into possession of a green suit filled with miraculous technology that protected the wearer from harm and allowed him to teleport around the world. Unfortunately, this was a case of the right tool in the wrong hands. Schwab's major character defect is his lack of linear logic, which gives him a skewed picture of the world. However, Schwab knows enough to want to use his costume and special abilities in the cause of good. Unfortunately, although he aspires to being a super hero, he always seems to get caught up in complicated events. Following the Infinite Crisis, Ambush Bug joined the short-lived replacement Justice League of America led by Firestorm. **RG**

PEST Ambush Bug tormented Superman before beginning his journey to become a hero.

ANIMAL MAN

DEFENDER OF THE RED

FIRST APPEARANCE STRANGE ADVENTURES #180 (September 1965)
STATUS Hero **REAL NAME** Bernhard "Buddy" Baker
OCCUPATION Stunt man; adventurer **BASE** Montana
HEIGHT 5ft 11½ in **WEIGHT** 172 lbs **EYES** Blue **HAIR** Blond
SPECIAL POWERS/ABILITIES Able to tap into the Lifeweb and temporarily replicate the powers and abilities of any animal on Earth.

ANIMAL ANTICS *Animal Man in his happier days, when being a super hero was a low-risk adventure compared with his later career. He had a reputation for sending fruit baskets after team-ups.*

THE PUBLIC STORY of Animal Man's origins is that an alien spaceship crashed in the Adirondack Mountains, in upstate New York, near film stuntman Buddy Baker, imbuing him with the ability to adapt and use animal powers. He then donned a costume and became Animal Man, part-time rocker and part-time hero. The truth is a little different. Buddy was actually the recipient of a spell cast by an ancient shaman that somehow connected him to the Lifeweb, or the Morphogenetic Field, a major source of primordial power. For former rocker turned stuntman Buddy, this was a life-altering experience that still has amazing repercussions for him and for his family.

MAKING A DIFFERENCE

After a time, Buddy retired his Animal Man costume and married Ellen Frazier, his longtime love. Ellen found work as an illustrator while Buddy did stunts for the movies, and they made a home in San Diego, California, raising their children, Cliff and Maxine. Buddy was persuaded to resume his Animal Man role by the Immortal Man, eventually joining Justice League Europe (*see* Justice League of America). Unlike most other heroes, Buddy was quite open about his alter ego, and his kids were well aware of their dad's extracurricular activities.

Over time, Buddy became increasingly concerned about the planet's animal life and the plight of endangered species. He combatted illegal hunting and animal testing aided by other heroes, such as Vixen. During these crusading days, he learned of his connection to the Morphogenetic Field from the scientist James Highwater. This knowledge further expanded Buddy's horizons, making him aware of his vital link to all life on Earth and his position as a role model for other activists.

A friend suggested Buddy start a new church to spread the word, and thus was born the Life Power Church of Maxine. This led to a pilgrimage and a relocation to the wilds of Montana. This upheaval had unforeseen effects on Buddy's life, including an extramarital affair with his friend Annie, which led to the birth of his second daughter (considered a human incarnation of the World Soul). Following the Infinite Crisis, Buddy spent a year stranded in space alongside Adam Strange and Starfire, fighting to end the menace of Lady Styx. He has since returned home to Ellen and his children. **RG**

WILD THING *Just learning to master his power, Buddy Baker handles runaway zoo attractions.*

ANIMAL INSTINCT *Buddy displays his power by getting close enough to a dog and impressing his wife, Ellen.*

KEY STORYLINES

• **STRANGE ADVENTURES #180 (SEPTEMBER 1965):** Buddy Baker first gains his animal powers.
• **ANIMAL MAN #1-9 (SEPTEMBER 1988–MARCH 1989):** Buddy returns to super-heroics as his family adjusts to events such as having a JLA transporter delivered to the house.
• **ANIMAL MAN #51-55 (SEPTEMBER 1992–JANUARY 1993):** Animal Man learns of his connection to the Red.

ANTHRO

FIRST APPEARANCE SHOWCASE #74 (May 1968)
STATUS Hero **REAL NAME** Anthro
OCCUPATION First boy on Earth **BASE** Prehistoric Earth
HEIGHT 5ft 2in **WEIGHT** 137 lbs **EYES** Brown **HAIR** Brown
SPECIAL POWERS/ABILITIES Skilled hunter and tracker.

RUNNING AMOK
Anthro's tendency to get in over his head nearly caused the destruction of the entire Bear tribe in a woolly mammoth stampede.

Anthro was the first of the Cro-Magnons, who would one day give rise to modern man. His father was a Neanderthal, the chief of the Bear tribe, and his mother was a mysterious figure from a tribe long thought destroyed. The Bear tribe viewed this strongly-built boy with suspicion, and Anthro had to push himself hard to win the respect of his tribe mates and his father, Ne-Ahn. Anthro's family included his brother Lart, his stepmother, Emba, and his uncle Do-Ahn. In time he met Embra, a Cro-Magnon like himself, and the two fell in love and married. During the Crisis (see Great Battles, pp. 186–7), Anthro experienced a number of temporal shifts that baffled him. Anthro recently appeared in the 21st century and joined a strange team of outcasts led by Doctor Thirteen. **DW**

ANTITHESIS

FIRST APPEARANCE TEEN TITANS (1st series) #53 (1978)
STATUS Villain **REAL NAME** Unrevealed
OCCUPATION Malevolent entity **BASE** Limbo
HEIGHT Variable **WEIGHT** Variable **EYES** Red **HAIR** None
SPECIAL POWERS/ABILITIES Telepathy; mental manipulation; psychic vampire that feeds off negative emotions.

The vile creature known only as the Antithesis was mysteriously imprisoned in the Justice League of America's computer mainframe. Unable to free itself, the Antithesis, whose past remains shrouded in secrecy, contacted Bromwell Stikk through his own computer. The Antithesis gave a mystical staff to Stikk, the fanatical descendant of a colonial landowner, who tried to enslave the youth of the town of Hatton Corners. Calling himself Mister Twister, Stikk was defeated and humiliated by the first Teen Titans. The Antithesis then used his powers to mentally manipulate the JLA, and the heroes went on a crime spree. The Titans stopped them, however, and, under Robin's leadership, hurled the Antithesis into Limbo, where the creature vowed vengeance against the Boy Wonder and his teenage teammates.

Soon after, the Antithesis transported the defeated Mister Twister into Limbo and

transformed Stikk into the hideous Gargoyle. The Gargoyle battled the Titans while using the mystical powers of the Antithesis. In their most recent attack on the young heroes, the Gargoyle used the Antithesis' mental powers to attack Nightwing's mind, but Nightwing and the Herald were able to teleport the villains back into Limbo, where they remain to this day, plotting their revenge. **PJ**

MISTER TWISTER *Stikk first battled with the Titans as Mister Twister.*

REVENGE
The monstrous Antithesis remains trapped in Limbo.

APPARITION

FIRST APPEARANCE ACTION COMICS #276 (May 1961)
STATUS Hero **REAL NAME** Tinya Wazzo
OCCUPATION Legionnaire **BASE** Legion World, U.P. Space
HEIGHT 5ft 6in **WEIGHT** 131 lbs **EYES** Blue **HAIR** Black
SPECIAL POWERS/ABILITIES Able to phase all or any part of her body into an intangible and translucent phantom state.

In one incarnation of the Legion of Super-Heroes, Apparition is the code name for the Legionnaire known elsewhere as Phantom Girl. Tinya Wazzo of Bgtzl joined the Legion after foiling a terrorist attempt. Tinya used her people's natural ability to become a living phantom as the Legionnaire Apparition. She apparently died defending Earth against a supremacist group known as the White Triangle.

However, Apparition still existed in a phantom-like state and was later fully restored during the Legion's brief foray to the 20th century. During that time, Tinya married longtime love and fellow Legionnaire Jo Nah (Ultra Boy), and gave birth to their son, Cub Wazzo-Nah. Legion membership and a lengthy separation during the Blight invasion strained Tinya and Jo's marriage. Furthermore, their son Cub has rapidly aged since his birth, further complicating all of their lives. **SB**

AQUAGIRL

FIRST APPEARANCE AQUAMAN (1st series) #33 (June 1967)
STATUS Hero (deceased) **REAL NAME** Tula
OCCUPATION Adventurer **BASE** Atlantis
HEIGHT 5ft 5in **WEIGHT** 119 lbs **EYES** Blue **HAIR** Brown
SPECIAL POWERS/ABILITIES As an Atlantean, she has a dense physique to allow her to withstand the crushing pressures under the surface, which, on land, gives her enhanced strength compared to humans; a superb swimmer.

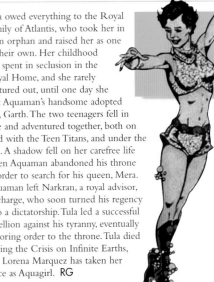

Tula owed everything to the Royal Family of Atlantis, who took her in as an orphan and raised her as one of their own. Her childhood was spent in seclusion in the Royal Home, and she rarely ventured out, until one day she met Aquaman's handsome adopted son, Garth. The two teenagers fell in love and adventured together, both on land with the Teen Titans, and under the sea. A shadow fell on her carefree life when Aquaman abandoned his throne in order to search for his queen, Mera. Aquaman left Narkran, a royal advisor, in charge, who soon turned his regency into a dictatorship. Tula led a successful rebellion against his tyranny, eventually restoring order to the throne. Tula died during the Crisis on Infinite Earths, but Lorena Marquez has taken her place as Aquagirl. **RG**

AQUAMAN

KING OF THE SEVEN SEAS

FIRST APPEARANCE More Fun Comics #73 (November 1941)
STATUS Hero **REAL NAMES** Arthur Curry; Orin
OCCUPATION Waterbearer of the Secret Sea, exiled King of Atlantis
BASE The undersea kingdom of Atlantis
HEIGHT 6ft 1in **WEIGHT** 325 lbs **EYES** Aqua blue **HAIR** Blond
SPECIAL POWERS/ABILITIES Can breathe underwater and communicate telepathically with sea life; can swim 100 m.p.h. underwater; possesses enhanced strength and toughness as well as limited sonar abilities; left hand is made of enchanted water and possesses healing powers as well as other magical abilities.

THOSE WHO UNDERESTIMATE AQUAMAN do so at their peril. This hot-headed monarch commands a kingdom that covers three-quarters of the Earth's surface and extends from the wave crests to the bottom of the Mariana Trench. Although he is, at present, a king in exile, his royal bearing is plain for all to see. Like many legendary kings, Aquaman's royal birthright was obscured by his upbringing as a commoner. The son of Queen Atlanna and a demigod, the spirit of Atlan, Orin was born with blond hair and the ability to communicate with sea life. These qualities sentenced the child to death by exposure on Mercy Reef, for the Atlanteans believed they were signs of the curse of Kordax, a legendary monster.

EARLY YEARS Aquaman got his own series in 1962, battling bizarre menaces such as these Fire Trolls.

FATHER FIGURE
Arthur Curry helped raise the young Atlantean, though he is no longer a presence in Aquaman's life.

STRANGER IN A STRANGE LAND
Found and raised by the dolphin Porm, Orin believed himself to be a misshapen dolphin until lighthouse-keeper Arthur Curry took him in. Absorbing some of the language and culture of the surface world from his adoptive parent, the boy took the name Arthur Curry and traveled north. He unknowingly fathered a child with an Inuit woman, Kako, then became the prisoner of Atlantean soldiers. Arthur befriended a fellow prisoner Vulko and escaped, wearing his prisoner's garb of orange-scaled shirt and green pants. He soon stumbled into a wave-top battle between the Prankster and the second Flash (Barry Allen). The Flash convinced Arthur to return with him to the U.S., where promoters dubbed him Aquaman.

OLD SCHOOL
Orin's dolphin family were perfectly suited for life underwater, but Orin kept pace by learning how to apply his opposable thumbs.

THE JLA
After he lost his hand in a piranha attack, Aquaman returned to the JLA, becoming a member of the modern team. He maintained ties with the organization he helped found and earned his place among the "magnificent seven" who comprise the icons of modern heroism.
   The awkwardness that Aquaman had expressed as a rookie JLA member now manifested itself as outright hostility, but he acquitted himself well in the battle to stop the White Martians of the Hyperclan from taking over the Earth. Aquaman worked sporadically with the JLA, often leaving to attend to business under the sea. Occasionally, hints have slipped out concerning his unspoken desire for his teammate Wonder Woman.

IMPERIAL Aquaman and Wonder Woman are the two JLA members who possess royal blood.

RETURN OF THE KING
Arthur found adapting to surface life hard, but discovered a kindred spirit in the Martian Manhunter. Like him, he became a founding member of the Justice League of America.
   Now a famous super hero, Aquaman returned to Atlantis to claim the throne. He made Vulko his regent and led his realm into a golden age. The exiled boy Garth became Aquaman's surrogate son, fighting threats to the kingdom as Aqualad. Mera then arrived from an alternate dimension and became Aquaman's queen. Aquaman defeated threats to the realm from super-villains including Black Manta, Fisherman, Scavenger, and his own half-brother Ocean Master. Aquaman and Mera eventually produced an heir—Arthur Jr., sometimes called Aquababy. The future of Atlantis looked bright.

ATLANTIS
The two largest cities in Atlantis are Poseidonis and Tritonis.

DEATH IN THE FAMILY
Aquaman cradles the dead body of his son, brutally murdered by Black Manta.

PLUNGE INTO THE DEPTHS

Shockingly, Black Manta killed Arthur Jr., setting off a string of tragedies that unraveled Aquaman's life. Mera blamed her husband for their son's death and abandoned him. An alien invasion shook the Justice League and Aquaman tried to reform it as a leaner, Detroit-based squad, but several new members died in the line of duty. A school of piranha chewed off Aquaman's left hand in a confrontation with the terrorist Charybdis, and Arthur's illegitimate son Koryak (product of his liaison with the Inuit Kako) took control of Atlantis.

Aquaman fought back from the brink of despair with the love of the adventurer Dolphin and the advice of Aqualad, now known as Tempest. Outfitted with a harpoon in place of a hand, Aquaman eventually won back rulership of Atlantis and defeated the sea god Triton, son of Poseidon.

A NEW CALLING

After Aquaman restored Atlantis to the modern era, the Atlanteans branded him an outcast. He exchanged his harpoon for a hand made of enchanted water from the Lady Of The Lake, and helped the transformed people of San Diego survive underwater after their city sank beneath the waves.

The Spectre destroyed Atlantis during the Infinite Crisis, and the sea gods transformed Aquaman into the mutated Dweller in the Depths. A new hero, Arthur Joseph Curry, arose in his absence, living up to his namesake's legacy by stopping Vandal Savage's scheme to flood the Earth.

AMERICAN TIDAL *An earthquake caused half of San Diego to sink into the ocean. Aquaman uncovered a mystery involving survivors who had evolved into water-breathers.*

IMPERIEX WAR

Intergalactic conqueror Imperiex, attempting to hollow out the Earth, chose Atlantis as one of his battlefronts (*see Great Battles, pp. 186-7*). Aquaman battled one of Imperiex's probes and seemingly died in battle, while Tempest used his magic to shift Atlantis more than 3,000 years back in time to the Obsidian Age of its ancient past. The other members of the JLA traveled back to restore Atlantis and find their lost teammate, Aquaman. Transformed into a water wraith by the evil sorceress Gamemnae, Aquaman merged with the entire ocean to re-sink Atlantis and restore it to its proper place in the timeline.

KEY STORYLINES

- *AQUAMAN: TIME AND TIDE #1-4 (DECEMBER 1993 – MARCH 1994):* The origin of Aquaman is tightened up and retold to fit within modern continuity.
- *AQUAMAN (3RD SERIES) #2 (SEPTEMBER 1994):* Aquaman loses his left hand in an issue that redefined the character for a new audience.
- *AQUAMAN (4TH SERIES) #15 (APRIL 2004):* The King of Atlantis returns to his classic look, and San Diego is submerged following an earthquake.

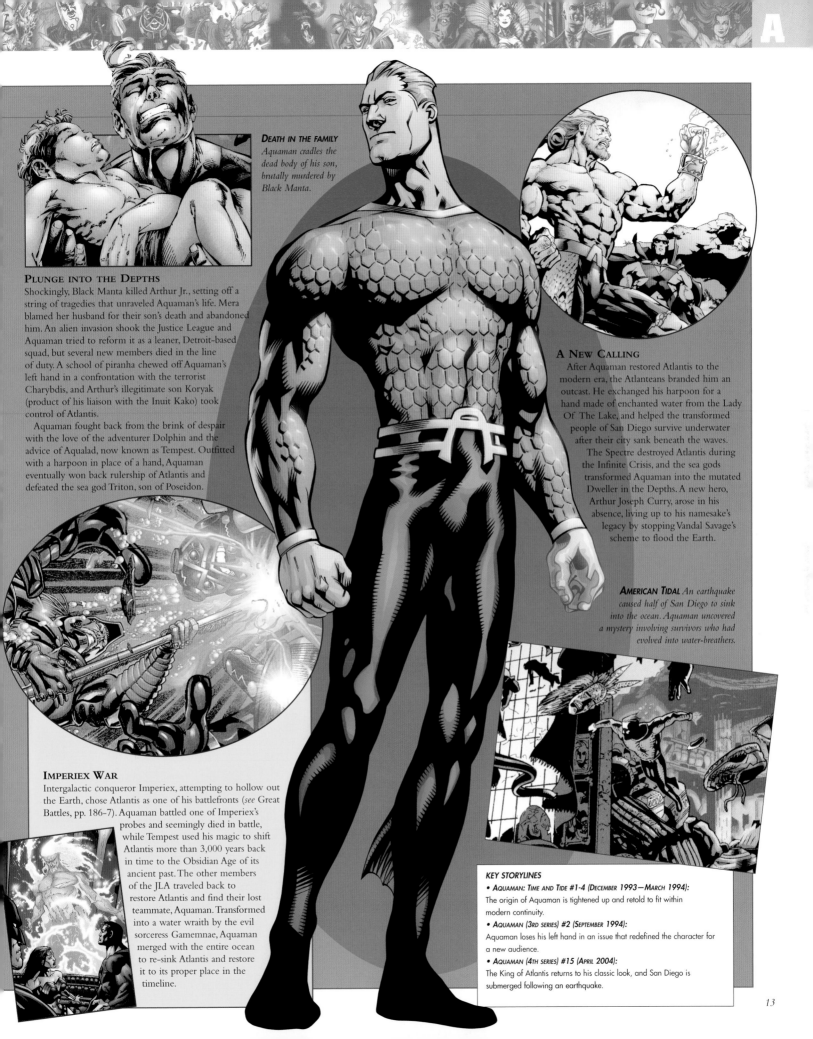

ALTERNATE EARTHS

Once there were an infinite number of universes – until a being called the Anti-Monitor annihilated all except five, and the surviving heroes collapsed those five into one. Yet this single, merged universe would not hold. The Multiverse burst forth again when Alexander Luthor, brilliant scientist from a reality the Anti-Monitor had wiped out, initiated the Infinite Crisis by constructing a tuning fork that replicated the existing universe fifty-one times. At first, these 52 parallel universes looked identical, until the Venusian worm Mister Mind retroactively altered their histories during a rampage through space-time.

The 52 realities are separated from one another by Source Walls that bound each universe; behind the Source Walls lies the Bleed, which allows certain individuals to make passage from one universe to the next. Intermingling between realities is discouraged by the Monitors, a corps of 52 watchers (one from each plane) who strive to maintain the purity of the Multiverse. The anti-matter universe, home to the Sinestro Corps and the Weaponers of Qward, exists on a separate plane than any of the 52 positive-matter realities.

Earth is a focal point of each universe, and "New Earth" – the first world among the 52 – is the Multiverse's cornerstone. The destruction of New Earth would trigger a chain reaction that would destroy the Multiverse, leaving only the anti-matter universe in its wake.

The 52 parallel universes are named after, and most easily distinguished by, the characteristics of the planet Earth in each.

New Earth
The foundation of the Multiverse, New Earth is home to the primary versions of all super heroes and similar cosmic champions. All other universes are altered copies of New Earth's reality.

Earth-2
On Earth-2, a slightly altered version of the Justice Society of America fought the Axis powers in World War II. In later decades, their descendents have taken up unique heroic identities.

Earth-3
On this evil mirror image of New Earth, the Crime Society of Ultraman, Owlman, Superwoman, Power Ring, and Johnny Quick rule with an iron hand, while rogue do-gooders like the Jokester (and the Joker's Daughter) fight for freedom.

Earth-4
Alternate versions of the Question, Blue Beetle, Nightshade, Captain Atom, Judomaster, and the Peacemaker inhabit Earth-4, where they work to find a role for super heroes in a sometimes shadowy world.

Earth-5
A sunny and colorful reality, Earth-5 is home to upbeat versions of Captain Marvel and the Captain Marvel family.

Earth-8
New Earth's heroes do not have any analogues on Earth-8, where a super-powered ruling class has taken root in the form of Lord Havok and the Extremists.

Earth-10
On Earth-10, Adolph Hitler achieved victory in World War II and conquered the planet. Alternate versions of Uncle Sam and the Freedom Fighters plot to end his reign.

Earth-12
Several decades into the future, new Batman Terry McGinnis has taken the mantle from Bruce Wayne to fight old threats in a high-tech Gotham City.

Earth-15

The highly-evolved super heroes of Earth-15 have eliminated nearly all crime. Their members include Jason Todd as Batman, Jessica Palmer as the Atom, Donna Troy as Wonder Woman, and Zod and his son Christopher Kent as dual Supermen. The world was recently destroyed by Superman-Prime.

Earth-17

Here, the Atomic Knights struggle to tame a savage planet in the wake of an apocalyptic Great Disaster.

Earth-18

On Earth-18, analogues of the Justice League heroes keep the peace on the Old West's frontier.

Earth-19

In the closing decades of the 19th century, a Victorian-era Batman fights crime in a Gotham City lit by gaslight.

Earth-21

Also known as the New Frontier reality, Earth-21 is where the planet's core heroes became famous during the 1950s and '60s

Earth-22

This universe, sometimes called the Kingdom Come reality and set several decades in the future, is distinguished by a mistrustful Earth where heroes fight heroes.

Earth-26

A cartoonish reality populated by anthropomorphic animals, Earth-26 counts Captain Carrot and his Zoo Crew among its furry champions.

Earth-30

Also known as the Red Son reality, Earth-30 is where baby Kal-El landed in Earth's Soviet Union during the Cold War of the 1950s, later using his abilities as a Soviet Superman to help Mother Russia dominate the globe.

Earth-31

In this reality, Earth's heroes are led by a pro-government, all-American Superman and a violent, aging Batman. Their differing methods define a world riddled with strife and oppression

Earth-34

Earth-34, also called the Amazonia reality, is where Wonder Woman first emerged in 19th century England and fought a male-dominated commonwealth in which Jack the Ripper ruled as king.

Earth-43

Batman is a vampire in this dark universe that seethes with the supernatural.

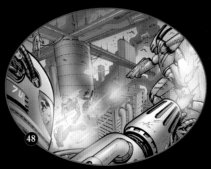

Earth-48[1]

Earth, a devastated scar in this reality, is used as a neutral warring ground for Martians, Venusians, and other species inhabiting the solar system. The cross-bred survivors of Earth have evolved to become the Forerunners—elite killing machines in the service of the Monitors.

Earth-50

This universe harbors a different lineup of heroes than those on New Earth, with teams including WildC.A.T.S, the Authority and Gen13

ARAK, SON OF THUNDER

FIRST APPEARANCE WARLORD #48 (August 1981)
STATUS Hero (dec.) REAL NAME Arak Red-Hand (Bright Sky After Storm)
OCCUPATION Shaman BASE 8th century Europe, Asia, N. America
HEIGHT 6ft WEIGHT 190 lbs EYES Brown HAIR Black
SPECIAL POWERS/ABILITIES Arak is an expert with an otomahuk and a sword. He also possesses undefined shamanic powers.

In the 8th century, after a surprise attack on the Quontauka Indians nearly wiped out the entire tribe, a 10-year-old boy favored by He-No, the Quontauka god of thunder, escaped into the Atlantic Ocean in a birchwood canoe. The boy was rescued by a roving band of Vikings, named Erik, and raised as one of their own. Pronouncing his name "Arak," the young Indian grew to adulthood among the Vikings. Living in Europe, Arak became a powerful Viking warrior, proficient with both a sword and his own weapon, his native otomahuk.

Tragically, the Vikings who saved and raised Arak were slaughtered. Arak survived the death of his Viking clan, however, and went off to seek Carolus Magnus, known as Charlemagne. Arak was accepted into Charlemagne's court and served the emperor for the rest of his life. Arak did return to North America, however, hoping to rediscover his tribal origins. When Arak was slain in battle, his spirit was summoned before the thunder god, He-No, who was actually Arak's father. He-No resurrected Arak as a mystical shaman, renewing his life energies and returning him to Earth to defend the tribes of natives across North America. During the time-spanning event known as the Crisis (see Great Battles, pp. 186-7), Arak briefly teamed up with the Golden Age heroes known as the All-Star Squadron. PJ

STORMING THROUGH Arak fought countless villains from the past, including bizarre mutations, supernatural threats, and demons.

NATIVE WARRIOR Blessed by the power of the He-No, Arak was a renowned warrior, feared across Asia and Europe for his skill with the otomahuk.

ARCANE, ANTON

FIRST APPEARANCE SWAMP THING #2 (January 1973)
STATUS Villain (reformed) REAL NAME Anton Arcane
OCCUPATION Scientist; demon BASE Hell
HEIGHT 5ft 1in WEIGHT 97 lbs EYES Obsidian HAIR White
SPECIAL POWERS/ABILITIES As a human, Arcane was a brilliant scientist; as a demon he was quick and sturdy.

HEAVEN AND HELL Arcane as a deformed monster from Hell (left), and in his mortal appearance (right).

Born in a Balkan state in 1895, Anton Arcane was obsessed with finding the secret of immortality. During World War II, Arcane was briefly in Adolf Hitler's employ. Later during the war, the time-traveling Swamp Thing took possession of the body of an Easy Company soldier and thwarted Arcane's bid for power. The Unknown Soldier infiltrated Easy Company, whose operatives gathered Arcane's collection of artifacts, including a replica of the Spear of Destiny.

By the time Arcane became immortal, his body was too old and feeble to be of any use, so he tried to create a new body. However, his experiments yielded only misshapen beings he dubbed the Un-Men. One experiment resulted in Arcane's brother, Gregori, becoming the Patchwork Man I. Arcane's hopes were raised when he discovered the Swamp Thing. Arcane survived the battle, and the Un-Men rebuilt his body.

Arcane began a vendetta against the Swamp Thing and his own niece, Abby Arcane, Swamp Thing's lover. Arcane was killed, but even confinement in Hell couldn't keep him from seeking vengeance, and he ultimately achieved demonhood. Arcane was summoned from Hell to be present at the first trial set by the Parliament of Flames for Swamp Thing, but by then he had found God. Because of this, Swamp Thing decided not to destroy humanity, and built Arcane a new body. Arcane was later reconciled with Abby. RG

ARASHI

FIRST APPEARANCE GREEN LANTERN PLUS #1 (December 1996)
STATUS Hero REAL NAME Arashi Ohashi
OCCUPATION Video game designer/adventurer BASE Tokyo, Japan
HEIGHT 5ft 5in WEIGHT 119 lbs EYES Brown HAIR Black
SPECIAL POWERS/ABILITIES High-tech weaponry includes a heavily armed motorcycle, right-arm flamethrower, and senses-augmenting cyber-helmet; no known superpowers.

One of Japan's super heroes, Arashi Ohashi helps defend her country from all manner of threats with advanced technology of her own design. Arashi once teamed up with Green Lantern Kyle Rayner and the Ray to thwart magnetic malcontent Doctor Polaris and prevent a giant tsunami from wiping Japan off the map. Polaris broke Arashi's arm and nearly killed her, but she has since recovered and resumed her adventurous activities. SB

LIFE SAVER While battling Doctor Polaris, Green Lantern saved Arashi with a power-ring-generated air-bag.

ARES

FIRST APPEARANCE WONDER WOMAN (2nd series) #1 (February 1987)
STATUS Villain **REAL NAME** Ares
OCCUPATION God of War **BASE** The Areopagus
HEIGHT 6ft 10in **WEIGHT** 459 lbs **EYES** Blue **HAIR** Blond
SPECIAL POWERS/ABILITIES Immortal; god-like strength and stamina; brilliant military strategist; indestructible armor.

The Greek god of war Ares thrives on bloodshed and is the implacable enemy of Wonder Woman, the Amazon peacemaker. Despite being Zeus's son, Ares never fit in with the other gods of Olympus (*see* Olympian Gods) and created his own realm, the Areopagus. When he plotted to destroy the mortals' world with a nuclear bomb, the AMAZON brought Princess Diana to life as the new Wonder Woman to combat the war god's evil.

Ares then made another bid for supreme power, killing Highfather in the process. He suffered torments for his treachery until he effected his escape. Later, Ares's children, Phobos, Deimos, and Eris, tried to ensure their father's place as ruler of Earth by raising the Areopagus in the center of Gotham City.

Ares has taken an interest in the new WONDER GIRL, and given her a magic lasso similar to Diana's. Ares continues to push Wonder Girl to become his champion, supplying her with powers that dwarf those originally given her by Zeus. **DW**

THE DECEIVER
During a battle with Darkseid, Ares merged with Zeus and the gods of other pantheons (Jove, Odin, and the New God Highfather). Ares would betray them all in due course.

SILVER TONGUE
Ares is just as skilled with flattery as he is with a sword, since both are weapons in the service of strife.

ARGENT I

FIRST APPEARANCE SECRET ORIGINS (3rd series) #14 (May 1987)
STATUS Hero team **BASE** Unknown
MEMBERS AND POWERS/ABILITIES
Control The mysterious leader. **Falcon** A master of disguise.
Fleur The daughter of notorious World War I spy Mata Hari.
Iron Munro He has superhuman strength and invulnerability.
Phantom Lady I A special device worn on her wrist emits a black light ray, creating total darkness. **Phantom** Mysterious master of disguise. **Dina** (deceased) wife of Control; Allied saboteur and spy.

Argent was created in 1951 as the civilian branch of Task Force X. The organization was designed to handle the threat of superpowered criminals after the JUSTICE SOCIETY OF AMERICA was forced to disband by the House of Un-American Activities Committee because they refused to reveal their secret identities. Unlike their counterparts in the Suicide Squad, Argent's missions were exclusively domestic, and the team operated in extreme secrecy. Their supervisor was known only as "Control," the mysterious former leader of the O.S.S. (Office of Strategic Services). This international intelligence and espionage organization was exposed by Control after he arranged the murder of a government operative indirectly responsible for the assassination of President John F. Kennedy in 1963.

SECRET SOCIETY *During the anti-Communist "Red Scare" of the 1950s, Argent exposed a number of threats to U.S. security, from foreign terrorists to costumed and superpowered villains.*

After the death of Control, his granddaughter began operating under the same guise. The group was finally disbanded after a confrontation with the Suicide Squad, and the U.S. government has no official record of their members or their existence. **PJ**

ARGENT II

FIRST APPEARANCE TEEN TITANS (2nd series) #1 (October 1996)
STATUS Hero **REAL NAME** Toni Moretti
OCCUPATION Adventurer **BASE** New Jersey
HEIGHT 5ft 8in **WEIGHT** 125 lbs **EYES** Blue **HAIR** Black
SPECIAL POWERS/ABILITIES Can generate silver plasma and shape it to whatever form she pleases; creates energy platforms and travels astride them at great speeds.

Teenager Toni Moretti first met the Teen Titans when the team saved her U.S. senator father from the Fearsome Five. She never dreamed she would ever join them. However, a few years later, her skin was mysteriously drained of pigment and her body started to generate silver plasma. Abducted by an alien race, the H'San Natall, Toni learned that she and several other teenagers were the results of a breeding program to create a superpowered advance guard for an attack upon Earth. Toni and her fellow hybrids rebelled against the H'San Natall and sabotaged the invasion. Since the Teen Titans were inactive at the time, the hybrids decided to form their own version.

As Argent, Toni had many tumultuous adventures with various incarnations of the Teen Titans. Toni then found out that her father was involved in drug smuggling, and she was eventually forced to turn him over to the authorities. Much later, the Titans disbanded again after the deaths of heroines Omen and Troia. Argent's current activities are unknown, although given her drive to succeed, one can safely assume that she is actively polishing her silver plasma skills. **SB**

SHINING LIGHT
Toni's silver plasma is not unlike the coherent light generated by Green Lantern's power ring.

ARION, LORD OF ATLANTIS

FIRST APPEARANCE WARLORD #55 (March 1982)
STATUS Hero   **REAL NAME** Ahri'ahn
OCCUPATION Atlantean sorcerer   **BASE** Mobile
HEIGHT 6ft 3in   **WEIGHT** 190 lbs   **EYES** Green   **HAIR** Brown
SPECIAL POWERS/ABILITIES Immortality; vast magical abilities drawn from the extra-dimensional Darkworld.

ATLANTIS! THE NAME IS LEGENDARY, and during its golden age no hero was greater than Arion. No mere mortal, Arion came into existence as the product of a union between two Atlantean gods more than half a million years ago. His father, Calculhah (a force of good), cared for Arion, then known by the name Ahri'ahn, while his mother, Dark Majistra (a force of strife), raised Arion's wicked older brother, Garn Daanuth. When the two evil entities tried to destroy primitive Atlantis, Arion sacrificed his life to stop them. His energies survived thanks to the extra-dimensional realm of the Darkworld—home to a cosmic entity who serves as the source of all Atlantean magic—and Arion existed for nearly 500,000 years in a state of intangibility.

PROTECTOR OF ATLANTIS

Approximately 45,000 years ago, Arion returned in physical form to serve as the protector of Atlantis. The civilization had reached a peak, with the *homo sapiens* offshoot species, the *homo magi*, making up a large part of the population and exhibiting a primal connection to the forces of the universe. Arion became Lord High Mage of Atlantis, residing in the City of the Golden Gate and fighting the creeping encroachment of ice. He soon fell in love with Lady Chian, and the two battled the still-surviving mage Garn Daanuth. Arion played a time-hopping role alongside heroes from other eras during the Crisis (*see* Great Battles, pp. 186-7).

The continent of Atlantis suffered its first great fracturing when Arion fought off an assault by alien invaders. A bolt of energy shattered the City of the Golden Gate and caused much of the continental shelf to slip into the ocean. Arion and Lady Chian rapidly dispatched teams to establish new Atlantean colonies across the globe, including one in the hidden realm of Skartaris. Atlantis's final sinking (involving the cities of Tritonis and Poseidonis) did not occur until tens of thousands of years later.

As an immortal, Arion wandered the Earth for the next 45,000 years, with his powers waxing and waning due to changes in the Darkworld. In the year 1659 he traveled to modern-day Metropolis and tried to convince Superman to retire from his role as humanity's protector to prevent a global catastrophe. Despite Arion's alternate-history visions of a devastated world, Superman remained unconvinced.

After living many more centuries into the modern era, Arion cast doubt on Power Girl's history by falsely claiming to be her grandfather. Arion died while helping the Justice Society of America fight the sorcerer Mordru. An impostor, Bill Knightley from Ohio, took up Arion's identity, helping the Shadowpact fight the Spectre. **DW**

AS TIME GOES BY
Arion's appearance has changed over the years in conjunction with the waxing and waning power of the Darkworld.

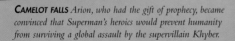

CAMELOT FALLS *Arion, who had the gift of prophecy, became convinced that Superman's heroics would prevent humanity from surviving a global assault by the supervillain Khyber.*

MAGIC ARCANA *His Atlantean heritage, coupled with centuries of study in the sorcerous arts, made Arion one of the greatest mages of any age. Arion, unfortunately, realized this, making him unbearably arrogant.*

KEY STORYLINES
• **ARION, LORD OF ATLANTIS #1 (NOVEMBER 1982):** Arion graduates to his own title after debuting as a backup feature in Warlord.
• **JSA #50 (SEPTEMBER 2003):** Arion passes onto another plane of existence, taking down Mordru, the Dark Lord, in the process.

ARSENAL

BATTLING BOWMAN

FIRST APPEARANCE ADVENTURE COMICS #250 (July 1958)
STATUS Hero **REAL NAME** Roy Harper
OCCUPATION Adventurer **BASE** Brooklyn, New York City
HEIGHT 5ft 11in **WEIGHT** 195 lbs **EYES** Blue **HAIR** Red
SPECIAL POWERS/ABILITIES One of the world's top archers with bow and crossbow, Arsenal is also an expert with most projectile weapons and is a natural leader.

ONCE THE TEEN SIDEKICK OF GREEN ARROW I, Roy Harper endured many painful years in the hero's shadow, but emerged as an adult with his own identity. Roy is well acquainted with loss, having been orphaned twice before his fourteenth birthday. When Roy was a baby, his forest ranger father, Will, died saving Navajo medicine chief Brave Bow from a wildfire. Out of gratitude, Brave Bow raised the boy as his own. Roy became a tireless long-distance runner and a fine archer, closely following the career of the world's greatest archer, Green Arrow. One day Green Arrow came to Roy's hometown, and Roy impressed his idol with his quick reactions foiling a robbery (earning him the nickname "Speedy").

WEAPONS MASTER
Arsenal still favors the weapons of his Navajo upbringing, but is also skilled with firearms.

SPEEDY *Roy has left behind the idealism of his early teens.*

LIAN *As a single father and a super hero, Roy struggles to find time for his daughter.*

SHARP SHOOTERS
Brave Bow died soon after, and Roy became the legal ward of Green Arrow's alter ego, playboy millionaire Oliver Queen. Green Arrow and Speedy's amazing archery skills put them in the same class as many of the super heroes emerging at the same time. Green Arrow joined the Justice League of America, while Speedy became a member of the Teen Titans alongside Kid Flash I, Wonder Girl, Robin, and Aqualad (*see* Tempest).

Yet Roy still felt adrift, and when Green Arrow left on a cross-country road trip with Green Lantern to "find America," Roy turned to drugs for comfort and became a heroin addict. Fortunately, Black Canary helped Roy kick his dependency, and he eventually joined the Central Bureau of Investigations. A mission to Japan brought him into intimate contact with the beautiful assassin Cheshire. When they eventually parted, Roy was unaware she was carrying his child. Cheshire later became a prisoner of the government and Roy gained custody of his daughter, Lian.

DRUG HELL *Feeling abandoned by Green Arrow, Roy hit rock bottom.*

While working for Checkmate, Roy retired the Speedy name for a more fitting identity as Arsenal. After stints leading the Titans and a new team of Outsiders, Arsenal returned to his roots by adopting an all-new costumed identity as Red Arrow. He gladly accepted membership in the new Justice League of America, and has struck up a romance with his teammate Hawkgirl. **DW**

OUTSIDERS *Arsenal led the new Outsiders against Gorilla Grodd and his ape-soldiers when the simian super-villain attempted to invade New York City.*

EMOTIONAL MOMENT *Roy is accepted into the JLA by his old friends Black Canary and Green Lantern.*

KEY STORYLINES
• *GREEN LANTERN #85 (SEPTEMBER 1971):* In one of the hero's most shocking moments, Speedy is revealed as a heroin addict.
• *NEW TEEN TITANS (2ND SERIES) #21 (JUNE 1986):* After a long tease, Cheshire discloses that Roy Harper is the father of her child.
• *NEW TITANS #99 (JULY 1993):* Speedy makes his debut as Arsenal.

ATOM

FIRST APPEARANCE (ATOM I) ALL-AMERICAN COMICS #19 (October 1940)
STATUS Hero (deceased) **REAL NAME** Al Pratt
OCCUPATION Professor of Nuclear Physics **BASE** Calvin College
HEIGHT 5ft 1in **WEIGHT** 150 lbs **EYES** Blue **HAIR** Red
SPECIAL POWERS/ABILITIES Skilled in the "sweet science" of boxing, Al Pratt packed an even mightier punch when he gained atomic strength, which also greatly enhanced his agility and kept him fighting fit many decades later.

FIRST APPEARANCE (ATOM II) SHOWCASE #34 (October 1961)
STATUS Hero **REAL NAME** Raymond "Ray" Palmer
OCCUPATION Professor of Physics **BASE** Ivy Town
HEIGHT 6ft **WEIGHT** 180 lbs **EYES** Brown **HAIR** Auburn
SPECIAL POWERS/ABILITIES Can shrink to any size, no matter how miniscule, either retaining the heft of his original 180 pounds or weighing next to nothing. He has mastered fighting techniques at various sizes. At sub-atomic size, the Atom can travel virtually anywhere on Earth via telephone transmissions, surfing microwaves or other electronic impulses.

FIRST APPEARANCE (ATOM III) DCU: Brave New World (2006)
STATUS Hero **REAL NAME** Ryan Choi
OCCUPATION Professor of physics **BASE** Ivy Town
HEIGHT 5 ft 8 in **EYES** Black **HAIR** Black
SPECIAL POWERS/ABILITIES Similar shrinking powers to those of Ray Palmer, powered by a size-changing belt.

AL PRATT WAS A "98-POUND WEAKLING" until he met former boxing champ Joe Morgan. Morgan transformed the young man into a "little superman" in less than a year, putting the pint-sized Pratt through a grueling exercise regime and increasing his weight. While Morgan groomed Pratt for a featherweight boxing career, his pupil had other plans. Pratt became the Atom, a diminutive costumed crime fighter with a formidable punch. A member of the Justice Society of America and All-Star Squadron, the Mighty Mite gained atomic strength and agility in 1948 as a result of radiation exposure during a battle with Cyclotron, a scientist forced into crime by the evil Ultra-Humanite. Later married to his sweetheart Mary, Pratt never hesitated to take his fighting togs out of mothballs if the need arose. Tragically, while aiding the JSA during the Zero Hour crisis (see Great Battles, pp. 186-7), the Atom died battling the villain Extant. Unknown to Pratt, a son—the young atomic-powered hero Damage— survives him.

LITTLE BIG MAN
Al Pratt punches above his weight in his first outing.

PART-TIMER
Ray Palmer preferred to be an auxiliary member of the JLA so he could continue his studies at Ivy University.

ATOM II

When Ivy University physicist Ray Palmer discovered a fragment of a white dwarf star, he believed he had found the key to success in his size-reduction experiments. Before Palmer could test the star fragment, he was trapped in a cave with a group of youngsters while on a nature outing. Palmer used the fragment and his size-reducing lens to find an escape route from the cave. Somehow, mineral-infused water in the cave and other factors combined with the reducing materials to allow Palmer to shrink safely. Palmer then fashioned a costume that would shrink and enlarge with him, and only appear when he was less than six inches tall. He also devised reducing controls which he placed on his gloves. Thus outfitted, he became the second super hero to call himself the Atom, a Tiny Titan packing a 180-pound punch at any size.

Tragedy struck when an insane Jean Loring killed Sue Dibny (wife of the Elongated Man) in order to win back Ray's affections. With his ex-wife committed to Arkham Asylum, Ray disappeared into the microverse to escape his emotional pain. At infinitesimal size he discovered a way to slip between dimensions, hopping among parallel worlds until finding a home on Earth-51. There, he assumed the identity of Earth-51's late Ray Palmer, until called back to prevent a foretold Great Disaster.

During Ray's absence, a new Atom took the stage. Ryan Choi, a junior professor at Ivy University, used his mentor's size-changing belt to explore the weird mysteries of Ivy Town. Despite his inexperience, Ryan received an invitation to join the Justice League of America. **SB/DW**

RYAN CHOI *The third Atom jumped into the role with enthusiasm, tackling everything from sewer monsters to vengeful ghosts while dating Giganta, teaming up with Wonder Woman, and somehow finding time to teach class.*

KEY STORYLINES

• **ZERO HOUR #3 (SEPTEMBER 1994):** The Atom I perishes alongside his JSA teammate Hourman I in an attempt to stop Extant's timestream tamperings.
• **THE ATOM #1 (JULY 1962):** The Atom II first battles the Plant Master (The Floronic Man).
• **SWORD OF THE ATOM #1 (SEPTEMBER 1983):** In the South American jungle, Ray Palmer befriends the alien Katarthans and becomes their sword-wielding super-heroic defender!

AZRAEL

THE AVENGING ANGEL

FIRST APPEARANCE BATMAN: SWORD OF AZRAEL #1 (October 1992)
STATUS Hero **REAL NAME** Jean Paul Valley
OCCUPATION Adventurer **BASE** Ossaville
HEIGHT 6ft 2in **WEIGHT** 210 lbs **EYES** Blue **HAIR** Blond
SPECIAL POWERS/ABILITIES Physically and psychologically programmed by scientists of the Order of St. Dumas to be an assassin; superb combat skills, great strength, speed, and agility; powers triggered by putting on special costume and using the name "Azrael."

As a Gotham University student, Jean Paul Valley had no inkling of the larger forces acting on his life. But when his dying father revealed the truth, Jean Paul willingly took up the mantle of Azrael, the champion assassin of a Crusades-era fraternity of warrior-priests, the Order of St. Dumas. In modern times, the Order had become a secret society with few members but uncountable riches. For centuries the "avenging angel Azrael" had been their silent enforcer—actually an Order member trained from birth to silence those who failed to observe the Order's strict code of secrecy. The role of Azrael was passed down from father to son, and Jean Paul suddenly realized he was heir to a long tradition. His life as the shadowy avenger Azrael would last for many years. Throughout this time, conflicting feelings toward the role that had been forced on him before he was even born plunged him into bouts of severe depression. His costume would also undergo a number of changes in design and equipment, the better to reflect the various alterations in his emotional state.

TEST-TUBE HORROR *Jean Paul's biological mother was horrified to discover that the egg she had donated to the Order of St. Dumas had been appropriated for a scientific program. The Order's fanatical scientists were busily mingling the fetus's genetic makeup with animal DNA to create a being of great strength capable of killing without remorse. The poor mother was condemned to die, but escaped thanks to a merciful priest, and has remained in hiding ever since.*

IMAGE CHANGES *Doubts over his Azrael role have led Jean Paul to revamp his warsuit several times.*

THE SYSTEM
In Switzerland, Jean Paul trained under the dwarf Nomoz, who triggered the deep hypnotic implants that Jean Paul had been unaware he possessed. "The System," a regimen of hypnosis and prenatal conditioning, turned Jean Paul Valley into a formidable fighter.

BACK AGAIN *It wasn't long before Bruce Wayne returned to the role he created.*

He tested his new skills on BATMAN, who had travelled to Switzerland on the trail of the St. Dumas renegade Carleton LeHah. As Azrael, Jean Paul lost the fight—but he nevertheless rescued Bruce Wayne from LeHah. Jean Paul then returned to Gotham City and continued his training as Azrael under Robin's guidance.

When the villainous Bane broke Batman's back, Jean Paul briefly took over as Gotham City's Dark Knight. He designed a new, Azrael-inspired bat costume with heavy armor, razor talons, and hidden weapons. Though he defeated Bane, he lost his internal struggle against the hypnotic goading of the System. Jean Paul became increasingly violent and finally lost his mind. Bruce Wayne, restored to full fitness, defeated him and reclaimed the mantle of Batman. Jean Paul, after a period of misery and soul-searching, became Azrael once more. Azrael moved against the Order's scientists who originally brainwashed him, culminating in a battle inside the Order of St. Dumas' headquarters, the Ice Cathedral. The destruction of the Cathedral wiped out the last traces of the Order. Jean Paul, however, did not live long enough to enjoy the fruits of his success—he apparently perished in a shootout, ending the career of Gotham's angel of vengeance. **DW**

KEY STORYLINES
• *BATMAN #500 (OCTOBER 1993):* Jean Paul Valley donned the Azrael/Bat armor for the first time and embarked on a career as Gotham's new Batman.
• *AZRAEL: AGENT OF THE BAT #100 (MAY 2003):* Azrael's life as a costumed vigilante came to a violent end when Jean Paul was seemingly killed.

AMAZING VEHICLES

NOT ALL HEROES can fly unaided or run at lightspeed. From Batman's Batmobile, which evolved from armored sedan into all-terrain tank, to Wonder Woman's invisible plane, an alien craft cloaked from Earthly technology, some of the world's greatest adventurers have the help of extraordinary vehicles. This fleet, created with magic or science (or both), are primed to sweep their owners to their destinations.

BATMOBILE

Equipped with a satellite dish for TV/radio/GPS linkage, anti-theft gas, hypersonic trilling sphere, gas nozzles, voice-activated controls, and gel-filled kevlar-reinforced wheels that are puncture and flame-resistant, the Batmobile has undergone many transformations over the years.

It remains one of the greatest weapons in Batman's arsenal, a sleek, fearful machine with no parallel for speed or maneuverability, even among the world's fastest race cars.

Able to attain speeds of 266 m.p.h., accelerate from 0 to 60 m.p.h. in under 3 seconds, and shielded in a bulletproof ceramic composite exterior, the Batmobile is almost as frightening to criminals as its legendary driver, who know they have little chance for escape from either.

BAT SECURITY *The Batmobile is equipped with security devices, including an electrified hull, hypersonic shrieks, and a self-destruct mechanism.*

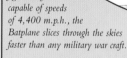

BAT PLANE
A stealth fighter craft capable of speeds of 4,400 m.p.h., the Batplane slices through the skies faster than any military war craft.

JUSTICE SOCIETY OF AMERICA'S SHUTTLE CRAFT BOX

When the alien marauder Imperiex came to reignite the Big Bang, President Lex Luthor (*see* Luthor, Lex) sent every member of the Justice Society of America on a space mission to save the planet. The JSA rocketed across the galaxy in their Star Racer space shuttle, defeated Imperiex and his probes, and saved the populace of Daxam (*see* Alien Races, pp. 86-7) from Imperiex's planet-sized ship.

The Star Racer is outfitted with protective shields, offensive weaponry, and warp-drive capabilities, and is paid for and maintained with monies left by the Dodd estate.

STAR RACER *The JSA's Star Racer can warp across galaxies, outfitted with technology from Earth and Thanagar. The Star Spangled Kid drove a flying car called the Star Rocket Racer, which was an inspiration for the Star Racer.*

ROBIN'S BIKES

The Supercycle isn't Robin's only specialized vehicle. While his primary mode of transportation is a customized sports coupé called the Redbird, Robin also rides a modified 491 c.c., liquid cooled, "motocross" Batcycle. One of many motorcycles in Batman's vehicular arsenal, the Batcycle's chassis and windshield are bulletproof. Capable of speeds of over 130 m.p.h., and armed with specialized shock dampers, the cycle is one of the sleekest machines on the road.

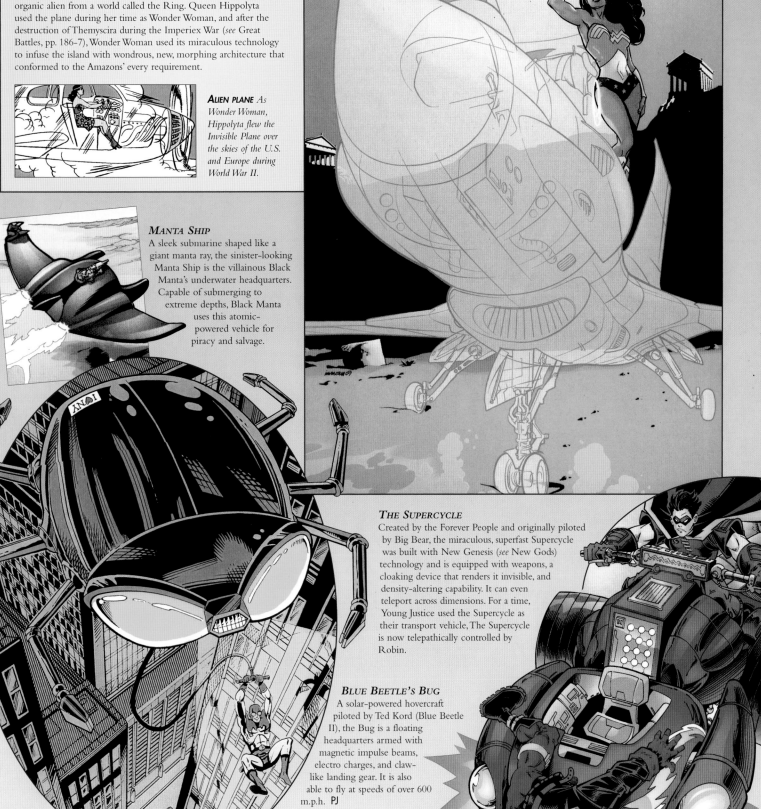

WONDER WOMAN'S INVISIBLE JET

A morphing, nearly invisible plane created by the alien Lansanarians, Wonder Woman's transparent transport is capable of changing into any number of shapes, from a fully submersible submarine to a spaceworthy chariot. Soon after accepting this incredible gift, Wonder Woman discovered that her invisible plane was a techno-organic alien from a world called the Ring. Queen Hippolyta used the plane during her time as Wonder Woman, and after the destruction of Themyscira during the Imperiex War (*see* Great Battles, pp. 186-7), Wonder Woman used its miraculous technology to infuse the island with wondrous, new, morphing architecture that conformed to the Amazons' every requirement.

ALIEN PLANE *As Wonder Woman, Hippolyta flew the Invisible Plane over the skies of the U.S. and Europe during World War II.*

MANTA SHIP

A sleek submarine shaped like a giant manta ray, the sinister-looking Manta Ship is the villainous Black Manta's underwater headquarters. Capable of submerging to extreme depths, Black Manta uses this atomic-powered vehicle for piracy and salvage.

THE SUPERCYCLE

Created by the Forever People and originally piloted by Big Bear, the miraculous, superfast Supercycle was built with New Genesis (*see* New Gods) technology and is equipped with weapons, a cloaking device that renders it invisible, and density-altering capability. It can even teleport across dimensions. For a time, Young Justice used the Supercycle as their transport vehicle, The Supercycle is now telepathically controlled by Robin.

BLUE BEETLE'S BUG

A solar-powered hovercraft piloted by Ted Kord (Blue Beetle II), the Bug is a floating headquarters armed with magnetic impulse beams, electro charges, and claw-like landing gear. It is also able to fly at speeds of over 600 m.p.h. **PJ**

23

BAD SAMARITAN

FIRST APPEARANCE THE OUTSIDERS (1st series) #3 (January 1986)
STATUS Villain   *REAL NAME* Unknown
OCCUPATION Agent provocateur   *BASE* Mobile
HEIGHT 6ft 2in   *WEIGHT* 190 lbs
EYES Unknown (hidden by dark glasses)   *HAIR* Black
SPECIAL POWERS/ABILITIES Is a superb hand-to-hand combatant and ruthless assassin; is both a master of disguise and covert espionage.

The Bad Samaritan is a spy-for-hire, a terrorist, or an insurrectionist, depending on his paymaster. His country of origin remains a mystery, and he claims allegiance to no particular organization, sovereign, or country. He has plied his trade for the U.S., the U.K., the former Soviet Union, and many other governments, although each will disavow any knowledge of covert operations involving him. While in the U.S.S.R.'s employ, the Bad Samaritan helped the Soviet government to obtain important information on meta-humans—the Outsiders and the Force of July in particular—to help the Communists to create a Soviet super-team of their own. Later, the Bad Samaritan shot down a plane carrying the Outsiders, leaving its member heroes stranded on an island somewhere in the Indian Ocean. The Bad Samaritan has recently joined the ranks of the United Nations peacekeeping operation Checkmate, acting as the White Queen's bishop. **SB**

BALLOON BUSTER

FIRST APPEARANCE ALL-AMERICAN MEN OF WAR #112 (December 1965)
STATUS Hero (deceased)   *REAL NAME* Steve Henry Savage, Jr.
OCCUPATION Lieutenant, U.S. Army Air Corps   *BASE* France
HEIGHT 5ft 11in   *WEIGHT* 178 lbs   *EYES* Blue   *HAIR* Blond
SPECIAL POWERS/ABILITIES A matchless marksman with any firearm, and an accomplished biplane pilot.

The son of legendary cowboy hero Brian "Scalphunter" Savage, Steve was raised in Mustang River, Wyoming, by a poverty-stricken farmer named Jennings.

The boy became a consummate marksman, and he learned that a gun is merely an extension of the man who wields it. At his dying adoptive father's bedside, Steve swore to make the old man proud of him by making Savage a name to be remembered. Enlisting in the U. S. Army Air Corps at the onset of World War I, Savage repeatedly disobeyed orders, breaking formation to attack and destroy German combat balloons, which earned him his nickname. Savage was one of the most aggressive warriors of that "war to end all wars," and he often dueled with the German flying ace Rittmeister Hans Von Hammer. Savage disappeared in South East Asia in 1924 while on an aerial investigation of a supposed dragon, which locals had blamed for a fever outbreak. **RG**

BANE

FIRST APPEARANCE BATMAN: VENGEANCE OF BANE #1 (January 1993)
STATUS Villain   *REAL NAME* Unknown
OCCUPATION Adventurer   *BASE* Gotham City
HEIGHT 6ft 8in   *WEIGHT* 350 lbs
EYES Brown   *HAIR* Brown
SPECIAL POWERS/ABILITIES Brilliant strategist and polylinguist, with near-superhuman strength while on the steroid Venom, mainlined into his system via tubing in his helmet.

Bane will forever be remembered as the man who broke the Bat! More than three decades ago, Bane's father received a life sentence from the Santa Priscan government for his role in a failed revolution. He fled the country, but Santa Priscan law demanded that his son take his place. The child that would become Bane was raised inside Pena Duro prison (mostly in a pit called the Cavidad Oscuro). Bane killed dozens of inmates and engineered a jailbreak when experiments with the drug Venom gave him monstrous strength.

Winding up in Gotham City, Bane exhausted Batman by freeing all the villains from Arkham Asylum. He then crippled the Dark Knight by snapping his spine. Jean Paul Valley (Azrael) donned the Batman garb and beat Bane into a coma.

Bane returned to a life of wickedness, shaking off his dependence on Venom and allying himself with Rā's al Ghūl. After a falling-out with the immortal would-be conqueror, he sabotaged Rā's al Ghūl's network of life-extending Lazarus Pits. After finding his father King Snake, Bane killed Judomaster during the Infinite Crisis, ending a brief period of semi-heroism. He has since led a revolution in Santa Prisca and joined the Suicide Squad, winding up on a prison planet alongside dozens of other villains. **DW**

CHILDHOOD TRAUMA *In prison, Bane found solace in books and a teddy bear given to him by a Catholic missionary.*

REDEMPTION *Now a blank slate, Bane must decide whether he will be an enemy or an ally in the Batman's future.*

BATGIRL

FIRST APPEARANCE BATMAN #567 (July 1999)
STATUS Hero   REAL NAME Cassandra Cain
OCCUPATION Adventurer   BASE Gotham City
HEIGHT 5ft 5in   WEIGHT 127 lbs   EYES Green   HAIR Black
SPECIAL POWERS/ABILITIES One of the greatest martial artists in the world; a deadly master of nearly all forms of unarmed combat; can "read" the body language of an opponent and predict their moves.

CASSANDRA CAIN IS THE THIRD YOUNG WOMAN to assume the mantle of Batgirl. A young orphan adopted by the master assassin David Cain to become his greatest pupil and heir, Cassandra was his most potent student, but was ultimately uninterested in extending his legacy. Seemingly unable to speak, the young Cassandra "spoke" with her body, and learned how to "read" the body language of those around her. Cain trained her in the world's deadliest martial arts, and the young Cassandra soon made her first kill, a Macauan crime kingpin. Sickened by the act, the mute girl fled Cain's estate and evil influence and began to travel the world, searching for a new home and a new way of life.

THE NEW BATGIRL

Cassandra found her way to Gotham City just before it was devastated by an earthquake and cordoned off from the rest of the U.S. During that time, she was recruited by mysterious computer hacker Oracle to act as a messenger in the city, now called No Man's Land. Years earlier, Oracle (Barbara Gordon), daughter of Police Commissioner James Gordon, had been the first Batgirl, until she was shot and crippled by the Joker. When Cain arrived in Gotham on a mission to assassinate Gordon, Cassandra saved the commissioner from her father's bullet. Impressed by Cassandra's skill and bravery, Batman took her under his wing and made her the new Batgirl.

Still without a voice, Cassandra quickly took to her new role, hoping to atone for the killing of the gangster all those years ago. Soon after, Batgirl saved a psychic named Jeffers, who was on the run from the mob. Jeffers used his powers to reorder Batgirl's brain, giving her the power of speech, but stripping from her many of her martial arts skills. Batgirl began retraining and sought out Lady Shiva, then the world's greatest martial artist, for a single lesson she hoped would help her remaster her skills. In a second confrontation with Shiva, Batgirl left her opponent for dead. She then assumed leadership of the League of Assassins, and joined other villainous outfits like Titans East. Batgirl has since redeemed herself by becoming a member of Batman's latest team of Outsiders. **PJ**

COMBAT Barely a child herself, Batgirl is nonetheless a frightening force to behold.

BODY LANGUAGE No ordinary criminal or super-villain can hope to hold their own against the martial-arts prowess of Batgirl, who was trained to communicate with her body, not with words.

KEY STORYLINES

• *BATMAN #556-559 (JULY–OCTOBER 1998):* After the Huntress forsakes her temporary role as Batgirl, a mute young girl named Cassandra Cain emerges and takes up the mantle of Batgirl.
• *BATGIRL #6 (JUNE 2000):* A psychic gives Batgirl the gift of speech, but strips her of some of her fighting skill.
• *BATGIRL #24 (APRIL 2002):* Batgirl and Lady Shiva face off in a duel to the death between the world's two greatest martial artists!
• *BATGIRL #45-50 (DECEMBER 2003–APRIL 2004):* When Doctor Death releases Soul, a rage-inducing pathogen, onto Gotham, Batgirl and Batman are forced into a confrontation spanning half of the city, including the destruction of Sprang Bridge!

BARBARA GORDON

Cassandra Cain was not the first Batgirl. Barbara Gordon, the daughter of Gotham City Police Commissioner James Gordon, dreamed of becoming Batman's partner-in-crime. Thus, Barbara became Batgirl, joining Batman and ROBIN to defend the innocent of the city. After she was crippled by the Joker, Barbara forsook her Batgirl identity and became the information broker Oracle.

25

BATMAN

THE DARK KNIGHT

FIRST APPEARANCE DETECTIVE COMICS #27 (May 1939)
STATUS Hero **REAL NAME** Bruce Wayne
OCCUPATION Industrialist; philanthropist; crime fighter
BASE Gotham City
HEIGHT 6ft 2in **WEIGHT** 210 lbs **EYES** Blue **HAIR** Black
SPECIAL POWERS/ABILITIES
Master detective with a brilliant deductive mind; quite possibly the greatest martial artist alive; Bat-costume is bulletproof and fire-resistant, featuring a weighted cape and a cowl outfitted with night-vision technology and communications arrays; utility belt contains an arsenal of crime-fighting gear, including various types of offensive Batarangs, de-cel jumplines and grapnels, micro-camera, smoke pellets, acetylene torch, gas mask, rebreather, and flexi-cuffs among other miniaturized non-lethal weapons; employs a variety of detective gadgets, including micro-computers and crime scene analysis kits; maintains a fleet of high-tech and high-powered vehicles, chief among them the Batmobile, Batcycle, Batboat, Batplane, and Batcopter; super-sophisticated Batcave headquarters houses training facilities, forensics laboratories, computer databases, and maintenance bays for all Bat-vehicles.

ALLEY SLAYING *Two bullets from a gangster's gun destroyed Bruce's young life.*

FIRST FLIGHT *Batman begins his war on crime with an aerial assault upon Gotham's goons.*

A FAMILY OUTING to the cinema ended in tragedy for young Bruce Wayne. Walking homeward, Bruce, his father, Thomas, and mother, Martha, accidentally ventured into Gotham City's notorious "Crime Alley" and were accosted by a mugger. Not content merely to rob the wealthy family, the hoodlum—whose identity was never determined—shot Dr. Thomas and Martha Wayne dead before fleeing into the darkness. As he knelt beside his parents' bodies, Bruce swore to avenge them. After the police arrived, Bruce was comforted by Dr. Leslie Thompkins. Dr. Thompkins and Alfred Pennyworth (*see* Pennyworth, Alfred) helped arrange matters so that Gotham's Social Services would not take Bruce into care. In this way, both Dr. Thompkins and Alfred enabled Bruce to realize his dream of becoming a crusader against crime.

THE YOUNG BRUCE WAYNE

At age 14, Bruce embarked on a journey that took him to every continent as he sought to learn all the skills he would need to keep his vow. He studied criminology, forensics, and criminal psychology, and learned from manhunters and martial artists, mastering every fighting style. In time, Bruce forged himself into a living weapon to wage war on crime and injustice. On his return to Gotham, Bruce stalked street thugs as a plainclothes vigilante. Beaten by the very people he intended to protect, he barely survived his first night out. As he sat bleeding in his study at Wayne Manor, Bruce knew that he had to first strike fear in the hearts of his foes. Just then, a bat crashed through the study window, giving Bruce the inspiration he needed.

BATMAN BEGINS

Establishing a secret headquarters in the caves beneath his mansion, Bruce became Batman, a Dark Knight to protect Gotham and its citizens from vice and villainy. Alfred Pennyworth remained his confidant, tending to injuries and offering sage advice—whether requested or not!

Batman became an urban legend, a cautionary tale that sent shivers through the city's underworld. This Caped Crusader found a friend in Captain James Gordon, a Gotham cop who didn't approve of Batman's methods, but appreciated the results of his nightly crime fighting. Batman's Rogues Gallery grew to include a host of bizarre criminals, such as the Joker, Catwoman, Two-Face, and the Penguin. As his enemies increased, help arrived in the form of another young boy left parentless by brutal crime.

DARK INSPIRATION *Wishing to strike fear among the criminal community, Bruce made the bat his symbol and totem.*

A FAMILY AFFAIR

The addition of Robin to his nightly crusade helped Batman in more ways than he would ever admit. However, when Dick Grayson embarked on his own path as Nightwing, the Batcave became a lonelier place for the Dark Knight, especially after Jason Todd's murder and the crippling of Barbara Gordon (see Batgirl and Oracle), both suffered at the hands of the Joker. For a time, Batman operated strictly solo until young Tim Drake convinced the Dark Knight that he needed a Robin to give him hope.

FAMILY *The Dark Knight counts Robin and Oracle among his trusted allies.*

HITTING BACK *Batman lashes out at the Joker for killing Jason Todd, the second Robin.*

BROKEN BAT

Tragedy again struck when the terrorist Bane, after forcing Batman to fight many of his most powerful foes, broke Batman's back. Jean-Paul Valley (Azrael) took on the Dark Knight's role while Bruce recuperated from his injuries. This interim Batman was more violent and unstable; Bruce returned to action as soon as his body had healed and he had regained his fighting spirit, with the help of the ruthless martial-arts mistress Lady Shiva. Bruce took back the mantle of the Bat by force, but Jean-Paul Valley remained a staunch ally as the hero Azrael until his death.

KNIGHTFALL *Bane delivers the final cruel blow to defeat an exhausted Batman.*

THE LONG HALLOWEEN

One criminal case still haunts Batman. Early in his career, the Dark Knight failed to identify the serial killer known as Holiday and prevent a string of murders targeting the Falcone crime family. "The Long Halloween" ultimately resulted in D.A. Harvey Dent's tragic disfigurement and led to Dent becoming murdering gangster Two-Face. In that regard, Batman lost both a friend and an ally.

DARK TIMES

The Dark Knight helped maintain law and order in Gotham City when a contagion struck, killing tens of thousands. He was also the city's saviour in the anarchic aftermath of a cataclysmic earthquake. With Gotham declared a No Man's Land by the government, Batman and his allies, including a new Batgirl, fought a yearlong struggle to take the town back block by block. Gotham City was eventually rebuilt, and Batman redoubled his efforts to make known to all returning criminals that a Dark Knight defender still ruled the night. More recently, Batman faced several more personal losses. The first involved the end of his "working" relationship with Commissioner Gordon, who left the police force after a near-fatal shooting. Batman's clandestine ties to the G.C.P.D. would never be the same with his friend and ally retired.

SOLOMON GRUNDY *The creature born on a Monday in Slaughter Swamp is among many monsters Batman battles every night of the week.*

KEY STORYLINES

• *BATMAN #401–404 (FEBRUARY–MAY 1987):* The Dark Knight's tumultuous beginnings as a costumed crime fighter are chronicled in "Batman: Year One."

• *BATMAN #492 (MAY 1993):* As the epic, multipart "Knightfall" begins, the Caped Crusader fights exhaustion to enemies set loose by Bane, the villain who would ultimately break the Bat.

• *BATMAN: CATACLYSM/BATMAN: NO MAN'S LAND (TPB COLLECTIONS):* Batman's greatest battle begins as Gotham City is rocked by an earthquake. This leaves the city reduced to rubble and abandoned to anarchy by all except the Dark Knight and his closest allies.

BRUCE WAYNE: MURDERER?

Not long after, Bruce was accused of murdering journalist Vesper Fairchild, actually slain by the assassin Cain on the orders of then-President Lex Luthor (see Luthor, Lex), a business rival. Bruce was vindicated, but Vesper's death served as a stark reminder why close relationships run contrary to Batman's mostly solitary mission. However, Batman still appreciates the aid of his crime-fighting partners, and the value of teamwork. He has long been a member of the Justice League of America and assembled the first Outsiders team to take action against criminals the authorities could not touch.

GUARDED LOVE *Bruce Wayne's latest romance was with his bodyguard, Sasha Bordeaux, now a government agent.*

BATMAN TODAY

Batman continues to watch over Gotham as its staunchest defender. Moreover, since his parents' killer has never been apprehended, Bruce knows that the Dark Knight's crusade could be an endless struggle to find "the one that got away." Meanwhile, Batman fights to ensure that no one else suffers the collateral damage of random crime and senseless violence. **SB**

TRUST *Batman's newest nemesis struck at him by being both friend and foe. Ultimately, Batman learned that Hush was his childhood chum, Tommy Elliot.*

BATMAN

HUSH

One of Bruce Wayne's oldest friends returned as one of Batman's greatest villains in a conflict that united the Dark Knight's foes. Dr. Thomas Elliot sought revenge on his former childhood companion as the bandaged villain Hush, allying with the Riddler to hatch a complicated scheme. Harvey Dent shot Hush and left him for dead, but the affair raised troubling hints that Jason Todd, the second Robin, had returned from the dead.

OLD WOUNDS As a boy, Tommy Elliot wanted his parents to die so he could collect their inheritance. When Dr. Thomas Wayne saved their lives, he swore revenge on the Wayne family.

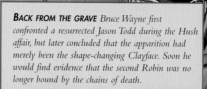

BACK FROM THE GRAVE Bruce Wayne first confronted a resurrected Jason Todd during the Hush affair, but later concluded that the apparition had merely been the shape-changing Clayface. Soon he would find evidence that the second Robin was no longer bound by the chains of death.

WITHOUT A TRACE Suspicious of the circumstances surrounding Jason Todd's death, Batman exhumed Jason's coffin – only to find it empty.

THE RETURN OF JASON TODD

Although killed by the Joker, the second Robin came back from the grave thanks to the timeline tremors that would soon signal the Infinite Crisis. Now an embittered adult, Jason Todd assumed the criminal persona of the Red Hood and set about cleaning up Gotham with brutal efficiency. Black Mask, Todd's primary target, fought back with increasing desperation, while Batman struggled to curb the violent zeal of his former protégé. Todd even kidnapped the Joker and forced Batman to explain why he had not avenged Todd's murder. Batman's refusal to kill drew a clear line between the veteran crimefighter and the rogue vigilante that Todd had become.

JASON'S REVENGE The Joker beat Jason with a crowbar before killing him in an explosion. After his return, Jason put the Joker's name on the top of his hit list

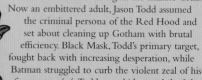

RED HOOD With a new identity, Jason Todd set about cleaning up the streets of Gotham even killing criminals and drug dealers to make a point. This put him at odds with Batman, and they soon came to blows.

WAR GAMES

Gotham City's underworld had always existed in a state of uneasy equilibrium between crime bosses, but events soon upset the balance and triggered gang-war chaos. Shortly before the shooting started, Tim Drake took leave from his Robin responsibilities out of concern for his father. Batman trained Stephanie Brown (Spoiler) as the fourth Robin, but rejected her after determining she lacked the needed experience. Anxious to prove herself, Stephanie prematurely activated one of Batman's long-range plans for dealing with Gotham organized crime. The operation soon spiraled out of control, with a victorious Black Mask emerging with nearly Gotham's entire underworld in his fist. Black Mask also captured and tortured Stephanie Brown, who died as Batman sat beside her hospital bed.

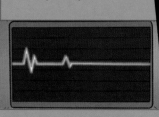

STRUCK DOWN *Black Mask's murder of Stephanie Brown is one of the most tragic outcomes of Gotham's 'War Games'.*

FLATLINE *The injuries suffered at the hands of Black Mask, as well as Dr. Leslie Thompkins' controversial treatment, led to Stephanie's death. This, however, would be mysteriously overturned."*

INFINITE CRISIS

Ever since Zatanna had mind-wiped him years earlier, Batman had harbored suspicions of his fellow heroes. With the Wayne Enterprises fortune, he built and programmed an observational satellite, the Brother Mark I, to keep tabs on superhuman activity. But the satellite's artificial intelligence soon named itself Brother Eye and initiated a program to eliminate all metahumans on Earth. As Brother Eye's nanotech virus transformed hundreds of thousands of humans into unstoppable OMAC agents, Batman led the charge to dismantle the satellite. His handpicked team, including Blue Beetle, Mister Terrific, Green Arrow, and Black Canary, took down Brother Eye in orbit, bringing victory to one battlefront of the Infinite Crisis. Although presented with an opportunity to kill enemy mastermind Alexander Luthor, Batman refused to take the easy way out. In one of the event's timeline ripples, reality shifted so that the killer of Batman's parents faced justice rather than getting away with murder.

SECRETS *Zatanna and other members of the Justice League agreed to perform mind-wipes on captured villains, an act that outraged Batman when he discovered the truth.*

OMAC AMOK *The spawn of Batman's own creation, the OMAC units swept across the globe during the lead-up to the Infinite Crisis.*

ONE YEAR LATER

Batman, Robin, and Nightwing left on an overseas ship for months of back-to-basics training, temporarily retiring their costumed identities. With Batman absent, protection of Gotham City fell to Harvey Dent – apparently cured of his split Two-Face personality. A string of murders, caused Dent to question his sanity, and when Batman returned after his year abroad, Dent returned to his criminal ways.

FALLING DOWN *After a year of working on the side of law and order, Dent used acid to re-scar his left side and become Two-Face once more.*

BATMAN

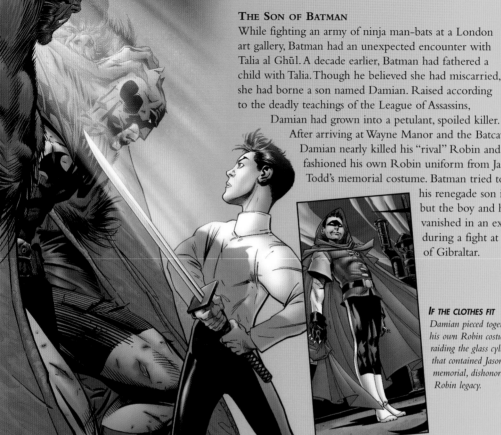

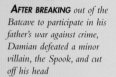

THE SON OF BATMAN

While fighting an army of ninja man-bats at a London art gallery, Batman had an unexpected encounter with Talia al Ghūl. A decade earlier, Batman had fathered a child with Talia. Though he believed she had miscarried, she had borne a son named Damian. Raised according to the deadly teachings of the League of Assassins, Damian had grown into a petulant, spoiled killer. After arriving at Wayne Manor and the Batcave, Damian nearly killed his "rival" Robin and fashioned his own Robin uniform from Jason Todd's memorial costume. Batman tried to bring his renegade son in line, but the boy and his mother vanished in an explosion during a fight at the Rock of Gibraltar.

AFTER BREAKING out of the Batcave to participate in his father's war against crime, Damian defeated a minor villain, the Spook, and cut off his head

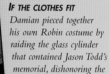

IF THE CLOTHES FIT Damian pieced together his own Robin costume by raiding the glass cylinder that contained Jason Todd's memorial, dishonoring the Robin legacy.

THE RESURRECTION OF RĀ'S AL GHŪL

Damian didn't stay underground for long. His late grandfather, Rā's al Ghūl, cheated death yet again and reappeared as a shambling, decaying corpse. Rā's hoped to transfer his soul into Damian's body, and Batman allied with Talia to ensure this fate did not befall their son. In the sacred city of Nanda Parbat, Batman battled Rā's al Ghūl in a duel to the death, with Damian, Robin, Nightwing, and even Alfred holding their own against the League of Assassins. Ultimately the monks of Nanda Parbat forced both sides to flee the battlefield, leaving Rā's a malignant threat and Damian back under the care of his mother. Among Batman's recent moves is the creation of an all-new team of Outsiders. DW

MUMMY WRAPS Rā's al Ghūl returned needing a fresh form taken from a member of his extended family to restore himself to full life.

LOW BLOW The fight against Rā's's minions in Nanda Parbat demanded contributions from the Bat-Family, including Bruce Wayne's butler Alfred.

FAMILY FEUD Although Batman and Rā's al Ghūl had fought many times before, the emergence of Damian put them into the new, and unfamiliar, roles of father and grandfather.

BATWOMAN

FIRST APPEARANCE 52 #7 (July 2006)
STATUS Hero **REAL NAME** Katherine "Kate" Kane
OCCUPATION Crimefighter **BASE** Gotham City
HEIGHT 5ft 11in **WEIGHT** 145 lbs
EYES Green **HAIR** Red
SPECIAL POWERS/ABILITIES Highly-trained acrobatic combatant
aided by an arsenal of high-tech gadgetry.

IN THE YEAR FOLLOWING the Infinite Crisis, Batwoman filled the void while Gotham City went without its primary protector. Batwoman, or Katherine "Kate" Kane, came from the same wealthy background as Bruce Wayne, with the Kane family rumored to own everything in Gotham that the Waynes did not. The circumstances that drove her to become a vigilante are still unknown, but Batwoman's martial arts skills are augmented by weapons and gadgets purchased with the Kane fortune.

HURT FEELINGS *Though they had once been in love, Kathy Kane and Renee Montoya had parted on bad terms. The Intergang plot pushed them together again, bringing raw emotions to the surface.*

NEW TITLE

Years prior to her debut as Batwoman, Kane shared a romance with Gotham City police detective Renee Montoya that ended painfully. After the Infinite Crisis, Montoya reached out to Kane for help in uncovering clues about Intergang activity in the city. As Batwoman, Kane tailed Montoya and her partner the Question to an ambush set by Intergang agent Whisper A'Daire. Smashing into the room, Batwoman knocked out A'Daire's animal-hybrid monsters, and Montoya recognized the new super hero as her former love.

Batwoman soon joined the Question and Montoya in their fight against Intergang. They learned that the Crime Bible, a book at the center of a cult led by Intergang boss Bruno Mannheim, contained a prophecy concerning the death of the "twice-named daughter of Cain"—a reference to Kane herself.

During the holiday season, Batwoman crossed paths with Nightwing, who gave her a Batarang. She also celebrated Hanukkah with Montoya, and the two renewed their relationship by sharing a kiss.

The final showdown with Intergang occurred when Mannheim's thugs kidnapped Kane and tied her to an altar, intending to offer her as a blood sacrifice to the evil spirits celebrated in the Crime Bible. Mannheim stabbed Kane in the chest, but she removed the knife and took down her attacker before passing out. After a period of recuperation, Kane returned to her role as Batwoman.

Batwoman continues to protect the citizens of Gotham, sometimes accompanied by Montoya in her guise as the new Question. The pair recently intercepted the Trickster and Pied Piper, after the two fugitive rogues fled the Penguin's Iceberg Lounge. **DW**

HAPPY HOLIDAYS *Nightwing happily welcomed Gotham's new adventurer to the Bat-Family, leaving her with a smile and the present of an official Batarang.*

KEY STORYLINES

• *52 #11 (JULY 2006):* Batwoman debuts against Intergang, saving Renee Montoya and the Question.
• *52 #48 (APRIL 2007):* Montoya, the new Question, saves Kathy Kane from Bruno Mannheim.
• *1-5 (DECEMBER 2007–APRIL 2008):* Montoya goes to uncover the Cult of Cain, leaving Batwoman to question their relationship.

ONE FOR THE ROAD
Bibbo hoists a cool one to toast his "fav'rit"!

BIBBO

FIRST APPEARANCE THE ADVENTURES OF SUPERMAN #428 (May 1987)
STATUS Hero/ally   **REAL NAME** "Bibbo" Bibbowski
OCCUPATION Tavern owner   **BASE** Suicide Slum, Metropolis
HEIGHT 6ft 3in   **WEIGHT** 250 lbs   **EYES** Gray   **HAIR** Gray
SPECIAL POWERS/ABILITIES A former boxer, Bibbo packs a mean punch and has started (and ended) more than a few bar fights.

OUT COLD *Not many can walk, let alone stand, after being on the receiving end of one of Bibbo's roundhouse punches. Even the Man of Steel is staggered!*

Ex-longshoreman and former heavyweight contender, "Bibbo" Bibbowski is proprietor of the Ace O' Clubs tavern, a down-and-dirty waterfront pub in Metropolis's seedy Suicide Slum. This same bar was formerly Bibbo's preferred watering hole during his days as a booze-soaked barfly. But despite his slovenly appearance, fortune has always favored Bibbo. He bought the Ace O' Clubs after finding a winning lottery ticket lost by Jose Delgado (Gangbuster). The first year's annuity from the $14,000,000 lottery jackpot put Bibbo on easy street. Happily, his sudden fortune did not change Bibbo's outgoing and relaxed attitude to life. A friend to SUPERMAN, Bibbo practically idolizes the Man of Steel, whom he regards as his "fav'rit" hero. Though he'd wallop anyone who calls him a snitch, by virtue of his role as barkeep in an area famous for criminal activity, Bibbo often overhears useful information that he passes along to Superman or his other pal, Jimmy Olsen (*see* Olsen, Jimmy). **SB**

GONE TO THE DOGS *Bibbo isn't choosy when it comes to poker buddies, even playing a hand with a pack of alien hounds!*

BIG BARDA

FIRST APPEARANCE Mister Miracle (1st series) #4 (September 1971)
STATUS Hero   **REAL NAME** Barda Free
HEIGHT 6ft 2in   **WEIGHT** 217 lbs   **EYES** Blue   **HAIR** Black
OCCUPATION Freedom fighter   **BASE** New Genesis
SPECIAL POWERS/ABILITIES Trained as a Female Fury; one of the deadliest hand-to-hand combatants alive; her mastery of the mega rod is unchallenged.

Barda was always destined to be someone special; she was the only child borne out of love by Apokolips' Big Breeda. The baby was taken by Darkseid, raised first in the Gestatron labs, then in Granny Goodness's vast orphanage, where the defiant look in Barda's eye could not be beaten out of her. Instead, Granny took her for special training and Barda excelled in all manner of combat. Barda was among the first selected to form the battalion known as the Female Furies. Barda became Granny's best squad leader, commanding the Furies to many successful victories. But then Barda fell in love with another of Granny's charges, Scott Free, a son of New Genesis. Scott met Barda, and she saw something in his spirit that touched a part of her she didn't know even existed. Barda found herself helping Scott escape from hellish Apokolips to Earth. She followed him, and their relationship deepened into lasting love. Finally, after Scott had established himself as master escape artist Mister Miracle, they married. Although Scott loved life on Earth, Barda could only barely tolerate it. This led to her serving two brief stints with the Justice League of America. Big Barda lost her life during the Death of the New Gods event, murdered in her home. Her husband Scott traveled to New Genesis and Apokolips to avenge her death. **RG**

BATTLING BARDA
Barda is one of the most feared combatants on Earth or New Genesis. She has even managed to fight Wonder Woman to a draw.

BIZARRO

IMPERFECT DUPLICATE OF SUPERMAN

FIRST APPEARANCE THE MAN OF STEEL #5 (October 1986)
STATUS Villain   **REAL NAME** None
OCCUPATION Imperfect duplicate of Superman   **BASE** Mobile
HEIGHT 6ft 3in   **WEIGHT** 225 lbs   **EYES** Blue   **HAIR** Black
SPECIAL POWERS/ABILITIES Superstrong, invulnerable, and able to fly like the Man of Steel, but possessing some powers opposite to that of Superman, including freezing vision and flaming breath.

COUNTLESS TIMES SUPER-VILLAINS have raised their eyes to the heavens and cursed in vain as the heroic Man of Steel flashes across the sky to save the day. *If only*, they fume, *if only* they had a SUPERMAN of their very own, a mindless, superpowered slave to do their evil bidding! Superman's arch enemy Lex Luthor (*see* Luthor, Lex) was the first rogue to try to make this dream a reality. In secret, Luthor called upon his top scientist, Dr. Teng, to scan Superman's genetic structure. Teng successfully duplicated Superman, but was unable to completely recreate the complex chromosomal structure of the Last Son of Krypton. The resulting Superclone quickly became a monstrous menace, a Bizarro creature that might have razed Metropolis to the ground had Superman not intervened. Yet this misbegotten Bizarro creature was not without its gentle side, for it allowed itself to be destroyed in a rain of disintegrating particles that somehow allowed Lucy Lane, blind sister of reporter Lois Lane (*see* Lane, Lois), to regain her sight.

CREATION At first, Dr. Teng's clone was the spitting image of the Man of Steel.

A BIZARRO IN LOVE

Luthor tried a second time to clone the Man of Steel many months later, and like the first imperfect duplicate, this second Bizarro became a superpowered nuisance. Retaining snippets of genetic memory of Superman's strong affections for Lois Lane, Bizarro #2 set about creating a ramshackle "Bizarro World" from junk and refuse, in his own way building a Bizarro Metropolis that would please his beloved "Lo-iz." Bizarro #2 then snatched up Lane and took her to his crooked city, where he held the reporter hostage while Superman searched frantically for her. However, all Bizarro #2 wanted was to please "Lo-iz," but like his predecessor, he succumbed to rapid cellular degeneration. He died in Lois's arms. The third Bizarro, however, had little to do with genetic tinkering. Instead, a boastful new Bizarro #1 was given a fresh lease on life via the twisted imagination of Batman's arch-nemesis, the Joker. After acquiring the reality-altering powers of fifth-dimensional imp Mister Mxyzptlk the Clown Prince of Crime envisioned a topsy-turvy Earth where evil replaced good and bizarre new villains occupied the seats of an anarchic Justice League Of America. Thus, Bizarro #1 came into being as counterpoint to Superman yet again. Though matching the Man of Steel muscle for muscle, Bizarro #1 possesses some abilities that are opposite to Superman's. He also *gains* strength when exposed to kryptonite, the radioactive element deadly to the Man of Steel. Bizarro has been used as a tool by Lex Luthor and others to achieve their ends. During the Infinite Crisis, Bizarro killed the Human Bomb while serving with the Secret Society Of Super Villains. Later he attempted to kidnap Clark Kent's foster son, Christopher Kent. Perhaps tiring of his role as a puppet for others, Bizarro fled the planet and created his own domain – a cube-shaped world populated with clones grown from his own body by using 'Bizarro vision.' These clones resembled crude versions of people whom Bizarro had known on Earth, including Lois Lane, Jimmy Olsen, and the Justice League Of America. Bizarro took things too far when he imprisoned Pa Kent on Bizarro World, forcing Superman's intervention.

SB

BIZARRO WORLD
To a Bizarro, Earth would be cube-shaped instead of a planetary orb. Anything to be different!

HARD LUCK Unable to have his revenge on Superman, General Zod punished Bizarro #3 instead.

LOOKING FOR LOVE In need of a father-figure, Bizarro kidnapped Pa Kent and imprisoned him on Bizarro World. For a while Bizarro even got the better of the Man of Steel.

KEY STORYLINES

- **SUPERBOY #68 (OCTOBER 1958):** Pre-Crisis, the very first Bizarro is an imperfect teen duplicate of Superboy!
- **SUPERMAN #87 (MARCH 1994):** Bizarro #2 is cloned, subsequently building his own Bizarro World before his untimely end.
- **SUPERMAN #160 (SEPTEMBER 2000):** The Joker uses Mr. Mxyzptlk's powers to create an upside-down world complete with an all-new Bizarro #1, more bizarre than any who came before!

BLACK CANARY

THE PRETTY BIRD OF PREY

FIRST APPEARANCE (BLACK CANARY I) FLASH COMICS #86 (August 1947)
STATUS Hero (deceased)   **REAL NAME** Dinah Drake Lance
OCCUPATION Adventurer; florist   **BASE** Gotham City
HEIGHT 5ft 5in   **WEIGHT** 128 lbs   **EYES** Blue   **HAIR** Black
SPECIAL POWERS/ABILITIES Trained in Judo, and a feisty fighter; often concealed smoke or tear-gas pellets in the amulet of her choker.

FIRST APPEARANCE (BLACK CANARY II) JUSTICE LEAGUE OF AMERICA #75 (November 1969)
STATUS Hero   **REAL NAME** Dinah Laurel Lance
OCCUPATION Adventurer   **BASE** Gotham City
HEIGHT 5ft 4in   **WEIGHT** 124 lbs   **EYES** Blue   **HAIR** Blonde
SPECIAL POWERS/ABILITIES Ultrasonic, earsplitting "canary cry," capable of shattering metal; martial arts and boxing expert.

IN 1947, DINAH DRAKE'S DREAMS of becoming a Gotham City policewoman were dashed when her police academy application was rejected and her doting father, Detective Richard Drake, subsequently passed away. Dinah used her small inheritance to open a florist's shop while pursuing a more clandestine career in crime fighting. Inspired by the brightly clad "Mystery Men" of the time, raven-haired Dinah designed her own stylish costume—black fishnets and leather, as well as a blonde wig to conceal her identity—and embarked on a vigilante career as the sultry Black Canary. At first passing herself off as a criminal to infiltrate Gotham's underworld, the Judo-savvy Black Canary eventually revealed her true colors upon teaming with fellow hero Johnny Thunder. She became a member of the Justice Society of America soon after, although eventually retired from costumed crime fighting. She married private detective Larry Lance and gave birth to a daughter (also named Dinah), who would carry on her mother's heroic legacy. Dinah Drake Lance died of radiation-induced cancer, an after-effect from battling the cosmic-powered villain Aquarius—an epic struggle during which Larry Lance sacrificed his own life—alongside her JSA teammates.

SOULMATES *The Canary often assisted paramour and private eye Larry Lance on his cases.*

BLACK CANARY II

While the original Black Canary hoped to spare her daughter the perils of a crime-fighting career, young Dinah Laurel Lance nevertheless grew up in the shadow of her mother's great exploits, tales often told to her by the JSA members who babysat her. Like her mother, Dinah was also a superb athlete and fighter. But young Dinah also possessed a metagene that bequeathed her a unique superpower: a hyper-pitched "canary cry." Despite her mother's wishes, Dinah took up the fishnets and leather outfit of Black Canary. Gifted in Judo, Dinah also learned boxing from her "uncle," Ted Grant (Wildcat I), as well as other fighting techniques from her mother's teammates in the original JSA.

As such, Dinah was one of the first "second-generation" super heroes. Operating as Black Canary II, Dinah had a string of solo adventures before joining the Justice League Of America, where she began a romance with Green Arrow Oliver Queen. Later she signed on as the primary "Bird of Prey" operative working for Oracle.

Following the Infinite Crisis, Black Canary traded places with Lady Shiva, training overseas while Shiva assumed duties with the Birds of Prey. In Vietnam Black Canary took Shiva's successor – the young girl Sin – under her wing, bringing her back to the U.S. to raise her. She also signed on as chairwoman of the new Justice League. She soon fell in love anew with Oliver Queen. But supervillains crashed their wedding, and Black Canary killed a man impersonating her husband. She later rescued the true Oliver from Amazonian imprisonment on Themyscira. **SB**

CANARY CRY *Dinah lost her canary cry after suffering a brutal beating. But this sonic superpower was restored after she was dipped in a restorative Lazarus Pit.*

SKRREEEEE

KEY STORYLINES

• **ALL-STAR COMICS #38 (DEC.–JAN. 1947–48):** Though not yet an official member, Black Canary I joins the JSA to defeat history's greatest villains!

• **JLA: YEAR ONE #1-12 (JAN.–DEC. 1998):** The second Black Canary's first year with the JLA is chronicled as the team battles the Appellaxian aliens and the organization known as Locus.

• **BLACK CANARY/ORACLE: BIRDS OF PREY (1996):** Black Canary II accepts her first assignment from ORACLE without knowing who her partner really is!

MELEE AT THE ALTAR
The superhero guests at her wedding proved an irresistible target for the villainous Society, who attacked in force. Black Canary helped crush their assault, but would soon discover her husband had been replaced by a shape-changer.

BLACK CONDOR

FIRST APPEARANCE CRACK COMICS #1 (May 1940)
STATUS Hero **REAL NAME** Richard Grey Jr., a.k.a. Thomas Wright
OCCUPATION Adventurer **BASE** Washington, D.C.
HEIGHT 6ft 2in **WEIGHT** 196 lbs **EYES** Blue **HAIR** Black
SPECIAL POWERS/ABILITIES Exposure to alien radiation granted him the ability to fly and to understand the language of birds.

Richard Grey Jr. was lost as an infant in the Mongolian mountains. There he was exposed to radiation from a meteor, which mutated the developing child. A family of condors rescued and raised him until he was found by Father Pierre, a missionary. He called the child Black Condor and taught him to speak, read, and write English. When Father Pierre was murdered, the Black Condor set out to avenge him. En route, he found the body of Senator Thomas Wright, who had been murdered by the deranged Jaspar Crow. Wright and the Condor looked identical in appearance, so the Condor assumed Wright's identity, complete with fiancée, Wendy Foster, who was none the wiser! Grey donned a costume to fight crime as the Black Condor, while serving justice in the senate. He was among the first costumed "mystery men" to serve with the All-Star Squadron and afterward its splinter group, the Freedom Fighters. His last recorded mission was in 1953, when he aided the Ray and Spitfire in fighting Doctor Spectron. The Condor subsequently moved on to a higher plane of existence—living with others "at the top of the world"—in an as-yet-unexplained manner. He made brief appearances on Earth, including helping to recruit Ryan Kendall as Black Condor II. **RG**

BLACK CONDOR II

FIRST APPEARANCE BLACK CONDOR #1 (June 1992)
STATUS Hero **REAL NAME** Ryan Kendall
OCCUPATION Adventurer **BASE** Opal City
HEIGHT 6ft 4in **WEIGHT** 170 lbs **EYES** Blue **HAIR** Black
SPECIAL POWERS/ABILITIES Flight, heightened senses, limited telepathy, and telekinesis; expert knife-thrower.

Though not a direct successor to the wartime hero known as Black Condor, Ryan Kendall has proven himself worthy of the Condor legacy and has become a hero in his own right. He received his powers thanks to a monstrous experiment conducted by his grandfather, Creighton Kendall, leader of the centuries-old Society of the Golden Wing. As part of the Society's program to create a flying man, Kendall irradiated Ryan while he was still a fetus. At the age of 21, Ryan fell into a coma which lasted two years. When he recovered, he flew off into the thick of New Jersey's Pine Barrens to find himself. Under the name Black Condor, Ryan Kendall assumed a super-heroic role in battles against the Sky Pirate and the Shark. He joined the Justice League of America following Superman's death, and later became a member of Primal Force. Black Condor then settled in Opal City working with the police. Kendall died during the Infinite Crisis. A third Black Condor, John Trujillo, now serves as a member of the Freedom Fighters alongside Uncle Sam. **DW**

FLYING SOLO Black Condor II is a loner who works with super-hero teams, but who doesn't socialize with them.

BLACK LIGHTNING

FIRST APPEARANCE BLACK LIGHTNING (1st series) #1 (April 1977)
STATUS Hero **REAL NAME** Jefferson Pierce
OCCUPATION Adventurer **BASE** Metropolis
HEIGHT 6ft 1in **WEIGHT** 182 lbs **EYES** Brown **HAIR** Black
SPECIAL POWERS/ABILITIES Olympic-level athlete; superb hand-to-hand combatant; internally generated electromagnetic field; can create and hurl bolts of supercharged electricity.

Jefferson Pierce escaped the squalor of Metropolis's Suicide Slum by devoting himself to athletics. He eventually won Olympic gold in the decathlon. Once qualified as a teacher, he returned to Suicide Slum. Pierce watched helplessly as his students fell victim to drugs, controlled by the 100 mob led by albino behemoth Tobias Whale. With a costume sporting an electronic belt to shock thugs senseless, Pierce became Black Lightning and brought the 100 mob, and Tobias Whale, to justice.

One of the most famous African-American super heroes of his time, Pierce became a founder member of the Outsiders. During his stint with the team, a latent metagene enabled him to internalize his lightning-like powers. Following the Outsiders' dissolution, Black Lightning became defender of crime-ridden Brick City. He then served under U.S. President Lex Luthor (*see* Luthor, Lex) as Secretary of Education. Pierce now serves with the Justice League Of America. His daughter Anissa (Thunder II) was recently a member of a new team of Outsiders. **SB**

BODY ELECTRIC Black Lightning continues to explore his electromagnetic abilities, including the power to travel via bolts of electricity.

HARD TO GET Black Lightning once turned down an offer of membership in the Justice League of America.

BLACKHAWK

FIRST APPEARANCE MILITARY COMICS #1 (August 1941)
STATUS Hero (missing in action) **REAL NAME** Janos Prohaska
OCCUPATION Squadron leader **BASE** England
HEIGHT 6ft 1.5in **WEIGHT** 195 lbs **EYES** Blue **HAIR** Black
SPECIAL POWERS/ABILITIES An expert pilot; a charismatic and quick-thinking field leader, in addition to being good with his fists.

POLAND'S JANOS PROHASKA served with the Bill Heywood Squadron of the International Brigades during the Spanish Civil War, gaining an international reputation as a flyer of amazing skill and courage. When, in 1939, Poland fell victim to Nazi Germany's *blitzkrieg* warfare, Prohaska, now nicknamed Blackhawk, joined with his friends Stanislaw "Stan" Drozdowski and Kazimierc "Zeg" Zegota and others to form the Blackhawk Squadron. They resisted the brutal invaders of their homeland from a secret base on Blackhawk Island.

THE BLACKHAWK SQUADRON

Blackhawk assembled a truly international band of air aces, all determined to fight for freedom. The pilots included Boris Zinoviev of Russia, Ian Holcolmb-Baker of England, André Blanc-DuMont of France, Olaf Friedriksen of Sweden, Ritter Hendricksen of Denmark, and Carlo "Chuck" Sirianni of the U.S. Sadly, Boris, Zeg, Ian, and Stanislaus were soon killed in action. Soon afterwards, 17-year-old Chinese-American "whiz kid" Weng "Chop Chop" Chan joined the group.

The C.I.A. later recruited the Blackhawks, and Blackhawk Airways was relocated to Washington, D.C. The U.S. government wanted more control over the team's missions, and when Blackhawk objected, the team was kidnapped until rescued by Blackhawk and new recruit Paco Herrera. The isle of Pontalba was then transformed into the new Blackhawk Island. Soon after, the Blackhawks severed all ties with the C.I.A. and the U.S. government.

In the 1960s, André was murdered by an assassin named Hardwire. Years later Blackhawk tracked the killer down in Saigon, just as the city was about to fall to the Viet Kong, and avenged his friend's death. Sadly, Olaf disappeared during the mission. Years after, Weng Chan formed an elite air courier service, Blackhawk Express. The company put together a team of doubles of the seven best-known Blackhawks, who fought crime in the decade ahead. President Lex Luthor (*see* Luthor, Lex) employed the new Blackhawk Squadron during the Imperiex War (*see* Great Battles, pp. 186-7), but the current whereabouts of Prohaska and the other members of the team is not known. **RG**

BRAVERY *Despite grave danger and frequent combat wounds, the Blackhawks never gave up.*

LEADING FORCE *Blackhawk was not only a great flyer and terrific fighter: even more importantly he was a charismatic leader.*

FIRST CLASS FLYERS *The Blackhawk planes were not only durable, they were also among the best engineered craft in the world.*

KEY STORYLINES

• *MILITARY COMICS #1 (AUGUST 1941):* This early story introduces the world to Janos Porhaska and his men.
• *BLACKHAWK #1-3 (MARCH–MAY 1989):* The tale spotlights Prohaska as he deals with a Russian conspiracy and life after the War.
• *BLACKHAWK #140 (SEPTEMBER 1959):* Lady Blackhawk is introduced to the team.

TWO-FISTED HERO *One-man blitzkrieg Blackhawk makes light work of a German army tank crew.*

BLUE BEETLE

BLUE BEETLE I

FIRST APPEARANCE BLUE BEETLE (1st series) #1 (June 1964)
STATUS Hero (deceased) *REAL NAME* Dr. Daniel Garrett
OCCUPATION Adventurer *BASE* Hub City
HEIGHT 6ft *WEIGHT* 189 lbs *EYES* Blue *HAIR* Red
SPECIAL POWERS/ABILITIES Superstrong; able to fly and discharge lightning-like energy from fingertips; chain-mail armor impervious to small-arms fire.

BLUE BEETLE II

FIRST APPEARANCE CAPTAIN ATOM (1st series) #83 (Nov. 1966)
STATUS Adventurer (deceased) *REAL NAME* Theodore "Ted" Kord
OCCUPATION Adventurer *BASE* New York City
HEIGHT 5ft 11in *WEIGHT* 184 lbs *EYES* Blue *HAIR* Brown
SPECIAL POWERS/ABILITIES The second Blue Beetle possesses no superpowers, but is a genius inventor and a capable hand-to-hand combatant. His BB-gun has several settings, including a walloping compressed-air blast and blinding strobe light. The Beetle's greatest weapon is his "Bug," a stealthy, solar-powered crime-fighting vehicle.

BLUE BEETLE III

FIRST APPEARANCE INFINITE CRISIS #5 (March 2006)
STATUS Hero *REAL NAME* Jaime Reyes
OCCUPATION High-school student, adventurer *BASE* El Paso, Texas
HEIGHT 5ft 8in *WEIGHT* 145 lbs *EYES* Brown *HAIR* Black
SPECIAL POWERS/ABILITIES Alien suit provides protection, flight, enhanced strength, and can generate many forms of weaponry.

After discovering a glowing azure scarab in the tomb of the evil Pharaoh Kha-ef-re, archaeologist Dr. Daniel Garrett gained miraculous powers when he uttered the words "Kaji Dha." Possessing superhuman abilities and clad in azure chain-mail armor, Garrett fought evil in Hub City as the first Blue Beetle. Years later, Garrett helped student Ted Kord thwart Kord's Uncle Jarvis and his plans for world domination. The battle left Blue Beetle mortally wounded. With his dying breath, Garrett made young Kord promise that he would carry on in his stead, thus ensuring that the Blue Beetle's heroic legacy would continue.

BEETLE POWER *With his mystic scarab empowering him, the original Blue Beetle was a veritable superman!*

TED KORD

When Dan Garrett was grievously injured thwarting the maniacal Jarvis Kord from dominating the world with his army of robots, Garrett asked his friend and protégé, Ted Kord, Jarvis's nephew, to carry on in his stead as Blue Beetle II. But before Garrett could pass on the mystic scarab that gave him his astounding abilities, the dying hero and his talisman were entombed under tons of rubble on the remote Pago Island, site of Jarvis Kord's failed plot. Undaunted, Kord trained himself in a variety of fighting skills and developed an arsenal of non-lethal weapons to let him operate as a non-powered Blue Beetle, whose sense of adventurous whimsy was in stark contrast to Dan Garrett's stalwart stoicism. Once more,

MAN ON A MISSION
Kord flies to Checkmate HQ to investigate Maxwell Lord's database on meta-humans.

there was a Blue Beetle to keep evil at bay in Hub City, where he added his own rogues gallery to villains inherited from Dan Garrett. Later, the Beetle moved to Chicago and made the Windy City safer during his tenure there. Unfortunately, super heroics haven't always been as easy for the second Blue Beetle as for the original Azure Avenger. Ted hasn't always been able to devote complete attention to running K.O.R.D. (Kord Omniversal Research and Development), a high-tech corporation he built up from the tiny company inherited from his father. And Ted can attest that he has had even less time leftover for his

infrequent romances. During Blue Beetle's investigation of Checkmate, Maxwell Lord shot the hero in the head. Ted Kord's death shocked the super-hero community, and inspired Booster Gold to attempt to reverse the event through time travel. A third Blue Beetle, the teenager Jaime Reyes, emerged in Texas during the Infinite Crisis and now serves alongside the Teen Titans.

MURDERED *Ted Kord is shot dead by Maxwell Lord in the headquarters of Checkmate.*

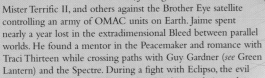

JAIME REYES

The scarab that gave Dan Garrett his powers found its way into Shazam's Rock of Eternity. When the Rock exploded before the Infinite Crisis, the scarab landed in Texas and bonded to Jaime Reyes's spine. After experimenting, Jaime could generate body armor, jet packs, and weapons. He became Blue Beetle, joining Batman, Green Arrow, Mister Terrific II, and others against the Brother Eye satellite controlling an army of OMAC units on Earth. Jaime spent nearly a year lost in the extradimensional Bleed between parallel worlds. He found a mentor in the Peacemaker and romance with Traci Thirteen while crossing paths with Guy Gardner (*see* Green Lantern) and the Spectre. During a fight with Eclipso, the evil being promised to bring Jaime's fantasies to life, revealing his deepest desire to be a comfortable living as a dentist. Jaime recently learned that his scarab is the creation of the alien species, the Reach. The scarab was to act as an advance agent, but through Jaime's influence, Blue Beetle III became one of the Reach's most persistent enemies. Jaime relies on friends and family to ease the stress of adventuring. He has formed a second family with the Teen Titans. **SB/DW**

STRANGE FIND
At first Jaime and his friends think the scarab is just a big bug.

KEY STORYLINES

• *JUSTICE LEAGUE #1 (MAY 1987):* Ted Kord hits the big leagues alongside Booster Gold, forming an inseparable, wisecracking friendship.
• *COUNTDOWN TO INFINITE CRISIS #1 (MAY 2005):* Former Justice League financier Maxwell Lord is revealed as a villain when he shoots and kills Ted Kord to preserve the secrets of the OMAC project.
• *BLUE BEETLE VOL. 7 #1 (MAY 2006):* El Paso teenager Jaime Reyes becomes the third Blue Beetle.

BOUNCING BOY

FIRST APPEARANCE ACTION COMICS #276 (May 1961)
STATUS Hero **REAL NAME** Chuck Taine
OCCUPATION Retired adventurer **BASE** Earth
HEIGHT 5ft 8in **WEIGHT** 221 lbs **EYES** Blue **HAIR** Black
SUPER POWERS/ABILITIES Able to inflate his body and bounce to great
heights; highly resistant to injury.

In an alternate timeline of the Legion Of Super-Heroes,
Chuck Taine of Earth received superhuman powers when
he accidentally drank an experimental serum. Now
able to inflate his body like a beach ball, he joined the
Legion as Bouncing Boy. Taine used his gift to bowl
over enemy combatants and shrug off most injuries. After
an adventurous career as a Legionnaire, Taine married
teammate Triplicate Girl and retired from active service.
    Bouncing Boy has yet to leave his mark in other
Legion timelines. In the reality created after the events
of Zero Hour, Chuck Taine
worked with the Legion
as an engineer and
mechanic, but did not
demonstrate his signature
bouncing abilities. DW

BOUNTY

FIRST APPEARANCE SUPERBOY (1st series) #225 (March 1977)
STATUS Hero **REAL NAME** Dawnstar
OCCUPATION Bounty hunter; Legionnaire **BASE** Earth; Starhaven
HEIGHT 5ft 6in **WEIGHT** 120 lbs **EYES** Brown **HAIR** Brown
SPECIAL POWERS/ABILITIES Wings enabled her to soar through space
without a Legion flight ring; able to track with unerring accuracy.

A mutant Amerind from the planet Starhaven, the bounty
hunter Dawnstar joined the pre-Zero Hour (see Great
Battles, pp. 187-6) Legion of Super-Heroes and used
her flying and tracking abilities in service to the United
Planets. When the LSH disbanded in 2992, Dawnstar was
among many members who departed Earth. The Legion
later returned to action and one of the new members
was Bounty, a mysterious mercenary. Bounty attempted
to apprehend the wanted criminal Sade, who mortally
wounded the Legionnaire. As her teammates watched, the
invisible entity known as Bounty departed the body of
Dawnstar. Later, it was learned that Bounty had possessed
Dawnstar and had changed her appearance, cutting off her
wings in order to act as a merciless bounty hunter and
sate the entity's bloodlust. Unfortunately, Dawnstar was
fully aware of Bounty's many murders.
Following Zero Hour, both Bounty
and Dawnstar were erased from the
timeline and ceased to exist. SB

BOY COMMANDOS

FIRST APPEARANCE Detective Comics #64 (June 1942)
STATUS Hero team **BASE** Europe
MEMBERS
Captain Eric "Rip" Carter
Alfy Tridgett
André Chavard
Daniel "Brooklyn" Turpin
Jan Haasan
Tex
Percy Clearweather

In 1942, Captain Eric "Rip" Carter led four resourceful
boys—Alfy Twidgett, André Chavard (see Chavard, André),
Daniel "Brooklyn" Turpin, and Jan Haasan—on missions
throughout war-torn Europe as the Boy Commandos.
Among their many successful missions, they pursued Agent
Axis, "the vengeful arm of Heinrich Himmler," who was
ultimately unmasked as a beautiful woman. In 1944, they
traveled Stateside to briefly join forces with the Guardian
and the Newsboy Legion to thwart gangster Boss Moxie and
Agent Axis.
    After the war, having achieved adulthood, several of the
team joined Metropolis' Special Crimes Unit. RG

THE BOY COMMANDOS 1) *Captain Rip Carter* **2)** *Alfy*
3) *Jan* **4)** *Percy* **5)** *Tex* **6)** *André* **7)** *Brooklyn*

BRADLEY, SLAM

FIRST APPEARANCE DETECTIVE COMICS #1 (March 1937)
STATUS Hero **REAL NAME** Samuel Emerson Bradley
OCCUPATION Private investigator **BASE** Gotham City
HEIGHT 6ft 1in **WEIGHT** 205 lbs
EYES Gray **HAIR** Dark brown with gray at temples
SPECIAL POWERS/ABILITIES Tough, two-fisted combatant and a highly
skilled, persistent detective; loyal to his friends no matter what.

Former soldier and cop, Slam Bradley became a P.I. so he
could be his own boss. Slam moved from city to city over
the decades, working with other respected detectives such as
Mysto, Pow-Wow Smith, and the Human Target. When his
partner Shorty Morgan fell victim to a murderer, Slam tracked
down the killer and solved a case that teamed him with
Batman. Years later, Slam's son, Slam Jr., was hired by the mayor
of Gotham City to find out whether Catwoman was alive
or dead. Slam Jr. was so smitten by her, he suffered beatings
to keep her existence secret. Slam Jr. fathered Catwoman's
daughter, Helena. DW

**SMITTEN KITTEN
SLAM'S PASSION** *was briefly returned
by Selina Kyle, the
Catwoman. Despite
the age difference,
the two loners found
that they had a great
deal in common.
Yet Slam realized
that he could never
be the one to tame
the enigmatic feline
fatale, and that only
heartbreak awaited
him if he got in too
deep. They remain
close friends and are
utterly loyal to
each other.*

PUNCHDRUNK *Slam earned his lifelong nickname as
a child on the streets of Cleveland when he knocked out
the local bully with a single punch. Slam can almost always
outthink his opponents, but he often swings first and asks
questions later. He likes a smoke and a drink—especially if
a dame's giving him the runaround!*

BRAINIAC

FIRST APPEARANCE ACTION COMICS #242 (July 1958)
STATUS Villain **REAL NAME** Vril Dox
OCCUPATION Cyber Conqueror **BASE** Mobile
HEIGHT Variable **WEIGHT** Variable **EYES** Red **HAIR** None
SPECIAL POWERS/ABILITIES A vast, superior intelligence limited only by the technology it currently inhabits. Knowledge of the universe is unparalleled, yet its hubris and emotions restrict its potential.

ONCE SCIENTIST PRIME on distant Colu, Vril Dox attempted to overthrow his technologically advanced world's Supreme Authority. Dox paid for his rebellion by being disintegrated. Yet somehow, his computer-like mind remained intact, traveling thousands of light years to Earth. Using his vast telepathic and psychokinetic abilities, Dox possessed the body of a sideshow mentalist named Milton Fine, to become the power-hungry Brainiac. When Fine's body proved too frail to contain Brainiac's power consciousness, he sought more suitable hosts, each time coming into opposition with SUPERMAN.

FOES *Brainiac's first meeting with the Man of Steel.*

REMAKE AND REMODEL

In the course of his attempts to conquer Earth, Brainiac has upgraded himself many times, even inhabiting the body of Superman's nemesis Doomsday. Brainiac downloaded his evolved alien psyche into a flawless android shell to become Brainiac 2.5 and threaten Earth with his Omega Spears. These weapons generated an energy web that could shatter the world. After Superman thwarted this scheme, Brainiac 2.5 attempted to increase his personal power by linking all the world's computers, but instead created a portal that enabled his massive, all-powerful future self, Brainiac 13, to enter the 21st century. It took the combined efforts of Brainiac 2.5, Lex Luthor (*see* Luthor, Lex), and Superman to stop the computer tyrant. While the B13 persona was trapped in a Kryptonian warsuit, Brainiac's modern-day incarnation was trapped within the infant body of Lex's daughter, Lena. To save Metropolis from both present and future androids, Luthor was forced to bargain away his own daughter! At least B13 did help Earth stave off the threat of the cosmic conqueror Imperiex. Superman helped teleport the android to the dawn of creation. There, Brainiac 13's energies, coupled with the "Big Bang" itself, created two vast explosions that scattered Brainiac's consciousness over 60 trillion light years of space and time. Brainiac came back even from this, using a future descendent, Brainiac 8 (Indigo) in a plot to destroy the OUTSIDERS. **RG**

MULTIPLE FORMS *Over the years, Brainiac has been constantly upgraded. The skull-shaped vessel (above) attempted an attack on the Earth. It took Superman and other heroes to repel the invasion and avoid panic in the skies.*

BRAINWAVE *The B13 incarnation nearly destroyed Superman and overwrote the entire city of Metropolis.*

EXCHANGE *Brainiac 2.5, seen here with Lex Luthor's daughter, a pawn in a greater game.*

GREAT MIND *Brainiac in his Coluan form of Vril Dox, before he was exiled for attempting to overthrow his homeworld.*

KEY STORYLINES

• *SUPERMAN Y2K (TPB, 2001):* Brainiac 13 reaches back from the 30th century to try to control Superman and Metropolis.
• *PANIC IN THE SKIES (TPB, 1993):* Brainiac launches an all-out assault on the Earth.
• *THE LUTHOR-BRAINIAC TEAM, SUPERMAN (2ND SERIES) #27-28:* Together, the two masterminds attempt to bring down the Man of Steel.
• *SUPERMAN: THE DOOMSDAY WARS (TPB, 1999):* Brainiac takes over Doomsday.

CAPTAIN BOOMERANG

First appearance FLASH #117 (December 1960)
Status Villain (deceased) **Real name** George Harkness
Occupation Criminal **Base** Keystone City
Height 5ft 9in **Weight** 167 lbs **Eyes** Brown **Hair** Brown
Special powers/abilities A boomerang-throwing expert, he has developed numerous boomerangs with specific functions.

CAPTAIN BOOMERANG II
First appearance IDENTITY CRISIS #3 (October 2004)
Status Anti-hero **Real name** Owen Mercer
Occupation Adventurer, government agent **Base** Mobile
Height 6ft 1in **Weight** 190 lbs **Eyes** Gray **Hair** Red
Special powers/abilities Skilled with boomerangs and other thrown weapons; can generate temporary bursts of super-speed

A NATIVE OF AUSTRALIA, George "Digger" Harkness was sent as a young adult to the U.S. by his mother, who was desperate to get her son away from his stepfather. He took a job demonstrating boomerangs for the Wiggins Game Company. Harkness, who had become an expert from years of throwing the wooden device as a kid, was given a uniform and the name Captain Boomerang. While demonstrating the boomerang to kids, Harkness liked to line his pockets with a spot of pilfering. This brought him into conflict with the second FLASH, whom Harkness opposed as Captain Boomerang with a variety of ever more bizarre boomerang gadgets. After the Flash's death, Captain Boomerang served on the government-sponsored Suicide Squad. However, he missed the thrill of stealing and secretly became Mirror Master II. After the Squad temporarily folded, Captain Boomerang returned to a life of crime in Central City, opposed by Flash III. He died during the Identity Crisis event, shot by ROBIN's father. His son Owen Mercer has since taken up the identity of Captain Boomerang II.

COME BACK Captain Boomerang applied his native talent to incredible devices such as this deadly trap for the Flash II.

TEAM REBEL The first Captain Boomerang often clashed with the Suicide Squad's director Amanda Waller.

VERSATILE WEAPON Some boomerangs carried by both Captains can slice through steel. Other varieties include explosive boomerangs.

THE NEXT GENERATION

Owen Mercer never knew his real father until the events of the Identity Crisis, when Digger Harkness – the first Captain Boomerang – reestablished contact. Mercer discovered that he shared his father's talent for hurling boomerangs, and also that he could call upon temporary bursts of super-speed. It eventually came out that Mercer was the product of a tryst between Harkness and Meloni Thawne, the 30th century mother of Bart Allen (see the Flash). Harkness died when shot by Robin III's father, and Mercer became the second Captain Boomerang.

Welcomed into the Flash's Rogues' Gallery by Captain Cold (who believed that Mercer might be his nephew and the son of his late sister the Golden Glider). Mercer ran with the Rogues until a jail sentence brought him into contact with a wrongfully-imprisoned Black Lightning. When Black Lightning's friends in the Outsiders sprang him, Mercer came too. With the Outsiders he found a slightly more respectable family to replace the Rogues, teaming with Checkmate to infiltrate the Oolong Island facility run by Chang Tzu. When Batman took control of the Outsiders, Mercer left the team. He found a new purpose with the U.S. government's Suicide Squad, hunting his former friends in the Rogues. Captain Boomerang II has established a close friendship with Supergirl as well as a mutual respect with Robin, despite the fact that their fathers killed one another. **RG/DW**

KEY STORYLINES

• SUICIDE SQUAD (1ST SERIES) #1 (MAY 1987): Captain Boomerang is recruited into a squad of costumed criminals, where his meanness and sarcasm make him standout.
• IDENTITY CRISIS #1–7 (JUNE–DEC. 2004): The original Captain Boomerang dies, making contact with his son just before his death.
• ROBIN #152-153 (SEPTEMBER-OCTOBER 2006): The new Captain Boomerang and Robin search Gotham to find a bomb planted by the Joker.

VILLAIN RETURNS Owen Mercer wears a patterned scarf to honor the criminal legacy of his father.

AT ODDS Their fathers killed one another during the events of the Identity Crisis, so Robin and Captain Boomerang II have had a hard time establishing a friendship.

CAPTAIN ATOM

FIRST APPEARANCE SPACE ADVENTURES #33 (March 1960)
STATUS Hero (missing in action) **REAL NAME** Nathaniel Christopher Adam, a.k.a. Cameron Scott **OCCUPATION** Super hero **BASE** San Francisco **HEIGHT** 6ft 4in **WEIGHT** 200 lbs **EYES** Blue **HAIR** White
SPECIAL POWERS/ABILITIES Alien alloy covering body enables him to tap into the quantum field, which gives him superstrength, anti-gravity, and the ability to emit focused blasts of atomic energy; capable of absorbing nuclear energy and quantum leaping one day to one week into the future.

KRYPTONITE CRAZY Batman comes face to face with Captain Atom who, after colliding with a kryptonite meteor, has become infused with vast amounts of radiation become a super-villain known as "Kryptonite Man." Fortunately Hiro Okamura, the new Toyman managed to drain the radiation from Captain Atom's body and return him to normal.

Decades ago, court-martialed Air Force Captain Nathaniel Adam volunteered for the top-secret Captain Atom Project in order to prove his innocence to charges of murder and treason. Adam's superiors theorized that a strange alien alloy would protect him from an atomic blast, a disastrous experiment that melded the alloy to Adam's body and catapulted him 18 years into the future. When the quantum-powered Adam reappeared, he was pardoned in exchange for service as the U.S.-sanctioned super hero, Captain Atom, a federally mandated member of Justice League International (see Justice League of America). Captain Atom ultimately left Justice League's European branch to form a more proactive but short-lived super-heroic strike force, Extreme Justice. After journeying to a parallel Earth during the Infinite Crisis, Captain Atom became the new Monarch. Assembling an army of super heroes from across the multiverse, he made war against the Monitors. **SB**

CAPTAIN COLD

FIRST APPEARANCE SHOWCASE #8 (May 1957)
STATUS Villain **REAL NAME** Leonard Snart
OCCUPATION Professional criminal **BASES** Central City/Keystone City
HEIGHT 6ft 2in **WEIGHT** 196 lbs **EYES** Brown **HAIR** Brown
SPECIAL POWERS/ABILITIES Cold-guns create ice slicks, shatter metal, or entomb victims in suspended animation in blocks of ice. Snow goggles minimize the flashes given off by Captain Cold's guns.

Raised by an abusive father, Leonard Snart found rare solace in the company of his grandfather, who drove an ice truck. Snart is one of the more sympathetic villains in the Flash's Rogues Gallery, able to chat over a coffee while plotting to break into the Keystone City Bank over the weekend. He began his crime career shortly after Barry Allen's debut as the Flash. Developing an experimental handgun to interfere with the Flash's superspeed, Snart accidentally irradiated his weapon and wound up with a tool that could freeze the moisture in the air. He donned a parka and goggles and declared himself Captain Cold. He committed a string of (non-lethal)

crimes throughout Central and Keystone City, but his main pleasure lay in matching wits with the Flash. After Barry Allen's death during the Crisis (see Great Battles, pp. 186-7), a disheartened Snart left crime to become a licensed bounty hunter with his sister Lisa, the Golden Glider. Captain Cold lost his eternal soul to the demonic Neron, but the third Flash, Wally West, brought him back to the land of the living. He soon returned to crime, this time as a member of Wally's Rogues Gallery. Captain Cold recently killed the villain Chillblaine in revenge for the death of his sister Lisa. He also helped an amnesiac Wally West defeat Mister Element. Yet, Snart remains an unrepentant crook, who *hates* being mistaken for Mister Freeze. **DW**

SLIPPERY SLOPE Even the great Barry Allen often fell victim to Captain Cold's ice tricks.

CAPTAIN COMET

FIRST APPEARANCE STRANGE ADVENTURES #9 (June 1951)
STATUS Hero REAL NAME Adam Blake
OCCUPATION Interstellar operative BASE The planet Cairn
HEIGHT 6ft 2in WEIGHT 190 lbs EYES Brown HAIR Brown
SPECIAL POWERS/ABILITIES Superstrength, superspeed, limited invulnerability, telepathy, telekinesis, flight, slowed aging, photographic memory, vast intelligence, and athletic prowess.

Born in 1931, Adam Blake began displaying his mutant abilities by age eight when he read and memorized every fact in a set of encyclopedias. By his 18th birthday he had mastered sports, music, and science, but kept his unusual abilities a secret. He finally revealed his amazing powers to physicist Emery Zackro. Blake discovered that he was a mutant born with the abilities of a man 100,000 years in the future. When aliens attacked Earth in the 1950s, Adam took the name Captain Comet and repelled their invasion force.

Captain Comet eventually left Earth to seek adventure in space, traveling across the galaxy. After serving with L.E.G.I.O.N., Captain Comet fought in the Rann-Thanagar War. Later killed by Lady Styx, he temporarily merged his consciousness with the Weird before reappearing in a new, younger body. PJ

REBIRTH After miraculously returning in a new, younger body, Captain Comet discovered that he now possessed limited powers of teleportation.

CAPTAIN COMPASS

FIRST APPEARANCE STAR-SPANGLED COMICS #83 (August 1948)
STATUS Hero REAL NAME Mark Compass
OCCUPATION Adventurer BASE The High Seas
HEIGHT 6ft WEIGHT 175 lbs EYES Brown HAIR Brown
SPECIAL POWERS/ABILITIES A skilled fighter with a keen deductive mind.

Mark Compass first acquired his sea legs as a frogman for the U.S. Navy, later commanding a few of the ships he had first served upon. In that regard, he became well-known as a capable and courageous captain, as well as a noted nautical investigator.

Following his naval stint, Compass was employed as a roving troubleshooter for Penny Steamship Lines. In his capacity as ship's detective aboard the S.S. Nautilus, Compass solved many mysteries on the high seas, as well as preventing crimes on the Nautilus and other vessels in the Penny Steamship Lines fleet.

At various times over the years, Compass even commanded the Nautilus himself. It is this ship in particular that he now calls his home. Captain Compass lives in his own personal cabin suite and enjoys semi-retirement while sleuthing the occasional seaborne mystery. SB

CAPTAIN FEAR

FIRST APPEARANCE ADVENTURE COMICS #425 (January 1973)
STATUS Hero (deceased) REAL NAME Fero
OCCUPATION Pirate BASE The Caribbean
HEIGHT 5ft 6in WEIGHT 160 lbs EYES Blue HAIR Black
SPECIAL POWERS/ABILITIES Excellent swordsman, sailor, and fighter, matched only by his skills as a leader and tactician; an average pilot and navigator.

Fero, a young Carib Indian, was taken captive in a Spanish raid sometime in the 16th century. Enslaved and put to work in a Spanish mine, Fero led the captives in a revolt against their oppressors. After stealing a Spanish galleon, losing its crew to a terrible storm at sea, and challenging and winning a duel with another pirate captain, Fero assumed the name Captain Fear. He sailed across the Caribbean, harrying the Spanish conquistadors of the day while protecting his fellow natives. When his wife was expecting their first child, Captain Fear planned to retire from life on the high seas after a final voyage with a man named Baron Hemlocke. Instead, Hemlocke's butchery during an attack on a Spanish vessel sullied the reputation of Fero and his crew, who vowed to take revenge. Tragically, Captain Fear and his men were killed by Hemlocke's demonic forces, and were doomed to wander the seas forever as spirits. RG

CAPTAIN HUNTER

FIRST APPEARANCE SECRET FILES & ORIGINS GUIDE TO THE DC UNIVERSE 2000 #1 (March 2000)
STATUS Hero REAL NAME Lucius Hunter
OCCUPATION Adventurer BASE Mobile
HEIGHT 6ft 1in WEIGHT 196 lbs EYES Blue HAIR Brown
SPECIAL POWERS/ABILITIES Excellent combatant and field leader; body enhanced through transplants.

The name Hunter has earned merit through six decades of service to the U.S. military. Lieutenant Ben Hunter turned a bunch of ex-convicts into a crack squad nicknamed "Hunter's Hellcats", seeing action in some of the worst battles of World War II. Ben Hunter's twin sons, Nick and Phil, became a major in the Air Force and a captain with the Green Berets respectively, serving with distinction in Korea and Vietnam. In more modern times, Captain Lucius Hunter leads the latest group of Creature Commandos for the top-secret Project M. DW

CAPTAIN MARVEL JR.

FIRST APPEARANCE WHIZ COMICS #25 (December 1941)
STATUS Hero   **REAL NAME** Frederick "Freddy" Freeman
OCCUPATION Adventurer   **BASE** New York City; Fawcett City
HEIGHT 5ft 10in   **WEIGHT** 164 lbs   **EYES** Blue   **HAIR** Black
SPECIAL POWERS/ABILITIES By saying "Captain Marvel" aloud, he gains
Solomon's wisdom, Hercules's superstrength, Atlas's stamina, Zeus's
raw power, Achilles's courage, and Mercury's superspeed. Captain
Marvel Jr. shares powers with Mary Marvel and Captain Marvel; if
either is using their powers, he has access to only half his power.

A WELL-MANNERED TEENAGER who excelled not
only academically but athletically, Frederick "Freddy"
Freeman was orphaned when his parents died in a
boating accident. After the accident, Freddy moved from
New York to Fawcett City to live with his grandparents,
Jacob and Elizabeth. Shortly after moving to Fawcett
City, Freddy was kidnapped by the demonic SABBAC,
who mistakenly believed Freeman to be Billy Batson, the
young alter ego of Captain Marvel, the World's Mightiest
Mortal. Freed from Sabbac's evil clutches by his idol,
Captain Marvel, Freddy subsequently became one of
Billy Batson's closest friends, unaware that the young
Batson was in truth the hero he so admired.

BRAVERY *The teenage Freddy
was crippled and nearly
killed by Captain Nazi.*

EVIL *Freddy rescued Captain Nazi from
certain death, only to watch the villain
murder Freeman's grandfather.*

THE WORLD'S MIGHTIEST BOY

Years later, however, Freddy learned Billy's secret identity after Batson
saved his sister, Mary (*see* Mary Marvel), from Ibac.
Soon after, on a trip with his grandfather Jacob, Freddy saw what
he took to be Captain Marvel plummeting from the heavens
and crashing into the lake where he and his grandfather were
fishing. Freddy tried to save the man, who turned out to be
the villainous Captain Nazi, awakened from a cryogenic sleep
after decades. Captain Nazi had been battling Captain
Marvel in a spaceship above Earth before he was knocked unconscious. Captain Nazi
killed Freeman's grandfather, broke Freddy's back, and escaped.

Captain Marvel and Mary Marvel, desperate to save the Freddy's life, took him to a
secret sanctuary in a deserted subway tunnel. There they beseeched the wizard Shazam,
who had given them their powers, to help them save Freddy's life. The mage cryptically told
them that he did not have the power they needed, but Mary cleverly deduced the logic behind
the Wizard's riddle, and she and Captain Marvel agreed to split their amazing powers with
Freddy. The Wizard, gratified by the wisdom of his charges, enchanted the dying boy. When
Freddy awoke and spoke the words "Captain Marvel," he was transformed into the World's
Mightiest Boy. The three Marvels began patrolling the skies of Fawcett City together, and
Freddy's romantic feelings for Mary grew. Captain Marvel, still technically a young teenager
himself, grew fiercely protective of his sister.

BOY ZONE *As
Captain Marvel
Jr., Freddy is the
World's Mightiest
Boy!*

After a fight between the two over Mary, the headstrong Captain Marvel Jr. moved to New
York City, and promptly fell in love with the schizophrenic villain Chain Lightning. Freddy
soundly defeated Captain Nazi and then changed his name to CM3, announcing his "split"
from the Marvel "family." CM3 served briefly with both the Teen Titans and the Outsiders,
but experienced a shock to his super-hero career following the Infinite Crisis. The murder
of Shazam at the hands of the Spectre caused Captain Marvel Jr. to lose his powers. Captain
Marvel, who had taken Shazam's place as keeper of the Rock of Eternity, arranged a series
of trials for Freddy to prove his worthiness to the gods that powered the Marvel family:
Solomon, Hercules, Atlas, Zeus, Achilles, and Mercury. **PJ**

KEY STORYLINES
• *POWER OF SHAZAM #8
(OCTOBER 1995):* The
modern Freddy Freeman
is introduced, nearly
dying at the hands of
Captain Nazi!
• *TEEN TITANS #17-18
(JANUARY–FEBRUARY 1998):*
Captain Marvel Jr. joins the Titans
after the teen heroes hold a recruitment
drive to swell their ranks.
• *POWER OF SHAZAM #37 (APRIL 1998):* Conquering
his internal demons—and the demon haunting his
dreams—Captain Marvel Jr. changes his name to CM3.
• *YOUNG JUSTICE #50 (DECEMBER 2002):* CM3 and
a horde of teenage heroes invade Zandia
and battle a host of super-villains lead
by Lady Zand and the Baron Agua
Sin Gaaz!

MARVELOUS *After defeating
Captain Nazi again, Captain
Marvel Jr. began calling
himself CM3.*

CAPTAIN MARVEL

THE WORLD'S MIGHTIEST MORTAL

FIRST APPEARANCE WHIZ COMICS #1 (February 1940)
STATUS Hero **REAL NAME** William Joseph "Billy" Batson
OCCUPATION Radio Personality; super hero
BASE Fawcett City
HEIGHT (as Billy) 5ft 4in; (as Captain Marvel) 6ft 2in
WEIGHT (as Billy) 110 lbs; (as Captain Marvel) 215 lbs
EYES Blue **HAIR** Black
SPECIAL POWERS/ABILITIES
Virtually invulnerable and able to fly; possesses the wisdom of Solomon, the strength of Hercules, the stamina of Atlas, the power of Zeus, the courage of Achilles, and the speed of Mercury.

WITHOUT A DOUBT, Captain Marvel is the world's mightiest mortal, with strength and powers on a par with Superman. But unknown to many, this stalwart and virtuous super hero—by all appearances a middle-aged man—is really teenager Billy Batson. With one magic word, youthful Billy assumes the appearance and abilities of one of Earth's greatest and most respected heroes; however, he remains very much an innocent in heart and mind.

ARRIVAL The Big Red Cheese was Fawcett Comics' answer to Superman and, for a time, was just as popular as the Man of Steel.

ORPHANED AND BETRAYED

When Billy was just a boy, his parents—archaeologists C.C. and Marylin Batson—were killed by their treacherous assistant, Theo Adam, while on a dig at the tomb of Rameses II at Abu Simbel, Egypt. Billy was separated from his sister Mary and left in the care of their unscrupulous Uncle Ebenezer, C.C. Batson's half-brother. Unfortunately, Ebenezer threw Billy out and stole the youth's trust fund, money set aside for Billy's care and welfare.

ORPHANED For the sake of a jeweled scarab of untold power, Theo Adam murdered Billy's parents.

DOWN IN THE SUBWAY

Left penniless and homeless, Billy eked out a sorrowful existence in Fawcett City as a newsboy. For shelter, he often slept in the subway terminals. One night, a mysterious stranger—later revealed to be the spirit of Billy's father, C.C. Batson—convinced the orphaned lad to follow him deep into the subway tunnels, where a marvelous train decorated in hieroglyphics and mystic runes awaited them. Billy and the stranger rode the train deep into the bowels of the Earth and arrived in a cavern that held statues epitomizing the Seven Deadly Enemies of Man: Pride, Envy, Lust, Hatred, Selfishness, Laziness, and Injustice.

THE WIZARD'S ADVICE

As Captain Marvel turned back into Billy, the magical lightning bolt also struck a stone block poised above Shazam, apparently crushing the old wizard beneath its great weight. Shazam, however, did not die, but instead disappeared to the Rock of Eternity, a distant peak outside time and space. When called upon by Billy in future, Shazam would offer guidance, but not without first reminding the lad to use the marvellous powers at his disposal. He particularly urged Billy to use the wisdom of Solomon when faced by the perils of adolescence and other emotional and practical problems.

ROCK OF ETERNITY Billy will make his home on this distant rock spire, assuming the mantle of Shazam.

THE MAGIC WORD

Within that strange cavern, Billy met the ancient wizard Shazam, a champion of mankind for thousands of years. Withered with age, Shazam sat on a throne poised beneath a giant stone block suspended above him as if by magic. Shazam chose Billy to succeed him and granted the young orphan all of his extraordinary powers. By speaking the wizard's name, a lightning bolt transformed adolescent Billy into the adult Captain Marvel, a hero possessing the wisdom of Solomon, the strength of Hercules, the stamina of Atlas, the power of Zeus, the courage of Achilles, and the speed of Mercury. With this great gift also came responsibility: he must vow to uphold the cause of good and to battle the Seven Deadly Enemies of Man, duties that Billy promised faithfully to fulfill every time he uttered the name "Shazam!"

ANGRY AT FIRST Billy was not sure if Shazam's great gifts were a blessing or a curse.

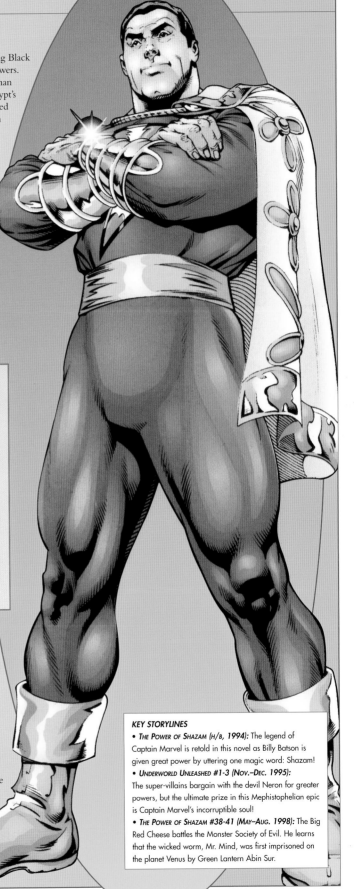

MERCY FOR A MURDERER

Captain Marvel's very first adventure found him battling Black Adam, his parents' killer enabled with his own superpowers. Theo Adam channeled the strengths of Teth-Adam, a man empowered with similar abilities by Shazam during Egypt's 19th dynasty via an ancient scarab amulet first discovered by Billy's parents. Captain Marvel defeated Black Adam by removing his amulet, thus stripping him of his powers, at least for a while. Instead of allowing the helpless Theo Adam to die in a collapsing museum, the good-hearted Captain Marvel spared the life of the man who murdered his family.

THE MARVEL FAMILY

Later, at the Rock of Eternity, Billy learned that the stranger who led him to Shazam was really his father. Billy chose to remain Captain Marvel and use Shazam's gifts for good, as well as to find his long-lost sister, Mary Marvel.

Eventually, Billy and Mary were reunited, and Captain Marvel decided to share his awesome abilities with her. He also gave some powers to their mutual friend, newsboy Freddy Freeman (*see* Captain Marvel Jr.), who had been crippled by the nefarious Captain Nazi. In the meantime, Captain Marvel became a member of the Justice League of America, although Billy often felt inferior to his more confident super-heroic peers.

DO THE RIGHT THING

Back home in Fawcett City, Billy returned to school and worked as an announcer for WHIZ radio. At the same time, Captain Marvel wielded Shazam's great powers to battle such evils as Mister Mind, Doctor Sivana, Mister Atom, and the Monster Society of Evil. Through it all, Captain Marvel fought with indefatigable spirit, perhaps the truest of any costumed champion. Captain Marvel's wholesome honesty and integrity made his spotless soul the prize most coveted by the demon Neron. However, Billy and his alter ego have always had the moral strength to resist temptation.

RADIO STAR *Billy often reports on the deeds of Captain Marvel.*

LOOKING TO THE FUTURE

Captain Marvel served with the Justice Society of America, helping curb Black Adam's excesses when his nemesis became dictator of Khandaq. He also aided Superman when Eclipso took control of the Man of Steel.

During the Infinite Crisis, the rampaging Spectre killed the wizard Shazam and destroyed the Rock of Eternity. Although the planet's magic-users helped rebuild the Rock, Billy Batson had no choice but to assume Shazam's former role as caretaker. Now known simply as Marvel, he sported an all-white costume and long, flowing white hair. He set a series of trials before Captain Marvel Jr. in the hopes of turning him into a worthy replacement. **SB/DW**

ENEMY ALLIED *Captain Marvel was forced to fight alongside his arch-foe Black Adam when both were members of the JSA.*

KEY STORYLINES

• *THE POWER OF SHAZAM (H/B, 1994):* The legend of Captain Marvel is retold in this novel as Billy Batson is given great power by uttering one magic word: Shazam!

• *UNDERWORLD UNLEASHED #1-3 (NOV.–DEC. 1995):* The super-villains bargain with the devil Neron for greater powers, but the ultimate prize in this Mephistophelian epic is Captain Marvel's incorruptible soul!

• *THE POWER OF SHAZAM #38-41 (MAY–AUG. 1998):* The Big Red Cheese battles the Monster Society of Evil. He learns that the wicked worm, Mr. Mind, was first imprisoned on the planet Venus by Green Lantern Abin Sur.

CATWOMAN

PRINCESS OF PLUNDER

First appearance BATMAN #1 (Spring 1940)
Status Unresolved   Real name Selina Kyle
Occupation Cat burglar/vigilante   Base Gotham City's East End
Height 5ft 7in   Weight 133 lbs   Eyes Blue-green   Hair Black
Special powers/abilities A formidable fighter with expertise in boxing and various martial arts disciplines; skintight cat costume features retractable razor-sharp claws in gloves and spring-action steel climbing pitons in boots; wields a variety of bullwhips and cat-o'-nine tails as offensive weapons and gymnastic accoutrements.

KEY STORYLINES
• CATWOMAN (1st series) #1-4 (February–May 1989) Selina Kyle's life on the mean streets of Gotham City is recounted.
• DETECTIVE COMICS #759-762 (August–November 2001) P.I. Slam Bradley is hired to find the missing and presumed-dead Selina.
• CATWOMAN (3rd series) #1-4 (January–April 2002) Catwoman stalks and defeats a shape-changing serial killer who is hunting Gotham's ladies of the evening.

SELINA KYLE'S CHILDHOOD was defined by tragedy. When Selina was just a girl, her brutalized mother committed suicide and her violent father drank himself to death not long after. Separated from her younger sister Magdalena and remanded to the Sprang Hall Juvenile Detention Center—an abusive state home for orphaned or delinquent girls—Selina opted instead to take her chances on the mean streets of Gotham City. Amid the crime and corruption of the poverty-stricken East End district, she survived through petty theft. Sharp wits and an amazing natural skill as a gymnast led to her becoming the slickest and slipperiest cat burglar the Gotham City Police Department had ever had to deal with.

PURPLE PRINCESS *Catwoman has worn a number of different costumes over the years, often preferring purple catsuits.*

THE FELINE FATALE

To protect herself from predators, Selina studied martial arts in a backstreet dojo where a Sensei taught her how best to use her claws. Later, ex-heavyweight champ Ted Grant taught Selina the "sweet science" of boxing. For a time, Selina was the most accomplished thief nobody knew. She was also one of the most generous, spreading her ill-gotten gains around the downtrodden and destitute of the East End, including the young prostitute Holly "Gonightly" Robinson, whom Selina befriended and watched over like the little sister she believed she no longer had. Selina would have continued to rob with impunity if not for the Batman. Spying the Caped Crusader from her window on one of his first outings, Selina watched him in action and was suitably inspired to take up her own costume when prowling the Gotham night. In a tight leather catsuit, Catwoman marked the city as her territory. However, she never killed, and she only stole from the wealthiest or the well-insured. For these reasons, Batman pursued other costumed criminals more relentlessly and gave Catwoman the chance to change her spots. Sometimes he even asked the Princess of Plunder to use her skills for the betterment of Gotham. Perhaps his altruism attracted her, because Selina ultimately did decide to make Catwoman more than just a thief in the night.

ALLEY CAT *Often, the alley cats of Gotham were Selina's only friends, especially after she was once beaten and left for dead.*

TOP THIEF *Few cat burglars can rival Selina Kyle's nimble-fingered thieving skills.*

THE CAT AND THE BAT

After faking her own demise, Selina left Gotham for a time, but eventually returned to the city's East End, where she defended the defenseless. Catwoman learned Batman's best-kept secret when the Dark Knight took her to his Batcave and revealed his identity to her. They finally admitted their feelings for each other (*see* Romantic Moments, p. 142-3) but then parted because Catwoman did not believe Batman trusted her. Selina began seeing private detective Slam Bradley, but Slam realized that Selina's heart would always belong to Batman. Catwoman enjoyed her adventures on the 'other' side of the fence, stealing only when necessary and usually if the loot would do someone other than herself a bit of good.

WHIP SMART *Her evil ways (mostly) behind her, Catwoman now fights for the downtrodden of Gotham.*

THE EXECUTIONER

Catwoman's path from villainess to reluctant hero hit a snag when she realized that her motivation might not come from within. Years earlier, during one of her stints with the Secret Society of Super Villains, Catwoman underwent an involuntary mind-wipe courtesy of the magic-wielding Zatanna. The act may have subtly nudged her psyche onto a less sinister track, yet Selina still proved capable of cold-blooded acts. In an apparent counterpoint to this revelation, Catwoman shot and killed the Gotham crime boss Black Mask when he threatened her friends.

DEATH MASK *Showing no remorse, Selina shot the crime boss Black Mask.*

HELENA *The birth of her daughter caused Selina to retire from costumed adventuring.*

ONE YEAR LATER

Over the course of the following year, Selina conceived a child with Slam Bradley's son Sam and gave birth to a daughter she named Helena. She also retired from adventuring, took the alias "Irena Dubrovna" and maintained a low-key lifestyle in an East End apartment. Catwoman continued on, however, her identity assumed by Holly Robinson in a duplicate costume. Most Gothamites didn't know that a second woman had donned the familiar catsuit. Neither did the GCPD. The police took Holly into custody for the murder of Black Mask, necessitating a breakout orchestrated by Selina. Selina's outings as Catwoman, battling threats to Gotham, became more frequent after this event.

Selina's baby became a easy target for her enemies—first Film Freak and Angle Man, and later the Russian team of Hammer and Sickle. Gradually Selina realized that her dangerous lifestyle would never be compatible with the needs of her child, and she began plotting an exit strategy. The Amazons invasion of Washington DC interrupted her plans, and Catwoman found herself in a unique position to infiltrate the Gotham wing of the Amazonian Bana sect. Her sabotage of the Bana prevented the city's decimation by a radioactive bio bomb.

HOLLY *During her time as Catwoman, Holly Robinson got in over her head.*

VULNERABLE *Hammer and Sickle, Angle Man, and Film Freak all threatened Selina's daughter.*

HEARTBREAK *To protect her daughter, Selina gave Helena up for adoption.*

CAT'S ROAR *Selina isn't loyal to anyone's cause.*

NEW BEGINNINGS

Saving Gotham from the Amazons was Selina's last great act before going underground. Batman helped her erase her former life when he posed as a terrorist and seemingly blew up both Selina and her daughter. The two left the city under new identities, and Selina then made the painful decision to put Helena up for adoption. Now truly alone, save for her few friends in the super hero community, Catwoman accepted Batman's offer to join his latest team of Outsiders. **SB/DW**

CHARYBDIS

FIRST APPEARANCE AQUAMAN (5th series) #1 (August 1994)
STATUS Villain **REAL NAME** Charybdis
OCCUPATION Would-be conqueror **BASE** The Seven Seas
HEIGHT 6ft 4in **WEIGHT** 237 lbs **EYES** Black **HAIR** Black
SPECIAL POWERS/ABILITIES Can absorb the latent talents of others;
in Piranha Man form, possesses superhuman strength and
ability to breath on land or in water.

Charybdis and his wife, Scylla, were freelance
terrorists named after two horrific beings from
Greek mythology (Charybdis was a whirlpool,
Scylla a multi-headed monster). Scylla
died when a bomb exploded in her
hands; her death drove Charybdis
insane. He appeared, seemingly
out of nowhere, displaying vast
powers and a hatred for the Sea
King, Aquaman. The self-proclaimed
terrorist easily defeated Aquaman in
battle, strapping him to a machine that
temporarily transferred his powers and abilities
to the usurper. Their battle resulted in Aquaman
losing his hand to piranhas before being shot by
Dolphin. Charybdis, who had not yet mastered
Aquaman's telepathic skills with fish, fell in the
water and was left for dead. Instead, he finally
made contact with the deadly fish, absorbing their
essence, thereby preserving his life and allowing
him to evolve into the even more formidable
form of Piranha Man. His aim was to absorb
every last shred of ability from Aquaman and
leave him for dead. The Sea King defeated
Piranha Man, but not before seeing his family and
friends suffer. RG

LOSING A HAND *Charybdis
achieved what other villains
could not, permanently scarring
the King of the Sea by forcing
his hand into a pool of hungry
piranha.*

TRANSFORMATION
*Now known as
Piranha Man, the
person once called
Charybdis is a
true monster.*

CHASE, CAMERON

FIRST APPEARANCE BATMAN #550 (January 1998)
STATUS Hero **REAL NAME** Cameron Chase
OCCUPATION D.E.O. investigator **BASE** New York City
HEIGHT 5ft 5in **WEIGHT** 129 lbs **EYES** Green **HAIR** Blonde
SPECIAL POWERS/ABILITIES Highly intelligent; skilled with both computers
and handguns; appears to possess a latent ability that allows her to
dampen the superpowers of meta-humans. This unconscious talent
has protected her in the past; she has yet to exploit it to the full.

Former private detective Cameron Chase is one of the top
agents in the Department of Extranormal Operations, a
branch of U.S. intelligence that keeps tabs on the Earth's
meta-humans and supernatural beings. Working under
Director Bones, Chase has discovered the alternate lives
employed by the shape-changing Martian Manhunter
and tried to deduce the true
identity of the Batman (she
mistakenly concluded that
he was Green Lantern
Alan Scott). Her dislike of
costumed crime fighters
stems from her childhood,
when the maniacal Dr.
Trap murdered her father.
Walter Chase had secretly
been Acro-Bat of the Justice
Experience, and Cameron
blamed his death on the
clandestine nocturnal
antics that had made him
a target. Chase often works
with Kate Spencer, the
current Manhunter. DW

CHAVARD, ANDRÉ

FIRST APPEARANCE BOY COMMANDOS #1 (July 1942)
STATUS Hero **REAL NAME** André Chavard
OCCUPATION Adventurer **BASE** Paris, France
HEIGHT 5ft 9in **WEIGHT** 165 lbs **EYES** Brown **HAIR** Black
SPECIAL POWERS/ABILITIES A natural leader, able to inspire respect and
loyalty in others; a capable marksman and hand-to-hand combatant.

A handsome young man
born in Bar-le-Duc, France,
whose parents were slain
in the early days of World
War II, André Chavard was
one of several orphans who
were mascots of an American
Army unit station in Britain
during the war. The orphans
became the Boy Commandos,
and the brave young soldiers
undertook dozens of special,
often dangerous missions
behind enemy lines until the
war ended in 1945.

Returning to his native
France soon after, André
chose to remain with the
military. He rose through the
ranks until he became the
commander of the spy agency
known only as Department
Gamma. His premiere spy in
the Department is Fleur-de-
Lis. PJ

CHECKMATE

FIRST APPEARANCE ACTION COMICS #598 (March 1988)
STATUS United Nations Security Council Agency   **BASE** The Castle, Switzerland.
PAST OPERATIVES Sasha Bordeaux, Mister Terrific II, Fire, Thinker, Count Vertigo, Mademoiselle Marie, Jessica Midnight, Tommy Jagger, Bad Samaritan, Rocket Red, August General In Iron, Master Jailer, Snapper Carr, Gravedigger, Cinnamon, Sebastian Faust, G.I. Robot

Checkmate was established by Amanda Waller as an independent arm of Task Force X, a bureau that also had administration over the Suicide Squad. Like the Squad, Checkmate engaged in top-secret missions vital to U.S. interests.

FORTRESS The mountain headquarters of Checkmate is impregnable to both conventional and magical assaults.

Mister Terrific II   Taleb Beni Khalid   King Faraday   Fire

Amanda Waller   Thinker   Tommy Jagger   Mademoiselle

Sasha Bordeaux   Shen Li Po   Jessica Midnight   Count Vertigo

FIRST INCARNATION

Structured after the hierarchy of chess pieces, Checkmate was led by a Queen or King, followed by administrative Bishops, field director Rooks, well-armed field agent Knights, and support-tech Pawns. The agency's first Queen was Valentina Vostok, formerly Negative Woman, later replaced by Waller herself. Checkmate was nearly destroyed by the terrorist group Kobra, a debacle referred to as the Janus Directive, which saw Waller unseated as leader. Maxwell Lord (see Lord, Maxwell) eventually rose to the position of King, murdering Blue Beetle II and unleashing the OMAC project.

FIELD ACTION Flanked by Count Vertigo and Fire, two Checkmate field agents.

RESEARCH SUBJECT Captain Boomerang II is tortured by Chang Tzu when his mission goes horribly wrong.

DOWN BUT NOT OUT Despite their imprisonment, Checkmate and the Outsiders prepared their escape.

MISSION BRIEFING With Thinker joining via hologram, the Checkmate 'royal family' prepares to send its knights to an international trouble spot.

AGENCY REBUILT

Lord's death and the Infinite Crisis left Checkmate in tatters. The UN revived the organization as a multinational group to monitor global metahuman activity. To stop superhumans dominating, each "powered" member had to have a normal human in a corresponding position. Alan Scott (Green Lantern) served as the first White King, with Amanda Waller as White Queen, Sasha Bordeaux as Black Queen, and Talib Beni Khalid as Black King. The new Checkmate faced off with China's Great Ten, became involved with rigged elections in Santa Prisca, deputized the Shadowpact to help a Checkmate Pawn infiltrate Kobra, and got the Outsiders to sabotage Chang Tzu on Oolong Island. Waller who had her own agenda, lost her rank. In a fight against Kobra, Checkmate deputized Superman, and unleashed Gravedigger, Cinnammon, Sebastian Faust, and G.I. Robot. SB/DW

CHECKOUT Nightwing and the Outsiders teamed up with Checkmate agents to infiltrate Oolong Island.

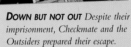

KEY STORYLINES
• *CHECKMATE VOL. 1 #15–18 (MAY–JUNE 1989):* The Janus Directive sees Checkmate crippled by inter-agency fighting while Kobra plots to rule the world.
• *COUNTDOWN TO INFINITE CRISIS #1 (MAY 2005):* Maxwell Lord, Checkmate's King, kills Blue Beetle to protect his involvement with the OMAC project.
• *CHECKMATE VOL. 2 #18–20 (SEPT–NOV 2007):* In the "Fall of the Wall" storyline, Amanda Waller's activities catch up with her and the Checkmate members force her resignation.

CINNAMON I

FIRST APPEARANCE WEIRD WESTERN TALES #48 (October 1978)
STATUS Hero (deceased) **REAL NAME** Kate Manser
OCCUPATION Bounty Hunter **BASE** The American West, circa 1898
HEIGHT 5ft 4in **WEIGHT** 110 lbs **EYES** Green **HAIR** Red
SPECIAL POWERS/ABILITIES Expert with pistol and knife; however, her weapon of choice was a shuriken, a Japanese throwing star.

Kate Manser was just a child when she saw her widowed father, the brave sheriff of a tiny Wyoming town, shot dead before her eyes by gunfighters fleeing a bank holdup. Kate was sent to a county orphanage, where her hatred for her father's murderers grew stronger as she matured.
She practiced with a six-gun and a star-shaped shuriken that reminded Kate of her late father's tin badge. On her 18th birthday, Kate rode off on a trail to vengeance. She became a bounty hunter, running down lawbreakers throughout the Old West. She was also romantically linked to gunfighter Nighthawk. No one knows whether Cinnamon found her father's killers or if she discovered she was the reincarnation of Egyptian Princess Chay-Ara. It has not been revealed how Cinnamon died. **SB**

CINNAMON II

FIRST APPEARANCE Cinnamon: El Ciclo (October 2003)
STATUS Hero **REAL NAME** Cinnamon (2nd name unknown)
OCCUPATION Gun-for-hire **BASE** Mobile
HEIGHT 5ft 9in **WEIGHT** 140 lbs **EYES** Green **HAIR** Red
SPECIAL POWERS/ABILITIES A crack shot, quick wits, and a savage street-fighting style; self-reliant.

As a child, a red-haired girl named Cinnamon, after the Old West gunslinger, watched in horror as her policeman father was gunned down during a bank robbery by seven criminals. Growing up alone, she became a crack shot, using copies of the wanted posters featuring the seven men as targets. Then she went looking for them. One by one they were found and shot dead. Cinnamon then became a gun-for-hire, protecting people or property. After one assignment, she heard that a woman was looking for her. This woman turned out to be Marisol "Macy" Samuels, the daughter of one of the men who had killed Cinnamon's father. Macy, who ran a home for runaway children, now wanted to take revenge on Cinnamon! However, after Cinnamon had helped Macy defeat a gang of kidnappers, Macy accepted Cinnamon's apology. Cinnamon, the lonesome gunslinger, headed off in search of her next job. **RG**

CIRCE

FIRST APPEARANCE WONDER WOMAN (2nd series) #17 (June 1988)
STATUS Villain **REAL NAME** Circe
OCCUPATION Sorceress **BASE** Mobile
HEIGHT 5ft 11in **WEIGHT** 145 lbs **EYES** Red **HAIR** Purple
SPECIAL POWERS/ABILITIES One of Earth's most powerful sorceresses, Circe is immortal; her hands project powerful bolts of energy and she can transform men into animals or animal hybrids called "beastiamorphs." She can also alter her appearance.

Circe is an immortal being who made a pact with Hecate, Greek goddess of sorcery, to exchange her soul for vast magical power. Circe then perfected her talents for transforming men into animals. Despising the peace-loving message of the Amazons, Circe used her agent Ariadne to kill Antiope, the sister of Queen Hippolyta.
Thousands of years later, Hippolyta's daughter Diana became Wonder Woman. Hidden away on the island of Aeaea, Circe tried to destroy Wonder Woman and her message of peace by turning her back into the primordial clay from which she had been originally molded. The evil sorceress failed, but returned to spawn a creation-shattering War of the Gods, pitting the mightiest deities against each other. Eventually, Wonder Woman and the heroes of Earth won the war and put an end to Circe, seemingly forever.

BEASTIAMORPHS *For 3,000 years Circe lived on the Grecian island of Aeaea, surrounded by her beastiamorph servants. After Circe's defeat at Wonder Woman's hand, the witch relocated to a stronghold in the Amazon rain forest and Greek villagers renamed Aeaea Dianata.*

But Circe survived; she returned to pit the Amazons of Bana Mighdall against their Themysciran relatives, and transported Paradise Island into a demon-filled dimension. Disguised as Donna Milton, one of Wonder Woman's closest friends, Circe infiltrated Wonder Woman's life. Circe joined Lex Luthor's criminal Injustice Gang (see Luthor, Lex), and then Cheetah II, in an all-out bid to take over the planet. Circe's most recent power play involved the resurrection of Queen Hippolyta and the manipulation of a war between the Amazons and Man's World. Spurring the Amazon armies to invade Washington DC, Circe met defeat and endured a sentence in Hades before returning to Earth. **PJ**

LYTA *The war god Ares is the father of Circe's daughter, Lyta.*

WONDER WOMAN'S NEMESIS *An ancient goddess devoted to stirring up jealousy and hatred, Circe has more than once used her vast power to destroy Paradise Island and its champion Wonder Woman. Circe's only known weakness is the herb moly, which acts as a protective charm against her magic.*

CLAYFACE I–IV

THE MUD PACK

FIRST APPEARANCE (I) DETECTIVE COMICS #40 (June 1940)
STATUS Villain   **REAL NAME** Basil Karlo
OCCUPATION Professional criminal   **BASE** Mobile
HEIGHT 5ft 11in   **WEIGHT** 178 lbs   **EYES** Brown   **HAIR** Black
SPECIAL POWERS/ABILITIES Originally a killer driven by revenge; now possesses shape-changing powers as the Ultimate Clayface.

FIRST APPEARANCE (II) DETECTIVE COMICS #298 (December 1961)
STATUS Villain   **REAL NAME** Matt Hagen
OCCUPATION Professional criminal   **BASE** Mobile
HEIGHT 5ft 10in   **WEIGHT** 173 lbs   **EYES** Blue   **HAIR** None
SPECIAL POWERS/ABILITIES Unique body chemistry enabled him to alter his body shape at will.

FIRST APPEARANCE (III) DETECTIVE COMICS #478 (July–August 1978)
STATUS Villain   **REAL NAME** Preston Payne
OCCUPATION Professional criminal   **BASE** Mobile
HEIGHT 6ft 4in   **WEIGHT** 264 lbs   **EYES** Red   **HAIR** None
SPECIAL POWERS/ABILITIES Shape-changing abilities; cursed with a more amorphous natural state (requiring him to wear a containment suit) and a killer touch that could melt others into protoplasm.

FIRST APPEARANCE (IV) (1st series) #21 (July 1987)
STATUS Villain   **REAL NAME** Sondra Fuller
OCCUPATION Professional criminal   **BASE** Mobile
HEIGHT 5ft 6in   **WEIGHT** 130 lbs   **EYES** Red   **HAIR** None
SPECIAL POWERS/ABILITIES Similar capabilities to Clayface II, with the added ability to duplicate the powers of those she copied.

MUD MASK OF TERROR

Horror actor Basil Karlo went off the deep end when he learned that Hollywood producers had undertaken a remake of his classic film, *The Terror*. Donning a clay mask to reprise his old role as Clayface, Karlo murdered several actors before Batman brought him to justice.

Treasure hunter Matt Hagen became the second Clayface when exposure to a mysterious oil altered his body chemistry and allowed him to assume almost any form. He died during the Crisis (*see* Great Battles, pp. 186-7) but his legacy lived on when Preston Payne, deformed by the chronic bone disease acromegaly, injected himself with Hagen's blood to develop his own shape-changing gifts and became Clayface III. Payne was a sad case, falling in love with a wax mannequin in between stints in Arkham Asylum, Gotham City's maximum-security prison for the criminally insane, before finding true happiness with Clayface IV, also known as Lady Clay. Born Sondra Fuller, Lady Clay received her morphing talents from the terrorist Kobra.

Basil Karlo soon returned to the Clayface family, forming an alliance with Clayfaces III and IV under the group name the Mud Pack. Karlo then shot his veins full of the distilled essences of his namesakes, transforming himself into a being he called the Ultimate Clayface.

Two creations have expanded the creeping reach of the Mud Pack. Preston Payne and Lady Clay have had a child named Cassius whose powers could dwarf those of his parents. During Gotham's earthquake, a tissue sample from Cassius bonded with the researcher Dr. Malley, altering him into a creature called Claything. **DW**

MENACE OF CLAYFACE Batman and Robin were confronted with a new kind of slippery foe when they first encountered the mud monster.

THE MALLEABLE MENACE that is Clayface has taken form as four distinct individuals over the years, all of them fierce opponents of the Batman. The presence of two new, offshoot Clayfaces in recent months may indicate the shape of things to come for the Dark Knight's Rogues Gallery. Though Basil Karlo started off as a non-powered killer, the name "Clayface" now describes a shape-shifter with a body formed of an amorphous, mud-like substance. Most Clayfaces can alter their bodies into almost any shape, including taking on the appearances of others.

Basil Karlo   Matt Hagen   Preston Payne   Sondra Fuller

SUPER SCARY Clayface is an old foe of both Batman and Robin, and one of the few super-powered foes in the Dark Knight's Rogues Gallery.

MUD STICKS *The Clayfaces have changed over the years, becoming more dangerous with each incarnation. Basil Karlo's upgrade into the Ultimate Clayface gave him the mimicking powers of Lady Clay and the deadly touch of Clayface III.*

KEY STORYLINES

• **DETECTIVE COMICS #604 (DECEMBER 1989):** All the surviving Clayfaces join together as the Mud Pack to menace Batman.
• **BATMAN: SHADOW OF THE BAT #27 (MAY 1994):** Clayface III and Lady Clay reveal that they have a child, Cassius, proving that even clay-creatures are capable of love.

CRIMSON AVENGER

FIRST APPEARANCE DETECTIVE COMICS #20 (October 1938)
STATUS Hero (deceased) **REAL NAME** Lee Travis
OCCUPATION Adventurer **BASE** New York City
HEIGHT 6ft **WEIGHT** 189 lbs **EYES** Brown **HAIR** Brown
SPECIAL POWERS/ABILITIES Expert combatant who carried a gas gun.

The Crimson Avenger is considered to be the first costumed hero of the Golden Age. He first donned his disguise in 1938 on the eve of the infamous *War of the Worlds* radio broadcast, when much of the U.S. was gripped with panic by the actor/director Orson Welles's vividly realistic dramatization of the H.G. Wells novel of a Martian invasion. In his civilian identity, the Crimson Avenger was Lee Travis, the crusading young publisher of the *Daily Globe-Leader*. His valet Wing became his sidekick. At the 1939 New York World's Fair, the Crimson Avenger helped a new hero, the Sandman I, to start his own heroic career.

During World War II, the Crimson Avenger and Wing adopted new costumes and joined the Seven Soldiers of Victory, fighting with great courage. During the Seven Soldiers' battle with a villain named the Nebula Man, the Crimson Avenger found himself sent centuries back in time to the days of the ancient Aztecs. Restored to the 20th century many decades beyond the point when he had left it, the Crimson Avenger discovered that he had been struck by a terminal disease. Lee Travis ended his life with a bang, bravely steering a doomed cargo ship away from New York's harbor so that it would explode safely in open water. **DW**

CRIMSON AVENGER II

FIRST APPEARANCE Stars & S.T.R.I.P.E. #9 (April 2000)
STATUS Villain **REAL NAME** Unknown
OCCUPATION Agent of vengeance; executioner **BASE** Mobile
HEIGHT 5ft 8in **WEIGHT** 136 lbs **EYES** Brown **HAIR** Black
SPECIAL POWERS/ABILITIES Wields twin pistols that never need reloading; bullet wound in chest symbolizes the violent deaths she is fated to avenge.

Decades later, another, very different Crimson Avenger arose in Detroit—a ruthless vigilante driven to kill. It all began when an unknown woman purchased two 1911 Colts from a pawnshop. The guns had once belonged to Lee Travis, Crimson Avenger I, and they were cursed. Once the woman had used them in an act of vengeance, they grafted themselves to her body.

Now that woman is an unwilling agent of powerful supernatural forces that cry out for the blood of sinners. Crimson Avenger II appears in a crimson mist to execute the guilty. She has also proved a threat to good guys, too, clashing with Wildcat II and taking away three of the hero's nine lives in the process. Tormented by doubts over the rightness of this mission, Crimson Avenger II tried to shoot herself with her own pistols. However, this desperate act had no effect, and she now knows that she is unable to escape her grisly calling, even in death. **DW**

CURSED *Crimson Avenger II is forced to relive the violent death of each victim before she is allowed to retaliate.*

CRIMSON FOX

FIRST APPEARANCE JUSTICE LEAGUE EUROPE #6 (September 1989)
STATUS Heroes **REAL NAMES** Vivian and Constance D'Aramis
OCCUPATION Publishers; adventurers **BASE** Paris, France
HEIGHT (both) 5ft 10in **WEIGHT** (Vivian) 143 lbs; (Constance) 147 lbs **EYES** Gray **HAIR** Red
SPECIAL POWERS/ABILITIES Martial arts; claws; costume tail used as a whip; pheromone triggers.

Vivian and Constance D'Aramis were the twin daughters of a research scientist for a multinational corporation. When they learned their mother had died of cancer caused by experiments the CEO of the corporation knew could have potential risks, they vowed revenge on the CEO and ruined his business by setting up the Revson Corporation. Creating a special shared identity that would allow one to run the business and the other to hunt criminals, the sisters became Le Renarde Rousse, the Crimson Fox.

As Crimson Fox, the D'Aramis sisters joined the Justice League of America's European branch in Paris, quickly rivaling the Elongated Man as France's favorite hero. Tragically, Vivian was killed by Paunteur, a mutant worm, and Constance was slain by Mist II. **PJ**

CRONUS

FIRST APPEARANCE THE NEW TITANS #51 (Winter 1988)
STATUS Villain **REAL NAME** None
OCCUPATION Titan **BASE** The Universe
HEIGHT 10ft **WEIGHT** 560 lbs **EYES** Red **HAIR** White
SPECIAL POWERS/ABILITIES Supernatural being of staggering strength and nigh-omnipotent power; carries a sickle capable of slaying gods.

Son of Gaea the Earth and Uranus the Sky, Cronus slayed his father to become lord of all creation. However, after siring the Olympian Gods and goddesses, Cronus was himself murdered by his three sons, Zeus, Poseidon, and Hades. The Olympian trio then divided the heavens, seas, and underworld between themselves. Millennia later, Cronus was magically brought back to life. He unleashed his terrible children—Arch, Disdain, Harrier, Oblivion, Slaughter, and Titan—upon the unsuspecting Earth. Hoping to rule the universe once more, Cronus set the Olympian and Hindu pantheons against one another in an epic war of the gods. However, Wonder Woman shattered Cronus's sickle, source of his power, and sent the Titan hurtling back into the arms of his mother. **SB**

CYBORG

FIRST APPEARANCE DC COMICS PRESENTS #26
(October 1980)
STATUS Hero **REAL NAME** Victor Stone
OCCUPATION Adventurer **BASE** San Francisco
HEIGHT 6ft 6in **WEIGHT** 385 lbs
EYES Brown **HAIR** Brown
SPECIAL POWERS/ABILITIES Enhanced vision, strength, and
endurance, as well as the ability to interface with any
computer system.

CYBERSKIN *Cyborg remains a cutting edge fusion between man and machine.*

ATHLETE *At heart, Victor would rather be a star athlete than a hero.*

Although Victor Stone's scientist parents encouraged Victor to pursue academic interests, he found athletic activity far more to his taste. During an experiment, Victor's mother accidentally unleashed a creature from another dimension that killed her instantly. If not for his father Silas's interference, Victor would have died as well. Silas rushed the injured boy to his lab and desperately grafted cybernetic parts to Victor's organs and computerized synthetic nerve bases to his spine. Once Victor was stable, his father replaced his limbs and part of his face with experimental molybdenum steel. Victor was outraged by his new body and felt cut off from the rest of society. However, when he crossed paths with the newly reformed Teen Titans, he quickly found acceptance with them.

Victor was later abducted by the alien computer intelligence from Technis which led to his humanity being restored. After learning that he could no longer exist away from this computer world, Vic agreed to be assimilated into Technis. The Technis entity, calling itself Cyberion, later captured every hero ever affiliated with the Titans.

CYBERWEAPON *Victor can adapt his components to a variety of uses, including his popular sonic generator.*

Changeling and the Titans eventually brought Vic to his senses. He freed the heroes and once more assumed the identity of Cyborg. Victor endured other physical changes until an encounter with the Thinker, the longtime villain, resulted in him once again taking on robotic form. After spending a year in a coma following the Infinite Crisis, Cyborg has made efforts to star an all-new Titans East team.'s teenage super heroes at Titans Tower in San Francisco. **RG**

CYBORG SUPERMAN

FIRST APPEARANCE ADVENTURES OF SUPERMAN #466 (May 1990)
STATUS Villain **REAL NAME** Hank Henshaw
OCCUPATION Mass murderer **BASE** Terran solar system
HEIGHT Variable **WEIGHT** Variable **EYES** Variable **HAIR** Variable
SPECIAL POWERS/ABILITIES Can control electronics and create new bodies
for himself out of machinery; possesses invulnerability due to his
Kryptonian organic material and alloys; seemingly impossible to kill.

MALEVOLENT FORCE *The Cyborg is living energy contained in an indestructible shell. He is more than a match for the Man of Steel.*

SUPERMAN's sinister duplicate once answered to the name of Hank Henshaw, crew member of the space shuttle *Excalibur*. A freak radiation accident melted Henshaw's body and turned him into pure energy. Horrified at what he had become, Henshaw beamed his consciousness into the Kryptonian birthing matrix that had brought Superman to Earth. He left the solar system, and his irrational hatred of Superman grew. In deep space he encountered the deposed tyrant Mongul, and the two hatched a plot against the Man of Steel. Henshaw used the birthing matrix to become a cyborg, with organic parts grown from Superman's DNA and limbs constructed of a Kryptonian alloy. Posing as a reborn Superman in the wake of Superman's battle with Doomsday, Henshaw diverted public attention while Mongul destroyed Coast City. Superman later demolished his cyborg copycat, but Henshaw came back in a new form.

Although Hal Jordan as Parallax slew the Cyborg in retaliation for Coast City, the villain again managed to return. Tormented by his former life and finding himself all but unkillable, Henshaw agreed to join Sinestro in the hopes that the Anti-Monitor would be able to finally end his life. The plan failed, and Henshaw now leads the robotic Manhunters. **DW**

HATE-MONGER *Hank Henshaw's baseless loathing for Superman is the key component of his paranoia*

AMAZING WEAPONS

SOME SUPER HEROES AND VILLAINS, such as Superman or Darkseid are, in effect, living weapons, their powers making them walking arsenals. But others, less naturally gifted, have developed incredible devices to help level the playing field between mere mortals and meta-humans. Some of these tools are marvels of alien technology, while others display the stubborn ingenuity of human inventors.

CEREMONY Green Lantern recites his oath as he recharges his power ring, an essential ritual performed every 24 hours.

GREEN LANTERN'S POWER RING

Limited only by the wielder's imagination, the emerald power rings of Oa have been described as the most powerful weapons in existence. The Guardians of the Universe created these rings eons ago for use by their peacekeepers in the Green Lantern Corps. Drawing energy from a Central Power Battery on Oa, the rings can create hard-light projections of almost anything, from a giant fist to a freight train to an atomic bomb. The rings also allow their wearers to fly, teleport, translate any language, and to draw upon a vast database of knowledge.

The traditional Oan power ring would not operate against anything colored yellow, though a clever Green Lantern could usually bypass this defect (by coating a yellow target in mud, for example), and the flaw was removed entirely in the creation of Kyle Rayner's ring. Earth's original Green Lantern, Alan Scott, possesses a similar ring, though his is based on magic rather than on Oan science and is vulnerable to wooden objects.

Black Hand

CRAZY CREATIONS

Obsessions are not a problem when you live in a world crawling with super-villains—just throw on a costume related to your mania and you've got an instant gimmick. Several fanatical fiends also happened to be geniuses of invention, and created themed gadgets that were memorable, if not always effective.

Black Hand, a methodical criminal who learned all his skills from books, developed many electronic gizmos, including one that could absorb the energy of Green Lantern's ring. The Fiddler, who destroyed objects with sound, employed an arsenal of specialized violins. Everything concerning the Key revolved around a "lock and key" theme, including his weapons and his crimes. The Sportsmaster, a gifted athlete, had a fondness for exploding baseballs.

The Fiddler

The Key

Sportsmaster

Green Arrow's Trick Arrows

Oliver Queen is not only renowned as one of the world's best archers; he is also famous for his array of trick arrows. Only Queen seems able to fire these arrows with any accuracy, and indeed their top-heavy designs would seem to defy the most basic laws of ballistics! Some of the specialty arrows that have found their way into Green Arrow's quiver have included the grappling-hook arrow, the boomerang arrow, the tear-gas arrow, the safe-cracking arrow, the smokescreen arrow, the suction arrow, the handcuff arrow, the net arrow, and the tiny mini-arrow.

Oliver Queen's son Connor Hawke, who preferred "regular" arrows in his career as Green Arrow II, was forced to break into his father's stash of trick arrows when the Key attacked the Justice League of America's lunar headquarters. Connor had to admit that Oliver's flamboyant weapons had some merit after he knocked the Key senseless with a hit from a boxing-glove arrow.

Combat arrow

Grappling-hook arrow

Net arrow

Tear-gas arrow

Cryonic arrow

Flash arrow

Boxing-glove arrow

STARMAN'S COSMIC ROD

One of humanity's greatest inventions, the cosmic rod was crafted by Ted Knight (the first Starman) to harness the "cosmic energy" emanating from the stars. Originally called the gravity rod, the device gave Starman the ability to fly, project force fields, and emit shattering blasts of stellar energy.

IMPERIEX'S ENTROPY AEGIS

The world-conqueror Imperiex employed scores of worker-bee Imperiex-Probes in his quest to hollow out the Earth and trigger a second Big Bang. Each Imperiex-Probe came encased in a suit of impenetrable alien armor. Earth forces captured a burned-out Imperiex shell and retrofitted it with Apokoliptian technology, creating what is arguably the most powerful suit of armor in existence. Originally intended to be worn by Superman, the Entropy Aegis suit became bonded to the hero Steel II after his resurrection during the Imperiex War (*see* Great Battles, pp. 186-7). The armor made Steel invulnerable and allowed him to emit cosmic energy, though it cost him his humanity.

SHOWDOWN
Steel's unbreakable suit lets him go toe-to-toe against Superman.

BATMAN'S BATARANGS

The Dark Knight has a billionaire's resources to fuel his crime crusade. Although he carries a host of gadgetry in his utility belt, his signature weapon is the Batarang—a sharp-edged crescent or disc modeled on the Australian boomerang. Batarangs can be used as grappling hooks or throwing stars, and some varieties can even be remote-steered. Other Gotham adventurers have been inspired by Batman to carry their own, similar variations on the weapon. Both Robin and Nightwing employ modified Batarangs, while the villainous Cat-Man has his "catarangs."

BAT GEAR *Batman carries other non-lethal weapons, including gas cartridges and flash grenades.*

WONDER WOMAN'S MAGICAL WEAPONS

Wonder Woman is an ambassador of peace and her weapons are largely defensive, including her bullet-deflecting Bracelets of Victory and her signature Lasso of Truth. Created from the Golden Girdle of Gaea and given to Princess Diana by the goddess Hestia, the magical lasso is unbreakable and compels anyone caught in it to speak the truth. The lasso has been destroyed only once, when the sorcerer Rama Khan unraveled the basic truths of the universe, but it was quickly reforged. Recently, the war god Ares gave Wonder Girl a replica of the lasso for his own shadowy reasons. DW

DARKSEID

FIRST APPEARANCE SUPERMAN'S PAL JIMMY OLSEN #134 (December 1970)
STATUS Villain **REAL NAME** Uxas
OCCUPATION Tyrant/world conqueror **BASE** Apokolips
HEIGHT 8ft 9in **WEIGHT** 1,815 lbs **EYES** Red **HAIR** None
SPECIAL POWERS/ABILITIES Utterly ruthless, unforgiving planetary overlord who rules underlings by fear; immensely strong and apparently invulnerable; eyes project Omega Beams, powerful rays that incinerate, annihilate, or transport beings.

Darkseid is the gravest threat to life in the DC Universe, representing all that is vile and corrupt. In the wake of the old gods dying, a race of New Gods were born, split between two planets, bright New Genesis and smoldering Apokolips, who were continually at war with each other. On Apokolips, Queen Heggra and her own son Uxas plotted and schemed against each other, one determined to retain power, the other seeking it. Uxas's drive for control resulted in his brother Drax's death. Uxas then evolved into the creature known as Darkseid.

APOKOLIPS
Born out of the cataclysm that claimed the old gods, a perpetually burning world.

RUTHLESS *Darkseid respects no-one and any person or god is but a means to his own ends.*

THE WARBRINGER

Against Heggra's wishes, Darkseid secretly married the sorceress Suli, and they had a son named Kalibak. Suli was murdered, at Heggra's command by the torturer Desaad and Heggra then ordered her son to marry Tiggra, with whom he had a son, ORION. To settle the war between New Genesis and Apokolips, a peace treaty was signed known as "The Pact," wherein the ruling gods of Apokolips and New Genesis give one another their sons to be raised by the other. The New Genesis ruler Highfather raised Orion as his own; Darkseid had Scott Free (Mister Miracle) raised by Granny Goodness at her brutal orphanage.

Martian philosophy led Darkseid to conceptualize the "Anti-Life Equation" as the object of his quest for power, and agents of Apokolips attacked Mars. Later, Darkseid turned his sights on Earth. Despite frequent setbacks, Darkseid continued his conquest of the universe, although he was frequently being opposed by his own son, Orion. Darkseid failed to recruit Supergirl into his Female Furies, and suffered the wrath of Superman who imprisoned him in the Source Wall for a time. The experience temporarily drained Darkseid of his Omega Effect, but despite the return of his abilities he remained unable to prevent the death of the New Gods and the end of the Fourth World. **RG**

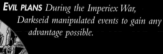

EVIL PLANS *During the Imperiex War, Darkseid manipulated events to gain any advantage possible.*

OMEGA BEAMS *The Omega Effect has no known limitations and can dissolve any organic being.*

KEY STORYLINES

• *JACK KIRBY'S NEW GODS (1997):* The initial storyline introducing Darkseid and his quest for the "Anti-Life Equation" plus a glimpse into the horror that is Apokolips.
• *LEGENDS (1987):* Darkseid attempts to besmirch the reputation of Earth's defenders, bringing down the heroes to make Earth an easier planet to pillage.
• *COSMIC ODYSSEY (2003):* Darkseid thinks he has found the "Anti-Life Equation" and will destroy entire planets to obtain it. However, he finds himself opposed by Highfather's handpicked champions—Superman, Orion, Batman, Green Lantern, and Bug.

DEADMAN

FIRST APPEARANCE STRANGE ADVENTURES #205 (September 1967)
STATUS Hero **REAL NAME** Boston Brand
OCCUPATION Acrobat **BASE** Mobile
HEIGHT 6ft **WEIGHT** 201 lbs **EYES** Blue **HAIR** Black
SPECIAL POWERS/ABILITIES Possesses human bodies for a limited period of time; converses with spirits; crosses realms of reality with ease.

TRAPEZE ARTIST BOSTON BRAND, the leading high-wire act for the Hills Brothers Circus, was murdered by an assassin's bullet. Rescued from the Afterworld by Rama Kushna, Goddess of Balance, for the many kindnesses he had performed during his life, Brand became the ghoulish spirit Deadman. He began to hunt for his assassin, knowing only that the man wore a hook for a hand. When Deadman learned that a villain called Hook was a member of the international League of Assassins, he was sure that it was Hook who had fired the fatal bullet. Along the way, Brand continued to interact in people's lives, doing good deeds in his distinctive style.

HIGH FLYER
Aerialist Boston Brand was killed in a random manner by the Hook.

HOW HE WORKS *Those inhabited by Deadman's spirit have no recollection of being possessed.*

SENTINEL OF MAGIC

Deadman eventually tracked down the Hook, only to watch him die at the hands of the Sensei, leader of the League of Assassins. With the aid of his brother Cleveland and Batman, Deadman then prevented the League seizing control of the fabled Himalayan land of Nanda Parbat.

Deadman was subsequently called upon to perform the kinds of duties expected of spirits such as himself, greeting those entering the Land of the Just Dead. In this role, Deadman guided the Phantom Stranger, the Spectre, Etrigan the Demon, and Swamp Thing to Hell in order to rescue the spirit of Abby Arcane after she was murdered by her uncle. Deadman has teamed up with other spectral heroes, joining the Phantom Stranger and Swamp Thing to combat the threat of a "primordial shadow" that imperiled Heaven and Earth. When Asmodel usurped the power of the Spirit of Wrath, Deadman formed part of a strike force of sentinels of magic with Doctor Occult, Felix Faust, Madame Xanadu, the Phantom Stranger, Ragman, Raven, and Sentinel assembled by Zatanna to oppose the fallen angel. Deadman continues to work with people on Earth, hoping one day to achieve a peaceful reward. **RG**

DEEP FEELINGS *Despite being only a spirit, Boston Brand still retains his emotions. Following the killing machine Doomsday's rampage through Metropolis, he was grief-stricken to come upon Lois Lane cradling the seemingly dying Superman in her arms.*

SPIRIT GUIDE *Deadman helps defend the mortal plane from all manner of malevolent spirits. However, he found himself in grave danger from a child called Zi with body-snatching astral powers the equal of his own.*

KEY STORYLINES

• **STRANGE ADVENTURES #205-216 (SEPTEMBER 1967–FEBRUARY 1969):** The initial run of Boston Brand's death and hunt for the Hook. Brand's tragic life and those left behind are introduced with stunning stories and art.
• **DEADMAN MINI-SERIES (1986):** The destruction of Nanda Parbat and the discovery of Rama Kushna's first champion, Joshua. Deadman's relationship with Kushna is re-examined.

DEMON, THE

FIRST APPEARANCE DEMON (1st series) #1 (September 1972)
STATUS Villain **REAL NAME** Etrigan
OCCUPATION Rhyming demon **BASE** Hell
HEIGHT 6ft 4in **WEIGHT** 352 lbs **EYES** Red **HAIR** None
SPECIAL POWERS/ABILITIES Adept at magic; however, has little patience for spell casting, preferring to simply blast his foes to cinders with his fiery breath; has attained the rank of Rhymer in Hell, which explains why he always talks in rhyming couplets!

THE DEMON ETRIGAN entered Hell, clawing his way out of the womb of his mother, a demoness. Son of the archfiend Belial, Etrigan quickly rose through the ranks of demonhood, and even the elder demons began to fear him. Belial arranged for his son Myrddin, who would become known as Merlin the Magician, to be trained in the arts of sorcery, so that Merlin might one day bind and control Etrigan, his half-brother. Merlin unleashed Etrigan to battle the forces of Morgaine Le Fey, intent on usurping King Arthur's Court at Camelot. After Le Fey's defeat and Camelot's fall, Merlin bound Etrigan to the druid Jason, who became Jason Blood.

SUPERMAN Etrigan's magical powers make him a match for the Man of Steel.

JASON BLOOD With the right mystic inducement, and chant, Etrigan's form is banished in favor of the body of Jason Blood.

THE DEMON WITHIN

Blood created a series of lives around the world and amassed occult knowledge, hoping either to free himself from Etrigan or at least tame the demon within. During World War II the Demon was unleashed, aiding the first Starman during a conflict with the Icicle and Nazi saboteurs. Etrigan also was called upon to help oppose occult forces such as Klarion, the Witch boy or Blackbriar Thorn. On more than one occasion, his ferocity was welcomed by occult conclaves with other powerful forces such as the Phantom Stranger, the Spectre, and Swamp Thing.

All the while Etrigan had his own agenda: to kill Blood, gain his freedom, and rule Hell. During one foray into Hell, Etrigan seemed to have gained his desire. However, moments after acquiring the Crown of Horns and becoming King of Hell, Etrigan was tricked by Jason Blood and Merlin into returning to Earth. It transpired that Etrigan's evil acts in recent years had been the result of a spell cast by Morgaine Le Fey and an aged incarnation of Merlin. The curse was temporarily broken but, without the stabilizing influence of the benevolent incarnation of Merlin (slain in a pit of hellfire along with his evil duplicate), the spell that made Etrigan an evil Rhymer soon took control of him again.

Recently, Etrigan tried to steal Blue Devil's Trident of Lucifer from the members of the Shadowpact in a bid to take control of Hell. Turned to stone after the failed attempt, the Demon became a coat rack for the patrons of the Oblivion Bar.
RG

DEMON IN JAPAN Etrigan is one of the most ambitious and dangerous demons in Hell or on Earth and he tends to let nothing impede that lust for power.

KEY STORYLINES

• *THE DEMON* #1-8 (1972–73): Jack Kirby's introductory story, setting up the conflict between Etrigan and Jason Blood. Jason's friends Glenda and Harry are also introduced.
• *THE DEMON MINI-SERIES (NOVEMBER 1986–FEBRUARY 1987)*: Matt Wagner's updated look at the Demon, his place on Earth, and his role in Hell. The series also looks at his relationship with Jason Blood.

DESTINY

FIRST APPEARANCE WEIRD MYSTERY TALES #1 (July 1972)
STATUS Unknown **REAL NAME** None
OCCUPATION Cosmic observer **BASE** Destiny's garden
HEIGHT Variable **WEIGHT** Variable **EYES** None **HAIR** Unknown
SPECIAL POWERS/ABILITIES God-like, all-seeing entity who carries a book containing the history of every event in the universe; casts no shadow, leaves no footprint.

The Endless, humanoid manifestations of the primal truths of the universe, oversee every aspect of the reality created by the supreme power. Destiny is the oldest of the Endless. He has existed since the birth of everything, and when the universe finally comes to an end his sister Death will come to claim him. Like Death and the other siblings Dream, Desire, Despair, Destruction, and Delirium, Destiny adopts human form when dealing with people. He appears as a tall, hooded man, believed by some to be blind and by others to have evolved beyond sight. The book he carries contains every event, no matter how infinitesimal, that has happened or will happen.

Destiny inhabits a garden in an unseen realm. Within the garden are infinite paths down which all souls must walk as they live their lives. Destiny does not control the destinations of those who walk the garden, but every possible choice and outcome has already been recorded in his book. Elsewhere in Destiny's garden is a stone structure containing a gallery of portraits that portray the Endless as they wish to be seen. Destiny recently discovered that the Challengers of The Unknown no longer existed in his book, and entrusted its safety to their care. **DW**

FATE Although chained to his book, Destiny would never dream of shirking his duties. He is the most serious of the Endless.

DEVASTATION

FIRST APPEARANCE WONDER WOMAN (2nd series) #143 (April 1999)
STATUS Villain **REAL NAME** None; calls herself "Deva"
OCCUPATION Creator of mayhem **BASE** Earth
HEIGHT 4ft 6in **WEIGHT** 82 lbs **EYES** Pale blue **HAIR** Red
SPECIAL POWERS/ABILITIES Supernatural shape-changer; possesses amazing strength; able to control the minds of humans to fulfill her goal of spreading chaos and despair all over the world.

Baby-faced and barely 12 years old in appearance, Devastation is the epitome of evil. She is yet another monstrous offspring of the mad Titan Cronus, father of the Olympian Gods. To counteract his enemy Wonder Woman, Cronus molded Devastation out of the very same clay from which peace-loving Olympian goddesses had sculpted the Amazon Princess. Deva's purpose was not to spread peace and love, of course, but to bring discord, prejudice, and brutality to the peoples of the Earth.

To do so, Devastation battled her Amazon "sister" Diana and learned all of Wonder Woman's secrets by ensnaring Diana in her own golden Lasso of Truth. Devastation then used her own supernatural powers to compel a terrorist group to plot an attack using a nuclear bomb. However, Devastation was unaware that a single drop of Wonder Woman's blood had been mixed into the clay that had also created her. Appealing to that scintilla of inherent goodness within Deva, Diana convinced her to allow the nuclear device to explode harmlessly underground, saving millions of lives. Deva then escaped. As Wonder Woman's spiritual opposite, Devastation is sure to return, older and wiser, and probably less likely to allow Diana to use their shared blood to appeal to her better nature again. **SB**

DETECTIVE CHIMP

FIRST APPEARANCE REX THE WONDER DOG #4 (August 1953)
STATUS Hero **REAL NAME** Bobo
OCCUPATION Detective **BASE** Oscaloosa County, Florida
HEIGHT 3ft 7in **WEIGHT** 76 lbs **EYES** Black **HAIR** Black
SPECIAL POWERS/ABILITIES Highly intelligent; can communicate with all forms of animal life.

Bobo is a chimpanzee from Africa, brought to the U.S. by animal trainer Fred Thorpe and promoted as the "Detective Chimp" in a novelty act in which Bobo learned to respond to simple cues and appeared to solve crimes. After journeying to the Fountain of Youth with Rex The Wonder Dog, Bobo received enhanced intelligence and the gift of speech. Bobo moved to the U.S. after he solved his first criminal case and was raised by Fred Thorpe, a world-renowned animal trainer.

Tragically, Thorpe was savagely murdered. Bobo then joined forces with Florida Sheriff Edward Chase and, using his advanced instincts and intuitive skills, discovered Thorpe's killer. Chase took on Bobo as his companion, and the two solved numerous cases over the years. Detective Chimp emerged from years of alcoholism when the Spectre attacked the Earth's magic-users. He became a member of the Shadowpact, battling supernatural threats and spending a year trapped in the town of Riverrock, Wyoming following the Infinite Crisis. **PJ**

DOCTOR FATE

FIRST APPEARANCE (Dr. Fate I) MORE FUN COMICS #55 (May 1940)
STATUS Hero **REAL NAME** Kent Nelson
OCCUPATION Archaeologist/physician **BASE** Salem, Massachusetts
HEIGHT 6ft 2in **WEIGHT** 197 lbs **EYES** Blue **HAIR** Blond
SPECIAL POWERS/ABILITIES Able to levitate and fly; nearly invulnerable; helmet, amulet, and mantle of Nabu are powerful mystic talismans, making Dr. Fate one of the greatest living sorcerers.

FIRST APPEARANCE (Inza Cramer) MORE FUN COMICS #55 (May 1940); (Dr. Fate III) DOCTOR FATE (3rd series) #25 (February 1991)
STATUS Hero **REAL NAME** Inza Cramer Nelson
OCCUPATION Adventurer **BASE** Salem, Massachusetts
HEIGHT 5ft 7in **WEIGHT** 125 lbs **EYES** Green **HAIR** Blonde
SPECIAL POWERS/ABILITIES Depending on who initiated the mystical merge, Kent or Inza Nelson, Fate manifested as a man or a woman.

FIRST APPEARANCE (Hector Hall) ALL-STAR SQUADRON #25 (September 1983); (Dr. Fate IV) JSA #3 (October 1999)
STATUS Hero **REAL NAME** Hector Hall
OCCUPATION Agent of balance **BASE** Salem, Massachusetts
HEIGHT 6ft **WEIGHT** 184 lbs **EYES** Blue **HAIR** White
SPECIAL POWERS/ABILITIES While wearing the helmet of Nabu, Hector hears the voice of the ancient sorcerer himself.

BULLETPROOF *With the helmet of Nabu, Dr. Fate can make himself intangible so that bullets whizz right through him!*

MANY CENTURIES AGO, the Lord of Order known as Nabu placed himself in suspended animation to allow his human host body to recover from the strain of wielding Nabu's magicks. Nabu was revived in 1940, when archaeologist Sven Nelson and his son Kent were exploring the Ur Valley in Mesopotamia. As Nabu was awakened, a deadly gas was released from the chamber that killed Sven Nelson. Nabu took Kent under his tutelage, transformed him into an adult, and schooled him in the ways of sorcery. After many years, Nabu bequeathed Kent his amulet, helmet, and cloak, mystic talismans of extraordinary might. Now an agent of the Lords of Order, Kent became Dr. Fate, one of the most powerful "Mystery Men" of the time, and a founding member of the Justice Society of America.

Inza Cramer Nelson

KENT NELSON AND INZA CRAMER

On his first adventure, Dr. Fate rescued Inza Cramer from the warlock Wotan and married her. During World War II, Dr. Fate was also a member of the Allied superpowered coalition known as the All-Star Squadron. In the decades that followed, Fate continued to combat eldritch evils based in his other-dimensional sanctum, a tower in Salem, Massachusetts that was also Kent and Inza Nelson's home. By virtue of Nabu's talismans both husband and wife retained their youth into modern times.

Eventually events conspired to bring about Kent and Inza's deaths, whereupon Nabu bestowed his arcane abilities upon Eric Strauss, a boy also transformed into an adult. While battling an agent of Chaos, Eric mystically merged with his stepmother, Linda Strauss, to become a Dr. Fate wholly independent of Nabu. who resurrected Kent Nelson's body in order to inhabit it and guide the Strausses as Fate's mentor. The second Dr. Fate later perished in battle, although Eric and Linda's spirits lived on inside the bodies of two friends, Eugene and Wendy Di Bella. Nabu then restored Kent and Inza Nelson to life and was reborn himself as the spirit of Wendy Di Bella's infant child.

Kent and Inza, meanwhile, both took up the mantle of Dr. Fate, merging as the Strausses once did. When Kent was unable to merge any longer, Inza was forced to go it alone. Both Kent and Inza perished during the Zero Hour crisis (*see* Great Battles, pp. 186-7). Fate's talismans then fell into the hands of Jared Stevens, who forged a mystic dagger from Nabu's helmet and amulet. His career as Fate was cut short by the sorcerer Mordru, thus setting in motion events that would bring a new, even more powerful Dr. Fate to the fore.

Hector Hall, son of Hawkman and Hawkgirl and the partner of Lyta Trevor (Fury II), was a spirit adrift in the ether until he was reborn as Nabu's champion of balance and justice. The Spectre ended Hector's term as Fate, leaving Nabu without a human host. After confronting the Spectre, Nabu passed on and allowed his helmet to find a new bearer – Dr. Kent V. Nelson, grandnephew of the original Doctor Fate. **SB**

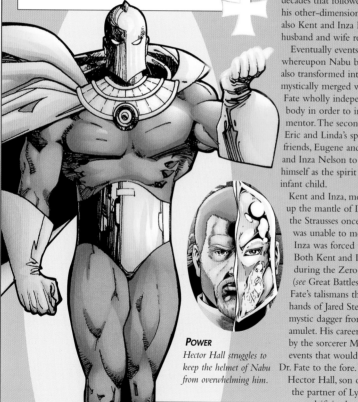

POWER
Hector Hall struggles to keep the helmet of Nabu from overwhelming him.

ATTACK *Nabu counsels Hector within the dreamscape of Fate's helm, spurring the latest Dr. Fate to strike out and use the full measure of his mystical might.*

DOCTOR FATE *Connection with the Lord of Order Nabu allows Fate to manipulate vast magical forces.*

KEY STORYLINES

• JSA #1 (August 1999): Jared Stevens, possessor of Nabu's talismans, is killed by the minions of Mordru, thus paving the way for the long-awaited return of Dr. Fate.
Doctor Fate (4th series) #1-4 (October 2003–February 2004): Hector Hall battles and destroys the Curse, a timeless evil that wrecked ancient Egypt, as he settles in at Dr. Fate's Salem tower.

DOCTOR PSYCHO

FIRST APPEARANCE WONDER WOMAN (1st series) #5 (May 1991)
STATUS Villain **REAL NAME** Edgar Cizko
OCCUPATION Psychotherapist **BASE** Mobile
HEIGHT 3ft 9in **WEIGHT** 85 lbs **EYES** Blue **HAIR** Black
SPECIAL POWERS/ABILITIES Able to alter and manipulate the perceptions of his victims by attacking through dreams; creates hallucinatory nightmare landscapes to torment foes with fear and despair.

One of the most powerful and persistent of Wonder Woman's enemies, the diminutive Dr. Psycho murdered Dr. Charles Stanton, psychiatrist to the Amazon Princess's teenage friend Vanessa Kapatelis, and usurped his identity. Dr. Psycho then used Vanessa's subconscious as a conduit to mentally manipulate Wonder Woman. Although thwarted in his initial psychic assaults, Dr. Psycho has been a lingering threat to Wonder Woman and her dearest friends, Vanessa especially. Psycho was later hired by power-hungry mogul Sebastian Ballésteros to further exploit Vanessa's damaged psyche and mold her into the second Silver Swan, a living weapon to battle Wonder Woman. Dr. Psycho became a key member of the Secret Society of Super-Villains during the Infinite Crisis, controlling Doomsday long enough to unleash him on the heroes assembled in Metropolis. He later escaped from a courtroom trial involving Kate Spencer (see Manhunter). **SB**

NIGHTMARE Dr. Psycho is a dwarf of uncommon ugliness. Even what you see here is an illusion created by the villain to appear more attractive than he truly is!

HEAD DOCTOR Bound and shackled to prevent his escape from imprisonment in a meta-human detention facility, Dr. Psycho must also wear a psychic-damping headband to prevent him from using his illusory powers.

CRAZY SCHEMES Time and again, Sivana and his family have tried to assume power or take over the world. They remain defeated at the hands of the Marvel Family.

DOCTOR SIVANA

FIRST APPEARANCE WHIZ COMICS #2 (February 1940)
STATUS Villain **REAL NAME** Thaddeus Bodog Sivana
OCCUPATION Adventurer **BASE** Fawcett City
HEIGHT 5ft 6in **WEIGHT** 123 lbs
EYES Gray **HAIR** None
SPECIAL POWERS/ABILITIES While possessing no powers, Sivana is a genius in any number of disciplines.

Dr. Sivana's scientific genius made him one of the wealthiest men in Fawcett City. However, his unethical business practices made him, as he observed, the man the media "loves to hate." Meanwhile, an extramarital affair led Sivana's wife, Venus, to leave him with their two children, Beautia and Magnificus, and the billionaire's empire collapsed when he was implicated in the murders of archaeologists C.C. and Marilyn Batson (see Captain Marvel). After the Sivana Building was destroyed in fire, the disgraced billionaire was presumed dead until he attempted to steal the scarab necklace of the wizard Shazam. He was thwarted by Captain Marvel, and in the process, Sivana learned that the hero was also young Billy Batson.

Sivana, despite his brilliant mind, was not a very good criminal, and despite frequent prison escapes, was always recaptured by Captain Marvel, whom he sarcastically dubbed "The Big Red Cheese." The Doctor upped the ante when he became embroiled with the Venusian worm Mister Mind who had plans to conquer Earth. However this came to nought when Mr. Mind allied himself with Captain Marvel. Sivana assembled a new grouping of the Fearsome Five, and after the Infinite Crisis he joined other mad scientists on Oolong Island. There, he devised weapons for Chang Tzu. The Venusian worm Mister Mind escaped from Sivana's lab and tried to devour the multiverse—after Booster Gold and Rip Hunter stopped Mister Mind's rampage, the worm wound up in Sivana's care once more. **RG**

DOMINUS

FIRST APPEARANCE ACTION COMICS #747 (August 1998)
STATUS Villain   **REAL NAME** Tuoni
OCCUPATION Destroyer of worlds   **BASE** The Infinite Domain
HEIGHT/WEIGHT Variable   **EYES** Red   **HAIR** None
SPECIAL POWERS/ABILITIES Creates multiple realities based on the worst nightmares of his opponents.

Once a benign Lord of Order named Tuoni, Dominus assumed his current malevolent form when he jealously struck against his former lover Ahti after she ascended to the coveted position of Illuminator of All Realities and became the godlike Kismet. His rash attack disintegrated him, but Kismet compassionately allowed him to live as an exile in the Phantom Zone. Kryptonian technology restored him to new life and Dominus escaped to Earth, where he tried to take his revenge on Kismet. Failing in that, he created alternate realities based on Superman's fears and convinced the Man of Steel that civilization would end unless he remained eternally vigilant. Proclaiming himself King of the World, Superman policed the planet with an army of Superman Robots. Superman shook off Dominus's influence, but the villain destroyed his Antarctic Fortress of Solitude. After a long struggle, Superman successfully banished Dominus to the Phantom Zone. **DW**

DON CABALLERO

FIRST APPEARANCE ALL-STAR WESTERN #58 (April–May 1951)
STATUS Hero (deceased)   **REAL NAME** Unknown
OCCUPATION Fencing instructor; adventurer
BASE Southern California in the early 19th century
HEIGHT 5ft 11in   **WEIGHT** 178 lbs   **EYES** Brown   **HAIR** Black
SPECIAL POWERS/ABILITIES Expert fencer and horseman.

Don Caballero moved to southern California from his native Spain in the early years of the 19th century and established an estate in the small community of Hawk Hill. His true name unknown, Don Caballero used his expert fencing skills to thwart local felons and desert pirates like the Jackal, and even supernatural threats like the ghost of El Feugo, becoming Hawk Hill's greatest hero in the process.

Over the years, Don Caballero came to instruct others in Hawk Hill, teaching them the fine art of fencing. Caballero used his own blade, the legendary *El Capitan*, and his own physical prowess and martial skills to defend his southern California home well into his senior years, although his final fate has yet to be recorded. **PJ**

DOOMSDAY

FIRST APPEARANCE SUPERMAN: THE MAN OF STEEL #17 (Nov. 1992)
STATUS Villain   **REAL NAME** None
OCCUPATION Destroyer   **BASE** Earth
HEIGHT 7ft   **WEIGHT** 615 lbs   **EYES** Red   **HAIR** White
SPECIAL POWERS/ABILITIES Bred to be the ultimate killing machine, each time he is defeated, he regenerates with a higher level of strength and endurance, making him an unbeatable foe.

CREATION The clone that will become Doomsday is jettisoned into Krypton's harsh environment.

Some 250,000 years ago, an alien scientist named Bertron arrived on Krypton and commenced cloning experiments to create the perfect warrior. Within decades, a cloned baby proved able to survive on harsh Krypton and withstand local predators. Turning on its creator, the creature killed Bertron before escaping Krypton. The monster traveled to other worlds, where it killed without mercy. Through the years, members of the Green Lantern Corps opposed this being, known as Doomsday until it threatened Oa, home to the Guardians of the Universe. Their champion Radiant defeated Doomsday and he was chained, wrapped in a protective garment, placed in a container, and ejected into space. The container crashed into the Earth, burying itself deep underground. Over the millennia Doomsday struggled to free himself, pounding his way to the surface until he emerged in North America. He beat back the Justice League of America before confronting Superman in Metropolis. The two fought an epic battle that laid waste to the city and resulted in the death of the Man of Steel. Since then, Doomsday has remained unstoppable, although he has since become a pawn for the likes of Brainiac and even Lex Luthor (*see* Luthor, Lex). **RG**

SUPERMAN SHOWDOWN Doomsday's kryptonian genetics allow him to cause Superman great pain.

KILLING MACHINE A rampaging engine of destruction, each new generation of Doomsdays adapts to new perils and new environments, making him the perfect weapon.

DOOM PATROL

SUPERPOWERED MISFITS

FIRST APPEARANCE MY GREATEST ADVENTURE #80 (June 1963)
STATUS Hero team **BASE** Midway City
CURRENT MEMBERS AND POWERS
BEAST BOY (GARFIELD LOGAN) Can transform into any animal
BUMBLEBEE (KAREN BEECHER) Can fly and fire electrical stingers
THE CHIEF (NILES CAULDER) Brilliant scientific mind
ELASTI-GIRL (RITA FARR) Can shrink or grow to various sizes
MENTO (STEVE DAYTON) Telepathy, mind control, telekinesis
NEGATIVE MAN (LARRY TRAINOR) Radioactive projection can fly, turn intangible
ROBOTMAN (CLIFF STEELE) Human brain housed in super-powerful robot body
VOX (MAL DUNCAN) Can emit sonic blasts and open dimensional gates

A TEAM OF SUPERPOWERED MISFITS, the Doom Patrol was assembled by the wheelchair-bound Dr. Niles Caulder to thwart threats to humanity. Caulder believed that these meta-humans—all marked by tragedy and ostracized from society—had nothing to lose and so would be willing to risk their lives as the world's strangest super heroes. As "The Chief," Caulder recruited Elasti-Girl, Negative Man, and Robotman II as the first Doom Patrol, a trio that soon learned to work as a team and live together as a family in Caulder's Midway City mansion. The Doom Patrol's greatest adventures involved saving the world from such menaces as the Society of Sin and General Immortus.

KEY 1) *Robotman II (Cliff Steele)* 2) *Elasti-Girl (Rita Farr Dayton)* 3) *The Chief (Dr. Niles Caulder)* 4) *Negative Man (Larry Trainor)*

KEY 1) *Vox* 2) *Beast Boy* 3) *Bumblebee* 4) *Negative Man* 5) *Elasti-Girl* 6) *Robotman* 7) *The Chief*

FAST FORWARD!

A huge number of meta-human heroes with all kinds of powers and abilities—ranging from the useful or miraculous to the weird or plain disturbing—have passed through the Doom Patrol's ranks. The most recent team was assembled by eccentric businessman Thayer Jost, who had purchased the rights to the Patrol's name from a Robotman doppelganger created by former team member Dorothy Spinner, who possessed the ability to turn her fantasies into frightening reality. This team of young meta-humans, which included Fast Forward—quickly dubbed "Negative Man" because of his overwhelming pessimism—Fever, Freak, and Kid Slick, had little experience wielding their powers.

The disbanding of this team, coupled with the reality-altering preshocks of the Infinite Crisis, allowed for the original Doom Patrol's return – including the Chief, Elasti-Girl, Negative Man, and Robotman. Caulder has since united other misfit heroes both old and new under his banner, including Mento, Bumblebee, Beast Boy, and Vox. The team continues to operate as outcasts, accepted by neither the public nor the super-hero community. **SB**

THE DEVIL *The Patrol went to Hell and back to beat Raum and free the souls empowering this fallen angel. Raum inspired the worst impulses in men and women, claiming their spirits after they committed suicide.*

FATHER FIGURE *As the Patrol's eldest (and most enduring) member, Robotman is the one constant among the Patrol's ever-changing roster.*

KEY STORYLINES

• **DOOM PATROL (1ST SERIES) #121 (AUGUST 1968):** The original Doom Patrol sacrifice their own lives to save Codsville, Maine, from Madame Rouge and Captain Zahl. All but Elasti-Girl truly perish.
• **SHOWCASE #94 (AUGUST 1977):** Dr. Will Magnus finds Robotman's broken body and rebuilds him in time to join a new Doom Patrol that includes Celsius, Negative Woman, and Tempest.
• **DOOM PATROL (2ND SERIES) #19 (FEBRUARY 1989):** Things get stranger for the world's strangest heroes as they emerge from further tragedy by adding Crazy Jane to the team. They embark on new adventures while battling menaces like the Scissormen, Red Jack, and the Brotherhood of Dada.

ELEMENT GIRL

FIRST APPEARANCE METAMORPHO #10 (February 1967)
STATUS Hero **REAL NAME** Urania "Rainie" Blackwell
OCCUPATION Former U.S. government agent **BASE** Mobile
HEIGHT 5ft 10in **WEIGHT** 142 lbs **EYES** Black **HAIR** Green
SPECIAL POWERS/ABILITIES Could shapeshift and transform into any combination of chemical elements.

Element Girl lived a sad life, transformed into a freak and then abandoned by those she loved. Many years ago, Urania Blackwell had been a spy working for the U.S. government who volunteered to expose herself to the same Orb of Ra radiation that had transformed Rex Mason into Metamorpho, the Element Man. The process worked—although Rainie's body became discolored and misshapen, she could shift between elemental states at will. She took the alias of Element Girl. Rainie worked with Metamorpho for several months, crossing the globe and falling in love. However she was spurned by Metamorpho, and soon her government agency declared it had no further use for her. Despairing, Rainie tried to live quietly in retirement but because of her hideous appearance, couldn't bear to leave her apartment. She tried to commit suicide on several occasions, but her body's natural defenses made the act impossible.

Element Girl ultimately received a visit from Death, who helped Rainie to make peace with herself and finally depart her mortal life. **DW**

ELEMENT LAD

FIRST APPEARANCE ADVENTURE COMICS #307 (April 1963)
STATUS Villain (deceased) **REAL NAME** Jan Arrah
OCCUPATION Legionnaire **BASE** 30th-century Earth
HEIGHT 5ft 5in **WEIGHT** 140 lbs **EYES** Blue **HAIR** Blond
SPECIAL POWERS/ABILITIES Could transmute any element into any other by using his mental powers to change its chemical makeup; could transmute his own body into any element; could even create life.

Jan Arrah was born to a race of element transmuters on the planet Trom in the latter half of the 30th century. With the ability to create literally anything they could think of, the Trommites were among the most powerful beings in the galaxy. The fear this engendered in others led to the rumored genocide of all Trommites, save one.

Sole survivor Jan Arrah joined the Legion of Super-Heroes as Element Lad, able to temporarily change the chemical structure of any object as long as he made physical contact. His powers made him one of the Legion's heavy hitters, yet he disdained fighting and maintained a quiet, spiritual demeanor. He often remained aloof from his fellow Legionnaires, declining to discuss his personal life, though he did go on one date with his teammate Triplicate Girl. Element Lad participated in the battles that drove back a Dominator invasion force intent on conquering Earth. **PJ**

ELONGATED MAN

FIRST APPEARANCE THE FLASH (1st series) #112 (May 1960)
STATUS Hero **REAL NAME** Ralph Dibny
OCCUPATION Detective **BASE** Mobile
HEIGHT 6ft 1in **WEIGHT** 178 lbs **EYES** Blue **HAIR** Red
SPECIAL POWERS/ABILITIES Consuming a Gingold extract every few days renders him super-elasticable to stretch or contort any portion of his body; brilliant deductive mind.

A fascination with the human body's powers of flexibility first led nine-year-old amateur detective Ralph Dibny to investigate the secrets of the "India Rubber Men" and similar contortionists that appeared at circuses and traveling sideshows. His determination to discover the source of their fantastic plastic abilities continued into adulthood.

Ralph traveled the world on this unusual quest and came to the conclusion that the greatest contortionists all had one thing in common: before a performance, each "rubber man" consumed a soft drink called Gingold, which contained the juice of the Yucatan gingo fruit. Ralph managed to isolate an unknown chemical present in the fruit's juices. When he drank a concentrated dose of this extract, his body acquired elastic properties far beyond the abilities of the sideshow freaks. As the Elongated Man, Ralph became a super-stretchable sleuth, frequently teaming with Batman and the Flash before joining the Justice League of America.

Tragedy shattered Ralph's life when his wife, Sue Dibny, died at the hands of the insane Jean Loring. Driven to despair, Ralph undertook a hunt to restore Sue to life, following what appeared to be Doctor Fate through various underworlds and magical realms. Ultimately he learned that Felix Faust and the demon Neron had been manipulating his quest. Ralph managed to trap both villains, but lost his life in the effort. In the afterlife, the reunited Ralph and Sue became "ghost detectives." **SB**

ELASTIC FANTASTIC
At first, Ralph felt no changes after drinking the Gingold extract. But when he walked beneath a falling flower pot, his arm rose to the occasion and stretched to catch it!

FLEXIBLE FRIEND *Ralph Dibny and Barry Allen (the second Flash) were fast friends and joined forces to solve several cases in Central City.*

DEVOTION *Ralph and Sue were inseparable. Even when Elongated Man was on a super heroic mission, Sue was never far behind! Sue died in a horrible attack by Jean Loring.*

ENEMY ACE

FIRST APPEARANCE OUR ARMY AT WAR #151 (February 1965)
STATUS Unresolved **REAL NAME** Hans von Hammer
OCCUPATION Pilot **BASE** Germany
HEIGHT 5ft 11in **WEIGHT** 161 lbs **EYES** Blue **HAIR** Auburn
SPECIAL POWERS/ABILITIES One of the greatest natural pilots ever seen.

The son of an aristocratic German family distantly related to Anton Arcane (*see* ARCANE, ANTON), Baron Hans von Hammer was among the first to enlist when World War I broke out in 1914. While in flight school, he engaged in a duel of honor with fellow cadet Heinrich Muller and received a permanent scar on his left cheek. An exceptional flyer, von Hammer soon became Rittsmeister of his own Jagdstaffel hunting squadron, and feared among Allied forces as the Enemy Ace. During the course of the war, he had over 70 kills to his credit; however, he took no joy in performing this duty. A solitary man, when not flying, von Hammer retreated to his home, wandering the nearby Black Forest, with his only companion, a wolf.

During World War II, von Hammer was persuaded out of retirement to fight on Nazi Germany's behalf on the Russian front. He crashed his plane in Leningrad and, before escaping back to his base, saw the horrors that Germany had inflicted on the Russian people there. After witnessing the atrocities at the Nazi concentration camp at Dachau in 1945, a shaken Hans von Hammer surrendered himself and his men to SERGEANT ROCK and Easy Company.

By the 1960s, the great von Hammer was broke, divorced, and confined to a German care facility. The former air ace spent his last days confiding his experiences to reporter and Vietnam veteran Edward Mannock, thereby bringing himself a measure of peace before he died. Some time later, von Hammer's exploits were popularized in a motion picture financed by Bruce Wayne, the BATMAN. **RG**

A SOLITARY MAN
Hans von Hammer took little pleasure in his wartime duty and when not in the air, remained an intensely private individual.

ACE HIGH
His tally of 70 kills during World War I made von Hammer the most feared fighter pilot of his day.

ERADICATOR

FIRST APPEARANCE ACTION COMICS #693 (November 1993)
STATUS Ally **REAL NAME** Dr. David Connor
OCCUPATION Preserver of Kryptonian heritage **BASE** Mobile
HEIGHT 6ft 3in **WEIGHT** 225 lbs **EYES** Red **HAIR** Gray
SPECIAL POWERS/ABILITIES Flight, super-strength, heat vision; can project and control various energy types; extremely difficult to kill.

The Eradicator was originally a Kryptonian superweapon devised to wipe out alien races on Krypton and alter the genetic structure of all Kryptonians making it impossible for them to leave the planet. Thousands of years after the destruction of the planet, this incredible thinking machine had become the repository of all Kryptonian culture. It built SUPERMAN's Fortress of Solitude and attempted to turn Earth into a replica of Krypton. It then assumed human form and even impersonated Superman following the Man of Steel's death at the hands of DOOMSDAY.

The Eradicator brought Superman back to the Fortress of Solitude and revived him with Kryptonian technology, allowing Earth's greatest hero to cheat death. The CYBORG SUPERMAN nearly destroyed the Eradicator, but it survived by bonding with the body of S.T.A.R. Labs scientist Dr. David Connor. Although Connor remained partially in control, a copy of the Eradicator program animated the ruins of Superman's shattered Fortress of Solitude (destroyed earlier by DOMINUS) and assembled a huge warsuit. Connor/Eradicator merged with this titanic construct and flew off into space. The Eradicator later returned to Earth, but by then it was clear that Connor had lost most of his sanity. During the JOKER's "Last Laugh" spree, an infected Eradicator went on a lunatic, Jokerized rampage. **DW**

FATAL FIVE

FIRST APPEARANCE Adventure Comics #352 (January 1967)
STATUS Villain team **BASE** Mobile
MEMBERS AND POWERS
Emerald Empress Vast powers stemming from the Emerald Eye.
Tharok Cyborg strength and advanced intellect.
Mano Can disintegrate with his touch
The Persuader Carries an atomic ax.
Validus Superstrength and invulnerability.

EARLY CLASH The Fatal Five often battled the Legion.

THE MEMBERS OF THE FATAL FIVE comprise some of the worst criminals of the late 30th century. Together, they are an almost unstoppable force for mayhem and murder. Their violent tendencies landed them behind bars long before anyone conceived the idea of a Fatal Five super-team. THAROK was a half-cyborg whose body had been reconstructed following a terrible accident; his electronically-amplified brain made him a brilliant strategist and leader. Empress' true name was Saryva of Vengar, and she delighted in destruction and pain. Mano was a mutant whose glowing right hand could disintegrate anything it touched; he used this power to destroy his polluted homeworld of Angtu. The Persuader carried an atomic ax that could slice through anything and shared he a psychic link with the weapon. Validus was a an invulnerable colossus of staggering strength.

FORCE FIVE Mutual mistrust hinders the team, but their powers can be terrifying when combined. Braniac 13 employed copies of the Fatal Five to protect his Warworld when venturing back into the 21st century.

THE WARMAKER

In one version of reality, the Fatal Five came into being when Earth's President Chu ordered their formation in order to spark a war. The Fatal Five soon came into conflict with the Legionnaires, triggering a fierce battle that ended in victory thanks to the involvement of the Legion Rescue Squad. The Legion executed a sting operation to prove President Chu's complicity in the affair.

The U.P. Council removed Chu from office and industrialist R.J. Brande became president in her wake. Later, the Empress bonded to the all-powerful artifact known as the Emerald Eye of Ekron, becoming the Emerald Empress. She freed the others and led the Fatal Five into other clashes with the Legion, including a hijacking of the Legion Outpost and a scuffle with new Legionnaire Timber Wolf.

As an odd side note to Fatal Five history, the tyrant Braniac 13 generated hard-light images of the team as guards for his Warworld when he traveled back in time to the 21st century.

Another version of the Fatal Five time-travelled to the modern era from the 31st century, threatening both Batman and the new Blue Beetle in their pursuit of a valuable relic. DW

VALIDUS
The powerhouse of the Fatal Five is a simple-minded giant largely under the control of Tharok. His bolts of mental lightning are powerful enough to fry Kryptonians and Daxamites.

THE FATAL FIVE 1) Mano **2)** Persuader **3)** Validus **4)** Tharok **5)** Emerald Empress

KEY STORYLINES

• *LEGION OF SUPER-HEROES #34 (APRIL 1996):* The Fatal Five battle the Legion of Super-Heroes, in the first Fatal Five storyline to appear in the new Legion chronology.

• *SUPERMAN #171 (AUGUST 2001):* A duplicate Fatal Five squares off against the Man of Steel, providing a yardstick for measuring the team's considerable might.

• *THE LEGION #16 (MARCH 2003):* New Legionnaire Timber Wolf receives a baptism of fire as he is forced to battle the entire might of the Fatal Five.

FIRESTORM, THE NUCLEAR MAN

FIRST APPEARANCE (II) FIRESTORM (2nd series) #1 (July 2004)
STATUS Hero **REAL NAME** Jason Rusch
OCCUPATION Student **BASE** Detroit, Michigan
HEIGHT 5ft 10in **WEIGHT** 165 lbs **EYES** Brown **HAIR** Black
SPECIAL POWERS/ABILITIES Flight; can rearrange the atomic and molecular structure of inorganic matter.

UNDERSTANDING THE HERO FIRESTORM is far from a straightforward proposition. Brought into being as the synthesis of two individuals, Firestorm later went through a number of alternate fusions whereby varied combinations of people united to create a single champion. The original Firestorm came about when high-school student Ronnie Raymond and physics professor Martin Stein fused into one superpowered "nuclear man" in an explosion at the Hudson nuclear facility. In their flame-topped Firestorm form, the two could fly and rearrange matter at the molecular level. Ron remained in control of Firestorm, while Martin hitchhiked along as a disembodied consciousness and took an advisory role, his scientific brain providing the complex atomic calculations needed for Firestorm's advanced powers.

MARTIN STEIN *The professor found his calling as a fire elemental.*

ELEMENTAL WARFARE

Operating out of Pittsburgh, Ron and Martin made an efficient team against the likes of Killer Frost and Black Bison. The Russian hero Pozhar later clashed with Firestorm above the Nevada desert. When a nuclear missile struck the two combatants, Ronnie and Pozhar merged into the second incarnation of Firestorm. Controlled by the amnesiac mind of Martin Stein, this Firestorm eventually learned that it had been fated to become Earth's fire elemental—but only with Martin as host. Ronnie and Pozhar had apparently been unnecessary roadblocks in the Earth spirit Gaea's plan. After Firestorm's involvement in an "elemental war" involving Swamp Thing (earth), Naiad (water), and Red Tornado (air), as well as the addition of another Russian, Svarozhich, to the mix, Firestorm fissioned off the superfluous personalities to become the "correct" Firestorm—a fire elemental, controlled by Martin Stein alone.

FROST AND FIRE *Normally a bitter enemy, the villain Killer Frost was hypnotized into loving Firestorm during the Crisis.*

Yet this wasn't the end of the Firestorm saga. Ron Raymond realized that the Firestorm powers had been written into his genetic code, and served with Extreme Justice and the Power Company before joining the Justice League Of America. The Ron Raymond Firestorm perished in a battle with supervillains, and the powers passed to a Detroit youth named Jason Rusch.

Rusch struggled to deal with his almost-limitless abilities. He fought in outer space during the Infinite Crisis, finding welcome help when Martin Stein returned from the cosmos to act as the other half of the "Firestorm matrix" that powered the merged superhero. Following the Crisis, Firestorm assembled a failed, second-string Justice League, then used Firehawk as his partner in the Firestorm matrix after Martin Stein's disappearance. **DW**

KEY STORYLINES

• *FIRESTORM, THE NUCLEAR MAN #90 (OCTOBER 1989):*
The Elemental Wars kick off, signaling the increasing complexity of this super-hero title.
• *EXTREME JUSTICE #5 (JUNE 1995):*
Raymond regains his Firestorm powers, and the Martin Stein fire elemental drops in for a visit.
• *JLA #69 (OCTOBER 2002):*
Firestorm joins the Justice League of America while the original team is trapped in the ancient undersea world of Atlantis.

APT PUPIL *As Firestorm, Jason Rusch soon accumulated his own rogue's gallery. Here he faces off against the brilliant Pupil.*

BURNING UP *Ron Raymond's reacquisition of the Firestorm powers led to a spot on the world's greatest super hero team. Recently, a young man named Jason Rusch has emerged as the possible inheritor of the Firestorm title.*

THE FLASH

THE SCARLET SPEEDSTER

JASON PETER "JAY" GARRICK (FLASH I)
FIRST APPEARANCE FLASH COMICS #1 (January 1940)
STATUS Hero **OCCUPATION** Research scientist
BASE Keystone City **HEIGHT** 5ft 11in **WEIGHT** 178 lbs
EYES Blue **HAIR** Brown, with gray temples
SPECIAL POWERS/ABILITIES Can run at near lightspeed; can vibrate his molecules and pass right through objects; ages at a far slower pace than most human beings.

BARTHOLOMEW "BARRY" ALLEN (FLASH II)
FIRST APPEARANCE SHOWCASE #4 (October 1956)
STATUS Hero (deceased) **OCCUPATION** Police chemist
BASE Central City **HEIGHT** 5ft 11in **WEIGHT** 179 lbs
EYES Blue **HAIR** Blond
SPECIAL POWERS/ABILITIES Could run at near lightspeed; could also pass through objects or phase into other dimensions.

WALLACE "WALLY" WEST (FLASH III)
FIRST APPEARANCE (as Kid Flash) THE FLASH (1st series) #110 (January 1960); (as the Flash) CRISIS ON INFINITE EARTHS #12 (March 1986)
STATUS Hero **OCCUPATION** Adventurer **BASE** Keystone City
HEIGHT 6ft **WEIGHT** 175 lbs **EYES** Green **HAIR** Red
SPECIAL POWERS/ABILITIES Can run at lightspeed; can vibrate through solid objects causing them to explode; can lend his speed to moving objects or people by touch; can form a protective costume from "living" Speed Force; traveling faster than lightspeed will hurl him across interdimensional timespace.

THEY HAVE BEEN CALLED the Fastest Men Alive—three generations of super heroes granted the power to tap into the extradimensional energy field called the Speed Force by a scientific experiment gone awry. Each hero named himself the Flash and became the progenitor of an age of champions, perpetuating a legacy of courage and valor that extends to the 853rd century and beyond.

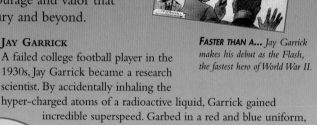

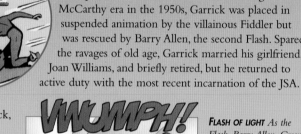

FASTER THAN A... *Jay Garrick makes his debut as the Flash, the fastest hero of World War II.*

JAY GARRICK
A failed college football player in the 1930s, Jay Garrick became a research scientist. By accidentally inhaling the hyper-charged atoms of a radioactive liquid, Garrick gained incredible superspeed. Garbed in a red and blue uniform, Garrick became the Flash and helped form the legendary Justice Society of America and the wartime All-Star Squadron. Forced into retirement during the McCarthy era in the 1950s, Garrick was placed in suspended animation by the villainous Fiddler but was rescued by Barry Allen, the second Flash. Spared the ravages of old age, Garrick married his girlfriend, Joan Williams, and briefly retired, but he returned to active duty with the most recent incarnation of the JSA.

NO TIME TO LOSE *The Flash and Dr. Flura must thwart Star Sapphire's deadly schemes or the Earth has only two minutes to live!*

BARRY ALLEN
Slowpoke police chemist Barry Allen idolized Jay Garrick, the super hero Flash. During a late, stormy night at the police station laboratory, a bolt of lightning crashed through the window and shattered the vials of chemicals surrounding Allen. Suddenly imbued with the power to move at near lightspeed, Barry took on the name of his Golden Age idol, the Flash, and, along with Green Lantern Hal Jordan and Aquaman, helped usher in the Silver Age of heroes.

As the Flash, Allen was one of the founders of the Justice League of America. When his fiancée, Iris, was apparently slain by the Reverse-Flash, Allen killed his hated foe. After a lengthy trial, the Flash retired to the 30th century, where he sired the Tornado twins. Tragically, Allen died saving the Earth from the nihilistic Anti-Monitor (*see* Great Battles, pp. 186–7) by destroying his antimatter cannon, aimed directly at the planet.

SLOW POKE *Police chemist Barry Allen was a notoriously methodical, plodding scientist known for being constantly late. When he was doused by chemicals, however, he gained the power of superspeed, becoming the second Flash.*

VWUMP!

FLASH OF LIGHT *As the Flash, Barry Allen, Green Lantern Hal Jordan, and several other heroes founded the legendary Justice League of America. Despite Allen and Jordan's differences— Allen was a quiet scientist and Jordan an adventurous hothead— the two became close friends. Their friendship would last for years, until each met their own tragic end.*

ZOOM *The name of Zoom has long haunted the Flash family. Recently, Zoom was responsible for Flash's wife, Linda Park, miscarrying their twins.*

THE DEATH OF BARRY ALLEN
Learning that his wife, Iris, was saved from death at the hands of Professor Zoom by a "psychic transplant" in the future into another body, the Flash traveled forward in time to be with her. Tragically, their happiness ended when the Flash was kidnapped by the Anti-Monitor, who planned to use a giant antimatter cannon to destroy the universe. Running faster than ever before, the Flash escaped the Anti-Monitor's bonds and destroyed the cannon. Allen's body disintegrated, but his energies rocketed back in time and became the lightning bolt that shattered the chemicals that originally gave Allen his superspeed.

KEY STORYLINES
- *GOLDEN AGE FLASH ARCHIVES:* The original adventures of Jay Garrick, the first Flash, during the 1940s.
- *THE FLASH (1ST SERIES) #123 (SEPTEMBER 1961):* Barry Allen meets his Golden Age namesake for the first time.
- *CRISIS ON INFINITE EARTHS (P/B, 2000):* Barry Allen makes the greatest sacrifice to save the universe from the marauding Anti-Monitor, and Wally West becomes the third Flash!
- *TERMINAL VELOCITY (P/B, 1995):* The Flashes learn that they are attached to the Speed Force, an ancient power.

WALLY WEST

The young nephew of Barry Allen, Wally West was visiting his uncle's laboratory when a bolt of lightning shattered a rack of chemicals in the room. The chemicals spilled on the boy, and duplicated the same accident that created the second Flash. West became the first Kid Flash, the junior partner of the Flash, and founded the TEEN TITANS with the first ROBIN (*see* Nightwing), Aqualad, Speedy (*see* Arsenal), and Wonder Girl. After Barry Allen died saving the universe, Kid Flash assumed his costume and identity.

GENERATIONS *Wearing a costume similar to his mentor, Barry Allen, teenaged Wally West learned to use his powers just as well—even vibrating through solid objects.*

THE SPEED FORCE

As the Flash, Wally discovered his link to the Speed Force, an energy source that gives all speedsters their power. Tapping into the Force made Wally the fastest Flash of them all, able to run at the speed of light. One of the founders of the current and most powerful incarnation of the JLA, West has garnered a lethal Rogues Gallery as the champion of Keystone City. The Flash revealed his secret identity to the world and, after several failed romances, fell in love with and married reporter Linda Park (*see* Park, Linda). After a battle with the villain Zoom ended in the miscarriage of their unborn twins, West asked the Spectre to remove all memories of his identity from the public consciousness—including Linda—to protect those he loved from the dangers he continues to face as the Fastest Man Alive.

LOVELY LINDA *Wally West is married to TV journalist turned medical student Linda Park.*

MAGIC RING *Like his predecessor, Wally West keeps his Flash costume in a special ring. The costume is made of the Speed Force itself, covering Wally in a protective sheath.*

FLASHES FROM THE FUTURE

John Fox was a speedster from the 27th century who traveled back to the 21st century to take over the Flash legacy when Wally West disappeared. After West's return, Fox leapt back into the timestream and resettled in the 853rd century. The third Kid Flash is the future daughter of Wally West, who inherited her father's heroic legacy when her slacker brother refused to do so. Walter West, the Flash from an alternate timeline whose wife Linda was slain by KOBRA, briefly replaced the Flash in our timeline, before entering Hypertime to rediscover his own. And Sela Allen, a sentient manifestation of the Speed Force, is the Flash of the 23rd century.

FUGITIVE *Fox, responsible for transplanting Iris Allen across the centuries, became a fugitive for violating the Time Institute's laws of time travel.*

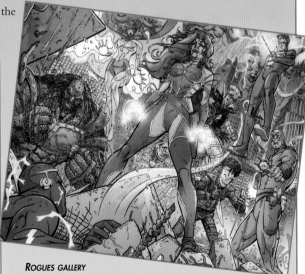

ROGUES GALLERY
The Flash has long had one of the most impressive collections of foes of any hero, and easily the most deadly.

THE FLASH

RETURN TO FORM

Wally's memories of his heroic past soon returned, and he took up the identity of the Flash once again. A time-bending adventure even undid Linda's miscarriage, and she gave birth to twins named Iris and Jai. The events of the Infinite Crisis changed Wally and his family forever. To stop a rampaging Superboy-Prime, Wally joined with Jay Garrick and Kid Flash (Bart Allen) to hurl the alternate-universe Kryptonian to the edge of the Speed Force. Just prior to crossing the threshold, Wally drew Linda and the twins with him into an alternate dimension, inhabited by long-departed speedsters including Max Mercury, Johnny Quick (see Quick, Johnny), and Barry Allen. Superboy-Prime escaped from this dimension after years of imprisonment, with Bart Allen following him back to Earth. Wally and Linda elected to stay behind and oversee the development of their twins, whose growth appeared to be surging in unpredictable bursts.

BART ALLEN (FLASH IV)

FIRST APPEARANCE FLASH (2nd series) #91 (June 1994) STATUS Hero (deceased) OCCUPATION Forensics student BASE Keystone City HEIGHT 5ft 11in WEIGHT 178 lbs EYES Yellow HAIR Brown SPECIAL POWERS/ABILITIES Can run at incredible speeds, generate whirlwinds, and vibrate molecules to pass through solid objects.

SUITING UP *Bart followed in Barry Allen's footsteps, even attending the police academy, but he died too young.*

BART ALLEN: THE FOURTH FLASH

Bart Allen, who first emerged on the heroic scene as Impulse before taking up the identity of Kid Flash while with the Teen Titans, became the fourth inheritor of the Flash legacy. To stop Superboy-Prime during the worst fighting of the Infinite Crisis, Bart joined with Jay Garrick and Wally West to hurl the homicidal teenager into the extra-dimensional energy that surrounded the Speed Force. Jay dropped out just before the point of no return, but Bart and Wally both carried Superboy-Prime into an alternate reality where they remained for several years of relative time. To observers on Earth only days had passed, but when Bart returned to Earth he had shed his adolescent gawkiness and grown into adulthood. Wearing Barry Allen's original costume, Bart battled the newly-escaped Superboy-Prime but seemingly exhausted his connection to the Speed Force during the fight. Bart retired from being a super hero, taking a job as an autoworker on a Keystone Motors assembly line. But the rise of the villain the Griffin—secretly Bart's coworker and roommate—revealed that the Speed Force had not abandoned the young man. Bart returned to fighting crime in Keystone and, after a move Los Angeles, studied forensics at the L.A. police academy.

KEYSTONE VICTORY *As the Flash, Bart puts the brakes on his former friend—turned super-villain—the Griffin.*

A HERO LOST

The return of Bart's twisted clone Inertia ushered in the fourth Flash's tragic and untimely death. Inertia gathered the core members of the Flash's Rogues' Gallery—Mirror Master, Pied Piper, Heat Wave, Captain Cold, Trickster, Abra Kadabra, and Weather Wizard—and promised that building a time-freezing device would make them all rich. Inertia activated the device at L.A.'s Getty Center, revealing the machine's true function when he used it to drain the Speed Force from Bart Allen. Though Bart defeated his foe, his lack of powers made him easy prey for the ruthless Rogues, who ended his life. Bart Allen's fellow heroes honored their fallen friend with a public funeral in Keystone and a memorial statue in the city's Flash Museum. In San Francisco, the Teen Titans erected a second statue of Bart outside Titans Tower.

THE END *Bart's clone Inertia led the Rogues in their deadly attack.*

FALLEN HERO *Bart Allen's girlfriend, Valerie Perez, mourns his death in battle.*

THE LIGHTNING SAGA

Wally West's return to Earth came about thanks to the Legion of Super-Heroes, who traveled a thousand years into the past to enact a strange ritual. By standing in precise locations while holding lightning rods, the members of the Legion hoped to restore a great hero—initially believed to be Barry Allen. It was Wally, however, who emerged through the Legion-created gateway, along with Linda and their (now school-aged) children. His colleagues welcomed Wally back and offered him a spot in the Justice League of America. Wally quickly learned of Bart Allen's murder at the hands of the Rogues. He tracked down Inertia, the mastermind behind the crime, and locked him in a moment of time—frozen forever in statue-like stasis on display in Keystone City's Flash Museum.

SPEEDY JUSTICE *On his super-heroic return, Wally's first order of business was to ensure that the villainous Flash-clone Inertia could never kill again.*

THE NEXT GENERATION

The Wests tried to return to a normal life in Keystone, but the abilities of their twins, Iris and Jai, caused headaches from the start. Iris manifested the power to vibrate her molecules through solid objects, while Jai added muscle mass to achieve temporary feats of super-strength. Though Iris appeared to be ten years old and Jai eight, both had lived slightly over a year in relative time. Their runaway metabolisms governed their development and their burgeoning powers were barely kept in check by mechanical treatments administered by their mother. By default, she had become the world's leading expert on "velocibiology." Iris and Jai got their first taste of their family's heroic lifestyle when they helped their father rid Keystone of intelligent starfish creatures. The fact that children so young have taken on life-threatening risks has raised concern among Wally's Justice League teammates. PJ/DW

UNWELCOME GUESTS *Aquatic aliens from another dimension are the latest threat to menace Keystone City.*

LEARNING THE ROPES *The limits of Jai's strength and Iris's phasing are still unknown.*

HIGH-TECH PARENTING *Advanced machines regulate the twins' metabolisms and help prevent premature aging spurts.*

AMAZING BASES

JSA HEADQUARTERS

The headquarters of the Justice Society of America is a mansion in Morningside Heights, Manhattan, north of Central Park in New York City. Equipped with personal suites, medical facilities, and a communications complex powered by WayneTech computers, the HQ has its own gas and electric power supply, recycles its water, and even has moveable walls that allow the JSA to reconfigure its architecture. There is a JSA museum and memorial open to the public on the first floor. Below the mansion are training facilities and computer monitors, as well as a high-speed rail link that follows a rebuilt submarine steam tunnel and a rocket ship (*see* Amazing Vehicles, pp. 22-3).

TITANS TOWER

Shaped in a giant "T," Titans Tower is located in the harbor of San Francisco. The first of several Towers was located in New York's East River. This tower was destroyed by Trigon, and the second was blown up by the Wildebeest Society. The latest Titans Tower, is full of state of the art technology and also has a garden, tended by Starfire, planted with the flowers of long dead worlds.

PARADISE ISLAND

Called Themyscira by its inhabitants, the immortal warrior women known as the Amazons, Paradise Island is the home of Wonder Woman. The first Themyscira was an island nestled in an otherdimensional pocket off the coast of Greece. Settled by the Amazons, it was a mystic land of Greco-Roman architecture, tropical forests, and eternal sunshine. The home of the Amazons for 30 centuries, the island was ravaged by Circe and two civil wars before being destroyed by Imperiex. Themyscira was recreated by several goddesses, and transformed into a floating chain of islands in the heart of the Bermuda Triangle. An architectural marvel of amazing science where weapons no longer worked, and whose population was dedicated to the democratic exchange of information, this Themyscira was destroyed in a jealous rage by Hera (*see* Olympian Gods), and replaced with an isle more similar to the original.

FROM SUBTERRANEAN CAVES to Arctic strongholds, technological fortresses on the moon to mythical islands in other dimensions, the world's greatest heroes find refuge in the most spectacular, and often secret, locales. Across the Earth and throughout the universe, the Justice League of America, the Teen Titans, and others maintain headquarters that lets them train together, collate information, and strike out at the forces of evil.

THE JLA WATCHTOWER

After inhabiting and abandoning several headquarters over the years, including a hidden cave in Rhode Island, a satellite in Earth's orbit, a Bunker in Detroit, and several embassies world-wide, the Justice League of America founded its greatest sanctuary on the moon. The JLA Watchtower was created using technologies from around the universe, and is equipped with the most advanced monitoring and transportation systems in the galaxy.

Equipped with specialized biospheres for each of its members and prison cells designed to contain the most destructive intergalactic criminals, as well as a Monitor Womb that records every transmission broadcast on Earth, the Watchtower is accessible from Earth by teleportation technology from Hawkman's homeworld of Thanagar.

MOONWATCH *Nestled in the Moon's Mare Serenitatis crater, the Watchtower is the headquarters of Earth's greatest hero team.*

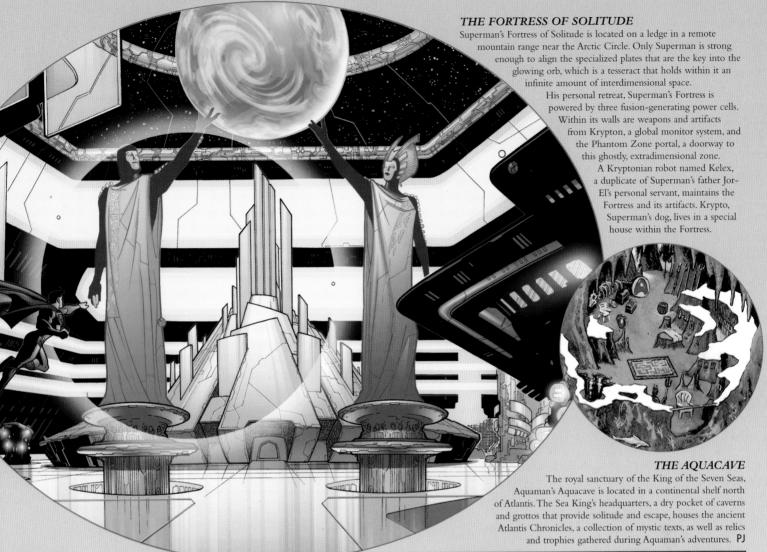

THE FORTRESS OF SOLITUDE

Superman's Fortress of Solitude is located on a ledge in a remote mountain range near the Arctic Circle. Only Superman is strong enough to align the specialized plates that are the key into the glowing orb, which is a tesseract that holds within it an infinite amount of interdimensional space.

His personal retreat, Superman's Fortress is powered by three fusion-generating power cells. Within its walls are weapons and artifacts from Krypton, a global monitor system, and the Phantom Zone portal, a doorway to this ghostly, extradimensional zone.

A Kryptonian robot named Kelex, a duplicate of Superman's father Jor-El's personal servant, maintains the Fortress and its artifacts. Krypto, Superman's dog, lives in a special house within the Fortress.

THE AQUACAVE

The royal sanctuary of the King of the Seven Seas, Aquaman's Aquacave is located on a continental shelf north of Atlantis. The Sea King's headquarters, a dry pocket of caverns and grottos that provide solitude and escape, houses the ancient Atlantis Chronicles, a collection of mystic texts, as well as relics and trophies gathered during Aquaman's adventures. *PJ*

THE BATCAVE

Carved out from the subterranean, bat-infested limestone caverns that run beneath his family estate, Wayne Manor, the Batcave is a sprawling underground headquarters equipped with the latest vehicles, weapons, and technology to help Batman in his constant crusade against crime.

The original Batcave was destroyed during the earthquake that leveled half of Gotham City. The new Batcave is a multi-level bunker, powered by its own hydrogen generators. Housing a vast array of vehicles, scientific equipment, a forensics lab, medical facilities, and training systems throughout its multi-tiered labyrinth, the Batcave's centrepiece is the central computer terminal. This is powered by seven Cray T392 mainframes, and incorporates a holographic projector. Stored on the computer is Batman's vast archive of crime and criminals.

For a time, Batman hired the hunchbacked mute Harold Allnut, a technological genius, to work in the cave. Harold was duped into revealing Batman's secrets to the villain Hush in exchange for a voice and a new body, and was murdered by the criminal. While several heroes—and a handful of villains—have seen the inside of the Batcave, very few know where it actually exists.

VIRTUAL REALITY *Batman's sophisticated computer is controlled by virtual reality telepads.*

BAT FORTRESS *The Batcave is equipped with the most sophisticated technology and weaponry Bruce Wayne's money can buy. Its many levels extend nearly a mile beneath Wayne Manor.*

GREEN ARROW

THE EMERALD ARCHER

OLIVER JONAS QUEEN (GREEN ARROW I)
FIRST APPEARANCE More Fun Comics #73 (November 1941)
STATUS Hero *OCCUPATION* Adventurer *BASE* Star City
HEIGHT 5ft 11in *WEIGHT* 185 lbs *EYES* Green *HAIR* Blond
SPECIAL POWERS/ABILITIES Has an excellent eye for archery; trained
hand-to-hand combatant with above average strength and
endurance.

CONNOR HAWKE (GREEN ARROW II)
FIRST APPEARANCE Green Arrow (1st series) #0
(October 1994)
STATUS Hero *OCCUPATION* Adventurer *BASE* Star City
HEIGHT 5ft 9in *WEIGHT* 160 lbs *EYES* Green *HAIR* Blond
SPECIAL POWERS/ABILITIES An expert marksman as well as one of
the top five martial artists on Earth.

WHILE ON A SOUTH SEA CRUISE, a business partner betrayed
playboy billionaire Oliver Queen and knocked him overboard.
Washing up on a remote island, Queen fashioned a crude bow
and arrow to take down a drug-running operation run by the
villainess China White. He soon returned to the social scene
in his hometown, Star City. Donning a Robin Hood costume
for a party, Queen foiled a robbery during the event, gaining
the nickname Green Arrow. Resolving to become a crime
fighter, he soon experienced firsthand the diseased underbelly
of society he had only previously read about.

*EARLY DAYS Early in his
career, the Emerald Archer
had his own Arrowcar,
complete with ejector seat.*

DARTING AROUND *Green Arrow and Speedy
sought out criminals wherever they lurked.*

ROY AND HAL

After a horrifying trip to Vietnam (where
he first met Hal Jordan, the second Green
Lantern), Queen sold off his armaments
division. He decided to become actively
involved in campaigning for good causes,
and adopted Roy Harper as his ward.
Roy became his first kid sidekick, Speedy
(*see* Arsenal). Together, they battled such
foes as the crime-clown Bull's-Eye, the Rainbow Archer, and the Red Dart. During this time, Queen
became the anonymous financier of the Justice League of America. He also used his fortune to finance
an Arrow Plane, Arrow Car, and a base called the Arrow Cave—clearly showing his respect for Batman.
A short time later, Green Arrow was formally inducted into the JLA. There, he met and fell in love
with beautiful Dinah Lance (the second Black Canary), despite the large gap in their ages. Soon
after, Queen was swindled out of his fortune by John deLeon, a former partner. Undaunted, Oliver
convinced Hal Jordan to join him as he explored America's heartland.
There they confronted issues such as bigotry, religious fanaticism,
and environmental destruction. They were frequently joined on their
journey by Black Canary II.

OLIVER QUEEN

Queen never talked about his parents or the events that
left him an orphan, heir to a manufacturing empire. Before
becoming the secret vigilante Green Arrow he had been
dissatisfied, restless, wrestling with an emerging social
conscience. Now he finally had the chance to do some
good in the world, fighting all manner of criminality. He
soon came to realize that crime and violence were global
problems, fueled in part by his own munitions division.

SHIELDED *Green
Lantern protects
Green Arrow and
a monk, Than,
from an explosion.*

SHADO, LONGBOW HUNTER

After Oliver Queen resigned from the JLA,
he and Dinah Lance moved to Seattle,
Washington, where she set up a flower shop
called Sherwood Florist. However, the pair
were soon imbroiled in tracking down a
drugs gang. The case led them to question
the future of their relationship—and then
Dinah vanished. She was brutalized and
tortured before Green Arrow rescued her
and killed the sadists holding her. During
the rescue, Green Arrow's life was saved
by a mysterious oriental archer named
SHADO, who was pursing her own vendetta
against a drugs cartel. The two eventually
become lovers for a time. Green Arrow
became a fugitive after being arrested
on false treason charges, and Dinah
Lance called Shado for help. Dinah
then discovered that Queen had
unknowingly conceived a son
with Shado, whom she
had named Robert.

CRISIS FOR THE GREEN ARROW

Feeling abandoned by his mentor, Speedy became a heroin addict. Black Canary II acted
as his surrogate mother and helped him kick the habit. Shortly thereafter, Green Arrow
accidentally killed a thief named Richard Hollinger and went into hiding. Black Canary II
and Green Lantern II searched for their friend, and the hunt took on extra urgency when
the Canary was gravely injured in an auto accident. Dinah needed a blood transfusion and
Green Lantern II realized that Queen possessed her rare RH Negative blood type. Green
Arrow returned in time to save his lover's life. This personal crisis averted, Queen began
to publicly question the JLA's goals and methods, putting him at odds with Hawkman, in
particular. Before long he had resigned his League membership.

LOVERS' TIFF *Black Canary may love Oliver, but she continues
to have problems with his infidelity and commitment issues.*

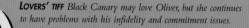

BACK FROM THE DEAD

Green Arrow attempted to prevent a terrorist from detonating a bomb over Metropolis, but gave his life in the process. His lifelong friend, Hal Jordan (formerly Green Lantern II, now a mad being named Parallax), used his cosmic power to restore Ollie to life, but without a soul.

With the help of his "family," Ollie regained his soul and made a concerted effort to put his life back in order. He reconnected with Connor Hawke and Roy Harper and took in Mia Dearden, a teen from the streets of his beloved Star City. Still restless, Ollie fought injustice while longing for Dinah.

His legend would grow and grow, eventually becoming so powerful that in the 853rd century the Earth would be watched over by a squad who called itself the society of Green Arrows.

MIA DEARDEN

Mia Dearden ran away from a violent home when she was a child. Homeless, she turned to prostitution to support herself. She subsequently met the recently resurrected Oliver Queen. He took her in and gave her a safe place to once again be a teen.

Mia trained with Connor Hawke until her skills at martial arts and archery rivaled those of the former Speedy, Roy Harper. Impressed, Oliver Queen allowed Mia to become the new Speedy. She also served a short term with the Teen Titans.

SAVIOR *Oliver sent Mia to the Star City Youth Recreational Center for safety.*

AMAZON PRISONER *Kidnapped on his wedding night, Green Arrow knew that Black Canary would come to his rescue.*

POLITICS AND MARRIAGE

After the Infinite Crisis, Green Arrow recuperated from an attack by Merlyn on a remote island. There, he recommitted himself to the martial arts, and took office as mayor of Star City upon his return. Mayor Queen did not serve a full term, instead resigning and rekindling his romance with Black Canary. The two were wed, though the shapeshifter Everyman temporarily took Green Arrow's place while Amazons took the real Oliver to Themyscira.

NEWLY WED *Her friends warned her it wouldn't last, but Black Canary accepted Oliver's proposal.*

CONNOR HAWKE

Oliver's son by Sandra Moonday Hawke, Connor Hawke was raised as a Buddhist monk and trained in martial arts. Though Connor sought inner peace, he also yearned for adventure, spurred by hero-worship for the father he had never known. A new path opened up for the teenager when Ollie visited the monastery where, years earlier, he had sought asylum. As the couple traveled together, Connor revealed that he was Ollie's son. When Ollie seemed to have been killed in an airplane explosion over Metropolis, Connor took on his father's crime-fighting role as a second Green Arrow.

DOUBLE HITTER *He's good with a bow, but Connor's major strength is martial arts.*

INNOCENT AND GOOD

When Oliver Queen returned to life, father and son decided to protect Star City together. Connor remains somewhat innocent about the world around him, confused over his magnetic attraction for women. He feels most free when patrolling the city's rooftops with his father. **RG**

KEY STORYLINES

• *GREEN LANTERN/GREEN ARROW (1ST AND 2ND SERIES) (2004):* Collections of classic stories as the heroic pair traveled the U.S. righting wrongs.

• *GREEN ARROW: THE ARCHER'S QUEST (2003):* Back from the dead, Ollie Queen uses keepsakes to reconnect with his family.

• *GREEN ARROW: THE LONGBOW HUNTER (1989):* Green Arrow saves Black Canary from being tortured; he also encounters the mysterious female assassin Shado.

• *THE BRAVE AND THE BOLD #85 (AUGUST 1969):* In "The Senator's Been Shot," Green Arrow dons a new outfit, a beard, and gains a new attitude toward his role as a crime fighter.

GREEN LANTERN

BRIGHTEST LIGHT IN THE UNIVERSE

ALAN SCOTT (GREEN LANTERN I)
FIRST APPEARANCE ALL-AMERICAN COMICS #16 (July 1940)
STATUS Hero *OCCUPATION* Crime fighter *BASE* Gotham City
HEIGHT 6ft *WEIGHT* 201 lbs *EYES* Blue *HAIR* Blond

HAL JORDAN (GREEN LANTERN II/PARALLAX)
FIRST APPEARANCE SHOWCASE #22 (October 1959)
STATUS Hero/villain (deceased) *OCCUPATION* Spectral guardian
BASE Utah desert *HEIGHT* 6ft 2in *WEIGHT* 186 lbs
EYES Brown *HAIR* Brown

GUY GARDNER (GREEN LANTERN III)
FIRST APPEARANCE GREEN LANTERN (2nd series) #59
(March 1968) *STATUS* Hero (deceased)
OCCUPATION Adventurer *BASE* New York City
HEIGHT 6ft *WEIGHT* 180 lbs *EYES* Blue *HAIR* Red

JOHN STEWART (GREEN LANTERN IV)
FIRST APPEARANCE GREEN LANTERN (2nd series) #87
(January 1972) *STATUS* Hero
OCCUPATION Architect *BASE* New York City
HEIGHT 6ft 1in *WEIGHT* 201 lbs *EYES* Brown *HAIR* Black

KYLE RAYNER (GREEN LANTERN V)
FIRST APPEARANCE GREEN LANTERN (3rd series) #48
(January 1994) *STATUS* Hero
OCCUPATION Crime fighter; cartoonist *BASE* New York
HEIGHT 5ft 11in *WEIGHT* 175 lbs *EYES* Green *HAIR* Black

SPECIAL POWERS/ABILITIES Green Lantern ring generates hard-light images, limited only by user's imagination; ring is also a database and language translator, and allows travel through space. Rings must be recharged using a lantern-shaped power battery.

ONCE THEY WERE a corps 3,600 strong, wearing the most powerful weapons ever devised on their fingers.
The Green Lantern Corps acted as an intergalactic police force, doing the bidding of the Guardians of the Universe. Each Green Lantern possessed a power ring that could create hard-light projections by drawing energy from the Central Power Battery on the Guardians' homeworld of Oa; however, the rings were ineffective against anything yellow. The Green Lantern Corps suffered a fatal blow at the hands of Hal Jordan, but Kyle Rayner may be the best hope for restoring this ancient force of justice and order.

BRIGHT LIGHT *Created by artist Martin Nodell, Alan Scott debuted in All-American Comics in 1940 before getting his own series a year later.*

ALAN SCOTT

Eons ago the Guardians of the Universe trapped most of the universe's magical energies into an orb called the Starheart. A fragment of this object gave rise to Alan Scott's ring and power battery. Unlike Corps equipment, Scott's mystical ring worked fine against yellow objects, but was powerless against wood. Scott helped establish the Justice Society of America during World War II. After many decades he discovered that his body had been infused with the energy of the Starheart and that he no longer required a ring. Scott briefly took the identity of Sentinel before reclaiming the Green Lantern mantle.

DOWN AND OUT
Sinestro fails to halt Parallax's rampage.

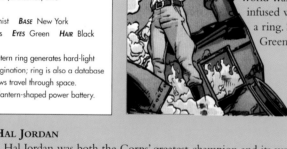

HAL JORDAN

Hal Jordan was both the Corps' greatest champion and its worst nightmare. As Green Lantern and protector of space sector 2814, Jordan founded the Justice League of America alongside Aquaman and the Flash. He battled a legion of galactic foes including the fallen Green Lantern Sinestro. But when the Cyborg Superman demolished Jordan's home, Coast City, he went mad with grief. Enraged when the Guardians barred him from resurrecting Coast City using his ring, Jordan destroyed the Guardians and their Corps—becoming the god-like villain Parallax. Though Parallax died during the Sun-Eater crisis, Jordan's spirit lived on as the universe's new Spectre.

TRANSITIONS
Guardian Abin Sur bequeaths his power ring to Hal Jordan.

GUY GARDNER

Originally passed over by Abin Sur in favor of Hal Jordan, Guy Gardner enjoyed a checkered career as Green Lantern. Gardner became known for his belligerent, cocky stance, marked by his constant attempts to prove himself as the one, true Green Lantern. Gardner served with the JLA but later lost his right to wear a power ring. He briefly wore Sinestro's yellow power ring, then embraced a new role when he discovered his heritage as a genetically-altered warrior engineered by the alien Vuldarians.

LIGHTS OUT *Guy Gardner takes a blow to his pride.*

PARALLAX *Hal Jordan achieved unimaginable power as the megalomaniacal Parallax. Ironically, he is even more powerful as the divinely-empowered Spectre.*

The Green Lantern insignia is worn by all members of the Corps.

The power ring is uniquely keyed to Kyle and cannot be used by others.

Art works Kyle's civilian job as a graphic artist helps him in his career as Green Lantern since he can physically create anything he dreams up in pencils. Viewed by some as irresponsible and too focused on Earth, Kyle has made amends by patrolling space and attempting to rebuild the Green Lantern Corps.

KYLE RAYNER

When Hal Jordan shattered the Green Lantern Corps, the last remaining Guardian gave a power ring to a new hero—Kyle Rayner of Earth. Although he seemed to have been selected at random, Rayner worked hard to prove himself worthy of the Green Lantern legacy. His upgraded ring has no weakness against the color yellow, and Rayner has handled himself well against the super-villain Major Force (who murdered Rayner's girlfriend) and the Lantern-hunting killer, Fatality. Kyle forged friendships with Green Arrow and the Flash, and has kindled a romance with Alan Scott's daughter, Jade. Rayner assumed the identity of the near-omnipotent Ion before bleeding off much of his power by resurrecting the Guardians. Kyle Rayner recruited members to restore the Corps to its former glory.

SWAN SONG

Although Kyle Rayner worked to restore the Green Lantern Corps, his actions seemed to bring about the twilight of his career. After returning from outer space, Kyle learned that his girlfriend, Jade, had moved on and that the JLA was doing well with John Stewart in the role of power-ring wielder. Kyle's subsequent battle with Fatality showed that he still had plenty of spirit, but other factors—including the revelation that Major Force had returned to orchestrate Fatality's attacks—were harbingers of change for Earth's Green Lantern. DW

EMERALD KNIGHT Kyle Rayner has grown from a rookie to a seasoned warrior.

JOHN STEWART

Originally Hal Jordan's backup Green Lantern, John Stewart has become one of the greatest ring-bearers, despite a career filled with unimaginable pain. Stewart accidentally destroyed the entire planet Xanshi, then suffered when his wife, Katma Tui, died at the hands of Star Sapphire. He earned a measure of peace as the caretaker of a patchwork "mosaic world" on Oa, and later became a member of the Darkstars (an intergalactic peacekeeping force that is a rival to the Green Lantern Corps). Injuries suffered in the line of duty left him paralyzed from the waist down, and he briefly worked as an architect until Hal Jordan, as Parallax, restored the use of his legs. Now, John Stewart works with the world's most powerful super heroes as a member of the JLA, and has helped quell interplanetary threats including Fernus, a Burning Martian who tried to trigger a nuclear holocaust. His most recent misfortune has been the breakup of his relationship with Merayn, a former Darkstar.

RESOLUTE Presented with several opportunities to retire, John Stewart has continued to serve as Green Lantern.

- *GREEN LANTERN (2ND SERIES) #76 (APRIL 1970):* This classic tale united Green Lantern Hal Jordan and Green Arrow Oliver Queen for what would become a road-trip exploration of America.
- *GREEN LANTERN (3RD SERIES) #48–50 (JANUARY–MARCH 1994):* Kyle Rayner took over as Green Lantern when Hal Jordan turned rogue in the series-changing "Emerald Twilight" epic.
- *GREEN LANTERN (3RD SERIES) #162–164 (JUNE–AUGUST 2003):* In an echo of his predecessor's journey, Kyle Rayner teamed up with Green Arrow Oliver Queen to investigate an intergalactic crime ring.

GREEN LANTERN

THE RETURN OF HAL JORDAN

Hal Jordan's penance came to an end with the revelation of Parallax's true nature. Parallax had existed since the beginning of time as the living embodiment of fear. Eons of imprisonment in the Green Lantern Central Power Battery, where it became known as "the yellow impurity," had contained its poisonous influence, and had given the power rings their traditional weakness against the color yellow.

In Jordan's case, Parallax had psychically weakened him after the destruction of Coast City, causing him to devastate Oa and crack the Power Battery. Now freed, Parallax had attached itself to Jordan's soul, remaining even while Jordan played host to the Spectre.

The ultimate showdown with Parallax united Green Lanterns John Stewart, Guy Gardner, Kilowog, Kyle Rayner, and Jordan himself – newly restored to life in his original body. The Lanterns locked Parallax within the Oan power battery, reintroducing the yellow weakness – but with Parallax's qualities revealed, the rings' flaw could now be overcome by mastering one's fear.

DUAL IDENTITY *Parallax appeared as an evil twin during Jordan's struggle.*

BACK IN UNIFORM *Hal Jordan's resurrection brought him back to Carol Ferris, his first love.*

UNITED FRONT *The combined efforts of five of the galaxy's best Green Lanterns beat Parallax into submission.*

THE SINESTRO CORPS WAR

Sinestro had not been killed during Jordan's Parallax rampage as originally believed. He gathered followers to forge a mirror opposite of the Green Lantern Corps. Instead of willpower, the yellow rings of the Sinestro Corps fed on fear. Jordan took the fight to the Sinestro Corps' headquarters on Qward in the anti-matter universe, then defended Earth when Sinestro made it his next target. Parallax, freed by the Sinestro Corps, possessed Kyle Rayner before being split into pieces and stored in the personal power batteries of Jordan, Stewart, Rayner, and Guy Gardner.

EVIL'S MIGHT *Sinestro's charisma makes him a popular leader among his monstrous troops.*

CHALLENGES AND CLASHES

Hal Jordan rejoined Earth's super-hero community. He also took up his duties as Green Lantern of sector 2814, sharing responsibilities with John Stewart. In his civilian identity Jordan worked as a test pilot and captain in the U.S. Air Force, operating out of the slowly-rebuilding Coast City. Jordan's former rogues' gallery was quick to notice his return. He soon clashed with Hector Hammond, Black Hand, and the Tattooed Man. After the Infinite Crisis, Jordan spent time in a POW camp after his jet went down over Russian airspace. Other challenges included a confrontation with Amon Sur (son of Abin Sur, who gave Jordan his first power ring) and his old nemesis Star Sapphire. Jordan served briefly with the Justice League of America until ceding his spot to John Stewart.

SUPERVILLAINY *The powers of the reborn Sinestro were enough to overwhelm Kyle Rayner and Green Arrow.*

VIOLET ENERGY *Star Sapphire is one of several villains to vex Jordan upon his return.*

JOHN STEWART AND THE GREAT TEN

After the return of Hal Jordan and the reorganization of the Green Lantern Corps, John Stewart assumed co-duties with Jordan as protectors of Earth's space sector 2814. Stewart was among the first to test the tense international standoff that followed the Infinite Crisis, when he chased a fugitive to the Chinese border and provoked a confrontation with the Great Ten. Stewart later accepted a position with the Justice League of America after Hal Jordan stepped down, and quickly found himself at odds with Lex Luthor's Injustice League Unlimited. He also used his architectural training to design the League's new Hall in Washington D.C.

GUY GARDNER'S MISSION

After enduring his body's genetic rejection of the Vuldarian DNA that had once transformed him into the Warrior, Guy Gardner returned to the Green Lantern Corps as an instructor for new trainees. He led his recruits to a victory over a resurgent Spider Guild and earned a promotion to the Corps' Honor Guard, but went behind the Guardians' backs to help Hal Jordan retrieve the "Lost Lanterns" believed killed during Jordan/Parallax's attack on Oa. As punishment, Gardner served on "Prime Duty," overseeing the floating prison cell in which Superboy-Prime had been locked since the end of the Infinite Crisis. Gardner later ran a mission with the top-secret agents of the "Green Lantern Corpse." During the Sinestro Corps War, he fought the escaped Superboy-Prime and an army of yellow-ringed soldiers during their invasion of Earth. **DW**

BODY'S REJECTION
With his Vuldarian DNA purged from his system, Gardner returned to the Corps.

KYLE RAYNER: MAGIC AND LOSS

At the edge of the universe Kyle Rayner was the first to uncover the truth of Parallax, bringing the knowledge back to Earth to help the other Lanterns defeat the fear entity. During the Infinite Crisis he witnessed the death of Jade and underwent a second transformation into Ion. Rayner eventually learned that Ion was a separate being, the living embodiment of willpower that fueled the Green Lanterns' emerald energy. The Guardians viewed Rayner/Ion as the next evolution of Green Lanterns, and gave him the title "the Torchbearer." Rayner suffered a new loss when his mother died of a debilitating illness. He soon learned her death had been no accident—Sinestro had arranged for her infection by the sentient virus Despotellis. Weakened by the knowledge that he hadn't saved her, Rayner became the new host for Parallax. During the Sinestro Corps War, Guy Gardner helped Rayner break Parallax's hold by showing him a painting that Rayner's mother had made before her death. After rejoining the Green Lantern Corps—now without the powers of Ion—Rayner helped Donna Troy, Jason Todd, and a rogue Monitor as they traversed the multiverse in search of Ray Palmer.

NEW BLOOD *During the Sinestro Corps war, Sodam Yat took over from Kyle Rayner as Ion.*

SAYING GOODBYE *Kyle Rayner tried to use his powers to sustain his mother's life, but ultimately had to let her go.*

HARLEY QUINN

FIRST APPEARANCE BATMAN: HARLEY QUINN #1 (October 1999)
STATUS Villain **REAL NAME** Dr. Harleen Quinzel
OCCUPATION Professional criminal **BASE** Gotham City
HEIGHT 5ft 7in **WEIGHT** 140 lbs **EYES** Blue **HAIR** Blonde
SPECIAL POWERS/ABILITIES An agile acrobat following exposure to
Poison Ivy's herbal remedies; once a gifted psychotherapist, she is
now dangerously unbalanced; like the Joker, often employs various
gag weapons in her bag of tricks.

Encountering the Joker, the inveterately evil Clown
Prince of Crime, was the very worst thing that could have
happened to young and impressionable Arkham Asylum
psychiatrist Dr. Harleen Quinzel. While attempting to
heal the Joker's maniacal mind, Quinzel found herself
captivated. As he spun heartrending—and probably
false—tales of an unhappy childhood, she was soon
falling head over heels in love with him.

CHILDREN Harley is certainly guilty of
child endangerment and contributing to the
delinquency of minors, but she actually likes kids
and hopes to have a few with the Joker someday.

COMIC CHARACTERS Fiercely loyal
to the Joker, Harley would clown
around for him at the drop of
a bat…Batman, that is!

COSTUMED CRIMINAL Dangerous
curves accentuate Harley's costume,
although she still finds places to hide
weapons of mass distraction!

Harley then proceeded to ruin her
career (and endanger her life) by helping
him escape from Arkham. Soon after, she
became the Joker's moll, slinking around in a
sexy jester's costume and white greasepaint to
become the giggling gangstress Harley Quinn.
Unfortunately, Harley's love for the psycho she calls
"Puddin'" was unreturned. Once free, the Joker found
her presence more and more irksome. He chose to
end their liaison by trapping Harley inside a rocket
and attempting to blast her into orbit. Harley survived,
thanks in part to the plant-manipulating rogue POISON
IVY, whose floral concoctions endowed the Clown
Princess with amazing acrobatic abilities.
After splitting from the Joker, Harley joined the
Secret Six. In a women's shelter the Amazons recruited
both her and Holly Robinson (see Catwoman) for
training on Themyscira, where they aided Hippolyta.
SB

HARRIGAN, HOP

FIRST APPEARANCE ALL-AMERICAN COMICS #1 (April 1939)
STATUS Hero **REAL NAME** Hop Harrigan
OCCUPATION Aviator **BASE** Mobile
HEIGHT 5ft 7in **WEIGHT** 145 lbs **EYES** Blue **HAIR** Blond
SPECIAL POWERS/ABILITIES A superb pilot and tactician with no formal
training as a fighter.

Hop Harrigan became an international
celebrity when a New York reporter rode
on one of the young man's humanitarian
transports of Chinese refugees aboard pilot
Prop Wash's experimental plane. A ticker-tape
parade greeted Hop upon his return to the
U.S. Harrigan's fame attracted the attention
of his abusive former guardian, Silas Crass,
who went to court and demanded that the
boy and the money associated with Hop's
name be placed in his custody. Thanks to
his pal Tank, evidence was provided that
Crass had never truly been authorized to be
Harrigan's guardian and had forged papers
to the contrary. In the aftermath, Prop
Wash became Hop's new legal guardian.
The young man had many flying adventures around the
world, occasionally aiding the All-Star Squadron. Hop
dabbled with becoming a costumed adventurer and
became the short-lived alter ego of Guardian Angel. After
the war, Hop Harrigan briefly became the Black Lamp,
but prefers just being himself. **RG**

HAUNTED TANK

FIRST APPEARANCE G.I. Combat #87 (May 1961)
STATUS Hero team **BASE** Europe during World War II
MEMBERS AND POWERS
Lt. Jeb Stuart Sherman tank commander.
Cpl. Arch Asher (deceased) Loader.
Sgt. Bill Craig (deceased) Gunner.
Pvt. Eddie Craig (deceased) Bill Craig's son.
Cpl. Gus Gray (deceased) Second gunner.
Pvt. Rick Rawlins Gunner.
Cpl. Slim Stryker (deceased) Driver.

The Haunted Tank was actually a series of tanks
commanded by Lieutenant Jeb Stuart during World War
II. The spirit of Alexander the Great assigned the spirit
of Confederate General James Ewell Brown (J.E.B.)
Stuart to become the ghostly guardian of a
Stuart M3 tank in Northern Africa. Initially
affronted by the idea of watching over the
tank's commander, a Yankee named Sergeant
Jeb Stuart, who shared his namesake, the
Confederate ghost was nonetheless impressed
by Stuart's platoon in battle.
Sgt. Stuart was able to see J.E.B.'s ghost and
flew the Confederate flag in honor of his
spirit guardian. Stuart's team was convinced
that their Sergeant imagined seeing the
ghost; nevertheless, J.E.B.'s loyalty to his
living namesake never wavered, and he watched over each
new tank under the Sergeant's care. **PJ**

HAWK AND DOVE

FIRST APPEARANCE (Hank & Don) SHOWCASE #75 (July 1968)
STATUS Heroes **REAL NAMES** Hank Hall, Holly Granger (Hawk);
Don Hall, Dawn Marie Granger (Dove)
OCCUPATIONS (both) Adventurers **BASE** (both) Washington, D.C.
HEIGHT (Hank) 5ft 10in (6ft 3in as Hawk); (Don) 6ft; **WEIGHT** (Hank)
181 lbs (320 lbs as Hawk); (Don) 175 lbs **EYES** (both) Brown **HAIR**
(Hank) Brown; (Don) Black and thinning **SPECIAL POWERS/ABILITIES**
(both) Faster-than-human speed; heightened body density.

Hank and Don Hall, two brothers with diametrically
opposed political and social philosophies, were
transformed as the result of an experiment by the Lords
of Order and the Lords of Chaos, into the super-strong
Hawk and Dove. They bickered but fought alongside
one another, briefly joining the Teen Titans until Dove
was killed during the Crisis (*see* Great Battles, pp. 186-7).
Dawn Granger, seeking help to save her mother, was given
powers by the Lords of Order and Chaos. Whenever she
said the word, "Dove," Dawn became Dove II, unwittingly
depriving the original Dove of his powers, leading to his death.
Dawn finally hooked up with Hank Hall and a new version of
Hawk and Dove were formed. In the mountain world of Druspa
Tau, they learned much about their abilities and origins even as
they found themselves on opposite sides in the war between the
Lords of Chaos and Order. When their creators died, Hawk and
Dove agreed to absorb the essence of their respective creators.
MONARCH, a future version of Hank Hall, murdered Dove and
fueled madness in Hawk that ensured that, in a temporal loop,
he fulfilled his destiny to become Monarch. With no Hawk or
Dove, the cosmic forces turned to others to fill these roles,
and U.S. Air Force pilot Sasha Martens and guitarist Wiley
Wolverman were transformed into the new Hawk and
Dove. However, Dawn Granger returned from the dead.
She came back to the role of Dove, and enlisted her sister
Holly as the latest Hawk. **RG**

HAWK, SON OF TOMAHAWK

FIRST APPEARANCE TOMAHAWK #131 (December 1970)
STATUS Hero (deceased) **REAL NAME** Unknown **OCCUPATION** Adventurer
BASE Echo Valley, American Midwest **HEIGHT** 5ft 10in
WEIGHT 166 lbs **EYES** Blue **HAIR** Brown with blond streak
SPECIAL POWERS/ABILITIES Expert marksman, horseman, and tracker;
his bravery and idealism made him an effective frontier diplomat.

As son of a legendary Revolutionary War hero, Hawk had
some big shoes to fill, but he became a hero in his own
right. Raised in a log cabin, Hawk learned the ways of the
frontiersman from his father and the secrets of America's
native people from his mother, Moon Fawn. Hawk
believed that all men were created equal and
fought fiercely against those who would
enslave or exploit their
fellow men. He had
one brother, Small
Eagle.

Late in life, Hawk
encountered the Swamp Thing
during the plant elemental's
time-traveling trip to the 1870s,
an adventure that involved other
famous Western heroes of the
time, including Bat Lash,
Madame .44, and Johnny
Thunder.

A mystical artifact Hawk
possessed sent Swamp Thing
back to his own time. Shortly
before his death, Hawk published his
autobiography, *Hawk, Son of Tomahawk*. **DW**

HAWKGIRL

FIRST APPEARANCE JSA SECRET FILES AND ORIGINS #1 (August 1999)
STATUS Hero **REAL NAME** Kendra Saunders
OCCUPATION Adventurer **BASE** St. Roche, Louisiana
HEIGHT 5ft 6in **WEIGHT** 131 lbs **EYES** Green **HAIR** Black
SPECIAL POWERS/ABILITIES Able to fly thanks to gravity-defying Nth
metal belt; uses giant wings to navigate during flight; aggressive
and adept hand-to-hand combatant.

Troubled orphan Kendra Saunders attempted suicide in her
teens and her body was inhabited by the spirit of an ancient
Egyptian princess, Chay-Ara. Inheriting Chay-Ara's soul and not
knowing why made Kendra mentally ill.

Kendra went to live with her grandfather, Speed Saunders,
a famous adventurer from the 1940s. Armed with the
secret knowledge that Kendra, the grandniece of Sheira
Saunders, the Golden Age Hawkgirl, had a great destiny
awaiting her, Speed began training the young woman
to become a super hero, and gave her Sheira's original
Hawkgirl wings. She had a daughter, Mia, at 16 and
gave her up for adoption.

Initially reluctant, Kendra became the new
Hawkgirl, joining the Justice Society of
America, and helping the team defeat Mordru
the Dark Lord. Later, Hawkgirl met Hawkman,
the reincarnation of Khufu, Chay-Ara's ancient
Egyptian soulmate. During the Infinite Crisis, an
outer space accident briefly transformed Hawkgirl
into a giant. She recently joined the new Justice League
of America. **PJ**

ACTION GIRL *Soaring
through the skies like her
avian namesake,
Hawkgirl is one of
the fastest—and most
ferocious—fliers on
the planet.*

SOUL MATES *United by love
and death for
thousands of
years, Hawkman
and Hawkgirl share
a unique bond.*

HAWKMAN

THE WINGED AVENGER

FIRST APPEARANCE FLASH COMICS #1 (January 1940)
STATUS Hero **REAL NAME** Carter Hall
OCCUPATION Adventurer **BASE** St. Roch, Louisiana
HEIGHT 6ft 1in **WEIGHT** 195 lbs **EYES** Blue **HAIR** Brown
SPECIAL POWERS/ABILITIES Thanagarian Nth Metal on boots and wing harnesses allow him to fly; artificial wings give great speed and agility; Nth Metal permits Hawkman to lift great weights and withstand extremes of temperature during flight; wields a variety of ancient weapons, including shield, dagger, mace, cestus, battleaxe, and more.

ARMED AND DANGEROUS
With ancient weapons amassed during his many lifetimes on Earth, Hawkman fights an eternal struggle against evil in any age.

THE STORY OF HAWKMAN begins many millennia ago, during the 15th Dynasty of Ancient Egypt. Prince Khufu and his beloved Chay-Ara discovered the wreckage of a spacecraft from the planet Thanagar. After exposure to the mysterious Nth Metal, the vehicle's anti-gravity alloy, Khufu and Chay-Ara were murdered by the sinister sorcerer Hath-Set. The Nth Metal initiated a cycle of reincarnation that would see Khufu and Chay-Ara reborn countless times throughout the ages.

BORN AGAIN LOVERS

Reincarnated during America's Wild West, Khufu was the gunfighting hero Nighthawk, while Chay-Ara was pistol-packing Cinnamon I. In the 1940s, Khufu was archaeologist Carter Hall and became Hawkman, while Chay-Ara found new life as Sheira Saunders, the heroine Hawkgirl and Carter's wife. Both winged wonders served with the Justice Society of America (Hawkman was chairman) and the wartime All-Star Squadron. Both Hawks later became members of the Justice League of America and flew with the team on its earliest missions. The Halls' cycle of death and rebirth was interrupted during the Zero Hour crisis (*see* Great Battles, pp. 186-7), when both Carter and Sheira merged with Thanagarian policeman Katar Hol, who adopted the mantle of Hawkman. Unfortunately, Sheira perished in the merging. Carter later freed himself from his union with Katar, who also died. Carter was resurrected yet again, this time possessing memories of his every previous reincarnation. Sheira, however, was reborn as

CURSED *Discovering a downed Thanagarian spacecraft gave Prince Khufu the power to fly and his immortal curse.*

her own grandniece, Kendra Saunders, with no past memories. Carter reclaimed the role of Hawkman, and rejoined the JSA alongside the new Hawkgirl. But for the first time in all their previous lives, Hawkgirl did not recognize Hawkman as her soulmate. Blinded by his love for Chay-Ara, in any form she exists, Hawkman followed Hawkgirl to St. Roch, Louisiana, as she began a quest to find the villain who murdered Kendra Saunders's parents. Hawkman spent a year on Thanagar following the Infinite Crisis, but later rejoined the JSA. **SB**

TOGETHER FOREVER *The Hawks are destined to find each other and fall in love time and time again.*

KEY STORYLINES

• *LEGEND OF THE HAWKMAN #1-3 (JULY–SEPT. 2000):* A retelling of Hawkman and Hawkgirl's connection to distant Thanagar.
• *JSA SECRET FILES AND ORIGINS #1 (AUG. 1999):* The return of Hawkgirl signals the reincarnation of Hawkman!
• *JSA #23-26 (JUNE–SEPT. 2001):* A reborn Carter Hall rejoins the JSA and leads the team to glory.

FEARLESS FIGHTER *Flying solo against fire-breathing monsters, soaring alongside Hawkgirl, or leading the assembled JSA, Hawkman is one of the greatest warriors ever known.*

HERALD (VOX)

FIRST APPEARANCE (as Mal) TEEN TITANS (1st series) #26 (April 1970);
(as Herald) Secret Origins Annual #3 (1989)
STATUS Hero **REAL NAME** Malcolm Arnold Duncan
OCCUPATION Restaurateur, musician, adventurer **BASE** San Francisco
HEIGHT 6ft 1in **WEIGHT** 210 lbs **EYES** Brown **HAIR** Black
SPECIAL POWERS/ABILITIES The now-destroyed Gabriel's Horn device
could open warps in space, allowing teleportation; Duncan was
a former Golden Gloves amateur boxing champion.

Malcolm "Mal" Duncan was raised in Harlem, NY, with his sister Cindy. When Cindy was harassed by a racist street gang, Mal single-handedly attacked them, and was soon helped by the Teen Titans, who had temporarily given up their costumed identities and happened to be nearby. Joining the Titans, but possessing no superpowers of his own, Mal began to feel like an outsider on the team, until Karen Beecher, the Bumblebee, helped him create the Gabriel's Horn, a special weapon with teleportational powers. Becoming the Herald, Mal helped the Titans defeat Doctor Light I.

Unknown to Mal, his special Horn had been corrupted by the villainous Gargoyle, who hoped to tear a hole in the dimensional fabric in order to release his master, the Antithesis. After the Titans defeated these villains, Mal destroyed the Horn. During the Infinite Crisis, Mal Duncan suffered an accident in space that left him unable to speak. After accepting a cybernetic voice box similar to the Gabriel's Horn, he joined the Doom Patrol as Vox. **PJ**

HERO

FIRST APPEARANCE SUPERBOY AND THE RAVERS #1 (Sept. 1996)
STATUS Hero **REAL NAME** Hero Cruz
OCCUPATION Adventurer **BASE** Metropolis
HEIGHT 5ft 9in **WEIGHT** 157 lbs **EYES** Brown **HAIR** Black
SPECIAL POWERS/ABILITIES Internalized H-Dial allows him to transform
into a new superbeing with new superpowers for one hour; he never
transforms into the same being twice.

Raised in a middle-class Puerto Rican family in Metropolis, Hero Cruz discovered a cache of technology stolen by the Scavenger. He took the Scavenger's Achilles Vest, using its invulnerability powers to join the Event Horizon, a cosmic rave party. Along with Superboy and the Ravers, Hero traveled across the universe with the Event Horizon party. When the Scavenger came searching for his Achilles Vest, he kidnapped several Ravers, including Sparx, whom he believed had stolen the vest. The Ravers tracked the Scavenger to his lair, and Hero discovered a mystical dial with the letters "H," "E," "R," and "O" on it. He used the dial to transform into different super heroes, rescuing Sparx and Superboy and defeating the Scavenger. Sparx fell in love with Hero, but Hero revealed that he was gay. He now lives in San Francisco. **PJ**

HERCULES

FIRST APPEARANCE ALL-STAR COMICS #8 (December, 1941)
STATUS Hero **REAL NAME** Hercules
OCCUPATION Demi-god **BASE** Olympus
HEIGHT 6ft 5in **WEIGHT** 327 lbs **EYES** Blue **HAIR** Black
SPECIAL POWERS/ABILITIES Super-strength and near-immortality
bestowed upon him by his father, Zeus. Hercules is resistant to most
injuries and has impressive stamina.

Hercules (or Heracles) is the champion of Greek myth and son of Zeus of the Olympian Gods. After performing legendary labors during the era of antiquity, Hercules and his warriors conquered the Amazons, with Hercules forcing himself on their queen, Hippolyta. The Amazons withdrew from the world of men to Themyscira, and the gods punished Hercules by forcing him to bear the weight of their island for centuries.

After gaining his freedom, Hercules returned to adventuring, aiding Wonder Woman during her time as Diana Prince of the Department of Metahuman Affairs. He matched his strength against both Superman and Superman's counterpart from Earth-22. He later joined with Wonder Girl (who, as a daughter of Zeus, is his half-sister) to investigate the mysterious disappearance of the Olympian gods. The trail put them into conflict with the Female Furies. Hercules continues to make his mark in the world of mortals. He may not be the brightest of the gods, but he makes up for it in sheer power. **DW**

TRIALS OF SHAZAM
While Freddy Freeman undertook a series of challenges meant to prove himself worthy of the Shazam mantle, Hercules took on a different form in order to aid the young hero.

HIPPOLYTA

FIRST APPEARANCE WONDER WOMAN (2nd series) #1 (February 1987)
STATUS Hero (deceased)   **REAL NAME** Hippolyta
OCCUPATION Former Queen of the Amazons   **BASE** Elysian Fields
HEIGHT 5ft 9in   **WEIGHT** 150 lbs   **EYES** Blue   **HAIR** Black
SPECIAL POWERS/ABILITIES Granted eternal life by the gods of Mount Olympus and gifted with amazing strength, speed, and agility; wore the Girdle of Gaea, which magically protected the Amazons from subjugation by man before it was forged into Wonder Woman's golden Lasso of Truth.

When a pregnant cavewoman was murdered more than 32,000 years ago by her brutish mate, her spirit was collected by the Earth Mother, Gaea, and deposited in the Well of Souls, which held the life essences of slain women from past ages. Zeus, King of the Gods (*see* Olympian Gods), called for the creation of a new race of humankind to bring glory to the gods, so the Olympian goddesses restored life to these waiting souls. Among the women reincarnated was that tragic cavewoman, reborn as Hippolyta, Queen of the Amazons.

NAZI FIGHTER *Hippolyta became a member of the Justice Society via time-travel. She also made Wonder Woman a legend during World War II.*

LEAVING MAN'S WORLD

The gods' chosen race dwelt in peace within their city-state of Themyscira until Ares, God of War, sent Zeus's son Heracles to seduce Hippolyta and defeat the Amazons. Her sisterhood divided, Hippolyta led a group of peace-loving Amazons to rebuild Themyscira on an island within the Bermuda Triangle, where they lived for centuries hidden from the outside world. Over time, Hippolyta's yearning for the unborn child slain within her all those millennia ago was heard by the gods. They instructed her to mold a daughter from clay; as soon as she did so, they breathed life into it. That child, Diana, would one day become Wonder Woman, a role Hippolyta paradoxically immortalized herself by time-traveling to 1942 and serving as a member of the wartime Justice Society of America.

In modern times, Hippolyta led the Amazons through civil wars and apocalyptic battles with Darkseid, who once decimated Themyscira and its people. Hippolyta ultimately gave her life defending both her homeland and Earth from the onslaught of the world-destroying Imperiex (*see* Great Battles, pp. 186-7). She is remembered as a fair and wise leader, a loving mother to Diana, and a Wonder Woman in her own right.

DEATH *Hippolyta helped to save Earth. The Olympian goddesses carried her soul into immortality.*

A QUEEN'S RETURN *Circe, mortal enemy of the Amazons, ironically brought their greatest leader back from the realm of the dead*

AMAZONS ATTACK

Hippolyta returned to life through the dark magics of Circe. Goaded to war on the news that the U.S. government had seized her daughter Diana, Hippolyta led an army of Amazons into Washington DC. As Greek monsters felled national monuments, the world's super heroes failed to stop Hippolyta's advance. Diana eventually persuaded the Amazon queen to lay down her sword, prompting the goddess Athena—Granny Goodness in disguise—to scatter the Amazons and banish them to live as mortal woman. Hippolyta remained alone on Themyscira, queen of an deserted kingdom.

THEMYSCIRAN EXILE

A strike team of fascist soldiers organized by Captain Nazi soon invaded Themyscira, opposed at first by Hippolyta and later by Wonder Woman and her gorilla shock troops. The Nazis found support in four imprisoned Amazons, who had once served as Hippolyta's Royal Guard until they tried to murder the infant Diana for being the first child to appear in a childless society.

Granny Goodness continued her deception as Athena by drawing false Amazons to Themyscira, including Harley Quinn and Holly Robinson (see Catwoman). The two newcomers discovered Hippolyta hiding in a cave and agreed to aid her in the fight to reclaim the island. Mary Marvel soon rounded out their resistance movement.
SB/DW

STRIKE TEAM *Holly Robinson and Harley Quinn proved worthy fighters.*

KEY STORYLINES
• ACTION COMICS #781 (SEPTEMBER 2001): Hippolyta gives her life to stop Imperiex's hollowing of Earth.
• AMAZONS ATTACK #1-6 (MARCH-AUGUST 2007): Hippolyta makes war against Man's World.

HITMAN

FIRST APPEARANCE THE DEMON (2nd series) Annual #2 (1993)
STATUS Hero (deceased) **REAL NAME** Thomas Monaghan
OCCUPATION Hitman; vigilante **BASE** Gotham City
HEIGHT 6ft **WEIGHT** 185 lbs **EYES** Black **HAIR** Black
SPECIAL POWERS/ABILITIES Infected with alien blood, Tommy had limited X-ray vision and telepathy; he was also a crack shot.

An attack by the alien parasite Glonth left hitman Tommy Monaghan with greatly enhanced senses and limited telepathic ability. Of course, the first thing Tommy did was kill Glonth. Some saw him as a hero, and although he operated far outside the law, he did have a better developed moral sense than your average hitman. He had earned the grudging respect of Batman, who recognized that Tommy kept one of the darkest corners of Gotham clean. Green Lantern Kyle Rayner also worked alongside Tommy.

Along the way, Tommy reunited with his old pal Natt the Hat, and the two became inseparable. Given his new powers, strange characters were soon drawn to Tommy. First came the would-be super heroes Six Pack, a group of costumed losers. Then there was the demon Baytor, who found hanging out with Tommy at Noonan's bar so fascinating that he went to work there as a bartender.

Tommy discovered the existence of the Bloodlines File, a government project hoping to create meta-humans using data from the earlier space-parasite outbreak. In the bloody aftermath of their attempt to shut down the facility, both Hitman and Natt were killed. **RG**

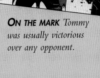

ON THE MARK Tommy was usually victorious over any opponent.

TROUBLE MAN
A previous survivor of the Bloodlines virus, Tommy Monaghan was kidnapped by Batman and brought to JLA headquarters. Batman hoped that Tommy's antibodies might help combat a new strain of the virus. However Tommy's controversial presence soon caused strife among the JLA heroes.

HOUNGAN

FIRST APPEARANCE THE New Teen Titans (1st series) #14 (Dec. 1981)
STATUS Villain **REAL NAME** Jean-Louis Droo
OCCUPATION Scientist turned criminal **BASE** Paris, France
HEIGHT 6ft 2in **WEIGHT** 205 lbs **EYES** Brown **HAIR** Black
SPECIAL POWERS/ABILITIES Computerized voodoo dolls trigger terrible pain and even death to his victims through an advanced bionic link.

Born in Haiti, Jean-Louis Droo became a top computer scientist in the U.S. He returned to Haiti to visit his dying father, only to see a local voodoo priest (a "houngan") effect a miraculous cure through the voodoo arts. Droo merged the old ways with the new by creating a computerized voodoo doll. This works by analyzing a victim's cell sample and generating a "bionic link." When Droo's stylus stabs the doll, pain signals travel via the link to the victim's equivalent body part.

Calling himself Houngan, Droo joined the New Brotherhood of Evil, later reorganized into the Society of Sin, and participated in epic events including the Crisis (*see* Great Battles, pp. 186-7). Houngan numbered among the criminals captured by the Suicide Squad and deposited on a prison planet during Operation: Salvation Run. **DW**

ALIEN RACES AND WORLDS

IN THE LAST FEW DECADES, humankind has learned that Earth is by no means alone in the universe as a planetary home to sentient life. From the galactic rim of the Milky Way to the furthest reaches of the known universe, advanced aliens abound. However, not all of these peoples are peaceful. Remarkably, some even resemble *Homo sapiens*, albeit with markedly different internal physiologies. A few exhibit superpowers, either a benefit of the atmospheres of their native worlds, or as a result of exposure to lesser gravities, the rays of a different colored sun, or any number of environmental factors. The following are the most notable alien races that have had more than close encounters with Earth, either as strange visitors from other planets or invaders from beyond.

THE KRYPTONIANS

From planet Krypton, some 50 light-years from Earth, the Kryptonian race were once renowned for their incredible advances in the science of cloning. For millennia, cloning banks extended the lives of the elite on Krypton and allowed them unfettered pursuit of knowledge and the arts. However, the terrorist group Black Zero, long opposed to cloning, launched civil wars that lasted thousands of years. In the year 105/892, Black Zero destroyed the capital city of Kandor with a thermonuclear device that initiated a slow-burning chain-reaction in planet's core. Eventually, Krypton's radioactive core spread "Green Death" across the planet, a plague that killed millions. In time, the planet exploded, killing every last Kryptonian save one, the infant Kal-El, who was rocketed to Earth and became Superman, whose legend spread throughout the universe.

KANDOR Krypton's greatest city paid a terrible price during the civil war over cloning.

SOCIAL DIVIDES Kryptonian hubris led to elitism, xenophobia, and isolationism. These attitudes permeated society, and led to individuals having little or no contact, physical or emotional.

TOWERING SPIRES Mile-high buildings lined the thoroughfares of Kryptonian cities before the planet's untimely doom.

THE DOMINATORS

The Dominators are a race of conquerors divided into a rigid caste system. On their homeworld, Dominion, thousands of light years from Earth, the Dominator hierarchy is determined by the size of a red disk worn on the forehead. The Dominators have invaded many worlds with advanced weapons created from a melding of technology and nature.

When the Dominators discovered that humans possessed a latent metagene capable of manifesting superpowers, they feared that Earth would spawn a super-race that would pose a threat to the Dominion. Assembling an alliance of nine alien worlds and extraterrestrial empires—including the Citadel, Daxam, Durla, Gil'Daan, Khundia, Okaara, the Psions, and Thanagar—the Dominators led an invasion of Earth and nearly wiped out its meta-human heroes with a power-negating metagene bomb (*see* Great Battles, pp. 186-7. The Dominators will remain a threat to galactic peace well into the 31st century, when the Legion of Super-Heroes will fight to thwart the Dominion from overrunning the United Planets.

DAXAMITES hail from the planet Daxam and are renowned for their biochemical research. The rays of a yellow sun have similar empowering effects on them as on Superman. Daxamites are fatally allergic to lead but, by the 31st century, they will have found an antidote, enabling them to become renowned space explorers. Notable Daxamites include Green Lantern Sodal Yat and Lar Gand, M'onel of the Legion of Super-Heroes.

DURLANS are shape-shifters, able to mimic any object or being's molecular pattern. Their home, Durla, was ravaged by the Six-Minute War, a nuclear holocaust that took place thousands of years ago. Durlans are nomadic, living in tribes who prohibit off-worlders from visiting their radiation-scarred planet, which the Durlans rarely leave. On the only occasion they have invaded Earth, they were defeated by the world's meta-humans.

THE KHUNDS

The Khund race are predisposed to aggression. On Khundia, it is not uncommon for citizens to challenge one another to physical combat, likely to the death, for the slightest offense or insult. While allied with the Dominators, the Khunds razed Melbourne, Australia, seeking to establish a beachhead in overrunning Earth. After Earth's super heroes routed this Dominion-led invasion, the humbled Khunds returned to their homeworld. For a thousand years, the Khunds remained confined to their own space. However, the war drums of Khundia will beat loudly once more in the 31st century.

THE PSIONS

Cold-blooded and utterly emotionless, the Psions were originally alien reptiles evolved to higher intelligence by Maltusian scientists. The Maltusians left their world to become the Guardians of the Universe and these creatures, who called themselves Psions, continued their evolutionary progress. Eventually the Psions traveled into space to find their creators. The Guardians, concerned with other matters, encouraged the Psions to continue their quest for knowledge. The Psions, however, took scientific experimentation to the extreme, often selling their cruel services to other alien cultures. Psion research under the banner of the Citadel gave Tamaranean sisters K'oriand'r and Komand'r their star-bolt powers as Starfire and Blackfire. The Psions added their scientific savvy to the Dominator-led invasion of Earth, and engaged in breeding experiments that crossed humans with the H'San Natall to create young superbeings briefly united as a team of Teen Titans.

THE TAMARANEANS

Although fierce fighters, Tamaraneans are a people who prefer peace to waging war. However, when the lush world of Tamaran was invaded by the Citadel, rulers of the Vegan Star System, King Myand'r's daughter Koriand'r, alongside her Teen Titans teammates, subsequently saved her homeworld from Citadel control.

Ultimately, Tamaran was destroyed by the Psions, forcing its people to settle on New Tamaran, which was in turn rendered uninhabitable by the star-consuming Sun-Eater. The Tamaraneans who were able to escape occupied Rashashoon, a world ruled by the reptilian Gordanians, former soldiers to the Citadel and lifelong enemies of Tamaran. Tamaraneans and Gordanians co-existed for a brief time before Rashashoon was obliterated by the world-razing Imperiex. The few remaining Tamaraneans are now a wandering people in search of a planet to call their own.

THE THANAGARIANS

The Thanagarians are known for their predatory civilization, based on the so-called "Hawkworld," Thanagar. Previously a slave planet of the Polaran Empire, Thanagar became a world markedly divided by class. Alien Downsiders live in the slums of Thanagarian cities, while native-born Thanagarians dwell aloft in floating cities high above the squalor and disease. Thanagarians also joined in the Dominators' invasion of Earth, supplying winged Hawkmen infantry for the planetary assault.

Following the Dominators' defeat, the Thanagarians returned to their own affairs. Unknown to many, Thanagarians traveled to Earth thousands of years prior to the Dominion-led invasion. Wreckage from a downed Thanagarian spacecraft provided the anti-gravity Nth Metal and presumably the inspiration for Egyptian Prince Khufu and his lover, Chay-Ara, to become Hawkman and Hawkgirl in countless reincarnations throughout the ages to follow. SB

DARK WINGMEN *Few sights inspire more awe (or fear) than watching a squadron of winged Thanagarian Hawkmen descending from the skies in battle.*

INJUSTICE SOCIETY

FIRST APPEARANCE (I) ALL-STAR COMICS #27 (Nov. 1947); (II) JSA #10 (May 2000) **STATUS** Villains **BASE** Mobile **MEMBERS/POWERS** *Brainwave I* (dead, psychic); *Fiddler* (violin-themed weapons); *Gambler* (dead, master of disguise); *Harlequin I* (creates illusions); *Icicle I* (dead, cold gun); *Per Degaton* (time-traveling despot); *The Shade; Hazard, Solomon Grundy; Sportsmaster* (martial arts); *Thinker I* (dead, evil genius); *Tigress I* (hunter); *Vandal Savage, Wizard; Johnny Sorrow, Black Adam, Count Vertigo, Geomancer* ('quakes); *Icicle II; Killer Wasp* (humanoid insect); *Rival* (superspeed); *Shiv* (cyborg); *Tigress II* (fighter); *Thinker II* (virtual consciousness).

THE INJUSTICE SOCIETY 1) *Icicle II*
2) *Rag Doll II* **3)** *Tigress II*
4) *Rival* **5)** *Kestrel* **6)** *Shiv*
7) *Solomon Grundy*

The first Injustice Society of the World was the criminal counterpart to the Justice Society of America in the 1940s. The Injustice Society's first attempt to conquer America was quickly foiled by the JSA. The Injustice Society soon resurfaced, however, committing a series of "Patriotic Crimes," whereby each villain, vying for leadership of the team, had to steal a famous historical object.

Another incarnation of the Injustice Society emerged decades later and fought both the JSA and the Justice League of America. Soon after, the Society formed an alliance with a race of underground beings and attempted to kill the JSA, but the villains were soundly defeated and parted ways.

More recently, the Wizard assembled a modern version of the Injustice Society, called Injustice, Unlimited. He recruited the Fiddler and the Shade as well as the Hazard I, the Icicle II, and the new Tigress. Injustice, Unlimited fought the combined forces of Infinity, Inc. and the Global Guardians at an international trade conference in Canada, but were ultimately defeated. The Wizard was apparently killed during the battle, but later resurfaced when Injustice, Unlimited returned under the command of the Dummy.

Years later, the Injustice Society was resurrected by the criminal Johnny Sorrow, who intended to use the team to engage the JSA while he resurrected the otherdimensional King of Tears. The JSA thwarted the new Injustice Society, though the villainous team has remained active. **PJ**

CARVING UP THE CONTINENT
The Earth's first team of supervillains, the original Injustice Society of the World, were nefarious criminals out to use the chaos of World War II to shape their mad schemes for world conquest and to destroy the JSA.

INSECT QUEEN

FIRST APPEARANCE LEGION OF SUPER-HEROES (4th ser.) #82 (July 1996)
STATUS Hero **REAL NAME** Lonna Leing
OCCUPATION Uncanny Amazer **BASE** Xanthu
HEIGHT 5ft 7in **WEIGHT** 137 lbs **EYES** Green **HAIR** Red
SPECIAL POWERS/ABILITIES Can transform part of her body into any insect form, thereby gaining that insect's abilities.

Lonna Leing was born in the 30th century on the planet Xanthu. She became Insect Queen, a member of Xanthu's team of government-funded teenage super heroes, the Uncanny Amazers.

Insect Queen was a prominent member of the Uncanny Amazers despite the rivalry between her team and Earth's team of teen heroes, the Legion of Super-Heroes. After the alien Blight took over much of the universe, Xanthu was invaded by C.O.M.P.U.T.O.'s cyborg world, Robotica. Insect Queen, Star Boy, and XS helped the Amazers evacuate millions of Xanthu's inhabitants from the Robotican forces that were consuming the planet. Along with the Legionnaires and Khund shocktroopers, Insect Queen helped destroy the Robotican transmitter that controlled the advancing droids. After BRAINIAC 5.1 disabled C.O.M.P.U.T.O. and Robotica, Insect Queen and the Amazers helped the populace of Xanthu recolonize their planet, settling in the megacity of Xanth Prime. **PJ**

INTERNATIONAL ULTRAMARINE CORPS

FIRST APPEARANCE JLA #24 (December 1998)
STATUS Hero team **BASE** Superbia
Original **MEMBERS AND POWERS**
  GENERAL WADE EILING (EX-LEADER) Possesses tremendous strength; has huge incisors that can rend limbs or metal.
  Lt. Col. Scott Sawyer No longer has material substance, but inhabits the stealth weapon Warmaker One.
  Capt. Lea Corbin Has been transformed into the dimension-shifting 4-D.
  Dan Stone Transformed into living liquid and given the name Flow.
  Capt. John Wether Utilizes the "unified field harmonic" to wield atomic powers as Pulse 8.

General Wade Eiling initiated the Ultramarines project to create meta-powered soldiers loyal to the U.S. Four Marine Corps officers were exposed to Proteum, an artificial isotope, and gained amazing powers, but lost their humanity in the process. Under Eiling's command, they battled the Justice League of America until they learned the general had gone insane. Following Eiling's betrayal, the Ultramarines became the new "Global Guardians" of Superbia, a city-state floating high above the nuclear ravaged ruins of Montevideo, Uruguay. After declaring themselves independent of any other nation, the team has since inducted Vixen, Jack O'Lantern III, Knight II and Squire III, and the Japanese hero Goraiko. However, an invasion by the far-future Sheeda decimated the Ultramarine Corps and destroyed their Superbia headquarters. **RG**

THE ULTRAMARINES 1) *Warmaker One* **2)** *Flow*
3) *4-D* **4)** *Pulse 8.*

INTERGANG

INSIDIOUS EMPIRE OF EVIL

FIRST APPEARANCE FOREVER PEOPLE (1st series) #1 (March 1971)
STATUS Villain team **BASE** Metropolis
ORIGINAL MEMBERS AND CRIMINAL ASSOCIATES
Morgan Edge, Vincent Edge (former leaders); *Bruno "Ugly"*
Mannheim (scarfaced former leader); *Boss Moxie* (current leader; clone of original); *Ferrous* (a trio of high-tech assassins); *Louis Gillespie* (no powers); *Mike "Machine" Gunn* (cybernetic gun-arms); *Thaddeus Killgrave* (evil scientist); *Ginny "Torcher" McCree* (wields fire); *Noose* (strangler with elongated fingertips); *Winslow Schott* (weapons inventor); *Zombie Twins* (killers).

During the Prohibition era of the 1920s, the Metropolis underworld was ruled by Boss Moxie's Intergang. Eventually, Moxie died in a hail of bullets beside his moll Ginny "Torcher" McCree, gun-toting Mike "Machine" Gunn, and the bald killer known as Noose. Decades later, WGBS media mogul Morgan Edge reformed Intergang with himself as chief of its enforcement division of Gassers, Shock Troops, and Wall-Crawlers. This Intergang packed serious heat in the form of Apokoliptian weapons supplied by Darkseid's master torturer Desaad, who aided and abetted the organization in its clashes with Superman and Orion.

WEAPON *"Machine" Gunn's clone had cybernetic arms that morphed into high-tech automatic weapons with self-replicating ammo.*

THE NEW BOSS *Bruno Mannheim, now head of Intergang, surveys Gotham, a city he regards as his new fiefdom.*

POWER STRUGGLES

Intergang's conflicts with the Man of Steel continued with future Toyman Winslow Schott providing high-tech weapons until Morgan Edge was convicted of racketeering and jailed. Second-in command Bruno "Ugly" Mannheim briefly led Intergang before Edge's father, Vincent, took it over. Fugitive and former Cadmus Project geneticist Dabney Donovan cloned cell samples from original Intergang hooligans to create an inner circle that included a resurrected Boss Moxie, "Torcher" McCree, "Machine" Gunn, and Noose. With Moxie back to being boss, Intergang became a smaller organization that made greater use of the latest technology and of superpowered thugs as hired muscle.

Intergang grew in power following the Infinite Crisis, expanding its operations from China to Bialya. Gang leader Bruno "Ugly" Mannheim fell under the influence of a cult that worshipped Cain—the first murderer—and celebrated the Seven Deadly Sins. The cult's sacred text, known as the Crime Bible, drove Mannheim to profane fervor as he reveled in blood and cannibalism. Armed with new weaponry from Apokolips, Intergang funded the mad-science inventions on Oolong Island run by Chang Tzu. It also made new inroads into Gotham City to prepare for a takeover. Batwoman, the Question, and Renee Montoya helped dislodge Intergang's Gotham foothold, but earned Mannheim's enmity. Convinced that Batwoman's alter ego Kathy Kane represented the "twice-named daughter of Cain" prophesied in the Crime Bible, Mannheim prepared to sacrifice her. Thwarted in this attempt, he next underwent treatments that grew his body to titanic size. Mannheim used technology provided by an alien benefactor to place Intergang in a position to control all organized crime in Metropolis. Superman, who used his enhanced hearing to zero in on the beat of Mannheim's enlarged heart, stopped this latest threat to the citizens of his city. **SB/DW**

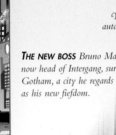

TIGHT SPOT *The Question and Renee Montoya run afoul of Intergang operatives Whisper A'Daire and Kyle Abbot.*

ONE-MAN CRIME WAVE *His body inflated to giant-size by experimental chemicals, Bruno Mannheim flexes his muscles in Metropolis.*

KEY STORYLINES

• *SUPERMAN'S PAL JIMMY OLSEN #133 (OCTOBER 1970):* Intergang debuts in this storyline by Jack Kirby. Intergang would grow to threaten the most powerful superheroes on the planet.

• *SUPERMAN #654 (SEPTEMBER 2006):* Through Intergang's extraterrestrial contacts, Bruno Mannheim has grown to the size of a giant and wields technology that could bring Metropolis to its knees.

ION

FIRST APPEARANCE GREEN LANTERN (3rd series) #142 (as Kyle Rayner); GREEN LANTERN: SINESTRO CORPS SPECIAL #1 (as willpower entity)
STATUS Embodiment of willpower   **REAL NAME** Not applicable
OCCUPATION Hero   **BASE** Mobile   **HEIGHT** (as Kyle Rayner) 5ft 11in
WEIGHT (as Kyle Rayner) 175 lbs   **EYES** (as Kyle Rayner) Green
HAIR (as Kyle Rayner) Black
SPECIAL POWERS/ABILITIES Flight, limited control of time and space, ability to manifest solid energy constructs

LIMITS OF POWER *Despite the abilities of Ion, Kyle Rayner chose to let his mother die in peace.*

Ion is an entity as old as the universe, existing as the embodiment of willpower. Green is the color of willpower on the emotional spectrum, and Ion appears in its purest form as a green, vaguely cetacean creature. It is the natural enemy of Parallax, the yellow, insectoids embodiment of fear. The Guardians Of The Universe learned to harness Ion's emerald energy to fuel the rings of the Green Lantern Corps. Parallax, imprisoned within the Green Lanterns' Central Power Battery on Oa, provided the "yellow impurity" that was the only weakness in the willpower-fueled weapons. Following Parallax's escape and Hal Jordan's subsequent destruction of the Central Power Battery (see Green Lantern), the Green Lantern Corps no longer existed. The universe's sole ringbearer, Kyle Rayner, absorbed the remaining willpower energies and unwittingly became the host for Ion. Adopting a new costume, Rayner expended his near-omnipotent abilities to reignite the Central Power Battery and resurrect the Guardians of the Universe. Rayner's sacrifice cleared the way for the return of the Corps, and the grateful Guardians named him "the torchbearer."

Rayner retired his Ion alter-ego, but the death of JADE in the Infinite Crisis funneled more emerald power into Rayner's body. Again a host for the willpower entity, Rayner reassumed the Ion identity. After clashing with old villains including Alexander Nero, Rayner faced heartbreaking tragedy when his mother wasted away and died of a mysterious disease. It later became known that her illness had been triggered by the sentient virus Despotellis, a member of the Sinestro Corps. A

SODAM YAT *The latest host of the Ion power is a superpowered Daxamite.*

shell-shocked Rayner became easy prey for a takeover by the fear entity, Parallax. On the anti-matter world of Qward, Rayner/Parallax killed attacking Green Lanterns while the Anti-Monitor performed experiments on the Ion entity, now purged from Rayner's body. The Green Lantern Corps rescued Ion from Qward, and later found a way to chase Parallax from Rayner's soul. The Guardians needed a new champion to wield the powers of Ion. The Daxamite Sodam Yat—hailed as the "ultimate Green Lantern"—became the willpower entity's latest host. During the Sinestro Corps war, Sodam Yat faced off against Superman-Prime. The two combatants battled along the eastern seaboard of America. Yat fell prey to the only weakness of Daxamites, suffering lead poisoning in a fight in a nuclear reactor.

He recovered, but struggles to the limits of his power as Ion.
DW

INVISIBLE KID

FIRST APPEARANCE ACTION COMICS #267 (August 1960)
STATUS Hero   **REAL NAME** Lyle Norg
OCCUPATION Legionnaire   **BASE** Legion World, U.P. Space
HEIGHT 5ft 6in   **WEIGHT** 140 lbs   **EYES** Brown   **HAIR** Brown
SPECIAL POWERS/ABILITIES Able to make all or part of his body invisible and, with great effort, is also capable of rendering others unseen.

Earthling Lyle Norg's prodigious interest in physics led him to the discovery of a serum that rendered him invisible at will by bending light around himself and his clothing to conceal either part or all of his body. His father, an officer with the United Planets' Science Police, tried to turn the serum over to Earth's repressive government, but Lyle ran away from home to join the Legion Of Super-Heroes as Invisible Kid. The Legion, which stood for independence and rebellion, welcomed Lyle into their ranks, though many Legionnaires viewed him with suspicion due to his inexperience and the stealthy nature of his powers. Invisible Kid found his closest peer to be Brainiac 5, who shared his genius for genetics and technology. He also developed a crush on Legion leader Supergirl during her time-traveling stay in the 31st century. When the alien Dominators invaded Earth, the Legionnaires teamed with the Wanderers to fight back. Invisible Kid lost his arm when his flight ring exploded, and temporarily wore a replacement limb taken from an alien donor. **DW**

IRON CROSS

FIRST APPEARANCE JUSTICE LEAGUE TASK FORCE #10 (March 1994)
STATUS Villain   **REAL NAME** Unrevealed
OCCUPATION Mercenary   **BASE** Mobile
HEIGHT 6ft 4in   **WEIGHT** 230 lbs   **EYES** Brown   **HAIR** Brown
SPECIAL POWERS/ABILITIES Appears to have meta-human strength and endurance, the limits of which have not been determined.

Pine Heights, Nebraska, seemed a quiet place, perfect to hide a white supremacist organization known as the Aryan Brigade. The group first caught the U.S. government's attention when it developed a virus designed to wipe out all people of non-European origin. The government, in turn, asked for the JL Task Force's help (see Justice League of America). A team consisting of Martian Manhunter, Elongated Man, Black Canary, Gypsy, and Hourman I took on the Brigade. Iron Cross was the Aryan team's major muscle; however, little or nothing was known about his background. He nearly proved a match for the Manhunter but finally beaten. He was subsequently recruited by the   for the second incarnation of the Cadre. The Joker killed Iron Cross on a prison planet during Operation: Salvation Run. **RG**

IRONS, NATASHA

FIRST APPEARANCE STEEL (2nd series) #1 (February 1994)
STATUS Hero **REAL NAME** Natasha Jasmine Irons
OCCUPATION Adventurer **BASE** Metropolis
HEIGHT 5ft 2in **WEIGHT** 106 lbs **EYES** Brown **HAIR** Black
SPECIAL POWERS/ABILITIES Wears armor that interacts with Metropolis's future tech, enabling her to grow 60ft tall and to fly. Metagene allows flight, enhanced strength, and the projection of light bursts and energy barriers.

A genius, a novice, a legacy. Natasha Irons is the niece of John Henry Irons (see Steel II) who, before his tragic death, owned a high-tech laboratory called the Steelworks in Metropolis's Suicide Slum. She spent her teenage years working alongside her uncle. Her cool, unconcerned façade concealed a scientist of formidable intellect, and her uncle was perhaps unaware that Natasha was in fact nearly as smart as he was. Despite Steel's best intentions, Natasha was drawn into the meta-human world. On more than one occasion she unobtrusively helped him in his role as the super hero Steel, working alongside the Justice League of America, the world's greatest hero team of heroes. She endured being exposed to the superstrength drug Tar, which briefly provides humans with enhanced strength but with addictive results, though she now seems fully recovered.

When John Henry was returned to Earth after being in Darkseid's thrall he chose to devote himself full time to being an inventor and engineer, and he crafted a new suit of armor, which Natasha happily donned. After the Infinite Crisis, Natasha received superpowers in Lex Luthor's Everyman Project (see Luthor, Lex) and briefly served with the new Infinity, INC. **RG**

ISIS

FIRST APPEARANCE 52 #3 (2006) **STATUS** Hero (deceased)
REAL NAME Adrianna Tomaz
OCCUPATION Super hero **BASE** Khandaq
HEIGHT 5ft 10in **WEIGHT** 139 lbs **EYES** Brown **HAIR** Brown
SPECIAL POWERS/ABILITIES Flight, super-strength, resistance to injury, healing abilities, power over nature.

BLACK ADAM was keen to make Isis part of his new "family," along with Osiris and Sobek.

Adrianna Tomaz first met Black Adam as a prisoner, captured by Intergang and presented to the superpowered Khandaq ruler as a slave. But he freed her, and she wasted no time confronting him about his confrontational style. The two fell in love, and Black Adam used the Amulet of Isis to transform Tomaz into a super hero. After their wedding, Isis and Adam located Isis's younger brother Amon, who became the gifted OSIRIS and the third member of the Black Marvel Family.

Their happiness ended when the Four Horsemen of Apokolips killed both Isis and Osiris, triggering Black Adam's descent into madness. An obsessed Adam later tried to resurrect Isis by immersing her corpse in a Lazarus Pit. He then traveled to the four corners of the Earth to retrieve missing pieces of her skeleton. Although Black Adam believed his quest was a failure, Felix Faust successfully restored Isis to a live as his mind-controlled servant. Because she possesses the abilities of many gods from the Egyptian pantheon, Isis' connection to mystical energies is unusually strong – indicating that death will not retain its hold on her for long. **DW**

AMID PUBLIC rejoicing, banners flew from Black Adam's palace in Shiruta, capital of Kahndaq, in celebration of his marriage to Isis.

THE JOKER

THE CLOWN PRINCE OF CRIME

FIRST APPEARANCE BATMAN #1 (Spring 1940)
STATUS Villain   **REAL NAME** Unknown
BASE Gotham City
OCCUPATION Anarchist; mass-murderer; professional criminal
HEIGHT 6ft 5in   **WEIGHT** 192 lbs   **EYES** Green   **HAIR** Green
SPECIAL POWERS/ABILITIES
Though not especially strong or skilled in fighting, the Joker is nonetheless a deadly combatant. Previously, he has demonstrated adeptness at chemistry, concocting his own poisonous Joker Venom, a weapon of mass distraction that leaves its victims with death-rictuses resembling his own maniacal leer. The Joker often wields deadly joke props or gags such as an acid-squirting boutonnière or BANG!-proclaiming flag pistol that doubles as a spear gun. However, he also plays the straight man in his blackly comedic campaigns of terror and will use conventional weapons—anything from a single-shot Derringer tucked in the brim of his hat to an operational nuclear warhead concealed within the trunk of his garish Jokermobile.

THE JOKER IS UNDENIABLY the most dangerous and unpredictable foe BATMAN has ever encountered. He literally reinvents himself each morning, concocting deadly new laugh-riots to bedevil the Dark Knight and his allies. While safely confined within the impregnable walls of Arkham Asylum for the Criminally Insane, the Joker has spun investigating psychiatrists various yarns concerning his troubled origins. Most of his tales can be dismissed, but a few facts remain that give some insight into how this leering lunatic came into being.

TWO-GUN CLOWN
The Joker mocks the Dynamic Duo in an early Detective Comics' cover appearance.

THE JOKER'S ORIGINS

The man who would become the Clown Prince of Crime was once a petty thief duped into donning the mask of the Red Hood and acting as costumed figurehead to thugs bent on robbing the Ace Chemical Plant in Gotham City. In that regard, he may have been a failed comedian coerced to crime following the sudden and tragic deaths of his wife and unborn child. Only the Joker knows the truth. Thwarted by Batman, the Red Hood fell into a vat of toxic chemicals that bleached his skin bone white, turned his hair emerald green, and left him with a crazed, ruby-red, malignant rictus for a smile. Driven utterly insane, the Joker fixated upon Batman as his arch-nemesis and has broken practically every law in Gotham City and beyond.

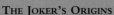
CHEMICAL PEEL *The Red Hood crawls from a toxic bath. From now on, villainy will wear a leering face.*

MASS MURDER, MALIGNANCY, AND MAYHEM

The Joker is probably the only criminal ever to qualify as a mass murderer, spree slayer, and serial killer. And that's just before lunch. He has committed robberies, assaults, extortion, and all manner of crime. His victims are innumerable. The Bat-Family especially has suffered from the Joker's sick humor. In a fit of anarchic glee, the Joker killed the second ROBIN (Jason Todd), beating him near to death with a crowbar before blowing the poor Boy Wonder and his mother to smithereens. He shot Barbara Gordon (Oracle) through the spine, ending her crime-fighting career as Batgirl. The Clown Prince of Crime then photographed Barbara's bleeding body, hoping the images would drive her kidnapped father, Commissioner Gordon, insane.

THE JOKER'S WEAPONS

The Clown Prince of Crime has no compunction against using weapons of mass destruction, including his own patented Laughing Gas, a nerve toxin that kills within seconds and leaves his victims giggling themselves to death. Not long ago, the Joker was imprisoned for attempting to bomb Broadway with a tactical nuclear weapon.

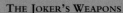

KILLING JOKE *The unsuspecting Barbara Gordon is viciously gunned down by the Joker as she opens her front door.*

HARLEY QUINN

Before he met Dr. Harleen Quinzel, the Joker's court-appointed psychotherapist, the Joker was more concerned with making mayhem than whoopee. But in Quinzel, he found a kindred spirit, winning her over to his side of the lunatic fringe. As Harley Quinn, she became murderous moll to the Joker's guffawing gangster. However, the Joker and Harley are now estranged, reuniting under passion, and breaking up when he tries to beat her to the punchline… often with a mallet!

ARKHAM ASYLUM

Certifiably crazed, the Joker was previously remanded to Gotham's Arkham Asylum for the Criminally Insane. However, Arkham has long suffered an almost revolving-door policy where its more dangerous charges are concerned, especially the Clown Prince of Crime. Despite his officially documented mental state, the Joker is cunning and crafty, knowing full well how to manipulate Arkham's doctors and administrators to achieve his anarchic ends.

THAT CERTAIN SMILE *The Joker enjoys putting on a happy face when his favorite foe Batman pays him a visit in his Arkham cell!*

PSYCHO KILLER *During No Man's Land, the Joker used defenseless babies to lure Commissioner Gordon's wife, Sarah, to her doom, shooting her in cold blood.*

PARTNERS IN CRIME *While most villains do not (or cannot) trust the Joker, some of Batman's arch-foes, including Rā's al Ghūl, have collaborated with him when it suits their roguish interests.*

THE LAST LAUGH

After gassing hundreds of victims during the "Last Laugh" event on the belief that he had a terminal disease, the Joker suffered a brutal beating from Jason Todd, who had returned from the dead after his murder at the Joker's hands. At the end of the Infinite Crisis, the Joker killed enemy mastermind Alexander Luthor.

Later shot in the face by a Batman impostor, the Joker spent months in the hospital rebuilding his body and psyche. Now more dangerous than ever, the Joker helped organize the latest incarnation of the Injustice League before the U.S. government exiled him and dozens of fellow villains to the distant planet Salvation." SB

PUSHED TOO FAR *Though he realizes it might be the death of him, the Joker continues to hurt those whom Batman cares about most.*

KEY STORYLINES

- **THE JOKER #1-9 (MAY 1975–SEPTEMBER 1976):** The Joker becomes the first Bat-Villain to star in his own comic book series, lasting nine issues.
- **BATMAN #426-429 (DECEMBER 1988–JANUARY 1989):** The Joker murders Jason Todd, the second Robin, leading Batman to pursue the Clown Prince.
- **BATMAN: THE KILLING JOKE (1988):** The Joker's origins are explored as he cripples Barbara Gordon to prove a point to the Dark Knight.
- **JOKER: THE DEVIL'S ADVOCATE (1996):** The Joker is finally made responsible for his sins and sentenced to Death Row, but for a crime he did not commit!

THE JUSTICE LEAGUE OF AMERICA

THE WORLD'S GREATEST HEROES

First appearance THE BRAVE & THE BOLD #28 (March 1960)
Status Team of Earth's greatest heroes
Base The JLA Watchtower, the Moon
Founder members and powers
Superman The Man of Steel; possessor of superpowers beyond those of mortal men.
Martian Manhunter Alien telepath; shape-changer; gifted with strength, flight, and enhanced vision.
Batman The Dark Knight; master combatant and strategist, coordinating the team's counterattacks.
Wonder Woman Princess from Themyscira; gifted with strength, speed, wisdom, and flight by the gods themselves.
Aquaman King of the Seven Seas; has incredible strength, ability to mentally control sea life, and a mystic hand.
Green Lantern V Wielder of the emerald power ring; protector of space sector 2814.
Flash III The fastest man alive, capable of hyper-velocities; channels the Speed Force to fight crime; Speed Force surrounds him with a frictionless protective aura.

They are Earth's premier defense team and for the last decade have seen to it that the basic human rights of liberty and justice remain paramount to all citizens. They are the Justice League of America, comprised of the best of the best. Ever since Superman ushered in the modern heroic age, Earth has needed protection, from megalomaniac supervillains and especially, from greedy alien tyrants with hitherto undreamed-of technologies and nightmarish weapons of mass destruction. Even when the team has suffered internal strife, they have rallied, recognizing their obligations to all of mankind. Their reputation has spread not only beyond this solar system but beyond this plane of existence.

PREMIER LEAGUE *The JLA heroes first came together to battle a giant alien starfish!*

JUSTICE LEAGUE DETROIT
Being a super hero is a tough life! Various stresses in the personal lives of the team caused rifts from time to time. In the wake of an invasion by the alien Debris, the JLA was reorganized by Aquaman, who called for full-time commitment from each League member. In the aftermath, only Aquaman, the Elongated Man, the Martian Manhunter, and Zatanna remained. However, the roster soon began to expand when Steel I, Vibe, and the Vixen joined. Hank Heywood I, Steel's grandfather and namesake, offered the JLA headquarters in a warehouse in Detroit that became known as the Bunker. This incarnation of the League was tragically cut short when Vibe and Steel II were killed in action.

THE DETROIT LINEUP *(clockwise from top)*
Martian Manhunter, Zatanna, Steel II, Elongated Man, Vixen, Vibe, Gypsy, Aquaman.

THE FIRST INCARNATION
When Earth was threatened by Appellax aliens, the Martian Manhunter, Flash II, Green Lantern II, Aquaman, and Black Canary II joined forces as the JLA to defeat these invaders. Inspired by the appearance of these powerful new heroes, J'Onn J'Onzz ended decades of hiding, publicly appearing as the Martian Manhunter. A short time later, plasma aliens invaded Earth, and the hero Triumph gathered Superman, the Martian Manhunter, Flash II, Green Lantern II, Aquaman, and Black Canary II to defeat them. During the fight, Triumph was trapped in a temporal anomaly and disappeared from the timestream.

THE SECRET SANCTUARY
The team's first headquarters, the Secret Sanctuary, was in Rhode Island, and secretly financed by Oliver Queen (the first Green Arrow). A teenage "cool cat" called Lucas "Snapper" Carr helped install the team's high-tech gear, designed by Ted Kord (later Blue Beetle II). Snapper became the team's official mascot. After functioning as JLA members in all but name, Superman and Batman formally joined.

JL INTERNATIONAL
This team was discredited by Glorious Godfrey's smear campaign, but a more powerful line-up was introduced, with the enigmatic Maxwell Lord pulling the strings. The United Nations formally recognized the JLA as global peacekeepers. Later, the JLI split into two branches, Justice League America and Justice League Europe. Lord decided to make use of the reformed members of the Injustice League, along with the former alien Green Lantern G'nort and the Scarlet Skier, as the short-lived Justice League Antarctica. The entire JLA, its reserves, and the JSA stopped Sonar's bid for power in Europe. Afterwards, Justice League Europe took the name Justice League International. The U.N. authorized the creation of a JL Task Force, a team led by the Martian Manhunter, intended for use on missions calling for discretion, and one which would recruit most members for a single case.

TOWER OF POWER
JL International continued to add team members, dispatching them via embassies scattered around the seven continents.

TASK FORCE *J'onn J'onzz supervised a team of fledgling heroes, training them between crises.*

DEFENDERS OF EARTH

The League continued to expand and contract as circumstances demanded, with a Justice League West unit led by CAPTAIN ATOM, a later addition. At the request of the U.N., the various Justice League splinter groups disbanded and Superman, Batman, Wonder Woman, Aquaman, the Martian Manhunter, Flash III, and Green Lantern V were acknowledged as the official JLA. They built a base on the moon known as the Watchtower.

As the external threats facing the world and its citizens grow more and more extreme, the JLA has sworn to repulse all threats from space or from parallel worlds. The League continually redefines the scope of its mission; thanks to the JLA's selfless, heroic protection, humanity continues to prosper.

VIRTUE AND VICE
The JLA and JSA combine to battle an evil conspiracy—apparently from within their own heroic ranks!

BRUTAL BATTLE *The JLA has faced all manner of opponents, from common criminals to intergalactic conquerors, but none has challenged them more than the Quantum Mechanics from another reality.*

THE JLA OF THE FUTURE

By the 853rd century, the Justice Legion A will be the premier protectors of the solar system. They will be aided by the Justice Legions B, L, S, X, Super-Zoomorphs, Union, Young Justice Legion S, and Primate Legion.

LATEST LINEUP

From their Watchtower on the moon, the JLA continues to monitor activity on Earth, dispatching the team as required. Their ranks have swelled to include the Native American mystic Manitou Raven and the reformed criminal Major Disaster. Others, such as the ATOM, remain available on an as-needed basis.

KEY STORYLINES

- *JUSTICE LEAGUE OF AMERICA #21–22 (1963):* The JLA teams up with the veteran heroes of the Golden Age, The Justice Society of America.
- *JUSTICE LEAGUE OF AMERICA #140-144 (MARCH–JULY 1977):* The planet Oa's Manhunter Robots threaten not only Earth but Oa as well!
- *JLA YEAR ONE (TPB, 1998):* Five distinct super heroes learn how to become a team.
- *JLA: WORLD WAR III (TPB, 2001):* Mageddon comes to Earth and it takes the JLA, plus many others committed to the cause, to save mankind.
- *JLA/JSA: VIRTUE AND VICE (TPB, 2001):* Earth's premier teams take on the combined threat of Johnny Sorrow and an enraged Despero.

THE JUSTICE LEAGUE OF AMERICA

Current members and powers (2008)

Black Canary (chairwoman) Ultrasonic, earsplitting "canary cry"; martial arts and boxing expert

Superman The Man of Steel; possessor of numerous superpowers.

Batman The Dark Knight; master combatant and strategist, coordinating the team's counterattacks.

Wonder Woman Princess from Themyscira; gifted with strength, speed, wisdom, and flight by the gods.

Green Lantern (John Stewart) Wielder of the emerald power ring; protector of space sector 2814.

The Flash (Wally West) The fastest man alive, capable of hyper-velocities; channels the Speed Force to fight crime.

Black Lightning Internally-generated electromagnetic field; can create and hurl bolts of supercharged electricity

Geo-Force Superhuman strength and powers of endurance; can fly, alter gravity, and project powerful blasts of heat from his hands

Hawkgirl Gravity-defying Nth metal belt enables flight on giant wings; adept hand-to-hand combatant

Red Arrow A top archer; expert with most projectile weapons

Red Tornado Can generate cyclones; some control over the weather.

Vixen Tantu totem gives her animal abilities.

CRISIS OF CONSCIENCE

After countless wins against the universe's most terrifying foes, infighting ultimately crippled the Justice League of America. With the shocking murder of Sue Dibny (wife of former member Elongated Man), a long-buried incident from the League's early years came to shameful light. At that time, the JLA members agreed to use Zatanna's magic to forcibly alter the memories and personality of Doctor Light, in response to the villain's assault on Sue. When Batman objected to the act, Zatanna had mind-wiped him too. The League imprisoned Jean Loring for Sue Dibny's murder, but the dubious morality of Zatanna's actions created a rift among the League. Batman was one of the most outspoken believers that the JLA had irrevocably betrayed its principles. With no trust remaining, the League members couldn't function as a team. An attack by the Secret Society of Super Villains—all of them victims of JLA brainwashing—became the trigger to the League's dissolution. The final blow came on the eve of the Infinite Crisis, when Superboy-Prime destroyed the lunar Watchtower headquarters.

MINDWIPE Erasing Doctor Light's memories created a rift in the Justice League.

PAYING RESPECTS *The super-hero community came out in force for Sue Dibny's funeral.*

MYSTERY MISSION *Even Superman, who had known the Legionnaires since childhood, could not uncover the reason behind their 21st-century visit.*

THE LIGHTNING SAGA

The newest League's first official mission saw it teaming up with the Justice Society of America and the Legion of Super Heroes. The latter group had traveled back in time one thousand years to restore a lost champion by using lightning rods and 31st century science. Superman, who had befriended the Legionnaires during his youth, set the tone for team interaction by countering Batman's suspicion of the Legion's cryptic plans. The affair ended with all three groups welcoming the return of Wally West, the third Flash, from an alternate dimension. Wally accepted a position with the new League, filling the JLA's need for a speedster.

TRINITY *Wonder Woman, Superman, and Batman assemble the latest JLA.*

A NEW START

Months after the Infinite Crisis, Firestorm made an abortive attempt to reform the JLA with third-string heroes including Ambush Bug, Bulleteer, Firehawk, and Super-Chief (who died in one of the team's only missions). But the true Justice League of America took shape again following the "World War III" affair, forged by backbone members Superman, Batman, and Wonder Woman. The three founders voted on the League's new roster, but simultaneous events helped pull together the worthy among the current heroic generation.

The theft of Red Tornado's android body spurred Black Canary, Green Lantern Hal Jordan, and Red Arrow (Roy Harper, formerly known as Arsenal) to aid in the hunt. Meanwhile, suspicious activity among Parasite, Doctor Impossible, and other supervillains drew the attentions of Vixen, Black Lightning, and Hawkgirl. Together the teams uncovered an elaborate plot from cybernetic genius Professor Ivo, who had determined a way to control others using technological replicas of the "starro" probes familiar as the trademarks of the alien Star Conqueror. Ivo's mind-puppets helped him piece together a composite android body that incorporated components from both Red Tornado and Amazo. This virtually unstoppable composite was to house the consciousness of Solomon Grundy, the mountainous zombie.

RETURN TO DUTY *Vixen also served with the Detroit incarnation of the JLA.*

BACK FROM LIMBO *Wally and Iris West and their twins returned from another dimension, thanks to Superman and his teammates.*

POWERED UP *Vixen easily dispatches an Amazo robot.*

WATCHTOWER
The satellite houses observational and training facilities.

THE NEW HQ

The heroes united to stop Ivo, and all accepted formal Justice League invitations soon after. To mark this new era, the JLA constructed a dual headquarters to replace its lost moon base. In high Earth orbit stood a reconstructed Watchtower satellite, containing a training room with the ability to replicate any environment or threat as a holograph. Groundside, a hall of Justice announced the JLA's presence in Washington DC, and featured a trophy room of captured (and deactivated) supervillain gadgetry. A "slideways" teleporter linked both facilities, accessed simply by stepping through a nearly-imperceptible energy portal. Similar portals could be activated from the Batcave and other secure locations, allowing instantaneous member travel in emergencies. RG/DW

ANTI-TRINITY *The Joker, Lex Luthor, and Cheetah assembled the Injustice League.*

THE INJUSTICE LEAGUE

Black Canary, the current chairwoman, led the Justice League of America into its most dangerous confrontation against its mirror opposite. Lex Luthor, the Joker, and Cheetah teamed up to create the Injustice League Unlimited, the latest incarnation of the murderous cabal which counted dozens of supervillains in its roster. Operating from a skull-shaped dome deep in the Florida everglades, the Injustice League fired its first shot before the JLA could counterattack, nearly killing Firestorm on the eve of the wedding of Black Canary and Green Arrow. With the JLA now counting Geo-Force and Green Lantern John Stewart among its members, the two teams clashed fast and forcefully.

The Injustice League withdrew, yet remains active. With the leadership of Luthor, the madcap ingenuity of the Joker, and the muscle of nearly every prominent member of the supervillain community, the Injustice League Unlimited will prove a match for the Justice League for years to come.

TROPHY ROOM *Continuing a longstanding JLA tradition, relics from past victories line one chamber in the Hall of Justice.*

WORLD'S FINEST *Top row (left to right): Green Lantern, Wonder Woman, Superman, Batman, Black Canary. Bottom row (left to right): Hawkgirl, Black Lightning, Red Arrow, Vixen, Red Tornado.*

THE JUSTICE SOCIETY OF AMERICA

THE BEST OF THE BEST

FIRST APPEARANCE ALL-STAR COMICS #3 (Winter 1940)
STATUS Hero team
BASE New York City
FOUNDER MEMBERS AND POWERS:
The Spectre Near-omnipotent control over space and time, but bound to a human host.
Doctor Fate Connection with the Lord of Order Nabu allows Fate to manipulate vast magical forces.
Sandman I Sharp detective's mind and dreams that can foretell the future; wields a gas gun that puts victims to sleep.
The Atom Expert boxer and hand-to-hand combatant; after the war gained super-strength and a radioactive "atomic punch."
Hourman I Superhuman strength, speed, and stamina for one hour as a result of ingesting a Miraclo pill.

OTHER MEMBERS HAVE INCLUDED:
Green Lantern, the Flash, Hawkman, Johnny Thunder, Doctor Mid-Nite, Mister Terrific, Hawkgirl, Starman, Miss America, Hippolyta, Atom-Smasher, Mister Terrific II, Star-Spangled Kid II, Stargirl, Black Canary II, Captain Marvel, Power Girl (see page 186 for current lineup).

THEY ARE THE WORLD'S FIRST and greatest super-group, formed at a time when "meta-humans" were still a new concept and free people everywhere faced the threat of annihilation from Adolf Hitler's Third Reich. They have survived throughout the decades, waxing and waning in synch with the national character to reflect the public's love–hate relationship with its super heroes. Several of the founding members are active today, even as they enter their nineties, thanks to a time-slowing radiation bath received during an early case. Living legends, they are the standard-bearers for all who followed in their footsteps. They are the Justice Society of America, the only hero team that Superman looks up to.

THE BEGINNING *With a cry of "For America and democracy," the JSA begins its adventures.*

WINGED WONDER *Hawkman's physical and mental strength make him the backbone of the JSA.*

A WORLD AT WAR
Costumed crime fighters started appearing in the late 1930s; by November of 1940 the numbers of these "mystery men," as they were called, had grown to permit the formation of the JSA. Eight of the U.S.'s top heroes—Green Lantern, the Flash, the Spectre, Doctor Fate, the Sandman I, the Atom, Hourman I, and Hawkman—banded together to stop Hitler's invasion of Britain and save President Roosevelt from Nazi assassins. The JSA continued to battle the Axis powers. In the wake of Pearl Harbor, the U.S. government established the All-Star Squadron, which brought together every costumed hero.

AN EVER-CHANGING LINEUP
The JSA became one of the All-Star Squadron's active sub-groups. During this time the JSA also went by the alternate name of the Justice Battalion. Throughout the war, members came and went as they cycled through active, reserve, and honorary status. Prominent JSAers included Johnny Thunder, Doctor Mid-Nite I, Mister Terrific I, Hawkgirl, Starman, Miss America, and the time-traveling Hippolyta, the Golden Age Wonder Woman.

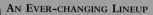

NO MORE HEROES
The All-Star Squadron ceased to exist after V-J Day, but the JSA remained, battling major villains such as Vandal Savage, and its villainous counterpart, the Injustice Society. However, now the war was over, public tolerance for super heroics was fading fast. In 1951, a joint congressional Un-American Activities Committee accused the JSA of harboring communist sympathies and demanded that its members publicly unmask as a sign of their patriotism. They refused, and regretfully retired the Justice Society. Decades passed, the flame of organized crime fighting kept alive through non-superpowered teams such as the Sea Devils and the Challengers of the Unknown and lesser lights like the Justice Experience. The JSA still existed, however, occasionally reforming for special cases.

ON THEIR WAY OUT *The retirement of the JSA marked the end of the Golden Age of super heroes.*

RAGNAROK!
The JSA seemed to have met its final end when the Flash, Green Lantern, Hawkman, Hawkgirl, the Atom, Doctor Mid-Nite, Hourman, Johnny Thunder, Starman, the Sandman, Wildcat, and Sand agreed to battle gods for all eternity in Limbo to prevent Ragnarok, the end of the world. Luckily "eternity" lasted only a couple of years, and the JSA soon returned. The crisis known as Zero Hour (*see* Great Battles, pp. 186-7) proved a deadlier threat. The villain Extant killed the Atom, Doctor Mid-Nite, and Hourman, and Flash and Green Lantern declared an end to the JSA.

THE MODERN ERA

The DARK LORD Mordru's murder of the Sandman triggered a new formation of the JSA, featuring old stalwarts (the Flash, Green Lantern, Wildcat, Hawkman, Sand), skilled veterans (Atom-Smasher), and new faces (Mister Terrific II, Star-Spangled Kid II, plus reincarnated versions of Doctor Fate and Hawkgirl). This JSA's greatest challenge was the "Darkness" crisis, in which Mordru, Obsidian, and Eclipso tried to plunge the world into eternal night.

INVASION *Black Adam made short work of Khandaq's defenders.*

FIGHTING THE GOOD FIGHT

The Black Reign incident deeply affected the JSA, causing many of them to struggle with the concepts of righteousness and appropriate force. Captain Marvel used the aftermath as an opportunity to tender his resignation. The group is still vital, however, as shown by the observations of the time-traveling villain Per Degaton, who recently visited several key JSA members to tell them that he had witnessed their deaths in the far future.

Significantly, Degaton admitted that, throughout all of future history, he was never able to defeat the JSA, and confided to Jay Garrick (the first Flash) that he "died like a man" in whatever fate yet awaits the Flash. Regardless of the predictions of would-be prognosticators, the multi-generational JSA will continue its fight against injustice and polish its reputation as the only super hero team that operates like an extended family.

DARKNESS FALLS
Obsidian's filial anger toward his father, Green Lantern, provided an added edge to the battle.

BLACK REIGN

The JSA's law-and-order approach to crime fighting is not universally revered. A vigilante team consisting of Black Adam, Eclipso, Northwind, Brainwave II, and Atom-Smasher recently took the law into their own hands. They spearheaded a violent coup in the terrorist nation of Kahndaq to put an end to their colleagues' meddling. In so doing they exposed the villainous manipulations of the Venusian worm, Mister Mind.

THE JSA 1) *Green Lantern I* 2) *Mr. Terrific II* 3) *Dr. Mid-Nite II* 4) *Sand* 5) *Hawkman* 6) *Hawkgirl* 7) *Atom-Smasher* 8) *Dr. Fate* 9) *Stargirl* 10) *Black Canary II* 11) *Flash I* 12) *Wildcat*

KEY STORYLINES

• *LAST DAYS OF THE JUSTICE SOCIETY SPECIAL (1986):* The JSA battles in an eternal Ragnarok in what was intended to be the team's final adventure.

• *ZERO HOUR: CRISIS IN TIME #3 (SEPTEMBER 1994):* Three of the JSA's oldest members perish in an issue that once again appeared to have killed off the team forever.

• *JSA #1 (AUGUST 1999):* The JSA returns in triumphant form in the first issue of the 'Justice Be Done' storyline.

THE JUSTICE SOCIETY OF AMERICA

CURRENT MEMBERS AND POWERS (2008)

Power Girl (chairwoman): Flight, super-strength, enhanced speed, and invulnerability.

Green Lantern I Wields solidified emerald energy generated by the Starheart.

Flash I Runs at super-speeds and vibrates through objects.

Wildcat I Championship boxer with mystical "nine lives."

Dr. Mid-Nite II Can see in non-visible wavelengths of light.

Mister Terrific Olympic-level athlete and genius in every field.

Hawkman Wings and harness made of anti-gravity Nth metal.

Sandman Transforms into sand-like form and can travel along the Earth's fault lines; sees the future through dreams.

Hourman Super strength, enhanced speed, and increased durability for one hour.

Liberty Belle Super-speed, enhanced strength.

Obsidian Can transform himself into an intangible shadow form.

Stargirl Cosmic staff projects energy and allows flight.

Jakeem Thunder Controls powerful, fifth-dimensional genie.

Starman Can increase the mass and gravity of objects.

Cyclone Can fly and generate tornados by controlling the wind.

Damage Enhanced reflexes and strength; emits power bursts.

Citizen Steel Super strength, indestructible organic steel shell.

Wildcat III (Tommy Bronson) Can transform into a werecat.

THE OLD GUARD *Green Lantern, the Flash, and Wildcat put together the newest Justice Society.*

REBIRTH

The Justice Society of America lay dormant following the Infinite Crisis, with many of its members swept up in the global fight to stop Black Adam known as World War III. JSA founders Green Lantern (Alan Scott), Flash (Jay Garrick), and Wildcat (Ted Grant) selected the aftermath as an opportunity to reform the group, taking a cue from Superman, Batman, and Wonder Woman who had simultaneously chosen to launch a new Justice League of America. The underlying tenet of the new JSA was a simple one: "the world needs better good guys."

With an eye for respect, family, and heart, the surviving JSA founders selected the latest lineup. The intergenerational legacies of the heroic age expressed themselves through the election of junior members including Damage (Grant Emerson, son of the original Atom), Starman (Thom Kallor, time-traveling inheritor of the Golden Age name), and the teenage wind-witch Cyclone (Maxine Hunkel, granddaughter of original Red Tornado Ma Hunkel). Others signed on to serve with a team that had welcomed them in the past, including Power Girl, Dr. Mid-Nite, Mister Terrific, Stargirl, Jakeem Thunder, Obsidian, Sandman, and the husband-and-wife team of Hourman and Liberty Belle, both of whom carry on the costumed identities of their respective parents. The new JSA lived up to its billing as a "society," not putting a limit on its sprawling roster. They began operating out of new headquarters in New York City's Battery Park, where they became a vital part of the neighborhood.

RED ALERT *The Justice Society scrambles to tackle a crisis. Its membership includes many legacy heroes now wearing the costumed identities of their late relatives.*

ARKHAM NIGHTMARE
Starman battled Doctor Destiny to rescue Dream Girl from the infamous asylum.

THE LIGHTNING SAGA

The JSA soon learned that Starman wasn't the only hero with ties to the far future. In Arkham Asylum, Starman helped rescue Dream Girl, his teammate from the Legion of Super-Heroes. Still more members of the Legion had made their way 1,000 years into the past and made their presence known. Earlier in the team's history the Legionnaires had brought one of their own back from the dead by channeling electricity into lightning rods—now, in an apparent duplicate performance, Legion members gathered around the globe to enable the return of another hero. The Justice Society, The Justice League, and the Legion joined forces—despite early misunderstandings between the three teams—and performed a ritual that successfully Wally West, the third Flash, back to life. The junior members of the JSA continued to grow into their roles under the mentorship of their elders. Citizen Steel learned that his new body was more than just a metallic prison when he rescued university students from a hostage standoff. Damage faced down his demons with help from Liberty Belle when he pursued the super-villain Zoom into Atlanta Georgia—a city he had nearly destroyed years before with his out-of-control powers.

ATLANTA STANDOFF *Damage defeated his nemesis Zoom when Liberty Belle convinced him to look past his pain and see the hero inside himself.*

TEAMS UNITED *The Lightning Saga saw the JSA team up with the Justice League and the Legion of Super-Heroes.*

THE FIRST TO FALL
Mister America's death launched the new JSA on its first case.

CALL TO ACTION

The Society's inaugural mission centered on a plot by Vandal Savage to stamp out bloodlines of the surviving Golden Age mystery men and their immediate relatives. Vandal's first victims included Mr. America, General Glory, and the Minute-Man. During the course of this mission, Wildcat discovered a grown son he'd never known—Tommy Branson. Upon first meeting, Bronson expressed no desire to follow his father into the family business. Once involved in a fight with Savage, however, Branson's own powers were revealed. He transformed through lycanthropy into a literal wildcat. Tommy joined the JSA under his father's name, becoming the third hero to take on the Wildcat identity.

LIKE FATHER, LIKE SON *Tommy Bronson didn't want to follow Ted Grant into superheroics, but his animalistic powers made him the only one who could stop Vandal Savage.*

MAN OF STEEL *Although disoriented by his trip through the multiverse, the original Superman soon proved his heroism.*

THE MULTIVERSE AND BEYOND

The existence of the multiverse hit home when the Justice Society extinguished a factory fire; accidentally summoning a Superman from a parallel Earth. This Superman, drawn through a miniature black hole from a reality known as Earth-22, remembered a grim near-future in which heroes had fought heroes in the face of fearful public resentment. In the Justice Society of America, this Superman found an example of the hopeful camaraderie his world had lost. **DW**

SAVAGE VENGEANCE

Vandal Savage's next Golden Age targets were in Ohio. Savage hired the neo-Nazis of the Fourth Reich to wipe out the family of Henry "Hank" Heywood, the original Commander Steel. Heywood's grandson Nate assisted Hawkman in fighting off the attackers, but became infected by living molten metal when he killed the villain Reichsmark. This new coating of organic steel made Nate indestructible and inhumanly strong, but—even after having a uniform sealed to his body in an iron foundry—he refused to embrace his family's military legacy. Instead, he joined the Justice Society as the first Citizen Steel. At the same time that new members found their footing, veterans took on greater responsibilities. Power Girl, a longtime JSA member, took over as the team's chairwoman.

SUPER-HERO GENOCIDE *Reichsmark and the Fourth Reich failed to wipe out the bloodline of Commander Steel.*

KILLER CROC

FIRST APPEARANCE BATMAN #357 (January 1984)
STATUS Villain **REAL NAME** Waylon Jones
OCCUPATION Alligator wrestler; gangster; murderer **BASE** Mobile
HEIGHT 7ft 5in **WEIGHT** 686 lbs **EYES** Red **HAIR** None
SPECIAL POWERS/ABILITIES Near superhuman strength; dense, but not
invulnerable, skin; razor-sharp teeth and claws; expert wrestler.

Born with a disease that made his skin green and scaly,
Waylon Jones was raised by an alcoholic aunt in a
northern Florida slum, and was relentlessly bullied because
of his appearance. Eventually he snapped, nearly killed
one of the bullies, and was sent to a reform school. With
little education and a sociopathic hatred for all "normal"
people, Jones became a petty criminal and, by his 18th
birthday, a fully fledged murderer.

After spending nearly 20 years behind bars, Jones
was released and found work in a traveling carnival as
an alligator wrestler known as Killer Croc. Croc soon
left the carnival and moved to Gotham City aiming to
become a gangster and amass a fortune. Despite Croc
employing experienced henchmen, such
as the Riddler and the Penguin, Croc's
criminal ambitions were continually
thwarted by Batman. After each failure,
Croc's body became more reptilian and
his psyche more psychotic, until the only
fit place for him was Arkham Asylum for
the Criminally Insane.

After a devastating earthquake
destroyed nearly half of Gotham
City, Killer Croc escaped
Arkham and was one of several
inmates to claim a section of
the town as his own. Croc was
defeated by ROBIN, however,
and jailed in Blackgate
Prison. The Riddler
and Hush freed the
reptilian thug, who
attacked Batman in the
Gotham City sewers, but
Croc was captured once
more and placed in
a maximum security cell
in Blackgate. **PJ**

MUTANT MONSTER *A psychopathic circus freak, Killer
Croc's body has mutated over the years, transforming
into a more hideous, reptilian form. Hating humanity,
Killer Croc has run afoul of the Batman more than
once, always swearing vengeance on the Dark
Knight, and always ending up back
in prison.*

KILLER FROST II

FIRST APPEARANCE FURY OF FIRESTORM #20 (February 1984)
STATUS Villain **REAL NAME** Dr. Louise Lincoln
OCCUPATION Professional criminal **BASE** Mobile
HEIGHT 5ft 3in **WEIGHT** 124 lbs **EYES** Blue **HAIR** Blue
SPECIAL POWERS/ABILITIES Projects waves of hyper-intense cold from her
body; able to create sheets of ice or icicle-like projectiles.

Dr. Louise Lincoln is the second
woman to be known as Killer Frost.
Lincoln assumed the abilities and
appearance of this frigid femme
fatale from Dr. Crystal Frost,
Lincoln's friend and colleague.
Years earlier, the shy physicist
Frost was locked inside an
experimental thermofrost
chamber that altered her body chemistry and transformed
her into a coolly confident super-villain able to generate
intense cold. As Killer Frost, Crystal Frost sought revenge
against male scientists she believed were prejudiced against
women, including fellow physicist Martin Stein, one half
of Firestorm the Nuclear Man and Frost's past paramour.
Louise Lincoln, believing that her tortured friend deserved
to live more than she did, transferred the powers of Killer
Frost to herself, becoming the second Killer Frost. Like
her predecessor, Killer Frost II is driven to
absorb heat from any source,
including the warmth of
human bodies, in order to
survive. Recently
she traded her frozen soul
to NERON for colder
power and an icy look all
her own. **SB**

SEWERS *Killer Croc kidnapped young heir Edward
Lamont IV from Gotham City and took him to
the sewers, demanding a multimillion dollar ransom.
The Dark Knight battled Croc beneath Gotham's
mean streets and saved the boy, only to discover that
Killer Croc's crime had been orchestrated by Hush,
a mysterious villain with ties to Batman's past.*

KRONA

First appearance GREEN LANTERN (2nd series) #40 (October 1965)
Status Villain (discorporated)   **Real name** None
Occupation Scientist; would-be tyrant   **Base** Nekron's dimension
Height 6ft 8in   **Weight** 349 lbs   **Eyes** Blue   **Hair** Black
Special powers/abilities Immortal and invulnerable; Krona's vast psionic abilities were increased by the demon Nekron to surpass the powers of the Guardians of the Universe.

Altering reality
Defying Oan taboos, Krona sought the secrets of the universe and nearly destroyed it in the process.

More than ten billion years ago on the planet Oa, the scientist Krona ignored his people's admonition against seeking the origins of the universe. He built a temporal viewer to peel back the veil of time. What Krona saw changed the whole fabric of the universe. As he gazed transfixed at the hand of creation reaching into a star-filled cosmos, Krona's machine exploded and reality changed irrevocably. One universe became two, splitting into positive-matter and anti-matter halves. The Monitor, and his evil doppelganger, the Anti-Monitor, were born and a wave of evil engulfed the 50 million worlds of the positive-matter universe (see Great Battles, pp. 186-7).

The Oan Guardians of the Universe punished Krona by turning his body into pure energy and shooting him across the breadth of the Multiverse. Billions of years later, Krona escaped his disembodied exile and entered the dimension of the dead ruled by the demon Nekron. He restored Krona to corporeal form and gave him the power to take revenge on the Guardians. Following massive battles with the Green Lantern Corps, Green Lantern Hal Jordan forced Krona's armies back into Nekron's demonic realm. No one knows whether Krona is aware that the multiverse has returned in the wake of the Infinite Crisis. **SB**

KRYPTONITE MAN

First appearance SUPERBOY #83 (September 1960)
Status Villain   **Real name** K. Russell Abernathy
Occupation Criminal scientist   **Base** Metropolis
Height 6ft   **Weight** 185 lbs   **Eyes** Black   **Hair** Black
Special powers/abilities Enhanced strength, ability to control and emit kryptonite radiation.

The Kryptonite Man is Dr. K. Russell Abernathy, a brilliant Metropolis researcher determined to use the unique radioactivity found in the pieces of Superman's homeworld for useful purposes. His early experiments used monkeys as test subjects, but Abernathy's growing boldness led to kryptonite infecting every cell of his body. Driven insane by the radioactive poisoning, he went on a rampage until stopped by Supergirl, who had taken over Superman's duties while the Man of Steel regained his powers following the Infinite Crisis.

Incarcerated for this crime, the Kryptonite Man became the prisoner of Lex Luthor (see Luthor, Lex), who used him as a power source during his hunt for a buried Kryptonian battleship. The Kryptonite Man escaped prison a second time with help from his irradiated lab monkey. His plans to obtain funding from underworld kingpins came to an end when Jimmy Olsen (see Olsen, Jimmy) burst into his lair under the identity of "Mister Action." The Kryptonite Man gained the upper hand until the surprise arrival of Krypto, The Superdog. **DW**

KRYPTO, THE SUPERDOG

First appearance ADVENTURE COMICS #210 (March 1955)
Status Heroic, but not always good   **Real name** Krypto
Occupation Superman's best friend   **Base** Fortress of Solitude
Height 25.5in   **Weight** 40 lbs   **Eyes** Blue   **Hair** White
Special powers/abilities Under Earth's solar radiation, Krypto is as enhanced among animals as Superman is among mortals with superior strength, invulnerability, and the power of flight.

In the doghouse
Lois discovers that having a super-powerful pooch to stay in the apartment definitely has its drawbacks.

Superman is believed to have met Krypto during his brief infancy on Krypton. After the planet's destruction, the El's family pet somehow traveled to Earth. He soon re-established contact with Kal-El, sharing many of his powers including flight, super-strength, and heat vision. With the sun's radiation enhancing his abilities, Krypto proved to be too exuberant for Superman's Metropolis apartment. Superman has installed his pet in his arctic Fortress of Solitude, although as the occasions require, he is freed to participate in adventures such as the recent Imperiex War (see Great Battles, pp. 186-7).

Krypto's keen abilities have been called into use by Superman, and even Batman, on more than one occasion. He formed a bond with Superboy during a stay on the Kents' family farm, but usually resides in the Arctic Fortress. **RG**

A Superman's best friend
Krypto currently resides in Superman's Fortress.

Down boy!
Fortunately for Mongul, the Man of Steel is on hand when Krypto loses his temper defending his master.

Beware of the dog
Even a super-villain like Poison Ivy has to watch out when Krypto bares his teeth!

L.E.G.I.O.N.

First appearance INVASION #2 (1989)
Status Heroes **Base** The planet Cairn
Key Members and Powers
Captain Comet (leader) Telekinetic and telepathic abilities.
Davroth Catto Flight, uncanny aerial agility.
Garryn Bek No superhuman abilities.
Marij'n Bek No superhuman abilities.
Darkstar (Lydea Mallor) Projects a negative energy field.
Vril Dox II (retired) 12th level intellect.
Amon Hakk Tremendous Khund strength.
Lobo (no longer active) Amazing regenerative abilities.
Zena Moonstruk Can absorb light and emit it in bursts.
Stealth Can manipulate soundwaves.
Strata Superstrength, invulnerability.
Garv Advanced telepathic abilities.

Formed during an alien invasion of Earth, the Licensed Extra-Governmental Interstellar Operatives Network (L.E.G.I.O.N.) is a heroic peacekeeping force protecting planets that subscribe to its service. The brilliant Coluan, Vril Dox II (son of BRANIAC), founded L.E.G.I.O.N. after he and its original core members escaped from a Dominator-run "Starlag" prison camp. On their first mission, Vril Dox and his compatriots liberated Dox's homeworld of Colu from the domineering grip of the ruling computer tyrants. They then cleaned out the riffraff from the vile planet of Cairn—the galaxy's "drug world"—and made it their headquarters. L.E.G.I.O.N.'s rapid run of successes lured several high-paying clients and attracted new members. The membership roster would remain in constant flux. L.E.G.I.O.N. continued its success until Dox's malevolent son Lyrl usurped control. Several members formed a rival team, R.E.B.E.L.S., to restore L.E.G.I.O.N.'s good name. Vril Dox returned as L.E.G.I.O.N. leader in time for the Rann-Thanagar War. **DW**

PEACE-KEEPING SQUADRON Some of the key members of L.E.G.I.O.N. past and present: **1)** Garryn Bek **2)** Telepath **3)** Garv **4)** Lady Quark **5)** Vril Dox II **6)** Phase **7)** Strata **8)** Lobo **9)** Captain Comet **10)** Marij'n Bek **11)** Stealth

LABRATS

First appearance LABRATS #1 (April 2002)
Status Heroes (deceased) **Base** The Campus
Members and Powers
Poe Possesses a high level intellect.
Alex Athlete.
Isaac The team strongman.
Trilby Computer whiz.
Dana Street-smart fighter.
Wu Possesses infiltration abilities.

Products of the mysterious institution known only as "The Campus," the Labrats were investigators, explorers, and guinea pigs. The Campus scientists, for their own mysterious reasons, exploited their eager test subjects by pitting them against various simulated dangers in specially designed virtual reality scenarios. The Labrats, whose oldest member was just 16, were trained in these simulations to handle extreme situations. Most of the Labrats were homeless teenagers, who exchanged their lives as street urchins for this high-tech training.

When their teammate Gia was killed during one of the training programs, they left the Campus, encountering for the first time the very real dangers they had faced only as laboratory simulations, including rogue scientific oddities, UFOs, Superman, and a theme park populated by genetically engineered monsters. Tragically, their Campus training could not prevent them all from being killed. **PJ**

VIRTUAL REALITY Scientist Robert Quinlan trained the young Labrats in virtual reality simulators to prepare them for the threats they might face, knowing full well that many might not survive. **1)** Alex **2)** Poe **3)** Isaac **4)** Trilby **5)** Wu

LADY BLACKHAWK

First appearance BLACKHAWK #133 (February 1959)
Status Hero **Real Name** Zinda Blake **Occupation** Pilot, adventurer **Base** Metropolis
Height 5ft 7in **Weight** 117 lbs **Eyes** Blue **Hair** Blonde
Special powers/abilities Expert flyer and markswoman with superior hand-to-hand combat abilities.

Zinda Blake, more commonly known as Lady Blackhawk, became an expert pilot during World War II with the intention of becoming the first female member of the legendary Blackhawks. Soon accepted among their number, Blake joined their wartime exploits and fought Killer Shark, who brainwashed her into becoming his queen. After the reality-warping event known as Zero Hour, Lady Blackhawk appeared in the modern era, showing no signs of having aged since the 1940s. When Oracle offered her a role as the pilot for the Birds of Prey Blake signed aboard, where her hard-drinking, rough-brawling lifestyle made her feel right at home among warriors such as Black Canary II and Big Barda. Lady Blackhawk resigned from the team when forced to take orders from Spy Smasher, but returned once Oracle's leadership role had been restored.

A second woman, Natalie Reed, also went by the code name Lady Blackhawk. Reed's tenure with the Blackhawks covered the end of World War II and many of the Cold War years. **DW**

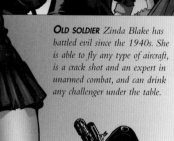

OLD SOLDIER Zinda Blake has battled evil since the 1940s. She is able to fly any type of aircraft, is a crack shot and an expert in unarmed combat, and can drink any challenger under the table.

LADY SHIVA

FIRST APPEARANCE RICHARD DRAGON, KUNG-FU FIGHTER #5 (January 1976)
STATUS Villain **REAL NAME** Sandra Woosan (Lady Shiva Wu-San)
OCCUPATION Martial artist **BASE** Mobile
HEIGHT 5ft 8in **WEIGHT** 141 lbs **EYES** Brown **HAIR** Black
SPECIAL POWERS/ABILITIES Lady Shiva is a master of virtually every known (and several forgotten) martial-arts disciplines; will stop at nothing to become the world's best and most lethal fighter.

When evil industrialist Guano Cravat falsely convinced Sandra Woosan that fellow martial artist Richard Dragon had murdered her sister Carolyn, Woosan vowed vengeance. As "Lady Shiva," Woosan fought Dragon before Cravat's deception was revealed. Lady Shiva then allied herself with Dragon and the Bronze Tiger (Dragon's friend and partner, Ben Turner) to dismantle Cravat's criminal consortium while serving as an operative of G.O.O.D., a U.S. government-sponsored spy organization. Later, Shiva opted for solo intrigue as a mercenary and hired assassin, honing her already formidable martial-arts skills to optimum efficiency. In this regard, Shiva has fought on both sides of the law.

AGAINST THE HIVE Shiva's blows can break bones and shatter armor, making her an unstoppable opponent.

CHALLENGERS Being the best martial-artist in the world requires Shiva to beat down the upstarts and pretenders.

LIVING WEAPON

She is credited with training the Question to become a better brawler, as well as helping Batman to regain the use of his legs and fighting spirit after the terrorist Bane had crippled him. However, both heroes know well that Lady Shiva's loyalties are capricious.

When it suits her, Shiva wields ninja and samurai arms with deadly grace. But her own body is a far more formidable weapon. In her years traveling the world, Shiva has blended the fighting finesse of judo, koroshi, karate, savate, capoeira, kung-fu, and countless other martial arts to create a style ideally suited for her size and frame. Opponents underestimate Shiva to their dying dismay.

TOP OF HER GAME Constant training and frequent life-or-death battles have kept Lady Shiva as skilled as ever as the years have passed.

MOTHER AND DAUGHTER

The emergence of BATGIRL Cassandra Cain shed new light on Lady Shiva's history. During Shiva's assassins' training, David Cain murdered her sister. Driven to even greater feats of martial artistry through her drive for revenge, Shiva achieved excellence within the League of Assassins, and eventually bore a daughter—Cassandra—with Cain.

After Cassandra took on the mantle of Batgirl, Shiva challenged her to a series of death-duels, never revealing the truth of their relationship. In their final confrontation, Cassandra died and returned to life in a Lazarus Pit, then defeated Shiva and left her for dead.

With her daughter taking the reigns of the League of Assassins, Lady Shiva chose to follow a new path. Following the Infinite Crisis, Oracle allowed her to join the Birds of Prey. Using the name "Jade Canary," Shiva took the place of Black Canary, who had agreed to undergo a recreation of Shiva's own training in Vietnam. Her time with the Birds of Prey did little to temper Shiva's ruthless instincts.

In Vietnam Black Canary befriended a young girl, Sin, who had been designated Shiva's eventual successor. After bringing the girl back to the United States, Canary did her best to raise Sin as her own daughter. Shiva recently took Bethany Thorne, daughter of the villainous Crime Doctor, as her new apprentice. **SB/DW**

SHOWDOWN Lady Shiva's daughter, Cassandra Cain, used her training as Batgirl to put up a formidable fight.

MEETING OF THE MINDS By exchanging lives for a year, Lady Shiva and Black Canary grew to understand one another and the choices each had made in life.

KEY STORYLINES
- **BATMAN #509 (JULY 1994)** After Bane snaps Batman's spine, Lady Shiva helps the Dark Knight work his way back to fighting strength.
- **BATGIRL #26 (MAY 2002):** Lady Shiva's daughter, Cassandra Cain, uses her Batgirl training to defeat her mother in combat.
- **BIRDS OF PREY #92 (MAY 2006):** Temporarily working for the good guys as a member of Oracle's Birds of Prey, Lady Shiva makes her debut as the Jade Canary.

LANE, LOIS

WORLD-CLASS REPORTER

FIRST APPEARANCE ACTION COMICS #1 (June 1938)
STATUS Hero **REAL NAME** Lois Joanne Lane
OCCUPATION Reporter **BASE** Metropolis
HEIGHT 5ft 6in **WEIGHT** 136 lbs **EYES** Blue **HAIR** Black
SPECIAL POWERS/ABILITIES Superb investigative journalist with an instinctive "nose" for a good story; trained in various hand-to-hand combat techniques and an adequate marksman.

A PULITZER PRIZE-WINNING JOURNALIST, Lois Lane specializes in reporting from the front lines of war zones and natural catastrophes for Metropolis's *Daily Planet* newspaper. One day a truly incredible story presented itself right in her own backyard. While covering a LexCorp-engineered disaster in Metropolis with young photographer Jimmy Olsen (*see* Olsen, Jimmy), Lois was rescued from certain death by a superstrong flying man. She became the very first reporter to record the exploits of the amazing costumed champion she named Superman. Her world, already full of activity, had just been turned upside down.

AWAY FROM IT ALL Superman and Lois take a well-earned break from saving the world.

DADDY DEAREST Sam Lane always wanted a son and was never close to Lois.

A NOSE FOR NEWS

The daughter of General Sam and Elinore Lane, Lois was born in a U.S. Army hospital outside of Wiesbaden, Germany. Sam Lane had always wanted a boy, and did not hide his disappointment from Lois, who became a model of self-sufficiency in response to her father's emotional distance. After high school, Lois moved to Metropolis and worked full time at the *Daily Planet*. She also attracted the attention of Lex Luthor (*see* Luthor, Lex); however, Lois spurned his every advance.

Lois rapidly became the *Daily Planet*'s leading investigative reporter, winning many awards and a daredevil reputation. After Superman's first appearance, she befriended both the Man of Steel and a new, mild-mannered reporter named Clark Kent. Of course, the biggest story was right under Lois's nose: Clark and Superman were one and the same person!

Over time and countless adventures, Lois and Clark fell in love and became engaged. Shortly after, Clark revealed his secret identity to Lois. Shocked as she was, she still agreed to marry him, as she loved Clark regardless and was moved that he had shared his secret with her. Tragedy struck when the Kryptonian creature Doomsday seemingly killed Superman during a violent rampage through the streets of Metropolis. Devastated, Lois cradled her dying lover in her arms as the life slowly ebbed from Superman's body. But Lois did not have to mourn for long, and upon Superman's return from the dead, the couple had a joyous reunion.

During one of the Joker's visits to the city, Lois was shocked to discover that Superman was willing to let her die rather than kill the villain to save her life. Her doubts fueled by this and other factors, she broke off her engagement to Clark and accepted an offer to become the *Planet*'s foreign correspondent. However, at the last minute she realized that she still loved Clark, and the happy couple were finally married.

Luthor then bought the financially troubled *Daily Planet* and closed it down. Lois was one of the few who retained jobs with Luthor's media enterprise, LexCom. Lex eventually sold the paper back to its editor, Perry White, having secretly arranged a deal whereby Lois agreed to kill one story of Luthor's choosing in the future. Lois's discovery that Luthor had had advance knowledge of the coming war with Imperiex (*see* Great Battles, pp. 186–7)

TRUE LOVE Despite separations, spats, and death-defying moments, Clark and Lois are deeply in love.

MR. MAJESTIC While an amnesiac Superman was trapped in the bottled city of Kandor, Lois dealt with the appearance of Mr. Majestic, who helped restore Metropolis.

INTREPID REPORTER
Lois never shies away from a good story.

became the scoop that she reluctantly agreed to kill. Meanwhile, Clark and Lois faced a different crisis: Lois had been impersonated for weeks by the Parasite, a villain who sought to destroy all that Superman stood for. With Batman's help, Superman rescued the real Lois after the Parasite died as a result of his backfired scheme. Lois's father was a casualty of the Imperiex War, and she grieved that their relationship would now never be repaired. She remains dedicated to her journalistic ideals, regardless of the danger they place her in, and her relationship with Clark has never been stronger.

KEY STORYLINES

- **ACTION COMICS #662 (1991):** Clark reveals the secret of his identity to his fiancée.
- **SUPERMAN: THE WEDDING ALBUM (1996):** Lois marries Clark in the wedding of the century!
- **SUPERMAN (2ND SERIES) #151 (2001):** Lois makes her deal with Luthor, in order to save the Daily Planet.
- **ADVENTURES OF SUPERMAN #631 (2004):** Lois is shot and gravely wounded while covering the U.S. occupation of Umec in the Middle East.

NEW FACES, NEW CHALLENGES

Lois helped ease Kara Zor-El's transition into Earth culture, welcoming her as a member of Clark's extended family and supporting her transition into Supergirl. But Lois' ties to Superman continued to put her at risk. During the "Crisis of Conscience," members of the Secret Society of Super Villains – all of whom had once been mind-wiped to forget the secret identities of the Justice League – temporarily regained their memories and lashed out at the League's loved ones.

ATTACKING THE INNOCENT *With knowledge of the Justice League's secret identities, the Secret Society took revenge on Superman by targeting Lois Lane and the Daily Planet.*

LIGHT AS A FEATHER *With all they have been through, Lois and Superman are still the perfect pair, with Lois providing a cynic's eye to complement her husband's too-trusting nature.*

GROUNDED FOR A YEAR

Crisis, Lois adjusted to life with a husband who had lost his powers. Clark's trip through the heart of a red sun had stripped him of his superhuman abilities, leaving him Clark Kent full time and making him a fixture at the Daily Planet and in their Metropolis apartment. Lois began to enjoy their new, low-key lifestyle and prepared for the possibility that the change might be permanent. But in time Clark's powers came back to him. Lois unequivocally supported his return to his role as Superman, explaining that his job was one of the reasons she loved him and that she's behind him all the way.

CHRISTOPHER KENT

A big change came into Lois' life when a mysterious Kryptonian boy arrived on Earth. After Superman removed the child from government custody in the Department of Metahuman Affairs, Lois and Clark agreed to give him a relatively normal life in Metropolis as their foster son.

Batman created false documentation establishing the boy as Christopher Kent. Lois helped teach him English and immersed him in the small joys of the big city. To conceal his abilities, particularly from his teachers and classmates, Christopher wore a wristwatch that mimicked the blocking qualities of a red sun.

Yet having a second Kryptonian in the house has brought substantial danger to Lois, particularly after the truth of Christopher's parentage became known. The boy had been born to Ursa and General Zod, conceived during their exile in the Phantom Zone and raised in a floating prison where the Phantom Zone's time-stasis did not apply. When General Zod escaped the Phantom Zone, he seized his son, captured Lois, and attempted a planetary takeover.

Shortly after Zod's rampage, outer-space marauders raided Earth on a hunt for the lost Kryptonian city of Kandor. Their vendetta against all Kryptonians put Lois and Christopher in peril until Superman, Power Girl, and Karsta Wor-Ul captured the enemy leader at the Fortress of Solitude. Despite the stakes and her vulnerability, Lois is determined to protect Christopher at all costs. RG/DW

RAISED BY THE ENEMY *As the son of the supervillains General Zod and Ursa, Christopher Kent experienced a troubled upbringing inside the Phantom Zone.*

THE LEGION OF SUPER-HEROES

TEEN DEFENDERS OF TOMORROW

FIRST APPEARANCE ADVENTURE COMICS #247 (April 1958)
STATUS Hero team
BASE Legion HQ, Earth

NOTABLE MEMBERS
Atom Girl (Salu Digby) Shrinking
Brainiac 5 (Querl Dox) Super-intellect
Colossal Boy (Gim Allon) Giant who can shrink to human size
Cosmic Boy (Rokk Krinn) Magnetism
Chameleon (Reep Daggle) Shapeshifting
Dream Girl (Nura Nal) Precognition
Dream Boy (Rol Purtha) Precognition
Element Lad (Jan Arrah) Transmutation
Invisible Kid (Lyle Norg) Invisibility
Karate Kid (Val Armorr) Martial artist
Light Lass (Ayla Ranzz) Gravity manipulation
Lightning Lad (Garth Ranzz) Electricity
Phantom Girl (Tinya Wazzo) Phasing
Princess Projectra (Wilimena Projectra Vauxhall) Illusion
Saturn Girl (Imra Ardeen) Telepathy
Shadow Lass (Tasmia Mallor) Darkforce generation
Star Boy (Thom Kallor) Gravity manipulation
Sun Boy (Dirk Morgna) Heat
Supergirl (Kara Zor-El) Flight, super strength, super speed
Timber Wolf (Brin Londo) Enhanced skills and senses
Triplicate Girl (Luornu Durgo) Splits into three beings
Ultra Boy (Jo Nah) Superpowers accessed one at a time

Through every crisis to come in the space-time continuum, one constant is that a group of young heroes and heroines will unite to defend their homeworlds from evil. Whether inspired by the boy who would become Superman or any of the costumed champions lost to history, the Legion of Super-Heroes will be that bright ray of hope in an uncertain future.

TIMELINE REBOOTS

The Legion has undergone numerous cosmic restructurings, with every universe-shaking crisis triggering major reworkings of the Legion's history and membership. The lineup from the original timeline drew its inspiration from young Clark Kent's adventures as Superboy, and featured a core team of Cosmic Boy, Saturn Girl, and Lightning Lad. Over time this team swelled to include dozens of members, who stood against the universe's most dire threats including Darkseid and the sorceress Glorith. Eventually the alien Dominators overran Earth and caused the planet's destruction. The clean-slate timeline that followed Zero Hour erased this Legion from history, replacing it with a similar lineup known for its alternate codenames ("Live Wire" for Lightning Lad) and fresh threats such as the Blight. The reality warps of the Infinite Crisis brought into existence a third Legion—but the rebirth of the multiverse indicates that all previous Legions currently exist in the future timelines of parallel worlds.

TOGETHER *Flight rings raised to the sky, the teenaged Legionnaires stand ready to defend the United Planets*

PHANTOMS *The dimension-phasing abilities of Phantom Girl allowed her to communicate with Mon-El, who had been trapped in the Phantom Zone for a millennium.*

SUPERGIRL AND MON-EL

Kara Zor-El, the Supergirl from the 21st century, traveled to the Legion's future during the Infinite Crisis. Stripped of her memories, she initially believed the entire experience to be a hallucination, but soon earned her place as a revered Legionnaire. Supergirl helped bring the 20th century hero Mon-El into the Legion. While visiting Supergirl in the re-enlarged Kryptonian city of Kandor, Saturn Girl detected Mon-El's ghostly presence in the Phantom Zone, where Brainiac 5's tinkering released him from his thousand-year prison.

SUPER-BRAWL Maddened by prison, Mon-El lashed out at Supergirl, nearly destroying Legion headquarters in the process.

HOME SWEET HOME *The Legion headquarters on Earth is a focal point for non-powered teenagers from all walks of life.*

THE LATEST LEGION

In the current continuity following the Infinite Crisis, the Legion of Super-Heroes emerged on a 31st century Earth governmental surveillance had become a way of life. With parents keeping obsessive tabs on their children, a teenage rebellion sprang up centered on admiration for the colorful superheroes a thousand years prior. The headquarters of the Legion of Super-Heroes served as a beacon for thousands of disaffected teenagers, who camped outside hoping for a glimpse of their champions. Brainiac 5 of Colu proved the mastermind of the team, designing their flight rings and keeping tabs on trouble spots across the United Planets. Cosmic Boy, Saturn Girl, and Lightning Lad remained the heart of the Legion, with Element Lad lending the ability to transmute objects, Ultra Boy serving as the team's powerhouse, the shapeshifting Chameleon excelling as a spy, and the rookie Invisible Kid providing a fresh perspective on the Legion's heroics. Colossal Boy, a member of a race of giants from Antarctica, possessed the ability to shrink to human size, and unsuccessfully petitioned for the name Micro-Lad. The United Planets wanted nothing to do with the team, and hoped to discredit them and their philosophy of non-conformity.

INTO THE FRAY *Although initially classified as outlaws, the Legionnaires now work with the Science Police and are recognized by the United Planets.*

THE WANDERERS

Mon-El became the latest recruit of the Wanderers, a militant superpowered team led by Mekt Ranzz, brother of siblings Lighting Lad and Light Lass. Originally the covert squad had assembled to combat threats to the United Planets, but Mekt rebuilt the team following a crushing defeat at the hands of the Dominators, making the extermination of the Dominators his top priority. Mekt tried to recruit many Legionnaires, but considered the Legionnaires ineffectual idealists who would only get in the way of his war. When the Dominators attacked Earth with genetically-modified warriors, the Legion and the Wanderers united to end the threat. The war ended with the invasion and apparent destruction of the Dominator homeworld. In reality, the planet had merely been shunted to the Phantom Zone, but Cosmic Boy took the blame for the seeming act of genocide and dropped out of sight. Supergirl became Legion chairperson in his absence, but soon returned to the 21st century.

THE LIGHTNING SAGA

After the Infinite Crisis, the original Legion lineup reasserted itself in Superman's life. The Legion's adventures with young Clark Kent returned to the timeline, and the members of this Legion reappeared in the 21st century during the "Lightning Saga." The Legionnaires had come to the past to restore a hero, using lightning rods in a ritual similar to the one that had once brought Lightning Lad

SHOCKING RETURN *In their time-traveling trip to the 21st century, the Legionnaires brought back the Flash from an alternate dimension.*

back from the dead. After allying with the Justice League and the Justice Society, the Legionnaires succeeded in bringing back Wally West, the third Flash. Most Legionnaires returned to their own timeline, but Karate Kid and Triplicate Girl—who had lost her duplicates and now called herself "Una"—undertook their own 21st century adventure and discovered a new strain of the OMAC virus. Karate Kid and Una later met Supergirl, who had returned from the 31st century with a different version of the Legion. Supergirl recognized these Legionnaires as alternate versions of the ones she had known in the future, proving that *both* versions of the Legion now existed in the multiverse. Superman traveled to this Legion's 31st century, where the planet's inhabitants were indoctrinated with anti-alien beliefs. Earth-Man led the "Justice League of Earth." With the human world no longer in the United Planets due to xenophobia, its inhabitants believed that the Superman of the 21st century was human, and the tales of his Kryptonian heritage were lies. The Legion of Super-Heroes, persecuted in this new society, went underground. Superman helped the surviving Legionnaires restore justice to Earth.
SB/DW

RED SUN *In the Legion's future, a powerless Superman helped battle the villainous Justice League that ruled all of Earth.*

THE LEGION OF SUPER-HEROES
1) *Supergirl* 2) *Brainiac 5* 3) *Ultra Boy* 4) *Brainiac 5.1*
5) *Karate Kid* 6) *Light Lass* 7) *Cosmic Boy* 8) *Lightning Lad*
9) *Sun Boy* 10) *Triplicate Girl* 11) *Star boy* 12) *Timber Wolf*
13) *Shadow Lass* 14) *Princess Projectra* 15) *Invisible Kid*
16) *Phantom Girl* 17) *Element lad* 18) *Atom Girl*
19) *Saturn Girl*

LIGHTNING LAD

FIRST APPEARANCE ADVENTURE COMICS # 247 (April 1958)
STATUS Hero **REAL NAME** Garth Ranzz
OCCUPATION Super-hero **BASE** Legion Headquarters
HEIGHT 6ft 2in **WEIGHT** 190 lbs **EYES** Blue **HAIR** Red
SPECIAL POWERS/ABILITIES Absorbs electrical energy;. generates and controls fields of electrical energy and can channel this energy through his hands, projecting it as a powerful super-heated discharge with properties similar to that of lightning; body is a natural insulator, so he is not harmed by his own powers.

GARTH RANZZ OF WINATH is Lightning Lad, a core member of the Legion of Super-Heroes in all versions of the Legion that have arisen throughout the timeline. Twins are common on Winath, and both Garth and his sister Ayla (Light Lass) have superpowers—Garth can generate bolts of electricity, and Ayla can manipulate gravity (and has possessed electrical abilities in other timelines). Their older brother Mekt has abilities similar to Garth's, but his status as a single-birth caused others to view him with suspicion and hostility. Mekt joined the United Planets as a covert commando, and later assembled the Wanderers to battle the alien Dominators.

FAMILY TIES The Ranzz siblings have all become adventurers, with Ayla manipulating gravity as Light Lass and Mekt heading up the Wanderers.

HOTHEAD Lightning Lad's short temper—and his short attention span—have made him an inconsistent and unpredictable Legion leader.

MAKING HIS MARK

Garth and Ayla, meanwhile, joined the more colorful Legion, with Garth helping found the organization alongside Cosmic Boy and Saturn Girl. The Legion stood for personal freedom on a repressive Earth that monitored its teenagers and frowned on uniqueness. As Lightning Lad, Garth numbered among the Legion's most powerful members, battling the insurgents of Terror Firma and even his own brother, who viewed the Legion as idealistic meddlers. Garth and Mekt later united to fight off a Dominator invasion of Earth.

Lightning Lad took over as Legion leader following Supergirl's return to the 21st century. His immaturity and short attention span led to problems, as he struggled to keep track of Legionnaire missions while dealing with the demands of the United Planets, who now enjoyed a formal relationship with the Legion. Garth's good heart kept him on track, as did the love of occasional girlfriend Saturn Girl.

An alternate version of Lightning Lad appeared in the mainstream Earth's timeline during the events of the "Lightning Saga," in which the Legionnaires traveled to the 21st century to restore a lost hero (Wally West, the third Flash). This Lightning Lad had previously died and experienced a resurrection via energy channeled through lightning rods, the same method used to bring back the Flash. Superman later traveled to the 31st century to visit this Legion later in their history, when the Earth's sun had turned red and its citizens had grown fearful and protectionist.

A third version of Garth Ranzz went by the code name Live Wire. In this timeline, he died battling an insane ELEMENT LAD, only to return trapped in Element Lad's crystalline body. **DW**

IN CHARGE Among Lightning Lad's duties as Legion chairman is the auditioning of potential new members, often with disastrous and embarrassing results.

DOMINATOR INVASION The alien Dominators have long been foes of the Legion. Their latest plan to conquer the Earth was foiled thanks to heavy-hitting Legionnaires like Earth Lightning Lad.

KEY STORYLINE
• ADVENTURE COMICS #312 (SEPTEMBER 1963): In this classic story, Lightning Lad is apparently resurrected from the dead by his teammates. Decades later, this tale provided the foundation for *Justice League of America's* "The Lightning Saga."

LOBO

FIRST APPEARANCE OMEGA MEN #3 (June 1983)
STATUS Villain **REAL NAME** Unpronounceable
OCCUPATION Contract killer; bounty hunter **BASE** Mobile
HEIGHT 7ft 6in **WEIGHT** 640 lbs **EYES** Red **HAIR** Black
SPECIAL POWERS/ABILITIES Vast superstrength and near invulnerability; superspeed and superhuman endurance; fantastic leaping ability; tracking ability allows him to trace prey across galaxies; can survive unaided in the vacuum of space; unparalleled brawler; can replicate himself into an army of clones.

HIS UNPRONOUNCEABLE REAL NAME roughly translates as "he who devours your entrails and thoroughly enjoys it." Once Lobo has targeted a victim, that person has little hope of escape and even less of winning any fight—for the only way to destroy Lobo is to vaporize every part of him, down to the last cell! Lobo loves his work and cares little for payment. When not pursuing prey, he keeps in practice by picking fights wherever he goes, marauding around the cosmos like a deep-space Hell's Angel on his intergalacticycle, the *Hog*. With his uncanny ability to sense an opponent's physical and mental weaknesses, Lobo is almost as notorious as a barroom brawler as he is as a killer-for-hire.

BAD TO THE BONE *Lobo's taken more than his share of lives, loot, and loves—and probably in that order!*

BOUNTY HUNTER *Lobo is known and feared throughout the galaxy as a tracker who never loses his prey.*

A ONE-MAN ARMY

Lobo is the sole survivor of the planet Czarnia, once renowned as a tranquil paradise. Lobo was trouble as soon as he was born, biting off the midwife's fingers, chasing the doctors with scalpels, and frightening the delivery nurse to death. As a child, he killed every caretaker he had. Finally, he committed global genocide, creating a horde of lethal insects that slaughtered every last Czarnian. Lobo then became a mercenary, leaving a trail of blood and corpses in his wake. Bizarrely, he also adopted a school of space dolphins as pets.

At length, after helping the OMEGA MEN vanquish the Spider Guild and the Citadel Empire, Lobo found Earth, and began challenging its greatest heroes—Superman, Warrior, the Justice League of America—to vicious battles to find the "Main Man."

Lobo worked with the interstellar police force L.E.G.I.O.N. for a time, along with their offshoot, R.E.B.E.L.S. During that time Brainiac 5.1 stripped Lobo of his amazing genetic ability to replicate himself into an army of exact clones.

Sometime later, Lobo was transformed into a younger version of himself by the magic of Klarion, the Witch Boy. Li'l Lobo was just as murderous as his adult self, and reclaimed his cloning ability. The child-sized Lobo then joined Young Justice for a while. He was incinerated by Darkseid on a mission to Apokolips during the Imperiex War (*see* Great Battles, pp. 3186-7). A Lobo clone, created from a drop of blood, returned to Earth with Young Justice. He called himself "Slobo," felt unworthy of the Khundian title "Lobo," and was condemned to a stony death in the 853rd century by Darkseid while trying to save his teammate SECRET from the New God's clutches. One of Lobo's many clones survived, however, to spread his brand of lethal rage across the galaxy. **PJ**

INDESTRUCTIBLE *Lobo's nearly impervious to physical attack.*

KEY STORYLINE
• *LOBO'S BACK #1-4 (MAY–AUGUST 1992):* Heaven doesn't want him, and Hell certainly doesn't either. Lobo rampages through the afterlife after being hacked to pieces by a rival hunter.

LASSOED! *Lobo became a pawn of the Olympian Gods in their battle against Circe. After murdering dozens of Amazons, he was captured by Wonder Woman!*

LORD, MAXWELL

FIRST APPEARANCE JUSTICE LEAGUE INTERNATIONAL #1 (May 1987)
STATUS Villain (deceased) **REAL NAME** Maxwell Lord
OCCUPATION Criminal mastermind **BASE** Mobile
HEIGHT 6ft 2in **WEIGHT** 185 lbs **EYES** Brown **HAIR** Brown
SPECIAL POWERS/ABILITIES Brilliant strategic mind, telepathic control
of others.

ACCEPTABLE LOSS
Wonder Woman
killed Maxwell Lord
to break his mind-
control of Superman;
the Man of Steel
did not agree with
the severity of her
actions.

Maxwell Lord was the billionaire who financed the JUSTICE
LEAGUE OF AMERICA during the period when it was most
commonly known as the Justice League International.
The explosion of a "gene bomb" during an alien
invasion triggered Lord's ability to control the minds
of others. He continued as the League's behind-the-
scenes leader until killed by a brain tumor.
Lord's consciousness spent time in the robotic body of
Lord Havok until he regained his human form.
By this time, his long-term ambitions to exterminate
the world's metahumans had begun to bear fruit.
As head of Checkmate, Lord had access to the
Brother Eye satellite and its army of O.M.A.C.
agents, which carried programming to
annihilate all superhumans. When Blue
Beetle II discovered the truth of the plot,
Lord shot him in the head. Lord then
used his mind-controlling powers to
take command of Superman and turn
him into a remote-controlled weapon.
Wonder Woman, faced with the decision to
eliminate Lord's threat for all time, killed
him instantly by snapping his neck.
DW

OMACS ARE GO
With Blue Beetle II eliminated,
Maxwell Lord launched the
OMAC Project which targeted all
superhumans on the planet.

LORD OF TIME

FIRST APPEARANCE JUSTICE LEAGUE OF AMERICA (1st series) #10
(March 1962)
STATUS Villain **REAL NAME** Unrevealed **OCCUPATION** Would-be
conqueror **BASE** Mobile **HEIGHT** 5ft 9in **WEIGHT** 159 lbs **EYES**
Blue **HAIR** Black **SPECIAL POWERS/ABILITIES** Access to the timestream
through Chrono-cube; armor assimilates weaponry from any era visited.

An immensely powerful being from the year 3786, the
Lord of Time attacked the Justice League of America,
using his miraculous chrono-cube to peel back the fourth-
dimensional veil of time. Since his initial defeat by the
JLA, this sinister fugitive from the future has learned to
move laterally and diagonally through history, accessing
armies and armaments spanning millions of years. He
desires nothing less than to conquer space and time.
To make sure that his bid to rule all reality is successful he
is quite capable of ensuring that the JLA have no power
to stop him by eliminating their ancestors and so erasing
them from existence.
At some point, the Lord of Time created a frozen
moment in history called Timepoint, and he will
eventually evolve into a being known as Epoch who
desires to master the timestream, changing events to grant
him power. **RG**

AGELESS ARMOR
Using armor from
the future, the Lord
of Time is able to
withstand assaults by
powerful opponents,
from Superman to
Green Lantern.

LORING, JEAN

FIRST APPEARANCE SHOWCASE #34
(September–October 1961)
STATUS Villain **REAL NAME** Jean Loring
OCCUPATION God of Vengeance **BASE** Mobile
HEIGHT 5ft 8in **WEIGHT** 130 lbs **EYES** Green **HAIR** Black
SPECIAL POWERS/ABILITIES None in normal form; as Eclipso, possesses flight, invulnerability, super-strength, and vast magical powers.

Jean Loring was once a notable attorney and the wife of Ray Palmer, the second Atom. The two divorced not long into their marriage, and Loring continued her law career in Ivy Town until suffering a complete mental collapse. Convinced that she could restore her marriage to Ray by threatening or killing the loved ones of the members of the Justice League of America, she murdered the Elongated Man's wife, Sue Dibny. When her crime became known, Loring served a term in Arkham Asylum until infected by the sinister spirit of Eclipso. Now Eclipso's human host, Loring seduced the Spectre into killing hundreds of Earth's magic-users to bring about an end to the Ninth Age of Magic. The Shadowpact fought the Spectre and sent Loring into orbit around the sun, but she returned, still armed with the powers of Eclipso. After fighting Blue Beetle III and Traci Thirteen, she attempted to corrupt Mary Marvel, only to be thwarted by the purity of Mary's spirit. **DW**

LOSERS, THE

FIRST APPEARANCE G.I. COMBAT #138 (November 1969)
STATUS Hero team **BASE** Europe and Asia during World War II
MEMBERS AND SPECIAL POWERS
CAPTAIN STORM (DECEASED) Indomitable will; a natural leader.
GUNNER Commando skills; expert marksman.
JOHNNY CLOUD (DECEASED) One of the greatest fighter pilots of World War II.
ONA (DECEASED) Expert markswoman.
POOCH (DECEASED) Specially trained military dog.
SARGE (DECEASED) Commando skills; expert marksman.

The Losers were Allied soldiers during World War II, each of whom had suffered serious failures during their military careers. Captain Storm's first command had been sunk by a Japanese submarine; a pilot flying alongside Johnny Cloud had been killed in combat; and a band of raw recruits led by Gunner and Sarge had been wiped out during their first patrol.

After Jeb Stuart persuaded the soldiers to help him destroy a Nazi radar tower, the four men stayed together, united by the Military High Command as a special task force. Briefly recruiting a fifth member, a Norwegian woman named Ona, the unit fought Axis tyranny throughout Europe and Asia, never quite shaking their self-imposed status as "Losers." Tragically, all four men and their K-9 sidekick, Pooch, died in action during the final days of World War II, but decades later Gunner was resurrected by Project M and recruited for the new CREATURE COMMANDOS. **PJ**

CRISIS IN TIME In the war torn country of Markovia, the Losers came face to face with Shadow Demons out to destroy the universe, and they succumbed to their explosive presence before time was reordered in the Crisis.

GUNNER
JOHNNY CLOUD
CAPTAIN STORM
ONA
POOCH
SARGE

LUMP

FIRST APPEARANCE MISTER MIRACLE (1st series) #7 (April 1972)
STATUS Villain **REAL NAME** None
OCCUPATION Warrior **BASE** Apokolips
HEIGHT 7ft **WEIGHT** 500 lbs **EYES** White **HAIR** None
SPECIAL POWERS/ABILITIES Can mold his misshapen body into any form he imagines to defeat opponents psycho-merged with him.

Deep within Granny Goodness's orphanage on Apokolips lies the dreaded Section Zero. Here, Scott Free (Mister Miracle) met the Lump, a horrendous hulk who encountered the enemies of Darkseid in the "Arena of the Gods," a mental realm within the creature's own Id. Strapped to Apokoliptian technology, Mister Miracle met the Lump inside this mind-world where the monster was master. Able to mold his body into any weapon, the Lump battled Mister Miracle to a standstill. To defeat the Lump, Miracle used a fission blast to turn the ground to glass. With a reflective shard, Mister Miracle showed the Lump his own vile visage. Horrified, the Lump retreated into the furthest reaches of his Id. Miracle then escaped with his beloved Big Barda. The Lump remains in Section Zero, imprisoned in his own private hell. **SB**

LYNX

FIRST APPEARANCE Robin (1st series) #1 (November 1990)
STATUS Villain (deceased) **REAL NAME** Ling
OCCUPATION Assassin; gang boss **BASE** Gotham City
HEIGHT 5ft 2in **WEIGHT** 119 lbs **EYES** Black **HAIR** Black
SPECIAL POWERS/ABILITIES One of the most formidable martial artists alive today; a courageous but ruthless killer.

Escaping from Wuzhong, China, a young girl known only as Ling begged for food on the streets of Marseilles. An adept thief, Ling was recruited by Sir Edmund Dorrance, the drug baron King Snake, to join his Ghost Dragons gang. When she was defeated by the third Robin, King Snake punished Ling, now renamed Lynx, by taking her left eye. Filled with hatred for Robin and King Snake, Lynx moved to Gotham City's Chinatown and wrested control of the Dragons from King Snake. Lynx has since clashed with Batman and Robin several times; however, she teamed with the Dark Knight in the aftermath of the Gotham earthquake, taking down a Chinatown gang using slaves to generate electricity for the crippled city. In a fight with Cassandra Cain (Batgirl), Lynx lost her life. **RG**

LUTHOR, LEX

SUPERMAN'S GREATEST ENEMY

FIRST APPEARANCE ACTION COMICS #23 (April 1940)
REAL NAME Alexander Joseph Luthor
BASE Metropolis; Washington D.C. (while U.S. President)
HEIGHT 6ft 2in **WEIGHT** 210 lbs **EYES** Green **HAIR** None
OCCUPATION Mastermind
SPECIAL POWERS/ABILITIES Luthor is one of the smartest men on Earth, able to invent technological marvels or manipulate entire nations. He believes in brute force and is an unskilled fighter, relying instead on weapons and armor.

LEX LUTHOR MAY BE the most gifted man alive but rather than use his supreme intellect and skills for the betterment of mankind, the sociopath has continually sought power and influence without regard for the pain and suffering he causes. The gifts are also wasted on his single-minded hatred of a more pure and noble man, especially given his alien origins.

EVIL GENIUS *Luthor's early attempts to kill Superman all failed.*

EVIL AND ALIENATED

One glance at Luthor's I.Q. test results, convinced his parents that their little genius would make them rich. They were determined he should excel, but their soul-destroying "guidance" bred a sociopath who engineered their deaths to capitalize on their life insurance. A budding astrobiologist, Lex then spent years searching for evidence of extraterrestrial life. His hunt took him to Smallville when he was 18. Lex befriended another seemingly alienated young man, Clark Kent. He turned his back on Smallville when a fire destroyed his lab and his scientific achievements, as well as his foster father. Refusing to take any responsibility for the accident, Lex blamed the town for "letting the Luthors burn," and to this day, refuses to admit he has ever set foot in Smallville.

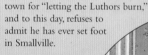

ONLY THE LONELY
Deprived of a normal childhood, Lex hid his personal pain behind a mask of arrogance.

TWO STRANGERS *Clark was the only person in Smallville who empathized with Lex's feelings of isolation.*

EXPLOSION *An accident physically and mentally scarred Lex so deeply he has erased all record of his ever being in Smallville.*

THE RISE OF LUTHOR

Years later, Lex appeared in Metropolis and built his technology company, LexCorp, into a powerhouse. Financial success led to political power, and he was considered the city's most powerful figure. Then came the day that Superman appeared in the skies above Metropolis and turned Lex's world upside down. Superman openly accused Luthor of being a criminal mastermind rather than a benefactor of mankind. Unwilling or unable to link this "meddling alien" with the boy he had known a decade earlier, Luthor swore to bring down the Last Son of Krypton. Over the years, he has used his power and influence to plague the Man of Steel time and again.

KRYPTONITE RING

Luthor got in his licks but continued to be thwarted by Superman both directly and indirectly. On one occasion, a ring Luthor had fashioned from kryptonite gave him cancer owing to the radiation inherent in the alien rock. Lex faked his death, and transferred his mind into the body of a clone, pretending to be Luthor's heretofore unknown son. This Luthor soon evolved to resemble the original, but continued to come second in his struggles with Superman.

METROPOLIS DESTROYED

Lex showed his true colors by refusing to sacrifice himself to help reignite the sun after the Sun-Eater had snuffed out its energy. When Lois Lane (*see* Lane, Lois) exposed his criminal dealings, Luthor triggered devices hidden within Metropolis that destroyed the city. Superman and his fellow heroes rebuilt Metropolis and the battle between Superman and Luthor continued. His manipulations extended to Metropolis's citizens, who sided with Superman over Luthor.

IN RUINS *Luthor destroyed Metropolis in a bid to avoid exposure by Lois Lane.*

LUST FOR POWER

Realizing the need to muzzle the press, Luthor bought and then sold the *Daily Planet* to Perry White on condition that Lois Lane killed any single story of his choosing. Feeling safe from exposure, Luthor ran for U. S. President to gain the power needed to bring Superman down. Surprisingly, he served the U.S.'s interests well, strengthening or forging relationships with many nations from Atlantis to Russia, and rallying the troops when Imperiex arrived to destroy Earth (*see Great Battles, pp. 186–7*).

CLASH OF WILLS *Perry White and Luthor never got along and it chafed when Luthor came to own Perry's beloved Daily Planet.*

FRONT PAGE NEWS
Lois found out that Luthor had known of Imperiex's threat earlier than stated. He demanded that this be the story the *Planet* killed, but the savvy reporter tricked him, giving her notes to Clark Kent, who wrote a scathing piece, exposing Luthor for the criminal he was.

WARSUIT *Luthor finally took matters in his own hands, attempting to destroy both Superman and Batman.*

DAILY PLANET
LUTHOR KNEW!

ADVANCE WARNING *Luthor had secretly known of Imperiex's invasion plans, but ordered Lois Lane to kill the story. However, Clark Kent printed the full truth, marring Luthor's term as U.S. President.*

KEY STORYLINES
• *SUPERMAN: PRESIDENT LEX (JULY, 2003):* The world looks on aghast as Luthor becomes U.S. President, following the most controversial election of all time.
SUPERMAN: BIRTHRIGHT #1–12 (SEPTEMBER 2003–SEPTEMBER 2004): Dating back to their childhood in Smallville, Luthor's tortured relationship with Clark Kent/Superman is redefined and explored.
• *SUPERMAN/BATMAN #1–6:* President Luthor becomes a kryptonite junkie and goes insane.
• *LEX LUTHOR: MAN OF STEEL #1–5 MAY–SEPTEMBER 2005):* Luthor's recovery from his downfall.

U.S. PRESIDENT *Luthor was quite effective in his post, improving diplomatic relations with Atlantis and other countries.*

ACT OF MADNESS

Luthor's presidential power still could not bring about the end of Superman and his costumed friends. When an asteroid neared Earth, Luthor detected kryptonite radiation and used that to try and turn the public against the Man of Steel. He even sent costumed champions after Superman, but this gambit also failed. Finally, he donned a LexCorp war suit and tried to take down not only Superman, but Batman as well. His efforts were in vain and his deception was made public. Driven from the presidency, Luthor was thought to have died but limped to freedom, an angry, vengeful man.

DKUSH

LUTHOR, LEX

The Superboy Plot

From a secret location, Lex Luthor plotted his return to power. With Lana Lang now in charge of LuthorCorp and Pete Ross stepping in to serve out the rest of Luthor's term as president, the stage seemed clear for a rebirth of Luthor's particular brand of genius. He began by activating buried programming in the mind of Superboy (Conner Kent), turning him against his teammates in the Teen Titans. The attack failed, but Luthor continued to think of Conner—a clone who shared 50% of his DNA with Superman and 50% with Luthor— as his own son. Lex's concern for Conner seemed uncharacteristic, but showed his protectiveness of the Luthor bloodline. By claiming Conner as his own, he had stolen a family member from Superman.

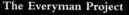

CLONE VAT *Luthor's ability to crack the genetic code also led to the first Bizarro.*

LIKE FATHER *Brainwashed, Conner Kent fights the Teen Titans under Luthor's orders.*

FALLEN SON *Conner died in the Infinite Crisis, with Luthor among his mourners.*

BEHIND THE CURTAIN *Luthor posed as the unseen Mockingbird in order to rally the Secret Six.*

Villains United

Just prior to the Infinite Crisis, Alexander Luthor— the adult son of a Lex Luthor from an alternate dimension —posed as this reality's Lex in order to unite the planet's supervillains under his banner. Assembling a new Secret Society of Super-Villains, this ersatz Luthor pitted the largest and most dangerous assemblage of criminals ever seen against the world's heroes. The true Lex Luthor, meanwhile, moved against the imposter by taking the identity of Mockingbird and forming a new Secret Six team to oppose the Society. Lex's vengeance came to fruition during the Infinite Crisis, when he arranged for Alexander Luthor's death at the hands of the Joker. Lex mourned Conner Kent, who had died trying to prevent Alexander's scheme to recreate the universe.

TABLES TURNED *For usurping his place as head of the Society, Luthor arranges the death of Alexander Luthor.*

The Everyman Project

Lex altered Alexander Luthor's corpse to resemble his own, then claimed that the late doppelganger had been responsible for the worst crimes of the Luthor presidency. The ruse fooled many, and Lex soon found himself the head of an ambitious experiment to transform ordinary citizens into superheroes. Dubbed the Everyman Project, the program attracted interest from thousands of hopefuls including Natasha Irons (*see* Irons, Natasha), niece of the hero Steel. Luthor granted Natasha superhuman abilities, then grouped her with several other charismatic young people and launched the team as the all-new, corporate-owned Infinity Inc. But the test subjects of the Everyman Project soon learned the limits of their genetic gifts. On New Year's Eve, as part of a scheme to humiliate the hero Supernova, Luthor triggered the instantaneous shutdown of all his subjects' powers. Suddenly powerless, dozens of hopeful heroes died as they plummeted from the sky. Steel and Natasha Irons confronted Luthor in his office, only to discover that he had temporarily acquired powers as well. The duo managed to outsmart Luthor and bring him to justice.

META-LUTHOR *The Everyman treatments worked on their creator as well. For a brief time, Luthor possessed the powers of Superman.*

PUBLIC ENEMY *The goodwill he earned as U.S. president now gone, Luthor burned for revenge on the citizens of Metropolis.*

Kryptonian Science

Yet Luthor managed to escape incarceration. Found innocent of all criminal charges related to the Everyman Project, Luthor tried to reassume his position as one of the Metropolis elite in the face of widespread public condemnation. Deciding that Superman was the obstacle preventing his return to fame, Luthor retrieved a long-buried Kryptonian battleship and led an assault on Metropolis using crystalline war machines not seen since the golden age of the long-dead planet. His plan was to discredit Superman as a failure. Luthor again went underground. Later he assembled a Revenge Squad consisting of the Parasite, Metallo, and Bizarro to battle the invading armies of General Zod.

MAD SCIENCE *His brain as sharp as ever, Luthor tortured the new Kryptonite Man to generate the energy he required.*

KRYPTON ON EARTH *Using self-assembling Kryptonian crystal technology, Luthor attacked Metropolis with an army of alien war machines.*

Injustice League Unlimited

Although no longer in possession of his vast business empire, Luthor put his organizational skills to work by amassing the Injustice League Unlimited, a team of supervillains so large it challenged Alexander Luthor's Secret Society. Luthor headed the new cabal with his lieutenants the Joker and the Cheetah. The group moved against the newly-reformed Justice League of America by capturing many of its members, then torturing them inside its secret headquarters in the Florida Everglades. The Justice League rallied to victory, but the Injustice League withdrew and remained coiled for a second strike.

Later, Luthor found himself one of the villains deposited on the distant planet Salvation and quickly assumed a leadership role.

Luthor's mind is as brilliant as ever. Since his fall from the presidency he has turned more of his genius to science. He now wears a modified version of his green and purple battle-suit in all encounters with enhanced combatants, and its built-in weapons make him a match for Superman. **RG/DW**

MAD HARRIET

FIRST APPEARANCE MISTER MIRACLE (1st series) #6 (February 1972)
STATUS Villain (deceased)   **REAL NAME** Unrevealed
OCCUPATION Shocktrooper   **BASE** Apokolips
HEIGHT 5ft 10in   **WEIGHT** 146 lbs   **EYES** Black   **HAIR** Green
SPECIAL POWERS/ABILITIES Ferocious combatant; fists are armed with power spikes that can slash through most materials.

Mad Harriet is a member of the FEMALE FURIES, an elite band of shocktroopers trained by the malevolent GRANNY GOODNESS as elite warriors for DARKSEID, dread lord of the planet Apokolips. Mad Harriet is a chilling, psychopathic killing machine, armed with special devices that let her cleave through any material, including the flesh of her prey.

The Female Furies were lead by BIG BARDA until she abandoned the team to be with her lover Scott Free, otherwise known as MISTER MIRACLE. When Barda moved to Earth, Mad Harriet and the Female Furies pursued her there and tried to capture her, but the Furies eventually turned when they were offered freedom from Granny's thrall. After working for a short time with Barda and Mister Miracle, Mad Harriet and the other Female Furies returned to Apokolips and to their roles as enforcers in Darkseid's Elite.

Mad Harriet met her apparent end in the weeks leading up to the Final Crisis. While pursuing MARY MARVEL through the streets of Apokolips, she ran into a hail of gunfire unleashed by Darkseid's own soldiers. **PJ**

MANIC MILLINER
No Man's Land gave many Gotham City rogues the opportunity to prey on the weak and defenseless. The Mad Hatter was mostly concerned with unearthing his collection of hats, buried in the Gotham City quake.

HATS OFF! *Superman helped a harried Dark Knight to defeat Jervis Tetch and put an end to his criminal chicanery.*

MAD HATTER

FIRST APPEARANCE BATMAN #49 (November 1948)
STATUS Villain   **REAL NAME** Jervis Tetch
OCCUPATION Professional criminal   **BASE** Gotham City
HEIGHT 4ft 8in   **WEIGHT** 149 lbs   **EYES** Blue   **HAIR** Red
SPECIAL POWERS/ABILITIES A master hypnotist, able to use chemical concoctions or electronic technology concealed in his oversized hat to enthrall his victims; short and slight in stature, the Hatter prefers to let his mesmerized minions do his fighting for him.

Insanely inspired by Lewis Carroll's children's book, *Alice's Adventures in Wonderland*, master mesmerist Jervis Tetch convinced himself that he was Carroll's chapeau-crazed Mad Hatter. In one of his very first crimes, Tetch hypnotized and kidnapped teenage girls to be "Alices" in a bizarre tea party before selling them into slavery. Fortunately, BATMAN and ROBIN foiled the Hatter's scheme and freed his unwilling guests, who included the Boy Wonder's very first crush, schoolmate Jenny Noblesse. Since then, the Hatter has committed even more sordid sins, usually involving his obsession with hats. However, what the prize Mad Hatter longs for most of all is Batman's famous headgear. He would gladly kill the Dark Knight to add the Bat-Cowl to his collection.

Mercurial in temperament, the Mad Hatter generally works alone. But for the sake of his hidden cache of chapeaus, buried under tons of rubble after Gotham City's cataclysmic earthquake, Tetch allied himself with the villain Narcosis, who planned to blanket the ruined city with his Bliss gas. Naturally, the Hatter bargained for Narcosis's hood to seal their partnership, short-lived though it was, since both were soon defeated by Batman.

In between his cap-themed crime sprees, Tetch is confined in the cells of Gotham City's notorious Arkham Asylum for the Criminally Insane, where hats are, as a rule, prohibited.

The Mad Hatter recently served with the new SECRET SIX, where he pitted his mind-controlling abilities against those of DOCTOR PSYCHO. **SB**

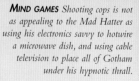

MIND GAMES *Shooting cops is not as appealing to the Mad Hatter as using his electronics savvy to hotwire a microwave dish, and using cable television to place all of Gotham under his hypnotic thrall.*

MAGENTA

FIRST APPEARANCE THE NEW TEEN TITANS (1st series) #17
(March 1982)
STATUS Villain   **REAL NAME** Frances Kane
OCCUPATION Criminal   **BASE** Keystone City
HEIGHT 5ft 7in   **WEIGHT** 134 lbs   **EYES** Blue   **HAIR** Purple
SPECIAL POWERS/ABILITIES Able to generate and manipulate magnetic
energy, controlling anything made of metal and bending it to her will.

Frances Kane grew up in Blue Valley, Nebraska, and
became a close friend of Wally West, the third Flash.
Kane's powers emerged one night while she, her father
and brother were driving on a narrow mountain road.
When her powers went out of control, the car fell off a
cliff, and Kane's father and brother were killed. France's
superstitious mother believed her daughter was possessed
by the devil and spurned her. With the help of Wally and
the Teen Titans, Frances was able to gain some control
over her powers, and the two became lovers in college.

Whenever Kane's powers emerged, however, she would
"split" into a second, evil identity known as Magenta.
Despite having helped the Teen Titans and the Flash in
their fight against villainy, Magenta has fought the Flash
as an enemy on more than one occasion. Having since been
forsaken by the Flash for another love, Magenta flutters
between her good and evil nature, and is now firmly
ensconced with other nefarious criminals in the Flash's
Rogues Gallery. **PJ**

PURPLE POWER *Once she was a victim of
circumstance. But now, corrupted by her powers,
troubled Magenta is one of the Flash's most tragic
villains—a former lover turned deadly enemy.*

MAGNO

FIRST APPEARANCE LEGIONNAIRES #43 (December 1996)
STATUS Hero   **REAL NAME** Dyrk Magz
OCCUPATION Legion ally   **BASE** Legion World, U.P. Space
HEIGHT 5ft 8in   **WEIGHT** 149 lbs   **EYES** Brown   **HAIR** Blond
SPECIAL POWERS/ABILITIES Formerly able to generate and control
magnetic fields to fly and manipulate metal objects; mystically
de-powered following a battle with Mordru.

Like his fellow Braalian Rokk Krinn (Cosmic
Boy), Dyrk Magz possessed highly developed
magnetic powers. When Cosmic Boy was
stranded in the 20th century for a
brief period, along with other members of
the Legion of Super-Heroes, his remaining
teammates in the 30th century initiated a
membership drive to replenish the Legion's
dwindled ranks. As Magno, Magz was recruited
from the planet Braal to replace Cosmic Boy,
at least until the founding member's return.
Magno's tenure as a Legionnaire was short-
lived, however, as he unfortunately lost his
magnetic powers following a battle with the
sinister sorcerer Mordru the Dark Lord.
Nevertheless, Magz remained
with the LSH and served as an auxiliary
non-powered member attending to
monitor duty full-time. Since the team
has relocated to the orbiting Legion
World and now employs entire staffs of
support teams, Magz's present role—if he
has one—is undetermined. **SB**

ATTRACTIVE *Like all Braalians, Magno possessed
highly developed magnetic powers until a battle
with Mordru negated his abilities.*

WEAK *Robbed of his powers,
Magno no longer serves the Legion of Super-Heroes
in an official capacity.*

MAN-BAT

GOTHAM'S NIGHT TERROR

FIRST APPEARANCE DETECTIVE COMICS #400 (June 1970)
STATUS Villain **REAL NAME** Robert Kirkland Langstrom
OCCUPATION biologist **BASE** A small town near Gotham City
HEIGHT 7ft 4in **WEIGHT** 315 lbs **EYES** Red **HAIR** Brown
SPECIAL POWERS/ABILITIES Transforms into a winged, super-strong batlike humanoid that has natural sonar, but limited daytime vision.

DOCTOR KIRK LANGSTROM was an expert in mammal biology, notably *chiroptera* (bats). Hoping to cure his growing deafness, he tried to create a serum that would give human beings the powers of echolocation that allow bats to use sound to navigate in the dark. When Langstrom tested the chemical on himself, the serum reacted with his genetic makeup and transformed him into a man-sized bat.

MAN-BAT ARMY
Once he became the Man-Bat, Langstrom's intellect seemed to vanish, and the crazed mutant began terrorizing Gotham City. Batman stopped Man-Bat's initial rampage, but Langstrom soon injected himself with another dose and became Man-Bat once again. He kidnapped his fiancée, Francine Lee, injected her, and she became a half-human/half-bat hybrid as well. After Batman once again captured Man-Bat and his mate, Langstrom refined the serum so that he could transform into his mutated state but maintain his intelligence. This Man-Bat occasionally helped Batman solve crimes. Langstrom and Francine eventually married and had a daughter, Rebecca, and a son, Aaron, a miniature version of his Man-Bat father.

KEY STORYLINES
• *DETECTIVE COMICS #400 (JUNE 1970)*: Man-Bat first appears in the skies of Gotham City, as a tragic figure who views his transformations as a curse.
• *BATMAN: MAN-BAT (MAY 1997)*: This Elseworlds story showcases a world in which Kirk Langstrom and his wife Francine have become full-time bats, raising a teenaged son and plotting to take over the world with man-bat hybrids.

CHEMISTRY EXPERIMENT *Dr. Langstrom's efforts to develop a serum to cure his condition have remained unsuccessful.*

SCREECHING THROUGH THE SKIES *Driven by madness instead of true villainy, Man-Bat has attacked Batman above the streets of Gotham.*

MAN-BAT IN LONDON
Back in his laboratory, Dr. Langstrom worked feverishly to refine the Man-Bat serum to reverse the changes it had made on his physiology and his sanity. One year after the Infinite Crisis, Langstrom earned the attention of Talia of the League of Assassins. Talia's agents kidnapped Langstrom's wife Francine in London, threatening her life unless Langstrom turned over the secrets of the Man-Bat formula. Desperate to save his wife, Langstrom rushed to assemble the ingredients, arousing the suspicions of Bruce Wayne, in London to attend a charity art exhibit.

Langstrom gave up the serum to Talia, who released Francine and used the genetic mutagen to shape a squad of assassins into ninja man-bats. The airborne killers crashed the gallery opening, forcing Bruce Wayne to do battle as Batman. Although he took down most of the man-bats, Batman fell prey to Talia's superior tactics and became her prisoner—an opportunity she exploited to introduce their mutual son, Damian.

Kirk Langstrom returned to Gotham City where he renewed his sporadic transformations into Man-Bat. Recently captured by the GCPD, he became one of the many villains deposited on a distant prison planet during the events of Operation: Salvation Run. PJ/DW

WORKING FOR THE ENEMY *Blackmailed by Talia Head, Dr. Langstrom created an entire strike force of Man-Bats that had been trained in ninja combat arts.*

MANHUNTER

FIRST APPEARANCE MANHUNTER (3rd series) #1 (October 2004)
STATUS Hero
REAL NAME Katherine Spencer
OCCUPATION Federal prosecutor, adventurer
BASE Mobile
HEIGHT 5ft 8in
WEIGHT 145 lbs
EYES Blue
HAIR Brown
SPECIAL POWERS/ABILITIES Suit provides enhanced strength and protection from injuries; carries a powerful energy staff.

THE scheming android MANHUNTERS have employed human agents over the years. The first was policeman Donald Richards who, with his robotic dog named Thor, battled crime in the 1940s. Big-game hunter Paul Kirk was also recruited during that period. He fought crime as Manhunter II, joining the All-Star Squadron during World War II. Decades later, idealist Mark Shaw became the third Manhunter. A master of many fighting styles, he helped the Justice League of America prevent the Manhunters from destroying the Guardians of the Universe. Star City musician Chase Lawler then had a brief career as a fourth Manhunter before suffering a heart attack. The fifth Manhunter is a clone of Paul Kirk named Kirk DePaul, who is a partner in the corporate team the Power Company. DePaul sometimes appeared to be more driven by financial gain than the idealism required to be a super hero, and has often clashed with his fellow partners over ethical and moral issues.

MANHUNTER I Donald "Dan" Richards had his own credo for tracking down villains: "Manhunter might get something on them when police methods fail!"

MANHUNTER II Former big-game hunter Paul Kirk, regarded tracking down criminals as a new challenge to savor. Genetic modifications meant that almost any injury he received healed rapidly.

MANHUNTER V Batman was highly suspicious of Kirk DePaul's motives when he discovered the former mercenary in Gotham City. The Dark Knight was sure DePaul was in town to kill an exile from the African nation of Oranga. Fortunately, on this occasion Batman's fears were groundless.

KATHERINE SPENCER

The sixth and latest Manhunter is Kate Spencer, a federal prosecutor who took up her adventuring identity in response to a legal system that too often let the guilty go free. When Copperhead escaped courtroom justice, Kate scavenged exhibits from an evidence room – including a strength-enhancing battle suit seized from a member of the Darkstars, Azrael's former wrist gauntlets, and a staff once carried by a former Manhunter – to piece together a costume and kill the villain. She continued as Manhunter while maintaining her secret identity as prosecutor, aided by her co-counsel Damon Matthews, DEO agent Cameron Chase, and Dylan Battles, a former gadgeteer for supervillains.

In the course of her crimefighting, Kate learned that she came from a proud lineage of super heroes, with her grandparents the Golden Age heroes Iron Monroe and the original Phantom Lady. Kate has served with the Birds of Prey, fought in the Infinite Crisis, and trained in hand-to-hand combat under Wonder Woman, even defending Wonder Woman in her criminal trial for the murder of Maxwell Lord (see Lord, Maxwell). Although still a second-tier adventurer, Kate has won the respect of many in the super-hero community and seems poised to take on greater challenges in the coming years.
RG/DW

SECRET IDENTITY During her day job as a prosecutor, Kate Spencer keeps her Manhunter costume inside her briefcase.

KEY STORYLINES

- **MANHUNTER (1ST SERIES) #1 (JULY 1988):** The Manhunter character appears in this self-titled series, this time as Mark Shaw, a public defender turned vigilante.
- **POWER COMPANY #1–18 (APRIL 2002–SEPTEMBER 2003):** Kirk DePaul, a clone of Paul Kirk, serves with the for-hire super-hero team organized by Josiah Power.
- **MANHUNTER (3RD SERIES) #1 (OCTOBER 2004):** Kate Spencer becomes the latest Manhunter, balancing her role as a prosecutor with her unlicensed, freelance adventuring.

BACK FROM THE DEAD Shadow Thief raises Copperhead from the grave—much to Manhunter's consternation. She believed she had put the killer in the ground for good.

MARTIAN MANHUNTER

FIRST APPEARANCE DETECTIVE COMICS #225 (November 1955)
STATUS Hero   **REAL NAME** J'onn J'onzz
OCCUPATION Adventurer   **BASE** JLA Watchtower, the Moon
HEIGHT 6ft 7in   **WEIGHT** 300 lbs   **EYES** Red   **HAIR** None
SPECIAL POWERS/ABILITIES Flight, superstrength, invulnerability, enhanced speed, shapeshifting, invisibility, telepathy, and "Martian vision," which provides a type of X-ray vision and allows J'onn to fire energy beams from his eyes.

TRUE TO FORM
J'onn still adopts his true Martian shape during moments of quiet meditation.

J'ONN J'ONZZ, THE MARTIAN MANHUNTER, has lost his wife, his daughter, and his newest love, yet he is never truly alone. His family is the Justice League of America. Eons ago, the Martians were one of the most powerful species in the universe, capable of shapeshifting, intangibility, flight, and a host of other incredible powers. J'onn J'onzz, a philosopher and peacemaker in his private life, worked as a Manhunter to keep the peace on his native planet.

H'RONMEER'S CURSE

J'onn J'onzz's calm life took a horrific turn when the mad priest Ma'alefa'ak (Malefic) unleashed the pyrokinetic plague H'ronmeer's Curse on the people of Mars. This pestilence, spread by telepathy, raced through the population and caused nearly every citizen to burst into flames, including J'onn's wife and daughter. J'onn imprisoned Ma'alefa'ak beneath Mars's highest mountain, Olympus Mons, and wandered the planet's surface for untold years until Dr. Saul Erdel brought him to Earth via a teleportation machine. J'onn J'onzz took steps to fit into this strange new society, first by assuming the identity of murdered Denver police detective John Jones and then by joining the Gotham City super-group "Justice Experience" under the alias Bronze Wraith. In Kansas, J'onn posed as a high-school civics teacher to keep an eye on a young Clark Kent (see Superman).

Eventually J'onn went public as the Martian Manhunter, becoming a founding member of the Justice League of America alongside Aquaman, Green Lantern, the Flash, and Black Canary. The League soon became his life. While other members came and went, the Martian Manhunter served with every subsequent lineup. His spirituality led many to consider him the League's heart and soul, while his vast array of powers put him in a physical class that even exceeded Superman's—suffering only from a vulnerability to fire.

The Martian Manhunter has battled foes from the Red Planet, including the White Martians (survivors from an ancient civil war between the Whites and J'onn's Green Martians) and Ma'alefa'ak, still alive and looking to complete his mission of genocide. J'onn faced his greatest challenge in the form of another forgotten Martian menace—the Burning. After the Infinite Crisis, J'onn went undercover to infiltrate Checkmate, and fought Black Adam during the event known as World War III. The experience caused him to withdraw from humanity and adopt an appearance more consistent with his true Martian form. He soon found a group of White Martians that claimed to be surviving Green Martians like himself, then served briefly with Batman's latest team of Outsiders. **DW**

SECRET IDENTITY *Hunting crooks as a detective allowed J'onn to become an Earth-based 'manhunter.'*

MALEFIC *Not content with the annihilation of a species, this Martian conqueror thirsts for blood.*

DARK MIRROR
Fernus, who needed fire in order to reproduce, represented all that was evil in J'onn's soul.

FIRE *J'onn's vulnerability to flame is caused by both genetic and psychological factors.*

KEY STORYLINES

• **MARTIAN MANHUNTER (2ND SERIES) #1 (DECEMBER 1998):** The quintessential team player gets a starring role for the first time in years.
• **JLA: YEAR ONE #1-12 (JANUARY–DECEMBER 1998):** J'onn's role as the heart and soul of the JLA is apparent in this retelling of the team's origin.
• **JLA #84-89 (OCTOBER–DECEMBER 2003):** J'onn turns against his JLA teammates during the Burning Martian storyline, showing why he is their most powerful member.

MARY MARVEL

FIRST APPEARANCE CAPTAIN MARVEL ADVENTURES #18 (Dec. 1942)
STATUS Hero **REAL NAME** Mary Batson **OCCUPATION** Adventurer
BASE Fawcett City **HEIGHT** 5ft 6in **WEIGHT** 139 lbs **EYES** Blue
HAIR Auburn **SPECIAL POWERS/ABILITIES** By saying "Shazam!" aloud, Mary Marvel gains Solomon's wisdom, Hercules' superstrength, Atlas's stamina, Zeus's raw power, Achilles' courage, and Mercury's superspeed. Mary Marvel shares her powers with Captain Marvel and Captain Marvel, Jr.; if either is using their powers, Mary Marvel has access to only half her power.

SHE IS THE TWIN SISTER OF BILLY BATSON, the mighty mortal known as Captain Marvel. Granted the abilities of the greatest Olympian Gods by uttering the name of the wizard Shazam, Mary Batson is Mary Marvel, one of the most powerful heroes on the planet! A sweet young woman in both guises, Mary nonetheless packs quite a punch, courageously defending her hometown of Fawcett City from mutant worms, Nazi terrorists, and ancient deities gone mad!

THE WORLD'S MIGHTIEST GIRL *Despite her power, Mary Marvel is still only a teenager.*

SHAZAM! *Mary summons a lightning bolt to change her into a super-hero.*

KEY STORYLINES

• POWER OF SHAZAM #30-31 (SEPTEMBER 1997): During the Genesis event, Mary's secret identity was revealed to her parents before she entered the Source to save all of creation!

• FORMERLY KNOWN AS THE JUSTICE LEAGUE #1-6 (SEPTEMBER 2003–JANUARY 2004): Mary joined the team, and nearly murdered Captain Atom in a hypnotic rage induced by Roulette!

THERE'S SOMETHING ABOUT MARY

Mary Batson's parents were killed by Theo Adam on an archaeological expedition in Egypt when she was nine. Mary, who had completely lost her memory, was taken back to the U.S. by Adam's sister, Sarah Primm, who worked for Nick and Nora Bromfeld, a wealthy family in Fawcett City. Adopted by the Bromfelds, Mary lived a sheltered life.

Years later, Mary was reintroduced to Billy Batson, who recognized her as his long-lost sister. Billy and his friend Freddy Freeman arrived at the Bromfelds just as the villain Ibac arrived to kidnap the family. Mary escaped, clutching the gift Billy had brought her to jog her memory, a stuffed animal the twins used to play with called Mister Tawky Tawny. As Mary hid from the kidnappers,

the toy transported her mind to another dimension, where she met the spirit of her slain mother, Marilyn, and the wizard Shazam. Mary's mental blocks vanished and her memory returned. She instinctively sensed that her brother Billy was Captain Marvel. Mary begged the wizard to help her save her family. He agreed and blessed her with a variety of powers she could summon forth by saying the word "Shazam!"

When the kidnappers burst into Mary's room, they found her garbed in a red and gold costume. Invulnerable to their bullets, she overpowered them, but not before her nanny, Sarah Primm, suffered a heart attack. As she lay dying, Sarah confessed her relationship with Theo Adam to Mary, and how she had tried to hide the amnesiac Mary, who had witnessed her parents' murder, with the Bromfelds to give her a chance at a decent life. Billy moved in with the Bromfelds soon after, and the Marvels became Fawcett City's champions, defending the town from master criminals like Doctor Sivana, Captain Nazi, and Mister Mind.

Mary Marvel lost her powers during the Infinite Crisis, but reacquired them as a "gift" from Black Adam. The transfer corrupted her, and a black-garbed Mary Marvel fell under the spell of Eclipso as she explored the depths of her new abilities. **PJ**

JUSTICE LEAGUER *Mary Marvel was once forced to use her power on her teammate Captain Atom in Roulette's fight club, the House.*

DARK DESIRES *Once considered the purest of heroes, Mary was corrupted by Black Adam's and turned against her friends in the months prior to the Final Crisis.*

MISTER E

FIRST APPEARANCE SECRETS OF HAUNTED HOUSE #31 (Dec. 1980)
STATUS Villain   **REAL NAME** Erik (last name unrevealed)
OCCUPATION Destroyer of supernatural evil; historian   **BASE** Boston
HEIGHT 6ft 3in   **WEIGHT** 190 lbs
EYES Blue   **HAIR** Black, white at temples
SPECIAL POWERS/ABILITIES Can time-travel at will; claims to be able to
see good or evil within a person; carries a thick wooden cane.

As a boy, Mister E was simply known as Erik, a child whose eyes were scooped out with a spoon by his insane father, who would rather Erik be blind than be "led into temptation." Traumatized by the abuse, Erik became the enigmatic Mister E in adulthood and used his "inner sight" to battle supernatural forces. E also acquired the ability to walk through time, a power he used to determine whether or not young Timothy Hunter—destined to become Earth's greatest sorcerer—might one day destroy the world. E at first believed it better to kill Tim than risk Earth's fate. However, after facing the Temptress, a being who manipulated the events of his youth leading to his own blinding, E decided not to kill Tim. Paradoxically, this decision broke the cycle of abuse begun by Erik's father. Mister E regained his sight and continues to combat supernatural evil wherever he sees it. **SB**

MISTER FREEZE   *SEE OPPOSITE PAGE*

MISTER MIND

FIRST APPEARANCE CAPTAIN MARVEL ADVENTURES #26
(August 1943)
STATUS Villain   **REAL NAME** Unknown
OCCUPATION Criminal mastermind   **BASE** Mobile
LENGTH 3in   **WEIGHT** 5 oz   **EYES** Black   **HAIR** None
SPECIAL POWERS/ABILITIES One of the planet's most formidable
telepaths, though his physical strength is negligible.

The world's wickedest worm comes from Venus and claims that his people once ruled the Earth between the extinction of the dinosaurs and the first Ice Age. His dreams of planetary re-conquest have so far come to nothing, but it may be only a matter of time!

Years ago, Mister Mind and his brethren plotted to escape their planet with the help of Doctor Sivana and launch an invasion, with Fawcett City as their beachhead. Captain Marvel saved Earth by transporting the worms into deep space, where most of them froze. Sarge Steel took custody of Mr. Mind's comatose form.

However, Mister Mind took mental control of Sarge Steel, orchestrated the release of the Mister Atom robot, which arrived in the Fawcett City suburb of Fairfield, and detonated an atomic bomb. The firestorm flattened Fairfield and killed thousands, but that was just Mister Mind's warm-up act. Mister Mind helped orchestrate the takeover of Khandaq by manipulating Brainwave II. During the Infinite Crisis, he evolved into a moth-like form and tried to consume the multiverse until sent back in time by Rip Hunter and Booster Gold. **DW**

ESCAPING SCOTT FREE *Aero Discs bearing him aloft, Mister Miracle crashes into action with his costume's Mother Box warning him of impending danger and healing any cut or scrape.*

GETTING FREE *Scott has traveled the world using his escape artistry to teach that freedom comes from within and that no prison is escape-proof. His skills have also come in handy when he and his wife, Big Barda, have found themselves in a spot of bother.*

MISTER MIRACLE

FIRST APPEARANCE MISTER MIRACLE (1st series) #1 (April 1971)
STATUS Hero   **REAL NAME** Scott Free
OCCUPATION Escapologist; adventurer   **BASE** Mobile
HEIGHT 6ft   **WEIGHT** 185 lbs   **EYES** Blue   **HAIR** Black
SPECIAL POWERS/ABILITIES Expert fighter; master escape artist; Mother
Box incorporated into costume; Aero Discs for flight; multi-cube fires
laser beams, emits sonic vibrations, or releases strong cable.

Mister Miracle is the son of Highfather of New Genesis, once the leader of the New Gods. As an infant, he was exchanged with Darkseid's son Orion, to secure a truce between the warring worlds of New Genesis and Apokolips. He was reared in one of the gulag-like orphanages overseen by the hateful Granny Goodness, who sarcastically dubbed him "Scott Free." Despite her attempts to turn him into another mindless minion of Darkseid, Scott remained incorruptible. He often broke out of the orphanage, meeting the insurgent Himon, as well as Big Barda, leader of the Female Furies.

Scott escaped Apokolips and journeyed to Earth, where he encountered escape artist Thaddeus Brown, known as Mister Miracle, and Oberon, Brown's manager. When Brown was murdered, Scott became Mister Miracle and brought the killers to justice. Scott reunited with Barda, who had also slipped from Granny's grasp. They wed and continued to thwart Darkseid's schemes on Earth. Mister Miracle joined the Justice League of America and remains an auxiliary member. Shilo Norman, the second Mister Miracle, served with the Seven Soldiers of Victory. Scott Free recently suffered the loss of his wife, Barda. **SB**

MISTER FREEZE

First appearance BATMAN #121 (February 1959)
Status Villain **Real name** Victor Fries
Occupation Professional criminal **Base** Gotham City
Height 6ft **Weight** 190 lbs **Eyes** Icy blue **Hair** White
Special powers/abilities Victor has a vast intellect, but has subsumed it in favor of brute force, using his Freeze Gun and super-cooling armor to get what he wants.

Describing Victor Fries as cold-hearted is just the tip of the iceberg. To escape the pressures of his brutal father, young Victor developed an unusual hobby: freezing animals. He thought he was preserving his pets forever, but his father saw things otherwise and sent the boy for counseling. The psychiatrist viewed this freezing tendency as Victor's way of controlling his world. Isolated and ridiculed at school and college, Victor believed he would never know the warm touch of humanity. Then came Nora, the beautiful athlete who stole his heart. They married and when his beloved was stricken with a rare malady, Fries left his teaching post to work for drugs company Gothcorp, hoping their technology would help him find a cure. Exposure to a hail of super-coolants altered his body chemistry, and the brilliant cryogenicist now wears a suit of air-conditioned armor to remain comfortably chilled.

COLD HANDS, WARM HEART

Nora loved the scientist and he idolized her, making her illness and subsequent death all the more heart-wrenching.

FROSTY RECEPTION *The need for a cold environment has always proven a challenge for the villain, and an inconvenience for his cohorts.*

COLD AS ICE

Desperate to cure Nora, Victor had placed her in suspended animation to halt the disease consuming her. Then disaster struck: Gothcorp decided to deny him the vital funding to save Nora's life. Wielding an ice-blasting cold gun, Mr. Freeze revenged himself upon the soulless corporation. He set about killing Gothcorp's executives, working his way up the organization and saving C.E.O. Ferris Boyle for last. An ensuing clash with the Batman, however, shattered any hope for Nora's recovery. Accidentally firing his cold gun at Nora's cryochamber, Freeze fractured her slumbering body into a million shards. Yet he still found a way for Nora to live, by immersing her in a Lazarus Pit. Unfortunately the experience transformed her into the insane villainess Lazara. **PJ**

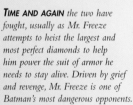

TIME AND AGAIN *the two have fought, usually as Mr. Freeze attempts to heist the largest and most perfect diamonds to help him power the suit of armor he needs to stay alive. Driven by grief and revenge, Mr. Freeze is one of Batman's most dangerous opponents.*

KEE-RACK!

KEY STORYLINES
- *UNDERWORLD UNLEASHED #1–3 (NOV 1995–JAN 1996):* Mister Freeze is given enhanced powers by Neron, but loses the ability to generate cold without his freeze gun.
- *BATMAN #635–638 (FEBRUARY–MAY 2005):* During the "Under the Hood" saga, Mister Freeze is hired to work for Black Mask, but can't prevent the return of Jason Todd.
- *BATGIRL #70 (JANUARY 2006):* Mister Freeze hopes Ra's al Ghul's daughter can restore his wife using the Lazarus Pit; but, she becomes an insane villainess called Lazara.

NEW GODS

HEROES OF THE FOURTH WORLD

FIRST APPEARANCE NEW GODS (1st series) #1 (March 1971)
STATUS Good and evil beings **BASE** New Genesis and Apokolips
NOTABLE NEW GODS
See individual entries for powers and abilities.
Bekka, Big Barda, Black Racer, Darkseid, Doctor Bedlam, Esak (deceased), Fastbak, Forager I (deceased), Forager II, The Forever People, Glorious Godfrey, Highfather (deceased), Himon (deceased), Kalibak, Lightray, Lonar (deceased), Mantis, Metron, Mister Miracle, Orion, Takion, Tiggra (deceased).

*The New Gods 1) Darkseid 2) Desaad
3) Glorious Godfrey 4) Heggra
5) Granny Goodness 6) Black Racer
7) Doctor Bedlam 8) Mokkari 9) Steppenwolf
10) Kanto 11) Kalibak 12) Mantis
13) Virman Vunderbar 14) Himon
15) Devilance16) Lightray 17) Mister Miracle
18) Fastbak 19) Metron 20) Highfather
21) Forager I 22) Big Barda 23) Avia
24) Lonar 25) Orion 26) Simyan 27) Bekka.
The New Gods of New Genesis know that Earth
will one day give rise to a Fifth World of super-
beings, already heralded by the abundance of super
heroes, to prevent the New Gods of Apokolips from
finding the Anti-Life Equation.*

Long, long ago, before time was even measured, there existed a race of Old Gods whose world was split apart in a fiery holocaust, unleashing a coruscating "godwave" of energy that swept across the universe. This godwave empowered the Olympian Gods and gave rise to latter-day human super heroes as it rebounded back and forth in continued, but diminishing, reverberation, seeding world after world with the potential for near-omnipotent power.

WAR OF THE WORLDS
On its fourth passing, the godwave infused the Old Gods' divided world. Out of the ashes arose two molten planets, New Genesis and Apokolips, collectively known as the Fourth World. New Genesis was home to the noble, near-immortal New Gods, who lived in harmony with their lush and verdant planet. Conversely, the denizens of nearby Apokolips were cunning and cruel, and dedicated to evil. For millions of years, New Genesis and Apokolips waged war upon one another until a peace pact was negotiated with the exchange of hostages, each the son of one world's leader. True to his nature, Apokolips's ruler Darkseid broke his pact with New Genesis's ruler Highfather by invading Earth in search of the Anti-Life Equation, the means to control all sentient life in the universe.

The New Gods met their end when a mysterious attacker ripped the souls from their bodies. Lightray, Magnar, and even the Black Racer numbered among the first casualties, and Takon, leader of New Genesis, found he could no longer access the omnipotent Source. Metron investigated the mystery and was the first to uncover the killer, while Darkseid waited for the inevitable. Big Barda's death proved one of the most shocking, prompting Mister Miracle to ally with Orion and Superman to avenge her death. **SB**

KEY STORYLINES
• *SUPERMAN'S PAL, JIMMY OLSEN #134 (DEC. 1970):* Darkseid's debut is harbinger to the introduction of the Fourth World.
• *THE HUNGER DOGS (1984):* Fourth World creator Jack Kirby's graphic novel marks his final story chronicling the New Gods.
• *COSMIC ODYSSEY #1–4 (1988):* Darkseid's quest for the Anti-Life Equation unites New Gods and heroes from Earth in a race to prevent universal destruction.

NIGHTWING

First appearance TALES OF THE TEEN TITANS #43 (July 1984)
Status Hero   **Real name** Richard "Dick" Grayson
Occupation Police officer; crime fighter   **Base** Blüdhaven
Height 5ft 10in   **Weight** 175 lbs   **Eyes** Blue   **Hair** Black
Special powers/abilities Second only to Batman in fighting skills and detective abilities; utility belt includes regurgitant gas pellets, smoke capsules, acetylene torch, flexi-cuffs, Batarangs, and shuriken-like Wing-Dings; bulletproof and fire-resistant costume is insulated and wired as single-shot taser to incapacitate attackers; right gauntlet carries hand-held 100,000-volt stun gun; preferred weapons are twin shatterproof polymer Escrima sticks, held in spring-loaded pouches in the back of costume for swift deployment in close-quarters fighting.

NIGHTWING IS DICK GRAYSON, the very first ROBIN now grown to manhood. Dick realized the need to leave the shadow of his mentor Batman and establish his own heroic presence. The Dark Knight accelerated Dick's decision by firing the young hero, who had just joined the Teen Titans, from his role as teen sidekick. Batman thought Robin would return to his side, but Dick accepted the decision and left the Batcave. Not long after, he ceded the role of Robin to orphan Jason Todd. For Dick Grayson, there would be no turning back. After much soul-searching, he adopted a new guise inspired by two of his childhood heroes. To remain a creature of the night like the Dark Knight, Dick became Nightwing. The name was recommended by Superman, a role model for Dick, after a mysterious hero of Kryptonian

FLYING GRAYSON *Having learned acrobatic skills from his parents, Dick is a gifted aerialist, perhaps surpassing even Batman in agility.*

NIGHTWING TAKES FLIGHT

Nightwing flew into action for the first time to save his fellow Teen Titans from Deathstroke the Terminator and the criminal consortium known as H.I.V.E (Hierarchy of International Vengeance and Extermination). He continued to lead the Titans thereafter, eventually reconciling with his former mentor Batman and reclaiming his status as the Dark Knight's closest and most trusted ally. When the Titans disbanded, Nightwing resumed solo crimefighting.

At Batman's behest, Nightwing left Gotham—his home since the deaths of his parents, the Flying Graysons—and moved to neighboring Blüdhaven, a crime-ridden port city desperately in need of its own defender. With Blüdhaven mired in corruption, Dick made law enforcement his day job also, enrolling in the city's police academy and eventually graduating to become a rookie cop with the B.P.D. Nightwing used his nocturnal hours to undermine mob boss Roland Desmond (Blockbuster) and the city's feuding gang lords. Nightwing even found time to join a fourth lineup of Titans before the group suffered the deaths of two longtime members. Soon after, Nightwing helped to establish a new team of heroes, dubbed the Outsiders after a defunct cadre of clandestine crime fighters Batman himself had once led. Rather than simply react to villainy, the Outsiders under Nightwing's leadership took a proactive approach to rooting out evil, hunting the world's Most Wanted and bringing them to justice. The Dark Knight's former squire continues to fight the good fight and make his mentor proud of both the man and the hero that he has become. **SB**

HALLEY'S CIRCUS *Before Dick's aerialist parents were murdered by gangsters they were a major circus act.*

KEY STORYLINES

• *TALES OF THE TEEN TITANS #41–44, ANNUAL #3 (APRIL–JULY 1984):* Deathstroke hunts the Teen Titans, leaving the all-new Nightwing the last Titan standing and the team's only hope!
• *BATMAN #440-442, NEW TITANS #60-61 (OCTOBER–DECEMBER 1989):* In "A Lonely Place of Dying," Nightwing meets his successor as Boy Wonder, Tim Drake, and fights alongside Batman to defeat Two-Face!
• *NIGHTWING #1 (1988):* At Batman's behest, Nightwing makes Blüdhaven his new home and brings costumed justice to the crime-ridden seaport.

TROIA'S DEATH *Nightwing's Titans teammate and closest friend, died in his arms. Despite strong feelings on both sides, the two were never romantically linked.*

THE OUTSIDER *Nightwing found an important role as leader of the Outsiders vigilante team, organized by Batman to track down criminals who were beyond the law's reach.*

COMBAT MASTER *Not even a posse of trained killers can subdue lightning-quick Nightwing!*

OLSEN, JIMMY

FIRST APPEARANCE SUPERMAN (1st series) #13 (November 1941)
STATUS Hero **REAL NAME** James Bartholomew Olsen
OCCUPATION Journalist; photographer **BASE** Metropolis
HEIGHT 6ft 2in **WEIGHT** 210 lbs **EYES** Blue **HAIR** Red
SPECIAL POWERS/ABILITIES Only an average athlete but has a keen photographer's eye; seemingly fearless in the face of danger; unswervingly loyal to his friends; periodically falls victim to bizarre mutant abilities he is usually powerless to control.

THE FIRST TWO PEOPLE ever rescued by Superman were Lois Lane (*see* Lane, Lois) and a fresh-faced photographer named Jimmy Olsen. Superman befriended Jimmy and the teen became one of the Man of Steel's most faithful admirers. In return, Superman gave Jimmy a special watch with a hypersonic signal only Superman could hear, which the teen used to alert the Man of Steel. Inspired by his hero, Jimmy has embarked on many adventures, risking life and limb to get prize-winning shots. Who else but Jimmy could have fearlessly photographed the deadly battle between Superman and Doomsday?

COUNTDOWN
Jimmy has earned Superman's trust and, with it, a signal watch to summon the Man of Steel!

LOOKING FOR TROUBLE

Jimmy was brought up by his mother Sarah in Metropolis's Bakerline section, after his father, Jake Olsen, a covert military operative, went missing. The boy proved to be highly intelligent and became an academic star. But what Jimmy really wanted was action. He signed on as an intern and then a junior photographer at the *Daily Planet* newspaper. He quickly developed a crush on the paper's star reporter Lois Lane, who tolerated the eager young pup and often brought him along on assignments. Jimmy also fell under *Daily Planet* editor Perry White's sway. White instilled in him the vital importance of photographs to truthful reporting, and the pair have something of a father-son relationship—which can turn explosive when Jimmy infuriates Perry by "accidentally" calling him "Chief." Strange superpowers manifested when Jimmy investigated the deaths of the New Gods. Discovering abilities including super speed, stretching, flame breath, and the power to grow porcupine quills or a turtle's shell, Jimmy branded himself as the superhero 'Mister Action.' He later traveled to Apokolips to help Forager investigate find the New Gods' killer. **RG**

SUPERMAN ARRIVES *When a costumed figure first flew over Metropolis, reporter Lois Lane grabbed her favorite photographer, Jimmy Olsen. They covered the year's biggest story, the arrival of Superman.*

THE CHIEF *Still learning, Jimmy is often given guidance by Perry White—in no uncertain terms!*

THIS IS A JOB FOR SUPERMAN! *The Man of Steel has rescued Jimmy from certain death almost as often as he has saved Lois Lane!*

MISTER ACTION *Jimmy's strange superpowers only appeared when danger threatened, prompting him to go into the superhero business. Approaching to the Final Crisis, Jimmy used his abilities to explore Apokolips and battle Darkseid.*

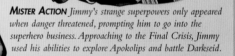

KEY STORYLINES

• *SUPERMAN'S METROPOLIS #1–12 (APRIL 2003–MARCH 2004):* Jimmy and Metropolis's Brainiac-created artificial intelligence learn from one another.
• *SUPERMAN'S PAL JIMMY OLSEN #133–134 (OCTOBER–DECEMBER 1971):* Jimmy learns of Darkseid's threat and begins a series of amazing adventures.
• *SUPERMAN #143 (MAY 1990):* Jimmy learns the truth about his father's disappearance and connection with Project Cadmus.

ONOMATOPOEIA

FIRST APPEARANCE GREEN ARROW (3rd series) #11 (February 2002)
STATUS Villain **REAL NAME** Unrevealed
OCCUPATION Assassin **BASE** Mobile
HEIGHT 5ft 11in **WEIGHT** 180 lbs
EYES Hidden by mask **HAIR** Unknown
SPECIAL POWERS/ABILITIES A superb athlete; expert with guns, knives, and swords; does things no normal human could accomplish, including biting one of Green Arrow's weapons in half.

The motivation that makes Onomatopoeia cross the country killing third-rate costumed heroes (i.e. Harrisburg, Pennsylvania's Buckeye) and assorted vigilantes remains an unexplained mystery. He seems to be deliberately working his way up from the bottom and moving on to more powerful and well-known adversaries; however, like so much about Onomatopoeia, this is mere conjecture. As his name suggests, he expresses himself using only onomatopoeic words. The last sound victims hear is Onomatopoeia's imitation of the noise made by the weapon he is about to use to murder them.

Green Arrow II Connor Hawke was one of Onomatopoeia's most notable victims. Ambushing the archer in the alley, the killer grazed his head with a gunshot…and then mistakenly left Connor for dead. A blood transfusion saved Connor's life, while his father, Oliver Queen (Green Arrow I) met the assassin with a sharp response on the top of a building. The enigmatic Onomatopoeia still managed to escape. **RG**

ONSLAUGHT, THE

FIRST APPEARANCE (Jihad) SUICIDE SQUAD (1st series) #1 (May 1987); (Onslaught) SUICIDE SQUAD (2nd series) #10 (August 2002)
STATUS Villain team **BASE** Qurac
MEMBERS AND POWERS
Rustam I and II (both deceased) Team leaders; each could summon and wield a blazing scimitar.
Djinn Digitized body of electronic code; density manipulation, phasing; can transform from digital code into a sentient droid.
Jaculi I and II (both deceased) Superspeed.
Manticore I, II, and III (all deceased) Lion-themed battlesuits with machine guns and grenade launchers.
Ravan Martial artist and weapons master; requires specialized body brace to move.
Agni Can create and manipulate fire.
Badb Sonic scream instills panic and hatred.
Ifrit An artificial intelligence based on the brain patterns of Mindboggler (a dead Suicide Squad member).
Koschei the Deathless (deceased) Could animate the dead.
Piscator Amphibious powers; limited telepathy.
Old Mother (deceased) The demon Dahak manifested in an old woman's body.
Dervish Superspeed.
Antiphon Superspeed.
Hyve Can split into multiple, smaller versions of himself.
Tolteca Warrior skills.

The Onslaught is a group of superpowered international terrorists for hire, operating out of the Middle Eastern country of Qurac. Originally called the Jihad, the Onslaught were created by then Quraci president, Marlo, in an attempt to kill the President of the United States. However, Nightshade and Nemesis I, two members of the American Suicide Squad, infiltrated the Jihad, allowing the Squad to launch a preemptive attack on the terrorists and cripple the team.

Later, reborn with new members, the Jihad launched a second attack on the United States. Once again, the Jihad came to blows with the Suicide Squad, this time in New York City, and many of the terrorist villains were captured or killed, including their leader, Rustam.

Years later, a third incarnation of the Jihad emerged and attacked the Hayoth, the Israeli supercommandos, as well as the Justice League of America, after the mercenary Cheshire detonated a nuclear warhead above Qurac, killing more than one million people. The Jihad, mistakenly believing American interests were responsible for the warhead's detonation, hijacked an American airliner heading to Gotham City from Paris. Fortunately, the Outsiders were also aboard the airplane, and the terrorists were defeated.

Recently, Njara Kattuah, the son of the first Rustam, created a new Jihad, now called the Onslaught, with new members. After successfully kidnapping Amanda Waller, the Onslaught was soundly trounced by the Suicide Squad and the Justice Society of America. Deadshot killed Rustam II, but the others escaped and remain at large. **PJ**

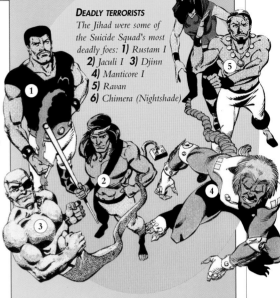

DEADLY TERRORISTS
The Jihad were some of the Suicide Squad's most deadly foes: **1)** Rustam I **2)** Jaculi I **3)** Djinn **4)** Manticore I **5)** Ravan **6)** Chimera (Nightshade).

ANTIPHON This Greek terrorist joined the Onslaught and fought against the Suicide Squad and the JSA. The Onslaught was responsible for the death of Amanda Waller's daughter, Havana.

DIGITAL DEATH The Digital Djinn kills computer hacker Modem.

HYVE This monster drips duplicates of itself that can change into other people and objects!

RUSTAM II The Onslaught leader could generate blazing scimitars of pure fire.

ORACLE

First appearance DETECTIVE COMICS #359 (January 1967)
Status Hero   **Real name** Barbara Gordon
Occupation Information broker   **Base** Gotham City
Height 5ft 11in   **Weight** 148 lbs   **Eyes** Blue   **Hair** Red
Special powers/abilities Superior computer hacker and information retrieval specialist; possesses a photographic memory and is a capable hand-to-hand combatant.

THE JOKER'S BULLET brought Barbara Gordon's high-flying career as Batgirl crashing to earth. However, despite being paralyzed and wheelchair-bound, she has accomplished far more as a crime fighter than she ever could have if she'd remained Batman's enthusiastic assistant in the realm of acrobatics

BEHIND THE SCREEN
Few heroes know Oracle's true identity. Often she appears only as a stylized, holographic head.

BARBARA GORDON
Barbara ("Babs" to her friends) became the adoptive daughter of her uncle James Gordon of the G.C.P.D. following the deaths of her parents. A brilliant student, she graduated from Gotham University at a very young age and took a job with the Gotham Public Library. Barbara admired the city's resident vigilante, Batman, and donned a homemade Batgirl costume to surprise her father at the Policeman's Masquerade. In this low-tech getup she foiled the despicable Killer Moth's attack on Bruce Wayne, and started a new life as a compatriot to the Dynamic Duo of Batman and Robin.

WayneCorp has helped Oracle obtain the latest technology.

KILLING JOKE *In an act that changed Gotham forever, the Joker shot and crippled Barbara Gordon.*

BIRDS OF PREY *Seen here flanked by the Huntress and Black Canary, Oracle is the director of Gotham's all-female crimebusting team.*

During her time as Batgirl, Barbara served a term in the U.S. Congress. After a near-fatal run-in with the assassin Cormorant, Barbara retired from active crime fighting. Shortly after, as part of a revenge plot against Commissioner Gordon, the Joker burst in on her and shot her in the spine. During rehabilitation she learned she would never walk again.

Barbara trained her upper body to physical perfection with the help of Richard Dragon and then packaged her skills as an information retrieval expert under the name Oracle. She worked with Amanda Waller of the U.S. government's Suicide Squad, becoming second-in-command under the alias Amy Beddoes.

Oracle began to operate out of Gotham City's imposing clocktower, behind banks of supercomputers running state-of-the-art hacking software. Soon, the "all-seeing, all-knowing" Oracle became a legend in the super-hero community. She recruited heroes into an informal "Birds of Prey" team (members have included Black Canary, Power Girl, and Huntress), to act on her data.

The destruction of Oracle's clocktower during a Gotham gang war prompted her relocation to Metropolis. She accepted a marriage proposal from Nightwing, but sidelined the romance due to the events of the Infinite Crisis. She recently survived Spy Smasher's challenge to her status as Birds of Prey leader. **DW**

KEY STORYLINES
• **BATGIRL: YEAR ONE #1–9 (FEBRUARY–OCTOBER 2003):** Batgirl battles Killer Moth in this retelling of her heroic debut.
• **BATMAN: THE KILLING JOKE (TPB, 1988):** A bullet from the Joker's gun paralyzes Barbara in a moment that shocked readers.
• **BIRDS OF PREY #1 (JANUARY 1999):** Working from Gotham's clocktower, Oracle begins a new career as a super-heroic string-puller.

THE OUTSIDERS

FIRST APPEARANCE Brave and the Bold #200 (July 1983)
STATUS Hero team **BASE** Brooklyn, New York City
CURRENT MEMBERS AND POWERS
BATMAN Master combatant, strategist, and detective
BATGIRL One of the world's greatest martial artists
GEO-FORCE Can manipulate gravity as well as powers linked to the Earth
GRACE Super-strong and near-invulnerable Amazonian
KATANA Skilled martial artist wielding an enchanted sword
METAMORPHO Can transmute body into chemical compounds

THE OUTSIDERS 1) *Batman*
2) *Catwoman* **3)** *Katanna*
4) *Metamorpho* **5)** *Grace Choi*
6) *Thunder III* **7)** *Martian Manhunter*

THE OUTSIDERS LIVE UP TO THEIR NAME by flatly refusing to work within the expected constraints of international law and propriety. The current version of the team is committed to taking proactive action—squashing meta-human and alien threats before they even have the chance to become threats! The original Outsiders included Black Lightning, Metamorpho, Looker, Halo, and the Markovian noble Geo-Force. Based in Gotham City and backed financially by Bruce Wayne, the hero team were an outgrowth of Batman's frustration with the political constraints under which the Justice League of America were forced to operate.

DIRECT ACTION

When Baron Bedlam kidnapped Lucius Fox in Markovia, the Justice League of America refused to interfere for fear of upsetting a nation's internal politics. Batman quit the JLA in disgust and formed his Outsiders to handle the Markovia incident and similar, unorthodox missions. Geo-Force fought with Batman over the Dark Knight's tendency to withhold information from team members. Batman quit, and Geo-Force led the team, which relocated to Los Angeles. During this period the Outsiders became agents of the Markovian government. Later additions to the roster included the airstream-manipulating Windfall and the armored Atomic Knight. Geo-Force eventually disbanded this team.

GEO-FORCE *The Outsiders' greatest leader.*

CRAKOOOM **KWOO-ONCK**

NEW BLOOD *Grace and Thunder are two brash young additions, lending their muscle to battle threats like Gorilla Grodd.*

Reunited in Markovia, the Outsiders became fugitives framed for the murder of the country's monarch), Queen Ilona. They cleared their names but split into two squads: one led by Geo-Force and including Katana and the warsuited Technocrat; the other led by the Kryptonian Eradicator and including Looker, Halo, Faust, and the bear-creature Wylde. The two teams united and the Outsiders remained active through the Imperiex War (*see* Great Battles, pp. 186–7), their last member being Doctor Light II.

Former Titan Arsenal founded a new team, led by Nightwing and featuring newcomers Grace, Thunder III, and Indigo. Operating outside the law to end threats before they could begin, the new Outsiders ran missions alongside Checkmate before Batman stepped in to take charge of the group once more. **DW**

KEY STORYLINES
• **BATMAN AND THE OUTSIDERS #1 (AUGUST 1983):** The classic Outsiders team makes its debut while meddling in foreign affairs.
• **OUTSIDERS (2ND SERIES) #1 (NOVEMBER 1985):** Without Batman, the Outsiders move to California.
• **OUTSIDERS (3RD SERIES) #1 (JUNE 2003):**

GREAT TEAM-UPS

TWO HEADS ARE BETTER THAN ONE is not an axiom that finds favor with all super heroes. Some hate to share, some combinations just don't click, and sometimes a spot of unresolved sexual tension clouds the issue. Before too long, all manner of hostility is bubbling to the surface. However, if two heroes are compatible, a team-up can lead to lasting friendship and mutual respect: a meeting of minds and talents. Here's a look at some classic combinations...

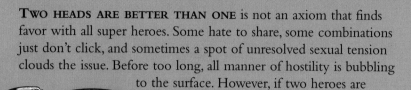

SUPERMAN/WONDER WOMAN

He thought she was mortal, like himself. She thought he was a deity, like her creators, the Olympian Gods. Despite their differences, these two champions and close friends share a common desire: to defend justice, protect the innocent, and help mankind.

ATOM/HAWKMAN

Given that opposites attract, it makes sense that a deep bond of friendship developed between the warrior Hawkman and the rational scientist Ray Palmer, alias the Atom. They work well together, mixing their abilities and knowledge to become a formidable duo.

ROBIN/BATGIRL

A Dynamic Duo in their own right, Robin and Batgirl's partnership began as an attempt by Batman to dissuade Batgirl from vigilantism. The couple's love found fuller expression in adulthood; by then Dick Grayson was Nightwing, and Barbara Gordon was known as Oracle.

CONSTANTINE/SWAMP THING

Alec Holland's essence was housed in the body of Earth's current elemental but unaware of the greater forces that controlled the world and even the cosmos. John Constantine, the ultimate manipulator, traded lessons and information for Swamp Thing's help when it mattered most. When Swamp Thing needed a human to impregnate his wife Abby Holland, he turned to Constantine. As a result, they share a bond of purpose, even friendship.

CYBORG/CHANGELING

Vic Stone, the Cyborg hated the cybernetic pieces that kept him alive, and as a result was sullen and withdrawn, coming to life only when the Teen Titans were in action. The younger, thrill-seeking Changeling, in contrast was always in action. Over time they learned much from each other, and a deep bond of friendship now exists, whether they are part of the Titans or on their own.

GREEN LANTERN II/GREEN ARROW I

Straight-laced Hal Jordan had his eyes opened by the older, more cynical Oliver Queen. They first met in Vietnam, where they teamed up to stop a dictator. They then toured America, gaining a vital understanding of the problems plaguing the common man. They learned much from each other; so much so that before sacrificing himself to save the world, Jordan used his extraordinary power as Parallax to bring Oliver back from the dead.

BOOSTER GOLD/BLUE BEETLE

They first met during a tour of duty with the Justice League of America, where a fraternal bond was quickly established. Both being single and well-to-do, they used their free time to chase women, fight crime, explore get-rich-quick schemes and periodically save the world. With age, though, came personal changes and the once firm friendship developed cracks.

ATTACKED FROM ALL SIDES

Accused of "crimes against humanity" by the administration of President Lex Luthor, Superman becomes a target for meta-human villains secretly acting on Luthor's orders. Fortunately Superman's JLA comrade-in-arms, Batman is on hand to help in a tight corner!

SUPERMAN/BATMAN

Superman takes on crises as they arise; Batman prefers a crushing, preemptive strike. Superman is good-natured, optimistic, and considerate; Batman suspicious, pessimistic, and brooding. Given their very different approaches to life and to their missions, it's odd to find the Man of Tomorrow working alongside the Dark Knight Detective. They have clashed on several occasions, yet, time and again they have found themselves helping one another or working together for the greater good of humanity. They respect one another's methods and secrets, while not wholly approving of the other's complete approach to the work.

FLASH II/KID FLASH

When Barry Allen, the second Flash realized that his nephew, Wally West had similar Speed Force powers, he gave him his own junior-sized Flash costume. Soon, Wally was partnering his idol as Kid Flash. Barry taught Wally some amazing tricks, such as how to vibrate right through solid objects. RG

PANTHA

FIRST APPEARANCE NEW TITANS #74 (March 1991)
STATUS Hero (deceased) **REAL NAME** None (originally designated X-24)
OCCUPATION Adventurer **BASE** Science City, Russia
HEIGHT 5ft 8.5in **WEIGHT** 136 lbs **EYES** Red **HAIR** Auburn
SPECIAL POWERS/ABILITIES Incredible predatory speed, strength, and
agility; indestructible claws on hands and feet; cat-like visual acuity.

The were-cat known as Pantha was
created by the Wildebeest Society. She
was one example of the Society's
attempts to alter human and animal
DNA and adapt suitable host bodies
for the vengeful souls of Azarath. These souls had once
belonged to peaceful, other-dimensional mystics who
had raised the Teen Titan known as Raven and shielded
her from the demonic Trigon. The Azarathians possessed
Raven's fellow Teen Titan Jericho, making him leader of
the Wildebeest Society as it worked in secret to fulfill
their master plans.

While the majority of the Wildebeest's
bio-engineered test subjects perished, Pantha
survived and escaped. Later, she helped the Titans and
Deathstroke defeat Jericho and the Wildebeests.
A Titan herself for a time, Pantha eventually departed
the team with Red Star and Baby Wildebeest.
The latter was the Wildebeest Society's final
experiment, a creature that bonded to Pantha,
who became its "mother." During the Infinite
Crisis, Superboy-Prime decapitated Pantha with
a superpowered punch. **SB**

CAT/WOMAN
*Since her escape
from the Wildebeests,
Pantha has sought to
learn whether or not she
is really a genetically altered
human or an evolved feline.*

PARALLAX

FIRST APPEARANCE GREEN LANTERN (3rd ser.) #50
(Mar. 1994)
STATUS Villain **REAL NAME** Inapplicable
OCCUPATION Fear entity **BASE** Mobile
HEIGHT Various **WEIGHT** Various
EYES Yellow **HAIR** None
SPECIAL POWERS/ABILITIES Feeds on fear and can instill
great fear in others; can possess other beings as hosts.

In Parallax is the living
embodiment of fear and the
natural enemy of the willpower
entity ION. Since the dawn
of time, Parallax has fed on
the terror of others, until
imprisoned in the Central
Power Battery on Oa by the
Guardians of the Universe. There,
Parallax's essence corrupted the
emerald energy used by the Green Lantern
Corps, making their power rings vulnerable to
the color yellow (a flaw referred to as the "yellow
impurity"). When the Cyborg Superman destroyed
Coast City, home of Hal Jordan (Green Lantern),
Parallax took root in Jordan's psyche and turned him into a
twisted version of his former self. Jordan made war against the Guardians and his
teammates, annihilating the Corps and attempting (with Extant) to wipe out all of
reality during the Zero Hour event.

Although Jordan eventually became the host for the Spectre, Parallax retained
a foothold. Only after purging Parallax could Jordan return as his true self.
Parallax in turn took possession of Green Lantern Kyle Rayner during the Sinestro
Corps War. Killing numerous Lanterns, Parallax spread fear throughout the cosmos
until Rayner fought his way free. Parallax then found itself quartered and locked
inside the power batteries of Hal Jordan, Kyle Rayner, Guy Gardner,
and John Stewart. **DW**

PARASITE

FIRST APPEARANCE ACTION COMICS #240 (August 1966)
STATUS Villain **REAL NAME** Rudy Jones; Torval Freeman
OCCUPATION Professional criminal **BASE** Metropolis
HEIGHT Variable **WEIGHT** Variable **EYES** Red **HAIR** None
SPECIAL POWERS/ABILITIES Absorbed the life essence of living
creatures, killing them; absorbed meta-human powers; could
shape-change; size and shape varied with energy absorbed.

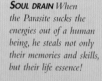

Rudy Jones was a maintenance worker at S.T.A.R.
Labs in Metropolis, who tried to smuggle scientific
waste out of the laboratory to sell illegally. Jones
opened one of the waste containers and was
irradiated with an isotope that transformed his body.
To survive, Jones was forced to absorb the life energies
of other living beings, much like a vampire. Searching for
the ultimate "meal," the Parasite began a lifelong pursuit
of Superman, whom he considered a living power
battery. The two clashed repeatedly, but the Parasite's
craving for the Man of Steel's solar-powered energy was always unfulfilled.

After absorbing the life energies of Doctor Torvell Freeman, the Parasite
retained Freeman's psyche and memories. The two personalities became
locked in a battle for supremacy for the Parasite's body, making him
more dangerous than ever. After the Parasite tried to absorb
SUPERGIRL's angelic energies, he found himself haunted by
the voices of every one of his victims, and was nearly
driven mad. The Parasite then kidnapped Lois Lane (*see
Lane, Lois*), from whom he learned Superman's secret
identity, and took her place. Although the Parasite
appeared to have died from kryptonite poisoning,
he recently reappeared offering his power-
draining services for a fee to metahuman criminals
hoping to temporarily avoid monitoring. **PJ**

SOUL DRAIN *When
the Parasite sucks the
energies out of a human
being, he steals not only
their memories and skills,
but their life essence!*

SUPER ABSORPTION *The leech-like creature's mightiest
meal proved its doom, as the Parasite absorbed not
only Superman's power, but kryptonite poisoning!*

PARK, LINDA

FIRST APPEARANCE THE FLASH (2nd series) #28 (July 1989)
STATUS Hero **REAL NAME** Linda Jasmine Park
OCCUPATION Television journalist; medical student
BASE Keystone City **HEIGHT** 5ft 6in **WEIGHT** 137 lbs
EYES Brown **HAIR** Black **SPECIAL POWERS/ABILITIES** She has no superpowers but is brave and resourceful; the Flash's equal for sheer gumption and his perfect partner.

Linda Park thought Wally West (Flash III) was brash and arrogant—which he was. But Linda also saw something else in him, the spark of a better man. As their relationship developed, that spark became the flames of love. So strong was their bond that it has enabled Flash to find his way home, regardless of time, dimension, or location, as they discovered when the Flash III pushed himself past his previous limits and joined the Speed Force.

Linda was seemingly killed by a supernatural entity called the Black Flash, which sent Wally West spiraling into a depression. The Flash ultimately rescued Linda from within the Speed Force and they made plans to wed.

SOULMATES
Linda loved the whirlwind life her husband led as the Flash.

As the marriage ceremony was about to take place, Linda was kidnapped by the villain Abra Kadabra and the world's memory of her was erased. Fortunately, the Flash sorted everything out, the couple married at last, and Linda enrolled at Central City Medical College. A short time later, pregnant with twins, she was attacked by Zoom and suffered a miscarriage. A time anomaly restored her pregnancy, and she gave birth to twins Iris and Jai. Linda struggles to keep pace with the twins' growing abilities. **RG**

END OF THE DREAM After her miscarriage, Linda came to question her life as a super hero's spouse and left to decide her future.

PARIAH

FIRST APPEARANCE CRISIS ON INFINITE EARTHS #1 (April 1985)
STATUS Hero **REAL NAME** Mossa
OCCUPATION Adventurer **BASE** Mobile
HEIGHT 5ft 11in **WEIGHT** 165 lbs **EYES** Black **HAIR** Purple
SPECIAL POWERS/ABILITIES Brilliant scientist; invulnerable to physical harm; innately teleports to the focal point of vast danger; it is undetermined whether he is immortal.

In another dimension, the scientist Mossa remained in an antimatter chamber for 13 months, hoping to unlock the secrets of the universe by witnessing Creation at the Dawn of Time. His chamber and world were destroyed in the process. The cursed scientist was renamed Pariah, and as penance for his actions, was forced to spend the next hundred million years witnessing the destruction of world after world and the deaths of countless billions of sentient beings. As red, stormy skies blanketed Earth during the summer heat of July, the Anti-Monitor attempted to destroy the positive matter universe (see The Crisis, Great Battles, pp. 186-7).

Pariah arrived on Earth to warn its people of the impending doom. The Monitor gathered heroes from across time and space to try and stop his evil twin, using the woman Harbinger to collect them. The Anti-Monitor plucked the Earth out of its universe and placed it in the anti-matter universe of Qward, unleashing millions of Shadow Demons across the planet, which slaughtered thousands. Pariah worked with the champions from across time and space to save all reality. Pariah apparently died when attacked by Alexander Luthor, a fellow survivor of the previous multiverse. **RG**

135

PENGUIN

FIRST APPEARANCE DETECTIVE COMICS #58 (December 1941)
STATUS Villain **REAL NAME** Oswald Chesterfield Cobblepot
OCCUPATION Criminal; stock trader; fixer **BASE** Gotham City
HEIGHT 5ft 2in **WEIGHT** 175 lbs **EYES** Blue **HAIR** Black
SPECIAL POWERS/ABILITIES Devious and ruthless, despite his small stature, he is surprisingly agile; usually prefers to flee rather than fight; formerly favored an array of bizarre umbrella weapons; also used his affinity with birds to assist in his crimes.

OSWALD CHESTERFIELD COBBLEPOT based a criminal career as the murderous gangster the Penguin on his fascination with birds and ornithology. This fascination dates back to his childhood, growing up with his widowed mother, who ran a pet shop specializing in exotic birds. Short, paunchy, and burdened with a prominent, beaky nose, his schoolmates nicknamed Oswald the Penguin. His fussy mother insisted he carry an umbrella, even on sunny days, making him the target of widespread ridicule.

EARLY BIRD *The Penguin sought gain wherever possible, even attempting to kidnap Arabian royalty.*

THE BIRD MAN OF GOTHAM

When he grew up, Oswald got his own back on the world by becoming a force to be reckoned with in Gotham City's underworld. He committed scores of crimes (often with a bird-theme), which inevitably led him to run afoul of the Batman and Robin time and again. The Penguin further increased his criminal profile when he met a scientific genius, a deformed mute named Harold, and convinced him to create a device that could control birds, directing them to commit crimes and various acts of terror for him.

LADIES MAN
The Penguin likes to surround himself with the finest acquisitions in life, both animate and inanimate.

Batman stopped this threat and later brought Harold to the Batcave, where he helped maintain the various Bat-vehicles. On parole, the Penguin tried to convince the public he had gone "legit" by playing the stock market. Though exposed for insider trading, the Penguin remained strongly attracted to the notion of concealing his criminal activities beneath a more socially acceptable façade.

To that end, Cobblepot became the owner of a premier Gotham nightspot, the Iceberg Lounge, and purportedly once more reformed. Secretly, he had formed an alliance with a number-cruncher known as the Actuary, who helped the Penguin pull off a series of spectacular robberies. Ultimately, the Actuary took the fall for his partner when Batman tracked them down.

The Penguin really came into his own when a cataclysmic earthquake struck Gotham and the government declared the city a lawless No Man's Land. Cobblepot saw his chance and made a fortune on the black market, trading essential goods and further strengthening his hold over the city's underworld. After Batman and his allies helped get the city back on its feet, the local government tried to shut down the Iceberg Lounge. Instead, Bruce Wayne bought the building, giving his alter ego the opportunity to keep closer tabs on the nefarious, slippery Penguin. **RG**

NO MANS LAND
During Gotham's exile, the Penguin amassed power through barter, favors, and guile.

TALK TO THE BAT *Time and again, the Penguin is pressured into telling Batman vital nuggets of information.*

PENNYWORTH, ALFRED

FIRST APPEARANCE BATMAN #16 (May 1943)
STATUS Heroic ally **REAL NAME** Alfred Pennyworth
OCCUPATION Butler for Wayne Manor **BASE** Gotham City
HEIGHT 6ft **WEIGHT** 160 lbs **EYES** Blue **HAIR** Black
SPECIAL POWERS/ABILITIES Expert medic, mechanic, chauffeur; former soldier and actor (professionally trained); vocal mimic; unswervingly loyal, and an endless source of good advice.

A GENTLEMAN'S GENTLEMAN
Alfred's manners are unimpeachable; his skill with a surgeon's blade is impeccable.

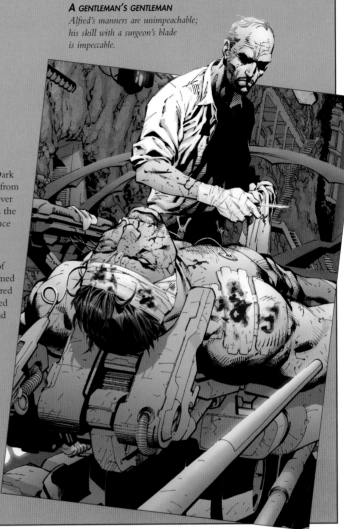

More than a butler, Alfred Pennyworth is the Dark Knight's squire—expert helpmate in every field from sewing to shotguns. The Batman's career could never have happened without the assistance of Alfred, who keeps the Batcave in working order and maintains the public illusion that Bruce Wayne is nothing more than a billionaire playboy.

Born and raised in England, Alfred chose to follow his mother into the theater rather than become a butler for the Wayne family of Gotham City, a job that both his father and grandfather had performed with distinction. After stints as both a soldier and actor, Alfred prepared to marry a young woman, then had his heart broken when he learned she had not been faithful to him. Soon Alfred's father passed away, and Alfred chose to abandon the stage to fulfill his father's obligation to Thomas and Martha Wayne as their family butler.

Two years later Thomas and Martha fell victim to a mugger. Alfred and physician Leslie Thompkins raised the Waynes' young son, Bruce, in Wayne Manor after a maze of paperwork shielded the case from the influence of Gotham Child Services. When an adult Bruce decided to become the vigilante Batman, Alfred became an aide to him and the subsequent string of Robins (*see* Robin): Dick Grayson, Jason Todd, and Tim Drake.

Alfred briefly left Batman's service but soon returned after trips to Antarctica and England. Since then he has survived the destruction of Wayne Manor during a cataclysmic earthquake that turned Gotham City into a lawless No Man's Land and his own near-fatal bout with the Clench virus. Because he knew Bruce as a boy, Alfred is perhaps the only person in the world utterly unfazed by Batman's grim façade. **DW**

PEOPLE'S HEROES, THE

FIRST APPEARANCE OUTSIDERS (1st series) #10 (August 1986)
STATUS Villain group (disbanded) **BASE** The Russian Federation
MEMBERS AND POWERS
Bolshoi A formidable martial artist and superspeedster.
Hammer He possesses superhuman strength and wields a hammer.
Molotov He has an explosive touch.
Pravda She possesses psychic powers.
Sickle A martial artist, her signature weapon is a razor-sharp sickle.

The People's Heroes were a group of superhuman agents created by Communist scientists using information learned through scientific analysis of the American super-team, The Force of July. The Peoples' Heroes were assigned to the Russian secret service and battled the American Outsiders twice to a standstill. The People's Heroes later came into conflict with the Suicide Squad during a kidnapping mission. The Squad squarely defeated the Heroes, leaving Pravda for dead.

After a failed attempt by Hammer and Sickle to execute Red Star, another Russian hero, on behalf of an extreme faction of the Russian government, the People's Heroes were disbanded. However, Molotov and Bolshoi were recruited by the Red Shadows, the Russian counterpart of the Suicide Squad. **PJ**

COMMUNIST AVENGERS *Before disbanding, the People's Heroes were Russia's most patriotic superteam. They are* **1)** *Bolshoi* **2)** *Pravda* **3)** *Molotov* **4)** *Hammer* **5)** *Sickle.*

PERIL, JOHNNY

FIRST APPEARANCE COMIC CAVALCADE #22 (September 1947)
STATUS Hero **REAL NAME** Unknown
OCCUPATION Private investigator **BASE** Unnamed Midwestern city
HEIGHT 6ft 2in **WEIGHT** 195 lbs **EYES** Blue **HAIR** Blond
SPECIAL POWERS/ABILITIES Above-average hand-to-hand fighter; quick-witted and good with a gun.

Johnny Peril's past is a mystery to all who know him. His name, synonymous with adventure and intrigue, is almost certainly an alias. He has been a reporter, a soldier-of-fortune, or a troubleshooter, taking on any high-risk job where more than money is at stake. Johnny is certainly well-traveled. However, despite his apparent addiction to adventure, Johnny isn't afraid to admit a longing for a nice, normal case every once in a while. That's why he currently makes his home in a mundane, Middle American city, having set himself up as a private investigator. He is frequently aided by psychic Heather Storm, in whom Johnny has shown more than a professional interest. **SB**

PLASTIC MAN

FIRST APPEARANCE POLICE COMICS #1 (August 1941)
STATUS Hero   **REAL NAME** Eel O'Brian
OCCUPATION Adventurer   **BASE** Chicago
HEIGHT 6ft 1in   **WEIGHT** 178 lbs   **EYES** Groovy goggles
HAIR Basic Black   **SPECIAL POWERS/ABILITIES** Capable of stretching
every atom in his body into any shape he wishes. He is seemingly
unbreakable and his shape-changing is limited only by his own
overactive imagination; also has a mercurial sense of humor.

EEL O'BRIAN STARTED OUT on the wrong side of the law, but is working hard to make up for it. In 1941, he was just a lowlife gangster. Shot by a guard at the Crawford Chemical Works, he stumbled into a vat of acid, which seeped into his wounds. He escaped and ended up at Rest Haven, a spiritual retreat. While there, he realized that amazing changes in his human form would also allow him to change his ways. He became the hero Plastic Man.

LUCKY BREAK Eel O'Brian's life changed for the better when he ought to have died in the accident.

YOUR FLEXIBLE FRIEND

After serving in both the All-Star Squadron and the Freedom Fighters with distinction during World War II, Plastic Man was employed by the F.B.I. and then its sister agency, the National Bureau of Investigations. To this day, he continues to handle cases for the N.B.I., usually paired with the sloppy, lazy, and dull-witted Woozy Winks. These two improbable partners have an impressive track record. Together they have brought down numerous villains, including, the Dart, Even Steven, and the Brotherhood of the Savage Caribou.

In more recent times, Plastic Man has successfully worked alongside Batman on several cases, despite their strikingly different temperaments. In fact, the Dark Knight recommended Plas for membership for the Justice League of America. Plastic Man has served the League well, despite his tendency to joke about everything.

Batman also learned that Plas had a son, born out of wedlock. Eel's son grew up to inherit his father's incredible "plastic man" abilities, although with greater control. Plastic Man's seeming death in the Obsidian Age, 3000 years ago, left the JLA traumatized. Reduced to atoms, he spent the next three millennia using his conscious mind to reassemble himself. Those millennia of isolation have had a profound affect on him, and O'Brian has rededicated himself to playing a positive role in his son's life, virtually forgetting his heroic persona in favor of becoming a daily presence.

When a demon from Mars's ancient past emerged on Earth, Batman forced Plastic Man to once again be a hero. Eel remains an occasional hero, a pal to Woozy Winks and a full-time father. RG

BUGGED OUT Queen Bee manages to get the drop on Plastic Man, a rare occurrence.

KEY STORYLINES
• **PLASTIC MAN** (3RD SERIES) #1–6 (FEBRUARY–JULY 2004): Plastic Man and Woozy Winks in one of their most madcap adventures yet.
• **JLA #65** (AUGUST 2002): Plastic Man reconnects with his son, thanks to Batman.
• **PLASTIC MAN** (3RD SERIES) #1-4 (NOVEMBER–FEBRUARY 1988-89): Plas and Woozy face the incredibly inept Ooze Brothers.
• **POLICE COMICS #1** (AUGUST 1941): Eel O'Brian turns from petty criminal to costumed crime fighter, thanks to a freak accident.

FIRED UP Plastic Man had to return to action in order to save America from the fiery Fernus, an ancient Martian threat.

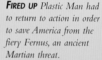

PLASTIC SOLUTION Batman shows the still reassembling Plastic Man—after 3000 years—to the JLA.

FATHER AND SON It took Batman to help, but Eel has rebuilt his relationship with his son, who also possesses his father's incredible stretching power.

PLASTIQUE

FIRST APPEARANCE FURY OF FIRESTORM #7 (December 1982)
STATUS Reformed villain **REAL NAME** Bette Sans Souci
OCCUPATION Former terrorist **BASE** Quebec, Canada
HEIGHT 5ft 6in **WEIGHT** 141 lbs **EYES** Blue **HAIR** Red
SPECIAL POWERS/ABILITIES Is able to cause objects to explode by touching them with her fingertips. A demolitions expert, Plastique has received training in urban terrorism and possesses an incendiary temper.

Plastique was a radical French-Canadian terrorist committed to winning Quebec's independence by any means necessary. Originally she possessed no superpowers, and so she wore a suit rigged with plastic explosives into the offices of the *New York News Express* in an attempt to extort the newspaper's owners.

Firestorm foiled her incendiary plot and sent her to prison, but behind bars Plastique received an injection of an experimental serum that gave her the ability to explode objects by touching them. A second criminal caper teamed Plastique with Killer Frost in a failed attempt to blow up the Niagara Falls power plant.

Plastique became semi-reformed when offered the opportunity to work with the Suicide Squad in exchange for a commuted sentence. Since then, she has changed her criminal ways and hooked up with Captain Atom, eventually becoming his wife. Plastique currently works with the Suicide Squad, and with the Electrocutioner as the two-person "Bomb Squad." **DW**

PLUNDER

FIRST APPEARANCE FLASH (2nd series) #165 (October 2000)
STATUS Villain **REAL NAME** None; a mirror clone of Joseph Morillo
OCCUPATION Bounty hunter **BASE** A mirror image dimension
HEIGHT 5ft 11in **WEIGHT** 190 lbs **EYES** White **HAIR** None
SPECIAL POWERS/ABILITIES Plunder is an expert hitman renowned for his unerring aim; he also possesses numerous handguns and other firearms in his armor; a powerful, if unsophisticated, hand-to-hand combatant.

Plunder was a bounty hunter that existed in a mystical "mirror world" housed within the diamond wedding ring of Linda Park (*see* Park, Linda), the wife of Wally West, the third Flash. A mercenary for the mirror world's Thinker, Plunder discovered that his dimension was fading into non-existence, and hoped to escape into our world. The Thinker hired Plunder to capture two of the Flash's Rogues Gallery, Mirror Master and Captain Cold, to lure the Flash into their mirror dimension. The Flash escaped the Thinker's trap and returned to our dimension. Plunder is the mirror image of Detective Jared Morillo, a Flash ally from the Department of Meta-human Hostility. Plunder shot Morillo, assumed his form, and briefly took his place. Discovered, Plunder forsook Morillo's identity and resumed bounty hunting. **PJ**

POISON IVY

FIRST APPEARANCE BATMAN #181 (June 1966)
STATUS Villain **REAL NAME** Pamela Lillian Isley
OCCUPATION Criminal; eco-terrorist **BASE** Gotham City
HEIGHT 5ft in **WEIGHT** 133 lbs **EYES** Green **HAIR** Chestnut
SPECIAL POWERS/ABILITIES Poison Ivy's altered body chemistry enables her to exude a venomous variety of floral toxins to which she alone is immune. She carries with her a plethora of pernicious plants that germinate from fast-growing seed pods.

PRETTY POISON *Ivy once grew wild in Wayne Manor, taking over Bruce Wayne's mind with her seductive pheromones. Little did Ivy know that she had Batman in her thrall!*

Botanist Pamela Isley was a shrinking violet when she went to work for famed scientist (and super-villain-in-the-making) Dr. Jason Woodrue. The future Floronic Man experimented on her, hoping to create a human/plant hybrid like himself. Woodrue succeeded all too well, creating the ravishing-but-deadly Poison Ivy. Where Isley was gangly and unremarkable, Ivy was gorgeous and unforgettable. Isley's porcelain skin soon took on a green pigmentation as chlorophyll replaced her human blood. Ivy even exuded man-maddening pheromones and natural toxins. She was Poison Ivy in more than name.

Ironically, the sun-loving Ivy found herself drawn to gloomy Gotham City, where she sowed the seeds of a criminal career to fund her true cause as a green guerrilla championing the world's diminishing fauna. Ivy also discovered a worthy foe in Batman, who has resisted Ivy's fragrant charms while uprooting her terrorist schemes. Ivy's victims, consumed by carnivorous plants, triggered the creation of the plant-monster known as Harvest. **SB**

GREENBACKS *Poison Ivy loves the color of money, especially because robbery and extortion help to fund her exotic environmental causes.*

POLAR BOY

FIRST APPEARANCE ADVENTURE COMICS #306 (March 1963)
STATUS Hero **REAL NAME** Brek Bannin
OCCUPATION Adventurer **BASE** Earth
HEIGHT 5ft 5in **WEIGHT** 140 lbs **EYES** Blue **HAIR** Blond
SPECIAL POWERS/ABILITIES Like all natives of Tharr, can generate subzero temperatures as a natural defense against a near-sun orbit.

Tharr's

Brek Bannin has the native power to generate cold. When there was an open call for recruits to join the Legion of Super-Heroes, Bannin was among the first to apply. He failed the tests but decided to join up with other rejects as the Legion of Substitute Super-Heroes. In the Legion's future, Polar Boy fought the anti-alien regime that had taken control of Earth, helping Superman and his fellow Legionnaires despite the loss of his arm. In an alternate Legion timeline, Brek Bannin became a member of the Wanderers under the leadership of Garth Ranzz. **RG**

QUANTUM MECHANICS

FIRST APPEARANCE JLA: HEAVEN'S LADDER (November 2000)
STATUS Cosmic beings **BASE** Mobile
SPECIAL POWERS/ABILITIES Possessed of virtually god-like powers and intellects, the Quantum Mechanics are capable of practically any feat that their imaginations can conceive, including teleporting entire worlds (including Earth) half-way across the universe.

Born at the Big Bang, the Quantum Mechanics roamed the universe, seeking celestial enlightenment. Fear of their own mortality, coupled with their inability to conceive of an afterlife, prompted the Quantum Mechanics to create a vision of heaven. They created thousands of agents to study the cultures of the universe, gathering information about each version of heaven to build the perfect hereafter for themselves. The JUSTICE LEAGUE OF AMERICA first discovered the Quantum Mechanics when these ancient beings abducted planet Earth, as well as hundreds of other worlds they had been studying, to create their own "ladder" to heaven. When a rogue faction of the Quantum Mechanics threatened to destroy them all these worlds, the JLA were forced to battle the cosmic creatures, eventually helping them cross over into a higher plane of existence. **PJ**

COLORBLIND *Zazzala's inability to see the color red aided several JLA members when they attacked her cloaked in Plastic Man's red costume. Big Barda made the Queen Bee see the error of her ways with a crunching blow from her Mega-Rod!*

QUEEN BEE II

FIRST APPEARANCE JLA #34 (October 1999)
STATUS Villain **REAL NAME** Zazzala
OCCUPATION Royal Genetrix **BASE** The planet Korll
HEIGHT 5ft 9in **WEIGHT** 226 lbs **EYES** Blue **HAIR** Gray-black
SPECIAL POWERS/ABILITIES Multifaceted eyes see in the ultraviolet spectrum; gauntlet on right arm fires poisonous barbed stingers from reflexive venom sacs; hypno-pollen capable of bending others' to her will; has a mindless army of drones at her disposal.

The first Queen Bee was a woman with hypnotic powers who seized control of the state of Bialya after murdering its dictator, Colonel Rumaan Harjavti (*see* HARJAVTI, RUMAAN & SUMAAN). She soon died at the hands of his brother, Sumaan.

The second Queen Bee, Zazzala, ruler of planet Korll and its ever-expanding empire, was far more dangerous. In her closest encounter with Earth, the Queen Bee and her swarms of Bee-Troopers joined Lex Luthor's INJUSTICE GANG in a plot to defeat the JLA and conquer Earth. In return for the firepower of her drones, Zazzala was offered a percentage of Earth's populace as slaves. The first to suffer were the citizens of New York City, which became the site of the Queen Bee's Royal Egg-Matrix and ground zero for her planned planetary domination (after betraying Luthor). After her defeat, the Queen Bee retreated to Korll. She re-emerged as a member of the SECRET SOCIETY OF SUPER-VILLAINS (*see* VILLAINS UNITED) at the head of the H.I.V.E., a global criminal syndicate. The SECRET SIX sabotaged her operations and left the H.I.V.E. in tatters. **SB**

QUEEN OF FABLES

FIRST APPEARANCE JUSTICE LEAGUE OF AMERICA #47 (November 2000) **STATUS** Villain **REAL NAMES** Unknown
OCCUPATION Sorceress **BASE** Other-dimensional space
HEIGHT Tall and willowy **WEIGHT** Light as a feather
EYES Twin sapphires **HAIR** Sleekest ebony
SPECIAL POWERS/ABILITIES Magical ability to make the monsters and myths of storybook fables real.

Centuries ago, the Queen of Fables arrived on Earth as an exile from another dimension. Possessed of vast magical power, she carved out an empire for herself and met defeat at the hands of the virtuous princess Snow White. Imprisoned within a storybook until the dawn of the 21st century, the Queen of Fables escaped to sow chaos in New York City by conjuring various ogres, witches, and goblins.

The JUSTICE LEAGUE OF AMERICA clashed with the Queen of Fables when she attacked WONDER WOMAN, believing the Amazon to be her old nemesis Snow White. With her unique brand of sorcery, the Queen drew the Leaguers into the realm of fairy tales, where they faced the worst monstrosities of the imagination. She even transformed Manhattan island into an enchanted forest festooned with hanging moss and creeping ivy.

Eventually, Wonder Woman used her lasso to defeat the Queen of Fables, forcing the Queen to confront the truth of her own mortality. She is now imprisoned inside a new book—the *United States Tax Code*. Within its dry, literal pages, the Queen of Fables is unlikely to find any magical elements she can use to escape. **DW**

STORY TIME *The Queen called to life elements from fairy tales including Snow White, Sleeping Beauty, and Hansel and Gretel.*

QUESTION I & II, THE

FIRST APPEARANCE BLUE BEETLE (3rd series) #1 (June 1967)
STATUS Hero (deceased)   *REAL NAME* Charles Victor Szasz
OCCUPATION Television journalist (as Vic Sage)   *BASE* Hub City
HEIGHT 6ft 2in   *WEIGHT* 185 lbs   *EYES* Blue   *HAIR* Reddish blond
SPECIAL POWERS/ABILITIES Trained by Richard Dragon, Vic is a
formidable fighter and martial artist.

FIRST APPEARANCE (as the Question) 52 #48 (April 2007)
STATUS Hero   *REAL NAME* Renee Montoya
OCCUPATION Vigilante   *BASE* Gotham City
HEIGHT 5ft 8in   *WEIGHT* 144 lbs   *EYES* Brown   *HAIR* Black
SPECIAL POWERS/ABILITIES Expert combatant, detective, and interrogator;
master of disguise.

CRIME BIBLE *Soon after assuming the identity of the second Question, Renee Montoya embarked on a globe-hopping quest to expose the evils of the Cult of Cain.*

Victor Szasz was an angry orphan who could not understand why people did the things they did. As Vic Sage, television reporter for K.B.E.L., he took on political corruption in Hub City. Those hypocrites he couldn't expose on television he went after as the Question, his features masked by a compound called Pseudoderm devised by his friend Tot (Dr. Aristotle Rodor). Sage was also aided by Mayor Myra Connelly, (widow of the former Mayor), and Izzy O'Toole, perhaps the only honest cop on the force.

After many adventures, Sage became disillusioned with his crusading role and, entrusted with Myra's daughter, journeyed to the Amazon rain forest to find himself.

He returned to Hub City a changed man after LADY SHIVA saved his life and Richard Dragon (see DRAGON, RICHARD) instructed him in martial arts. Vic Sage died of cancer following the Infinite Crisis. His protégée, G.C.P.D. detective Renee Montoya (see MONTOYA, RENEE) has taken his place as the new Question. **RG**

CRUSADER *Vic Sage became an Everyman figure, using his fists to find truth in corrupt Hub City.*

QUICK, JESSE

FIRST APPEARANCE Justice Society of America (2nd series) #1 (August 1992)   *STATUS* Hero (retired)   *REAL NAME* Jesse Chambers
OCCUPATION C.E.O. of Quickstart Enterprises   *BASE* Keystone City
HEIGHT 5ft 9in   *WEIGHT* 142 lbs   *EYES* Blue   *HAIR* Blonde
SPECIAL POWERS/ABILITIES Superspeed, superstrength, flight, martial arts.

Jesse Chambers is the daughter of Johnny Quick (see QUICK, JOHNNY) and LIBERTY BELLE, two heroes of World War II. Jesse inherited her parents' powers and gained superspeed by reciting her father's formula ("3x2(9YZ)4A"), which allowed her to tap into the Speed Force.

An ally of the FLASH, MAX MERCURY, and Impulse (see KID FLASH), Jesse Quick, as Chambers called herself, became a prominent speedster in Keystone City. She was also a member of the JUSTICE SOCIETY OF AMERICA and the TEEN TITANS. After her father's death at the hands of SAVITAR, Jesse inherited his role as C.E.O. of Quickstart Enterprises.

Jesse retired the Jesse Quick identity when she became the new Liberty Belle. She now serves with the JSA alongside her husband, HOURMAN II. **PJ**

QUICK, JOHNNY

FIRST APPEARANCE MORE FUN COMICS #71 (September 1941)
STATUS Hero   *REAL NAME* Johnny Chambers
OCCUPATION Super hero   *BASE* New York City
HEIGHT 5ft 11in   *WEIGHT* 170 lbs   *EYES* Blue   *HAIR* Blonde
SPECIAL POWERS/ABILITIES Superspeed; can pass through objects by
vibrating his molecules and briefly "fly".

At the dawn of the 1940s, Johnny Chambers's guardian, the celebrated Professor Gill, discovered a miraculous formula written on a piece of papyrus in the temple of Egyptian king Amen. When young Johnny said "3X2(9YZ)4A" he received the gift of superspeed, and he could close off this link by saying "Z25Y(2AB)6." So began a new life as the costumed Johnny Quick.

The outbreak of World War II caused all of America's mystery men to unite under the banner of the ALL-STAR SQUADRON. Johnny Quick worked with Jay Garrick (the original Flash), and dated and later married LIBERTY BELLE.

Unlike others Johnny Quick did not enter forced retirement when the House of Un-American Activities Committee ordered all mystery men to unmask themselves in the 1950s. Nevertheless, Johnny spent gradually less time in the hero game in order to build up his communications business and to spend time with his daughter, Jesse (see Quick, Jesse).

Though Johnny Quick claimed he didn't believe in the Speed Force, his magic formulas acted as mental mantras that channeled the extra-dimensional speed energy into his body. He became one with the Speed Force when he sacrificed himself in battle against the foul SAVITAR. He is survived by Jesse, who adventured as Jesse Quick (see QUICK, JESSE) before assuming her mother's role as the new Liberty Belle. **DW**

AND HE'S OFF *Although less well-known than his fellow speedster Flash I, Johnny Quick was a critical member of the wartime All-Star Squadron.*

ROMANTIC MOMENTS

CLARK KENT AND LOIS LANE

Perhaps no pair is more different, yet more perfect for one another, than the ace reporter from Metropolis and the farmboy from Smallville, Kansas. As co-workers at the *Daily Planet*, they gradually put aside their professional rivalry (as well as Lois' infatuation with Superman) and learned to embrace all that they had in common. Eventually Clark revealed his secret identity to Lois and the two were married. Fortunately—because so few know of Clark Kent's famous alter ego—the happy ceremony remained unmarred by super-villains or other occupational hazards.

To date, Lois has not expressed any jealousy over the fact that, by necessity, she has to share Superman with the world. Recently, however, Clark and Lois' relationship has come under new strain as Clark deals with work-related stress at the *Daily Planet*. Lois still provides the human grounding the Man of Steel desperately needs.

OFFICE ROMANCE *When Lois first met Clark the air crackled with tension; but eventually mutual competitiveness turned to lasting love.*

SUPER HEROES ARE ESSENTIALLY SOLDIERS, ready to go into battle at a moment's notice and regularly brushing up against death. With this as a backdrop, it's understandable that these amazing superbeings form desperate, passionate, often short-lived liaisons. Although a few relationships belie that stereotype, having lasted for years, tellingly, few steady romances exist where *both* partners are costumed heroes.

GREEN LANTERN AND CAROL FERRIS

The head of Ferris Aircraft, Carol Ferris was first and foremost Hal Jordan's boss, but the cocky test pilot did not let their professional relationship prevent him from striking up a steamy romance. Their connection became increasingly complicated when the Zamarons made Carol their unwitting queen (Star Sapphire) and pitted her against Green Lantern. Immediately after Hal became the supremely powerful Parallax, he shared a final kiss with Carol before sacrificing his life to reignite Earth's sun.

NIGHTWING AND ORACLE

Dick Grayson, as ROBIN, fell for Barbara Gordon early in her career as Batgirl, calling her the "first person to make my heart sing." Mutual affection soon led to passion, though the only thing that remained consistent in their relationship was the inconsistency of their on-again, off-again romance. Their love survived Barbara's paralysing injury by the Joker and her subsequent role as Oracle, but they eventually split up, with Barbara citing Dick's reckless disregard for his own safety as Nightwing as the cause. Yet how long can Nightwing and Oracle ignore their destiny?

BLACK CANARY AND GREEN ARROW

Dinah Lance and Oliver Queen are two of the world's most outspoken heroes. She is a brash self-promoter. He is a blunt liberal activist. Their strong personalities seem to draw them irresistibly together—for passionate arguments or for passionate kisses. They toured the U.S. on a cross-country road trip and still team up on the occasional mission, riding tandem on a motorcycle. It's amazing they can ever agree on a route!

ANIMAL MAN

Suburban super hero Buddy Baker led the perfect family life with his wife, Ellen. High-school sweethearts, Buddy and Ellen raised two children, Cliff and Maxine, in between Buddy's adventuring stints as Animal Man. Eventually his powers overtook his life, causing him to start his own religion based on animal-power. This placed severe strain on Buddy's relationship with Ellen.

THE FLASH AND LINDA PARK
Remarkable among super-heroic romances for its permanence, the marriage between Wally West (Flash III) and Linda Park (see Park, Linda) echoes the bond between Wally's mentor Barry Allen (Flash II) and Barry's wife, Iris (see Allen, Iris). Linda maintained her own identity (formerly a TV reporter, now a medical student) and did not allow her husband's career as Keystone City's protector to overshadow her goal of starting a family. The couple's greatest happiness came when Linda announced she was pregnant with twins. Tragically, the super-villain Zoom stole their future when his attack caused Linda to miscarry. The couple must now rebuild their relationship without any super-heroic complications.

SUPERBOY AND WONDER GIRL
These two powerful teens have tried to push away their troubles by seeking comfort in each other's arms. Superboy wrestles with the knowledge that he is a clone created with DNA extracted from Superman and Lex Luthor (see Luthor, Lex). Wonder Girl strives to live up to the high expectations of her mother, top archaeologist Helen Sandsmark, her mentor Wonder Woman, and the entire pantheon of Olympian Gods. A stolen kiss atop San Francisco's Titans Tower typified the way outside pressures seemed determined to cut this young romance short. Wonder Woman, determined to control all outside influences on Cassie Sandsmark's life (including Superboy's affections), yanked Superboy off the roof in mid-smooch and launched him a quarter-mile over San Francisco bay!

BATMAN AND CATWOMAN
The Dark Knight and the Feline Fatale have enjoyed an ongoing flirtation for years, spurred by Catwoman's playfulness and the professional attraction between the two best rooftop adventurers in Gotham. When the villain known as Hush united Batman's worst foes in a crusade of vengeance, Catwoman joined her rival in a partnership that soon led to romance. Unfortunately, Batman is an expert at everything except relationships. His suspicious nature led him to question Catwoman's motives, and the two coldly parted ways... for now. DW

PLAYING CATCH-UP Batman and Catwoman's passion is fueled by death-defying pursuits through the Gotham night. It is not always clear who is chasing whom.

RAG DOLL II

FIRST APPEARANCE VILLAINS UNITED #1 (March 2005)
STATUS Villain   **REAL NAME** Unrevealed
OCCUPATION Professional criminal   **BASE** Mobile
HEIGHT 5ft 11in   **WEIGHT** 120 lbs   **EYES** Green   **HAIR** None
SPECIAL POWERS/ABILITIES Double-jointed contortionist achieved through extensive surgery; expert grappler.

The second Rag Doll is the son of the original Rag Doll, but did not inherit his father's double-jointedness. Desperate for parental approval, he underwent surgery that replaced his joints with 360-degree sockets, damaging his skin to such a degree that he now needs to lubricate it every day to prevent splitting.

As Rag Doll II, he joined the new SECRET SIX that arose prior to the Infinite Crisis, running missions

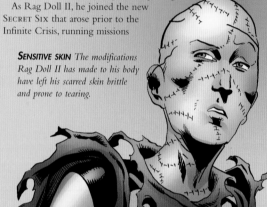

CONTORTIONIST Rag Doll's amazing flexibility makes him a versatile combatant who is often fatally underestimated by opponents.

SENSITIVE SKIN The modifications Rag Doll II has made to his body have left his scarred skin brittle and prone to tearing.

against the Society (see VILLAINS UNITED) on behalf of the mysterious MOCKINGBIRD. Rag Doll also shared a relationship with his teammate Parademan, who enjoyed the laughter triggered by this strange "clown."

During a final battle with the Society, Rag Doll II briefly faced his father, before Parademan sacrificed himself to allow the Secret Six to escape. Rag Doll II remained with the team. He immediately found himself at odds with a new recruit, the MAD HATTER, believing that the Hatter had usurped his role as the team's "dandy freak." **DW**

RAJAK, COLONEL

FIRST APPEARANCE ADVENTURES OF SUPERMAN #590 (May 2001)
STATUS Villain   **REAL NAME** Ehad Rajak
OCCUPATION Dictator   **BASE** Bialya
HEIGHT 5ft 6in   **WEIGHT** 155 lbs   **EYES** Blue   **HAIR** Black
SPECIAL POWERS/ABILITIES No superpowers, but a charismatic and willful commander who leads an army of fanatical followers.

The African country of Bialya has seen its share of iron-fisted leaders come and go. After Rajak evicted Sumaan Harjavti (see HARJAVTI, RUMAAN AND SUMAAN) from power, the Colonel took control of Bialya and perpetuated the anti-American stance for which the country had become well known. Bialy remains under economic sanctions from the U. S., which does not help the political situation. President

Luthor (see LUTHOR, LEX) asked SUPERMAN to help rescue *Newstime* journalist Andrew Finch, hoping to avoid direct military intervention. Finch, however, was a C.I.A. assassin working under Luthor's orders. Superman rescued Finch but stopped him eliminating Rajak. The strongman remains a threat to the Middle East peace process and has a personal score to settle with Luthor. **RG**

RAGMAN

FIRST APPEARANCE RAGMAN 1st series #1 (September 1976)
STATUS Hero   **REAL NAME** Rory Regan
OCCUPATION Defender of the weak   **BASE** Gotham City
HEIGHT 5ft 11in   **WEIGHT** 165 lbs   **EYES** Blue   **HAIR** Brown
SPECIAL POWERS/ABILITIES Costume grants superhuman strength, speed, agility, and the ability to float on air. It claims the souls of the wicked by engulfing them within the Ragman's tatters.

To protect themselves from persecution, the Jews of 16th century Prague animated a soulless Golem from river clay. Wary of the monster they created, the Council of Rabbis decreed that the Golem should be replaced with a human defender. The Rabbis chose rags to clothe their new champion who, like the Golem, was empowered by a verse in the Kaballah. Thus, the "Ragman" was first woven to guard over the Warsaw Ghetto. During World War II, Jerzy Reganiewicz took up the patchwork mantle of Ragman to protect Warsaw's Jews from the Nazis. Tragically, Jerzy failed to spare his people from the horrors of the Holocaust. Years later, Jerzy (renamed Gerry Regan after emigrating to the U.S.) passed down the Ragman's suit to his son, Rory, who first wore it to defend the oppressed denizens of Gotham City's slums. From his "Rags 'n' Tatters" junk shop, Rory continues to add new rags to the garish garment of the "Tattered Tatterdemalion," Ragman. Ragman joined the SHADOWPACT prior to the infinite Crisis, fighting the maddened SPECTRE alongside his teammates and spending a year trapped inside a mystical sphere encasing Riverrock, Wyoming. **SB**

RAMULUS

FIRST APPEARANCE WORLD'S FINEST #6 (Summer, 1942)
STATUS Villain   **REAL NAME** Unknown
OCCUPATION Scientist   **BASE** The Magic Forest, upstate New York
HEIGHT 6ft 3in   **WEIGHT** 185 lbs   **EYES** White   **HAIR** Green
SPECIAL POWERS/ABILITIES Can control vegetation with his mind, specifically giant vines, his so-called Tendrils of Terror.

Originally committing crimes under the name Nightshade, the green-skinned Ramulus created mechanized, murdering plants to terrorize his victims in a "magic forest" in upstate New York. In 1942, Wesley Dodds, the SANDMAN, and his protégé, Sandy the Golden Boy, ran afoul of Nightshade when the villain kidnapped the parents of one of Sandy's friends. While Sandman and Sandy rescued the kidnapped couple, Nightshade lost control over his electronic plants and was seemingly murdered by them, while his "magic forest" burned to the ground.

Miraculously surviving, Nightshade was discovered by the Aztec priestess NYOLA. Given greater control over his technological flora, and the ability to mentally manipulate living vegetation, Nightshade changed his name to Ramulus and joined Nyola's MONSTER SOCIETY OF EVIL. **PJ**

RĀ'S AL GHŪL

ENVIRONMENTAL TERRORIST

FIRST APPEARANCE BATMAN #232 (June 1971)
STATUS Villain (deceased) **REAL NAME** Unknown
OCCUPATION International terrorist **BASE** Mobile **HEIGHT** 6ft 5in
WEIGHT 215 lbs **EYES** Blue **HAIR** Gray with white streaks
SPECIAL POWERS/ABILITIES A master swordsman and ruthless hand-to-hand combatant, Rā's al Ghūl has lived for many centuries, amassing great wealth and power, as well as a treasure trove of knowledge, during his near-eternal existence.

ALTHOUGH NOT TRULY IMMORTAL, the international terrorist Rā's al Ghūl was one of the most long-lived men on the planet. In Arabic, his name translates as "The Demon's Head," a fitting sobriquet for someone so sinister. Rā's al Ghūl's primary purpose during his extended life was to restore the Earth's ecological balance. Unfortunately, this seemingly altruistic goal led to him committing global genocide to reduce mankind's polluting numbers.

ECO-TERRORIST

For centuries, Rā's al Ghūl maintained his existence by periodically immersing himself in "Lazarus Pits," pools filled with an alchemical mix of acids and poisons excavated above the electromagnetic ley lines crisscrossing the Earth. Following his emergence from the liquid in the Lazarus Pits Rā's al Ghūl would, for a short time, be consumed with insane fury. For this reason, Rā's demanded solitude when rejuvenating himself.

BODYGUARD Ubu shadows every move Rā's makes. Ubus are chosen in mortal combat matches and will give their lives to protect the Demon's Head.

LAZARUS PITS
Like a macabre fountain of youth, these fiery pits sustained Rā's al Ghūl incredible vim and vigor.

Rā's al Ghūl's schemes to restore Earth to an Eden-like splendor have been thwarted time and again by BATMAN. The Dark Knight first met the enigmatic eco-terrorist when Rā's al Ghūl, desiring an heir for his crime empire, kidnapped ROBIN in an attempt to coerce the Dark Knight into marrying his daughter, TALIA. Naturally, Batman refused, and although he had deep feelings for the beautiful Talia, he continued to oppose Rā's al Ghūl schemes.

Rā's al Ghūl's most ambitious attacks upon humanity occurred with his creation of the Ebola Gulf-A plague that decimated the population of Gotham City. This plague, dubbed the "Clench" due to its victims' writhing ends, was halted by the Dark Knight and his squires, who later learned that Rā's al Ghūl had deciphered the virus's genetic code from an ancient "Wheel of Plagues." With it, Rā's al Ghūl would have unleashed even more virulent contagions if not for the intervention of the Bat-Family.

Rā's al Ghūl continued to seek a suitable heir, even considering the musclebound terrorist Bane, before Talia spurned this potential suitor. The dejected Bane then set about sabotaging Rā's al Ghūl's Lazarus Pits to get revenge.

MASTER SCHEMER Not content with making Batman's life miserable, the Demon's Head has involved other super heroes, including the Man of Steel, in his "world-saving" plots.

SWORDPLAY A renowned swordsman with centuries of fighting experience, Rā's has challenged Batman to duels on many occasions in order to put the Dark Knight's mettle to the test.

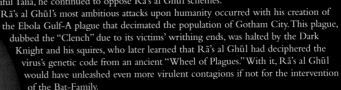

DAUGHTER DEAREST Nyssa succeeded where others could not, ending the long life of the Demon's Head!

Meanwhile, Rā's al Ghūl created worldwide anarchy with his electronic "Tower of Babel," which rendered all languages unintelligible until the JUSTICE LEAGUE OF AMERICA destroyed it. Talia left her father's side soon after, hired by Lex Luthor (*see* LUTHOR, LEX) to run his company LexCorp.

Other challengers to Rā's's throne emerged, including his second daughter Nyssa, who killed her father and attempted to take over his worldwide empire. But Rā's al Ghūl did not stay dead for long. Brought back in the body of a decaying corpse, he tried to transfer his soul into the body of Damian, the young son of Batman and Talia. Thwarted, he instead inhabited of the form of his estranged son, the White Ghost. **SB**

KEY STORYLINES
• **BATMAN #232 (JUNE 1971):** Rā's al Ghūl makes his first appearance, kidnapping the Boy Wonder to force Batman to do his bidding!
• **DETECTIVE COMICS #700 (AUGUST 1996):** As the multipart "Legacy" storyline begins, Rā's al Ghūl uses the ancient Wheel of Plagues, responsible for Gotham City's Clench outbreak, to unleash an even worse contagion!
• **BATMAN: DEATH AND THE MAIDENS #1-9 (OCTOBER 2003–JUNE 2004):** Nyssa, daughter of Rā's al Ghūl, plots her father's demise in order to take over his worldwide criminal empire! Is this the end for the Demon's Head, or the beginning of another villainous dynasty?

RESURRECTION MAN

First appearance RESURRECTION MAN #1 (March 1997)
Status Hero **Real name** Mitchell "Mitch" Shelley
Occupation Former lawyer; adventurer **Base** Mobile
Height 6ft 1in **Weight** 190 lbs **Eyes** Brown **Hair** White
Special powers/abilities An immortal champion imbued with new superpowers each time he is reborn; his distinctive coat and hat are remade by the tektites when damaged.

Mitch Shelley is an immortal man, and for a brief time believed he was the Immortal Man, imbued with eternal life after exposure to the same meteor that created the villain Vandal Savage. In truth, Shelley was lawyer, experimented upon by the Lab, a clandestine organization that injected tektites—microscopic nanobots—into his bloodstream. With the tektites rebuilding his body each time he died, Shelley possessed the closest thing to immortality. Moreover, the tektites also imbued him with a different superpower each time he was resurrected. At first, Shelley suffered from amnesia and traveled the U.S. in search of his lost memory while helping those in need. In the course of his adventures, he fought Amazo, the Body Doubles, and other threats while making the acquaintances of the Justice League of America, Supergirl and other costumed heroes. Shelley ultimately discovered that he was not the Immortal Man, although he did come into conflict with Vandal Savage and, as has been revealed, will continue to battle Savage through many lives and deaths well into the 853rd century. In the present, however, Shelley joined forces with the true Immortal Man to stop Savage from obtaining the Temporal Meteor. Mitch Shelley made a temporary home for himself in Viceroy, South Carolina with the love of this life, private eye Kim Rebecki. **SB**

HEROIC PATHS
Despite not considering himself a costumed champion, Mitch Shelley has sided with Supergirl and other heroes while attempting to recover his lost memories.

GHOST OF A CHANCE *Resurrection Man tries to give a suddenly intangible Supergirl a helping hand.*

REVERSE-FLASH

First appearance FLASH (1st series) #139 (September 1963)
Status Villain (deceased) **Real name** Eobard Thawne
Occupation Super-villain **Base** 25th century Central City
Height 5ft 11in **Weight** 179 lbs **Eyes** Blue **Hair** Reddish-blonde
Special powers/abilities Could run at near-light speeds, vibrating through solid objects or temporal dimensions; though not a skilled combatant, his brilliant mind led him to use his speed dangerously.

The evil Reverse-Flash, also known as Professor Zoom, hailed from the far future of the 25th century. Eobard Thawne became obsessed with the 20th century's second and most prominent Flash, Barry Allen, even going so far as to try to duplicate his incredible powers. He found one of the Flash's old costumes in a time capsule and the suit's residual Speed Force energy provided the boost he needed. Now possessed of superspeed, Thawne traveled back five centuries to meet his idol but arrived several years after Allen's death during the Crisis (see Great Battles, pp. 186-7). Conclusive evidence Thawne discovered in a museum stating that he would one day become the evil Reverse-Flash sent Thawne into psychological shock, and he briefly posed as a resurrected Barry Allen before returning to his own time.

Thawne now harbored a hatred of Barry Allen. He dyed his costume in opposite-spectrum colors and returned to the 20th century as Professor Zoom, the Reverse-Flash. His attempts to win the heart of Barry Allen's wife, Iris, failed dismally, so a bitter Thawne apparently murdered her. Barry Allen sent his nemesis into another dimension, but Thawne returned to menace Allen's new fiancée, Fiona Webb. This time, Allen accidentally killed the Reverse-Flash by snapping his neck. In the aftermath, Barry Allen was acquitted of manslaughter and Iris Allen revealed that she had survived as a citizen of the 30th century. **DW**

DERANGED
The Reverse-Flash was a menace to everyone he encountered.

MEASURING UP *A fixation on Barry Allen quickly drove Thawne mad.*

RIDDLER, THE

FIRST APPEARANCE DETECTIVE COMICS #140 (October 1948)
STATUS Villain **REAL NAME** Edward Nigma (née Nashton)
OCCUPATION Professional criminal **BASE** Gotham City
HEIGHT 6ft 1in **WEIGHT** 183 lbs **EYES** Blue **HAIR** Black
SPECIAL POWERS/ABILITIES Brilliant in his own twisted way, but a poor hand-to-hand fighter. His addiction to leaving "enigmatic" clues to his crimes for Batman always proves his undoing.

EDWARD NIGMA'S SCHOOLTEACHER once held a contest to see which one of her pupils could assemble a puzzle the fastest. Little Edward secretly photographed the assembled puzzle, which he had found in the teacher's desk, and studied its formation so he could easily win. After this event, puzzles became his life. Failing in school, he took a job as a carnival barker, running a rigged puzzle booth. From there, it was only a matter of time before he turned to crime full-time as one of Gotham City's most famous rogues, the Riddler.

TRICKS FOR KICKS *The Prince of Puzzlers loved matching wits with the Dynamic Duo.*

ASKING THE QUESTIONS

The Riddler seemed psychologically incapable of committing a crime without first posing a riddle to Batman or the G.C.P.D. An admirer of the late, great escape artist Harry Houdini, the Riddler's tangled traps display a similar flair for showmanship. For years, he was considered a second-rate criminal, meeting defeat not only at the Dark Knight's hands, but also in matches against the Elongated Man, Flash, Green Arrow, Black Canary, and the QUESTION. Recently, however, he has shown a more dangerous side, which seems to have attracted a score of followers. He is usually accompanied by Diedre Vance and Nina Damfino, known as Query and Echo, who handle the rough stuff.

RIDDLER'S GANG *Over the years, the Riddler has used many costumed henchman, mere pawns in his master game.*

The Riddler was eventually diagnosed with terminal cancer, setting him on his most deadly path yet. He found one of RAˉS AL GHUˉL'S Lazarus Pits and healed himself. Hoping to profit from this, he turned to his doctor, Philadelphia physician Thomas Elliot. Many years before, Elliot had tried to kill his parents but Thomas Wayne (Bruce Wayne's father) had saved Elliot's mother's life. Elliott hated the Waynes for spoiling his childhood plot and conspired with the Riddler to gain revenge on Batman. Thus began an involved scheme organized and planned by the Riddler, who learned Batman's identity in the process. The Riddler spent most of the year following the Infinite Crisis in a coma, recuperating from injuries sustained in the fight. When he awoke he had lost much of his memory, including his knowledge of Batman's secret identity. He then announced a break from his criminal past, and opened a private detective agency. He has occasionally teamed with Batman to solve cases. **RG**

NO JOKING MATTER *Out for only himself, the Riddler has crossed many fellow rogues, including Harley Quinn.*

RETURN OF HUSH *When the Riddler's usefulness seemed at an end, he had good reason to fear the wrath of his former partner, Hush.*

KEY STORYLINES

• *BATMAN #608–619 (DECEMBER 2003–NOVEMBER 2004):* Paired with Hush, the Riddler set out an elaborate scheme to kill Batman after learning his secret identity.
• *BATMAN #452–454 (AUGUST–SEPTEMBER 1990):* In "Dark Knight, Dark City," the Riddler is possessed by the spirits of Gotham's founders as Batman learns about the city's gruesome beginnings.
• *SECRET ORIGINS SPECIAL (1989):* How Edward Nigma turned from cheater to master criminal.
• *THE QUESTION #26 (MARCH 1989):* Fleeing Gotham for Hub City, the Riddler wants to make a clean start, but fails once again.

ROBIN

THE BOY WONDER

DICK GRAYSON (ROBIN I)
FIRST APPEARANCE DETECTIVE COMICS #38 (April 1940)
STATUS Hero   **REAL NAME** Richard "Dick" Grayson
OCCUPATION Crime fighter; police officer   **BASE** Gotham City
HEIGHT 5ft 10in   **WEIGHT** 175 lbs   **EYES** Blue   **HAIR** Black

JASON TODD (ROBIN II)
FIRST APPEARANCE DETECTIVE COMICS #526 (September 1983)
STATUS Hero (deceased)   **REAL NAME** Jason Todd
OCCUPATION Crime fighter; student   **BASE** Gotham City
HEIGHT 5ft 2in   **WEIGHT** 105 lbs   **EYES** Blue   **HAIR** Black

TIM DRAKE (ROBIN III)
FIRST APPEARANCE (as Tim Drake) BATMAN #436 (August 1989);
(as Robin) BATMAN #457 (December 1990)
STATUS Hero   **REAL NAME** Timothy Drake
OCCUPATION Student; crime fighter   **BASE** Gotham City
HEIGHT 5ft 5in   **WEIGHT** 125 lbs   **EYES** Blue   **HAIR** Black
SPECIAL POWERS/ABILITIES
Like the previous Robins, Tim Drake was trained by Batman in martial arts, as well as sleuthing skills. He is adept in the use of electronic devices, especially computers. Tim's utility belt carries the standard complement of Batarangs, gas capsules, de-cel jumplines, and other tools. His R-insignia doubles as a razor-sharp shuriken. Robin's costume is lined with Kevlar and Nomex fabrics, making it bulletproof and fire-resistant. His mask is fitted with Starlite night-vision lenses. Typically, Robins have ridden customized Batcycles in their own colors, but Tim prefers his Redbird, a crime-fighting car second only to the Batmobile.

As a member of the Flying Graysons acrobatic family, young Dick Grayson thrilled audiences nightly on the high wire beside his circus aerialist parents. But when gangster "Boss" Zucco sabotaged the high wire because the owner of Haly's Circus refused to offer up protection money, the elder Graysons paid with their lives. Billionaire Bruce Wayne was in the audience that night; however it was BATMAN who visited the grieving Dick Grayson, offering the boy a chance at retribution by becoming Robin, the Dark Knight's squire in his personal war on crime.

SENSATIONAL DEBUT *The introduction of Robin brought a ray of hope to the Dark Knight's nocturnal vigil.*

DICK GRAYSON
The first Robin was carefully schooled by Batman, learning all the skills he would need to bring "Boss" Zucco to justice. Before long, Dick was ready for action. Swearing a solemn oath, he joined the Dark Knight's crusade as his most trusted partner, Robin the Boy Wonder.
After several years in service to the Dark Knight, Grayson—then leader of the Teen Titans—relinquished the mantle of Robin when Batman forced him to choose between his duties with the Titans and his promise to aid the Dark Knight. Adopting the identity of Nightwing, Dick continued to battle crime while remaining Batman's close ally.

BRUCE WAYNE'S WARD
To give the orphaned Dick Grayson a home, billionaire Bruce Wayne became the boy's legal guardian. Wayne's trusted valet, Alfred (*see* Pennyworth, Alfred) was just as much a surrogate father to Dick as Bruce was. While the Dark Knight's alter ego trained Dick in fighting and detective skills to become his second in the war on crime, Alfred made sure that Dick kept up with a more "classical" education. Bruce avoided adopting Dick because he didn't want to replace Dick's real father. However, he made Dick his legal heir in adulthood, and the two are as close as any father and son could be.

JASON TODD
Batman met juvenile delinquent and presumed orphan Jason Todd when the boy literally tried to steal the tires right off the Batmobile. With original partner Dick Grayson having given up the role of Robin, Batman decided to take Jason in and offer him both a home and a purpose. Jason began the same training regimen Grayson once undertook to become the Dark Knight's partner. However, Jason was a troubled soul who lacked maturity and was quick to anger.

A DEATH IN THE FAMILY
When Jason discovered clues that his long-lost mother was alive, he secretly travelled to Africa to find her. Tragically, the trail also led him straight into the clutches of the Joker, who savagely beat the second Boy Wonder within an inch of his life. Robin died in the subsequent explosion, but returned to life years later as a result of the reality-altering effects of the Infinite Crisis. Now an angry adult, Jason Todd assumed the identity of the Red Hood and set to work eliminating the Gotham gangs. He later joined with Donna Troy and Green Lantern Kyle Rayner on a search through the multiverse for Ray Palmer.

THE DEATH OF ROBIN *Batman cradled Jason in his arms, blaming himself for not rescuing him in time, consumed with rage at the Joker's latest, cruelest crime.*

Robin's costume carries most of the same crime fighting equipment wielded by his mentor, Batman.

TRAINING With Batman, Nightwing, Batgirl, and Azrael as sparring partners, Robin is prepared for combat with any opponent.

TIM DRAKE

Tim Drake was barely more than a toddler when he sat in the stands at Haly's Circus and watched the Flying Graysons fall to their doom. Tim was transfixed as the Dark Knight swooped down to comfort young Dick Grayson. The moment was burned into his memory. Years later, Tim saw news reports of an unhinged Batman becoming more and more violent following the death of the second Robin, Jason Todd. Using his detective skills, Tim deduced the secret identity of Batman and the first Boy Wonder, Dick Grayson.

MODEL STUDENT
Tim went to Brentwood Academy until his father had money trouble. Public education made it easier for Tim to operate as Robin.

THE THIRD ROBIN

After revealing this knowledge to the original Dynamic Duo, Tim argued the need for a Robin to give the Dark Knight hope, especially when faced with a seemingly hopeless and unyielding war on crime. Though reluctant at first, Batman gave Tim the opportunity to prove that he was as good as his word. After months of grueling training, Tim Drake became the third Robin.

It is a job at which Tim excels, despite the constant struggle of balancing his crime-fighting life with the day-to-day battles of just being a teenager. A former member of Young Justice, Tim presently belongs to the latest incarnation of the Teen Titans.

STEPHANIE BROWN

The fourth Robin, Stephanie Brown, served for a short time after Tim Drake abandoned the job. Fired by Batman due to her lack of experience, Stephanie accidentally triggered a Gotham gang war. Black Mask captured and tortured her, and she later died from her injuries.

THE TEEN TITANS

Tim Drake once led Young Justice. This group of teenage heroes disbanded, and members Robin, Kid Flash II, Superboy, and Wonder Girl II graduated to an all-new incarnation of the Teen Titans that includes Titans teammates Beast Boy, Cyborg, and Starfire, all mentors to the less-experienced junior Titans.

- *BATMAN #426-429 (DECEMBER 1988–JANUARY 1989):* While searching for his biological mother, Jason Todd is murdered by the Joker! Batman's resolve is sorely tested as "A Death in the Family" brings terrible tragedy to the Batcave.
- *BATMAN CHRONICLES: THE GAUNTLET (1997):* Dick Grayson's "final exam" to become Batman's partner involves surviving a night alone in Gotham!
- *ROBIN: YEAR ONE #1-4 (OCTOBER 2000–JANUARY 2001):* Dick Grayson's first year as Boy Wonder includes victories against Mad Hatter and Mr. Freeze, but a near-fatal encounter with Two-Face!

SCARECROW

THE FEAR MASTER

FIRST APPEARANCE WORLD'S FINEST COMICS #3 (Fall 1941)
STATUS Villain **OCCUPATION** Professor and professional criminal
REAL NAME Jonathan Crane **BASE** Gotham City
HEIGHT 6ft **WEIGHT** 150 lbs **EYES** Blue **HAIR** Brown
SPECIAL POWERS/ABILITIES A psychologist and biochemist, Crane used his knowledge to create a fear-inducing gas that creates nightmarish hallucinations in the mind of anyone who inhales it; costume also designed to strike terror; a manic hand-to-hand combatant.

GAWKY AND UNCOORDINATED as a child, Jonathan Crane was often the physical and emotional target of neighborhood bullies. Initially frightened by their horrible taunts, Crane eventually decided he would turn the tables on his attackers, and began voraciously studying phobias and the nature of fear.

HARMLESS TEASE?
Jonathan was a spindly nerd, easily fooled by a sexy girl like Sherry.

TERROR master
A psychiatrist turned psychopath, the Scarecrow uses his fear gas to terrorize his victims, often leaving their minds permanently crippled.

As an adult, Crane became an expert psychologist, specializing in fear. He also acquired some knowledge of chemistry, studying how certain combinations of chemicals could affect the human psyche. Crane became a professor at Gotham City University, but was summarily dismissed for his unorthodox teaching methods and his refusal to follow the school's safety codes.

Crane's fragile mind snapped after his dismissal and he adopted the guise of the Scarecrow, vowing to use his knowledge of fear and his own specially designed "fear gas" to gain revenge. Using this chemical, the Scarecrow killed several of Gotham University's regents by literally scaring them to death. The Scarecrow was then confronted by the Batman, who ended the villain's reign of terror and incarcerated him in Arkham Asylum for the Criminally Insane. Escaping from custody over and over again, the Scarecrow used stolen funds to constantly upgrade the potency of his fear gas, mixing powerful synthetic adreno-cortical secretions with potent hallucinogens to create a pathogen strong enough to prompt almost instantaneous, terror-induced heart attacks in his victims.

A constant foe of Batman and his allies, and a spooky threat to the citizens of Gotham City, the Scarecrow is obsessed with fear in all its manifestations and relishes inflicting it. Perhaps fortunately, Crane is prey to a phobia of his own: *Chiropteraphobia*, a chronic fear of bats or, more specifically, of Batman! **PJ**

TORMENTING TEENS
More cruel pranks fractured his already fragile psyche.

HUSH Scarecrow was one of several Arkham inmates the villain Hush used in his war against Batman. Scarecrow's used his fear toxins and psychological expertise to frighten and manipulate Joker, Poison Ivy, Killer Croc, and the Huntress into battling the Dark Knight.

KEY STORYLINES
• *WORLD'S FINEST COMICS (FALL 1941):* The Scarecrow makes his debut, ensuring sleepless nights for citizens of Gotham City.
• *BATMAN #626–630 (JUNE–SEPTEMBER 2004):* In "As the Crow Flies," Scarecrow is infected with a mutation that transforms him into a monstrous Scarebeast during times of stress.
• *DETECTIVE COMICS #820 (AUGUST 2006):* During the "Face the Face" storyline, Scarecrow faces off against both Batman and Robin, confronting each with their greatest insecurities.

SCANDAL

FIRST APPEARANCE VILLAINS UNITED #1 (March 2005)
STATUS Villain **REAL NAME** Scandal Savage
OCCUPATION Professional adventurer **BASE** Mobile
HEIGHT 5ft 9in **WEIGHT** 160 lbs **EYES** Brown **HAIR** Brown
SPECIAL POWERS/ABILITIES Enhanced damage resistance, expert combatant with bladed weapons..

LOOK OF DEATH
Scandal wields her lamentation blades with deadly efficiency, making her the equal of her murderous father.

Scandal Savage is the daughter of the immortal Vandal Savage, one of Earth's greatest villains. She apparently shares her father's resistance to injury, and is a deadly combatant with her wrist-mounted "lamentation blades."

She first appeared as a member of the new Secret Six, working for Mockingbird to sabotage the worldwide criminal operations of the Society (see Villains United). During a mission to Brazil, she explained to her teammates that she had grown up in that country; later revelations included the news that she was in a romantic relationship with Knockout who had infiltrated the Society as a mole. Once Knockout joined up with the Secret Six, the two grew even closer – raising the anger of Vandal Savage, who wanted his daughter to bear him an heir.

Knockout lost her life during the Death of the New Gods event, leaving behind a despondent Scandal who spurned the Suicide Squad's efforts to recruit her. She later found herself among the supervillains exiled on an alien world during Operation: Salvation Run. **DW**

TEAM PLAYER
Her time with the Secret Six gave Scandal the opportunity to romance her teammate Knockout. The murder of her lover pushed Scandal into despair.

SCARAB

FIRST APPEARANCE SCARAB #1 (November 1993)
STATUS Hero **REAL NAME** Louis Sendak
OCCUPATION Adventurer **BASE** New York City
HEIGHT 5ft 10in **WEIGHT** 170 lbs **EYES** Brown **HAIR** Brown
SPECIAL POWERS/ABILITIES The Scarabaeus allowed him to command mystic energies, either as raw power or in subtle manifestations.

Louis Sendak was born in Staten Island, N.Y. during the 1920s. In 1924, Louis's father brought home various mystic artifacts including the Door and the Scarabaeus. Louis later used this talisman to become the occult adventurer Scarab.

He was a successful hero, teaming with other mystics to form the Seven Shadows. When Johnny Sorrow murdered six of the Seven Shadows, their deaths caused Scarab to suffer a mental breakdown. During his convalescence, Louis's wife Eleanor was drawn into the Door and vanished. Decades later, Sendak teamed up with the Justice Society of America on their quest for the Fate child, only to be attacked by the Dark Lord. Stripped of his magic powers, he became the unwitting vessel chosen by Johnny Sorrow to enable his master, the King of Tears, to return to the known world from the plane of non-reality he was trapped in. **RG**

SCAVENGER

FIRST APPEARANCE SUPERBOY (2nd series) #4 (March 1994)
STATUS Villain **REAL NAME** Unknown **OCCUPATION** Plunderer
BASE Mobile **HEIGHT** 5ft 10in **WEIGHT** 160 lbs
EYES One white; one cybernetic **HAIR** White
SPECIAL POWERS/ABILITIES Long-lived; possesses several cybernetic implants; wields weapons pillaged from various heroes and villains.

His origins a closely guarded secret, the Scavenger travels the world using stolen teleportation technology, searching for mystic talismans and items of power. He claims he was once wronged by a godlike hero and is gathering weapons for a coming battle with this mystery foe. The Scavenger also believes that all heroes are conspiring against humanity and cannot be trusted.

The Scavenger has battled Superboy on several occasions, and he also engaged in a cyberspace auction hoping to outbid Green Arrow for a vintage Arrowcar. The Scavenger continues to prepare for conflict with his unnamed nemesis. **SB**

SCORCH

FIRST APPEARANCE JLA #61 (February 2002)
STATUS Villain (reformed and deceased) **REAL NAME** Aubrey (second name unknown)
OCCUPATION Unrevealed **BASE** Pisboe, VA
HEIGHT 5ft 9in **WEIGHT** 140 lbs **EYES** Red **HAIR** Black
SPECIAL POWERS/ABILITIES Does not sleep and seems to have complete mastery over fire, from generating it to controlling its intensity.

The sultry young woman Aubrey, known as Scorch, escaped from a variation of reality when the Joker briefly gained Mr. Mxyzptlk's fifth-dimensional, cosmic powers. She battled both Superman and the Martian Manhunter as she tried to make a name for herself in the world of crime. Although offered a chance to reform and become a force for good by Superman, she refused. Later, the Manhunter asked Scorch to help him overcome his psychological fear of fire in exchange for helping her calm her tortured mind. During the resulting sessions they became lovers, although Superman remained suspicious of her motives. His doubts seemed justified when she unwittingly unleashed an ancient Martian horror; however Scorch sacrificed herself to save not only her beloved but the entire JLA. **RG**

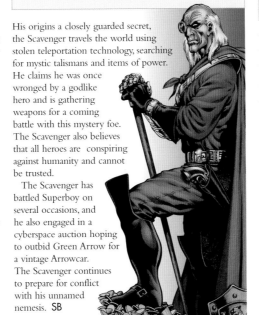

SEVEN SOLDIERS OF VICTORY

FIRST APPEARANCE LEADING COMICS #1 (Winter 1941–1942)
STATUS Hero team **BASE** Mobile
MEMBERS AND POWERS
Bulleteer Invulnerable metal skin and enhanced strength
Frankenstein Enhanced strength, undead body provides extreme resistance to injury
Klarion the Witch Boy Spellcasting and monstrous transformations
Manhattan Guardian Top physical condition; skilled fighter
Mister Miracle II One of the world's greatest escape artists
Shining Knight II Skilled fighter and excellent swordswoman
Zatanna Vast magical powers triggered by saying spells backward

SOLDIERS OF THE GOLDEN AGE
(left to right) Klarion the Witch Boy, Shining Knight II, Zatanna, Frankenstein, Manhattan Guardian, Bulleteer, Mr. Miracle II.

Independently stopping the villainous agents of the Iron Hand, seven heroes joined together to become the Laws' Legionnaires, more commonly referred to as the Seven Soldiers of Victory. Founding members included the Crimson Avenger, the Spider, the Shining Knight, Vigilante I and Billy Gunn (later succeeded by Stuff), and the Star-Spangled Kid, and Stripesy. The Avenger's aide, WING, was the unofficial eighth member. In 1948, the Seven Soldiers of Victory were betrayed by one of their own, the Spider, and engaged in battle with the entity known as the Nebula Man. Wing sacrificed his life to destroy the creature in Tibet, but the resulting explosion of temporal energies cast the rest of the group across the timestream.

SPELLCASTER Zatanna, arguably the most famous of the new Seven Soldiers, never met the other team members.

SOLDIERS OF THE GOLDEN AGE 1) Vigilante I
2) Green Arrow **3)** Shining Knight
4) Star-Spangled Kid **5)** Speedy
6) Crimson Avenger I **7)** Stripesy.

Decades later, DEADMAN organized a short-lived new edition of the SSV including Adam Strange, Batgirl, Blackhawk, Mento, Metamorpho and the Shining Knight II to defend the planet Rann from attack by the Injustice League. Soon after that, six of the time-displaced original Soldiers were rescued by the united Justice Society of America and Justice League of America before Red Tornado II sacrificed his life to save Earth from the Iron Hand.

A modern incarnation of the Seven Soldiers appeared prior to the Infinite Crisis. The Sheeda, a faerie race from the far future, prepared to annihilate humanity by striking down heroic teams of seven—the only thing (according to prophecy) that could stop them. VIGILANTE assembled I, Spyder, Gimmix (daughter of Merry, Girl of a Thousand Gimmicks), Boy Blue, Dyno-Mite Dan (using replicas of the rings worn by T.N.T. and Dan the Dyna-Mite), and the granddaughter of the WHIP. Numbering only six (after Bulleteer dropped out at the last minute), they fell prey to a Sheeda invasion in the American southwest.

Forces conspired to unite a new Seven Soldiers against the Sheeda, with one critical distinction—these soldiers, though working on parallel paths, would never actually meet. This loose team consisted of Mister Miracle II (Shilo Norman), the Spawn of Frankenstein, Zatanna, Klarion the Witch Boy, Shining Knight II (Sir Ystina), the Manhattan Guardian, and the Bulleteer. The Sheeda Queen, having tortured the Shining Knight aboard her flagship the Castle Revolving, found her invasion fleet sabotaged by Frankenstein (now an elite commando working for the S.H.A.D.E. department of the U.S. government). While the Manhattan Guardian rallied citizens to fight the invaders in the streets, I, Spyder returned and shot the Sheeda Queen with an arrow. She fell from her flagship, landing in the roadway, where a car driven by Bulleteer struck her.

Klarion, having obtained a powerful Sheeda artifact from Zatanna's apprentice, took control of Frankenstein with a Croatoan binding spell, then used his new powers to become king of the Sheeda. Mister Miracle II, shot by Darkseid, became the only casualty among the Seven Soldiers—though death may be only a temporary challenge for this master of escape. **RG**

KEY STORYLINES
• JUSTICE LEAGUE OF AMERICA (1ST SERIES) #100–102 (AUGUST–OCTOBER 1972): The Justice League rescue the time-lost of the Seven Soldiers.
• STARS AND S.T.R.I.P.E. #9 (APRIL 2000): The original Seven Soldiers shown again in this tale of how Alias the Spider betrayed his teammates and caused their defeat by Nebula Man.
• SEVEN SOLDIERS #1 (OCTOBER 2006): The Seven Soldiers are reborn for a new age to battle the Sheeda, faerie-like people from the distant future who want to consume human history.

SERGEANT ROCK
THE COMBAT-HAPPY JOE

FIRST APPEARANCE OUR ARMY AT WAR #81 (April 1959)
STATUS Hero   **REAL NAME** Frank Rock
OCCUPATION Former leader of Easy Company   **BASE** Mobile
HEIGHT 6ft   **WEIGHT** 183 lbs   **EYES** Blue   **HAIR** White (formerly red)
SPECIAL POWERS/ABILITIES Expert combatant, marksman, and battlefield leader; is skilled with almost every known firearm and can operate most varieties of tanks and other heavy equipment.

THE ALL-STAR SQUADRON earned much of America's attention during World War II with their brightly-colored costumes and their superhuman powers. Yet no one is considered a greater wartime hero than a simple, G.I.-uniformed Army sergeant named Frank Rock. Rock suffered unfathomable tragedies before he ever saw combat. His father died in World War I. His stepfather suffocated during a mine collapse. A father figure Rock looked up to while working at a Pittsburgh steel mill also lost his life. Many of his siblings similarly perished, but patriotic Rock enlisted in the army the day after the Japanese attacked Pearl Harbor in 1941 and received an immediate assignment to the European theater of war.

IN PRINT Sergeant Rock was immortalized by writer Kanigher and artist Kubert.

THE GOOD SOLDIER
Private Rock didn't truly distinguish himself until the D-Day invasion in 1944. Soon after, at the Battle of Three Stripes Hill, he received a battlefield promotion to sergeant. Sergeant Rock's unit, Easy Company, quickly became one of the most distinguished fighting forces in Europe. Moving from North Africa to Italy to France to Germany, the "combat-happy Joes" included such stalwarts as Wildman, Little Sure Shot, Bulldozer, Farmer Boy, and the Ice Cream Soldier. Pulling off impossible missions, the company lived up to their motto, "Nothin's ever easy in Easy."

Sergeant Rock struck up a battlefield romance with French resistance fighter Mademoiselle Marie and served a brief tour in the Pacific theater. He refused promotions so often he received the nickname "the general of sergeants." According to legend, he died when struck by the last enemy bullet fired on the last day of the war.

Rock, however, survived. Performing postwar covert missions for the U.S. government, he battled his old foe the Iron Major and teamed up with Easy Company veteran Bulldozer on an assignment to Dinosaur Island.

Recently, U.S. President Lex Luthor (*see* Luthor Lex) named General Frank Rock—by then in his eighties—Chairman of the Joint Chiefs of Staff. Rock died during the Imperiex War (*see* Great Battles, pp. 186-7) and was buried with full honors at Arlington National Cemetery. A short time later a similar Frank Rock appeared at the head of a reconstituted SUICIDE SQUAD. It is debatable whether this Rock was the original or merely an impostor. DW

QUIET HERO Rock never thought twice about advancing on an enemy machine-gun nest or charging into a firefight to rescue a pinned-down comrade. His men would follow him anywhere.

OLD SOLDIER Rock had never sought out promotions, but in the modern era he re-emerged as a general. Part of President Lex Luthor's cabinet, he distinguished himself from his shady commander-in-chief by leading the military effort to destroy Imperiex.

DEFENSIVE General Rock prevents Imperiex from invading Washington.

KEY STORYLINES
• *OUR ARMY AT WAR #81 (APRIL 1959):* Sgt. Rock (here called "Rocky") makes his debut. The series would be renamed for him in issue #302.
• *SGT. ROCK: BETWEEN HELL AND A HARD PLACE (2004):* This moody, recent graphic novel was illustrated by the legendary Joe Kubert.
• *SUPERMAN #166 (MARCH 2001):* President Lex Luthor reintroduces Frank Rock into the DC universe's modern era.

5 2

IN THE YEAR following the Infinite Crisis, the world persevered without its greatest heroes: Superman, Batman, and Wonder Woman. While the legends avoided the spotlight, lesser figures claimed the stage and ushered in a new era with the rebirth of the multiverse.

ELONGATED MAN

Following his wife Sue's murder at the hands of Jean Loring, Ralph Dibny retired his Elongated Man identity and sank into a deep depression. News that a Kryptonian "resurrection cult" had vandalized his wife's gravestone prompted Dibny to investigate the cult's most prominent member, Wonder Girl. She believed its rituals could restore life to Conner Kent (Superboy). Dibny sought to expose the cult as a fraud, but experienced a shock when his wife's soul appeared to animate a straw effigy. Shaken, Dibny agreed to follow the helmet of Doctor Fate through a string of magical realms and netherworlds on a search for Sue's spirit. Dibny ultimately learned that the journey was a ruse: Fate's helmet had been controlled by the magician Felix Faust to lure Dibny into the clutches of the demon NERON. Dibny outsmarted his enemies, trapping both in Doctor Fate's tower, but lost his life in the effort. Yet in the afterlife he found a happy ending. He reunited with Sue and the couple became mystery-solving "ghost detectives".

RESURRECTION CULT *Cultists promised they could bring Sue Dibny to life by animating a straw effigy.*

THE EVERYMAN PROJECT

Lex Luthor (*see* Luthor, Lex) announced to an eager public that superpowers no longer had to be the sole possession of an elite. The genetic manipulations of his Everyman Project provided hundreds of ordinary citizens with enhanced abilities, including Natasha Irons (*see* Irons, Natasha), niece of the hero Steel. Natasha and several others became the first inductees into Luthor's new Infinity Inc. team. On New Year's Eve, the limits of Luthor's benevolence became apparent when he shut down all of his subjects' powers, causing dozens of helpless flyers to plunge from the sky. Luthor also gave himself superpowers, prompting a showdown with Steel and Natasha Irons that resulted in Luthor's capture and disgrace.

SPACE EXILES

ANIMAL MAN, Adam Strange, and Starfire found themselves stranded in deep space after the Infinite Crisis, swept up in a war of conquest by the armies of Lady Styx. The intergalactic mercenary Lobo became their ally, thwarting Lady Styx's schemes despite setbacks including Adam Strange's blindness and Animal Man's death and resurrection. After a year-long journey, the trio at last found their way home.

THE QUESTION

Vic Sage, the faceless investigator known as the Question, teamed with ex-Gotham City police detective Renee Montoya to investigate Intergang's inroads into Gotham City. The trail led to Black Adam's country Khandaq, where the two prevented a suicide bombing at the wedding of Black Adam and Isis. They later journeyed to Nanda Parbat in the Himalayas, hoping that the region's mystics could halt the Question's terminal lung cancer. Back in Gotham, the Question and Montoya teamed with Batwoman to stop Intergang's Bruno Mannheim and his Crime Bible cult. In the end Vic Sage died, passing the Question identity on to Montoya.

SAGE ADVICE *The original Question passed on his knowledge to Renee Montoya so she could continue his legacy.*

BOMBER DOWN *She hated taking a life, but Renee Montoya (kneeling in red dress) had no other choice to prevent a suicide bomber at the wedding of Isis and Black Adam.*

NANDA PARBAT *The holy mountain city became Vic Sage's refuge as he battled cancer.*

OOLONG ISLAND

Will Magnus, the genius behind the Metal Men, became the newest inductee into a "Science Squad" of evil geniuses on Oolong Island in the Pacific. The operation's mastermind proved to be Chang Tzu (Egg Fu), an Apokoliptian creation working for China's Great Ten. Magnus refused to build lethal robots for his captors, escaping Oolong after incapacitating Tzu by cracking his eggshell with a lead bullet.

WELCOMING PARTY *Oolong Island had plenty of distractions to keep its scientists occupied.*

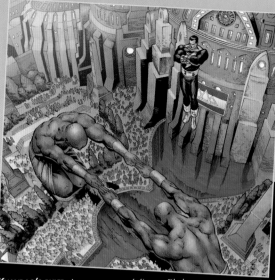

KHANDAQ'S RULER *As a superpowered dictator, Black Adam held absolute power in his home country.*

BLACK ADAM AND WORLD WAR III

As the leader of isolationist Khandaq, Black Adam had grown beyond his role as a foil to Captain Marvel. Black Adam found a calming influence in his life in Adrianna Tomaz. She became his wife after assuming the powers of Isis. Her younger brother Amon joined them as the superpowered Osiris, and the addition of the talking crocodile SOBEK rounded out what appeared to be a happy family unit.

Yet treachery arose when Sobek revealed himself as Famine, one of the Four Horsemen of Apokolips ordered to bring down the Black Marvel Family. Sobek devoured Osiris, and Isis died at the hands of Pestilence, before Black Adam unleashed his revenge. Black Adam blasted the Horsemen's launching point of Bialya, killing everyone within the country's borders. He then stormed across the globe in a bloodbath of destruction called World War III, until stripped of his powers by Captain Marvel.

ADAM'S FALL *World War III ended with Black Adam powerless. It took a worldwide quest for him to regain his abilities.*

EVIL SKEETS *The malevolent intentions of Skeets became clear in the Kandor showdown. It wasn't until later that Mister Mind revealed himself as the true culprit.*

BOOSTER GOLD AND MISTER MIND

This second-string super hero saw an opportunity to become a major player with the knowledge of future events stored in the memory banks of his robot sidekick Skeets. But Booster discovered that the timeline was unfolding differently than had been recorded, making his data worthless. Desperate to make his mark, Booster sold out to corporations and staged mock battles with super-villains, quickly developing a rivalry with Metropolis' newest hero, the mysterious Supernova. Booster seemingly perished in an oil tanker explosion, but soon revealed himself as the masked Supernova. He had used Rip Hunter's time machine to skip backward in history, the better to uncover Skeets' suspiciously sinister actions. Rip Hunter and Booster confronted Skeets in the bottle city of Kandor, but their attempt to trap him in the Phantom Zone failed. In a chase through time, Skeets revealed himself as Mister Mind, the Venusian worm who had cocooned inside Skeets' robot shell before undergoing a monstrous metamorphosis. Mister Mind began to "eat time," altering the histories of the multiverse's 52 parallel realities. Booster and the new Supernova (Booster's ancestor Daniel Carter) stopped Mister Mind by hurling him backward through a time loop.

The end of the year saw the return of Superman, Batman, and Wonder Woman. Yet the actions of Booster Gold and others had changed the multiverse forever. **DW**

FIGHT FOR FAME *Booster Gold dispatched Mammoth in his early, desperate bid to become Metropolis's champion.*

SPECTRE

THE SPIRIT OF VENGEANCE

JIM CORRIGAN (SPECTRE I)
FIRST APPEARANCE More Fun Comics #52 (February 1940)
STATUS Hero *REAL NAME* James Brendan Corrigan
OCCUPATION Police detective; spirit of vengeance
BASE New York City
HEIGHT (as Corrigan) 6ft 1in *WEIGHT* (as Corrigan) 184 lbs
EYES (as Corrigan) Blue *HAIR* (as Corrigan) Red, with white streak

HAL JORDAN (SPECTRE II)
FIRST APPEARANCE (AS THE SPECTRE) Day of Judgement #5 (November 1999) *STATUS* Hero *REAL NAME* Harold "Hal" Jordan
OCCUPATION Former test pilot, Green Lantern; the Spirit of Wrath
BASE Mobile
HEIGHT (as Jordan) 6ft *WEIGHT* (as Jordan) 186 lbs
EYES (as Jordan) Brown *HAIR* (as Jordan) Brown

SPECIAL POWERS/ABILITIES The Spectre is among the most powerful beings in the universe. Limited only by its need to bond with another host, the Spectre possesses the ability to fly at nearly any speed, become intangible, inhabit and animate objects, read minds, teleport, and psychically project hideous fears into the hearts and souls of his victims. He can turn invisible, cast illusions, create impenetrable mists, travel across the astral planes, grow to incomprehensible size, and manipulate magics to nearly any end his spiritual mind can conceive!

GHOSTLY *The Spectre arrived in a swirl of mist to pass his sentence on criminals.*

LOOSED ON EARTH by the almighty Presence in 776 BC, the Spectre is the mystical embodiment of God's wrath. When the angel Raphael, who rebelled against Heaven with Lucifer, repented his sins, God transformed him into an avenger that would inflict His wrath on sinful souls. The Spectre destroyed Sodom and Gommorah, spread the ten plagues across Egypt, and brought down the walls of Jericho. After the birth of Jesus, whose mission was to teach people compassion, the Presence decreed that the spirits of vengeance and forgiveness should not exist on Earth at the same time. The Spectre bided in Limbo until Christ's death. Then, forced to bond with mortal souls to manifest his power, the Spectre leaped forth, meting out vengeance down the centuries.

JIM CORRIGAN

James Corrigan was the only child of the Reverend Jedediah Corrigan, a fundamentalist preacher who physically and emotionally abused his son to discourage him from the temptations of sin. As a teenager, Corrigan ran away to New York City and enrolled in the police academy, excelling at detective work. Self-righteous, arrogant, Corrigan became a pitiless cop.

Corrigan's brutality caught up with him, when he was killed by mobster Gat Benson in 1940. Corrigan's soul cried out for vengeance and was answered by the Spectre. Infused with the Spectre's power, Corrigan's spirit, returned to his body and took revenge on Benson. The Spectre was subsequently encouraged to use his power for good by Percival Poplanski, a patrolmen who witnessed Benson's demise. Manifesting itself as a ghostly spirit, the Spectre joined the Justice Society of America as one of its most powerful members.

After World War II, the Spectre fought the demon Azmodus, who trapped the Spirit of Vengeance in Corrigan's undead frame for nearly two decades. The Ghostly Guardian quarreled often with his earthly host over methodology and the nature of humanity itself.

AVENGING ANGEL *The Spectre uses his powers to horrify criminals, visiting upon them grisly retribution in its most hideous form.*

MURDER! *Gat Benton stuffed Jim Corrigan's body in a cement-filled barrel and drowned him.*

THE CRISIS

During the Crisis (*see* Great Battles, pp. 186-7), the Spectre traveled back to the dawn of time and used his vast power to save all of Creation as its heroes battled the universe-consuming Anti-Monitor. The Spectre's powers were greatly diminished, and he was once again separated from Corrigan. Exhausted by his life on Earth, and forgiving his father for his abuses, Corrigan pleaded with the Presence to allow his soul to travel to its final resting place. The Spectre, nearly omnipotent, was once again left without a human focus.

HAL JORDAN

Hal Jordan was one of the most powerful officers in the legendary Green Lantern Corps and a founding member of the Justice League of America. When Mongul and the Cyborg Superman destroyed Jordan's hometown, Coast City, slaughtering its seven million inhabitants, Jordan went insane, usurping the power of the Corps and transforming into the universe-threatening Parallax.

Parallax first tried to recreate Coast City by tampering with time during the Zero Hour crisis (*see* Great Battles, pp. 186–7). Failing time and time again, Parallax nonetheless helped reignite the Earth's sun, which had been extinguished by an alien creature, at the cost of his own life. His spirit consigned to Purgatory for his sins, Jordan bonded with the Spectre's energies after they briefly inhabited Asmodel.

Returned to Earth in this new, ghostly form, the spirit of Hal Jordan and the essence of the Spectre wander the globe, seeking redemption while inflicting punishment on the guilty. PJ

HELPING YOUNG JUSTICE

As the Spectre, Hal Jordan used his omnipotent power to help Secret learn the truth about her past. The elder ghost helped the younger discover that her death was a sacrifice to a demon, and that she had been transformed by the Lords of Light into a spirit guide. The Spectre used his power to help Secret accept her dismal past, and hopeful future.

JLA ALLY *Hal Jordan uses his new power to aid his former teammates in the JLA. While Jordan's vast power worries Batman, Jordan's diligence in hunting evil earns Batman's trust, and the trust of Earth's Greatest Heroes.*

KEY STORYLINES

- *MORE FUN COMICS #52 (FEBRUARY 1940):* The first appearance of the ghostly avenger.
- *DC SPECIAL #29 (SEPTEMBER 1977):* The Spectre becomes a founding member of the Justice Society of America.
- *Crisis on Infinite Earths* (tpb, 2000) The Spectre stops the Anti-Monitor from destroying all creation, and reignites the universe.
- *DAY OF JUDGEMENT #1–4 (NOVEMBER 1999–FEBRUARY 2000):* Hal Jordan rescues the spirit of God's wrath from Asmodel and becomes the new Spectre.

SPECTRE

UN-TETHERED SPIRIT

Hal Jordan's penance as the Spectre's host ended with the purging of Parallax—an ancient fear entity that had been sharing space in Jordan's soul alongside God's Spirit of Vengeance. By defeating Parallax, Jordan won the right to resume his former life on Earth, leaving the Spectre a rogue ghost. Lacking the grounding of a human spirit, the Spectre lost touch with the concerns of mortal justice. He lashed out with irrational, disproportionate punishments, including executing a girl for talking back to her father. In this disturbed state, the Spectre became an easy target for Eclipso—God's ex-Spirit of Revenge who had taken over the body of Jean Loring. Eclipso's seductions convinced the addled Spectre that magic represented a perversion of God's orderly laws, and that only by eliminating all magic could he purge the universe of evil. Because he existed as a creature of magic himself, as his final act the Spectre planned to extinguish his own life. The Spectre's rampage against spellcasters and mystical realms marked an end to what had been known as the Ninth Age of Magic. His first targets included the "big guns" of the magical community. The Spectre burned out the eyes of Madame Xanadu so she would be incapable of reading tarot cards, and imprisoned Doctor Fate inside his enchanted helmet. Although the Spectre lacked the power to kill the Phantom Stranger, he left him powerless by transforming him into a mouse. Dozens of lesser magicians perished when the Spirit of Vengeance attacked their mass gathering, and even the kingdom of Atlantis fell beneath the Spectre's boots.

DARK SEDUCTIONS *Eclipso, in the body of Jean Loring, manipulated the Spectre into wiping out her magical competition.*

THREE DOWN *In short order, the Spectre neutralized his greatest threats: the Phantom Stranger, Doctor Fate, and Madame Xanadu.*

SHADOWPACT SHOWDOWN

The surviving magic-users gathered in the Oblivion Bar to plan a counterattack. Their plans hinged on Nightmaster, Ragman, Nightshade, Blue Devil, the Enchantress, and Detective Chimp, who had formed a super-group known as the Shadowpact. In Budapest, the new team faced off against the combined forces of Eclipso and the Spectre, with the Shadowpact's efforts aided by Captain Marvel and the channeled magical energy of the planet's population. The Spectre fled, but regained his strength for a second clash with the Shadowpact. This time, Black Alice temporarily sapped his powers. Teleporting to the Rock of Eternity, the Spectre executed the wizard Shazam, causing the Rock to explode above Gotham City and freeing the spirits of the Seven Deadly Sins. Led by the Lord of Order Nabu, the Shadowpact and other magic-users collected the Deadly Sins and again earned the Spectre's anger. This time, however, the Spectre finally grabbed the attention of his heavenly master, who removed the renegade spirit and forced him to seek a new human host.

CLASH OF TITANS *Grown to colossal size due to an influx of magical energy, Captain Marvel slugs it out with the Spectre in Budapest.*

END OF THE NINTH AGE *The maddened Spectre eliminated most of the Earth's sorcerers and magic-users. The destruction of the Rock of Eternity signaled the end. The release of the Rock's evil spirits brought terror to a battle-scarred Gotham City.*

CRISPUS ALLEN (SPECTRE III)
First appearance Detective Comics #742 (March 2000)
Status Instrument of retribution **Occupation** Police detective;
Spirit of Vengeance **Base** Gotham City
Height 6ft **Weight** 180 lbs **Eyes** Brown **Hair** Black
Special powers/abilities The Spectre is among the most powerful
beings in the universe. Limited only by its need to bond with
another host.

CRISPUS ALLEN

The Spectre's third host came from the ranks of
the Gotham City Police Department. Detective
Crispus Allen struggled to make a difference
in a city overrun with costumed killers and
masked vigilantes, with his wife and two sons
helping keep him sane. Allen worked alongside
fellow detective Renee Montoya in the GCPD's
Major Crimes Unit. Allen's life took a tragic turn
when he crossed paths with crime scene technician Jim
Corrigan—who bore the same name (but was otherwise
unrelated to) the Jim Corrigan who
had originally served as the Spectre's
host. During an investigation gone
bad, Allen saved his partner's life by
shooting and killing the villain BLACK
SPIDER. An Internal Affairs inquiry
into the incident went awry when
Corrigan stole the bullet from the
scene, casting a cloud over Allen's
actions. Enraged by Corrigan's
interference, Montoya forced him
to give up the bullet, but by this
point the crooked cop knew that
Internal Affairs was closing in on
him. To cover his tracks, he shot Allen in the back. In the morgue,
the body of Crispus Allen became the newest host for the Spectre.

BACK FROM THE DEAD
*Murdered in cold blood,
Detective Crispus Allen
became the Spectre's
unwilling host.*

Allen's spirit soon rejected the ghostly invader, despite the
latter's pleas for an Earthly lifeline to help him continue
his mission of retribution. Yet life as a phantom—rendering
him incapable of interacting with his family or striking back
at Corrigan—proved unsatisfying for Allen. After nearly
a year, he accepted the Spectre into his body and began
to mete out punishments to the worst of Gotham City's
sinners, always in a gruesomely ironic fashion. Victims were
impaled by wads of cash, speared by fishhooks, burst apart
like balloons, and devoured by rats and spiders. Allen took
grim satisfaction in his methods of justice, since the Spectre's mission
prevented him from simply stopping atrocities before the murderers
could take action. He collaborated with both the Batman and the
Phantom Stranger, gradually coming to the realization that, despite
the Spectre's near-omnipotence, punishment was a more merciful
action when meted out on an individual basis. Crispus Allen's final
test came when his young son Mal avenged his father's death by
shooting Jim Corrigan. To exact retribution for the murder, Allen, as
the Spectre, took his son into the afterlife. PJ/DW

BLIND JUSTICE *Realizing that the
Spirit of Vengeance must treat all
crimes with equal weight, Crispus
Allen uses the powers of the
Spectre to pass judgment on his
own son for the sin of murder.*

STARMAN

THE STARRY KNIGHT

STARMAN I
FIRST APPEARANCE Adventure Comics #61 (April 1941)
STATUS Hero (deceased) *REAL NAME* Theodore Henry Knight
OCCUPATION Astronomer, adventurer *BASE* Opal City
HEIGHT 6ft *WEIGHT* 165 lbs *EYES* Blue *HAIR* Gray
SPECIAL POWERS/ABILITIES A wealthy amateur scientific genius who helped develop the atomic bomb. He also invented a method for collecting energy radiated by stars and the Gravity Rod, which allowed him to fly; an average hand-to-combatant.

STARMAN II
See DR. MID-NITE I
SPECIAL POWERS/ABILITIES Paul "Robotman" Dennis and Jim "Red Torpedo" Lockhart designed and constructed a sophisticated star-shaped hovercraft that served as Starman II's transportation.

STARMAN III
FIRST APPEARANCE First Issue Special #12 (March 1976)
STATUS Hero *REAL NAME* Mikaal Tomas
OCCUPATION Adventurer *BASE* Opal City
HEIGHT 6ft 3in *WEIGHT* 160 lbs *EYES* Pale blue *HAIR* Purple
SPECIAL POWERS/ABILITIES The sonic crystal that was seared into his flesh allowed Mikaal to fire sonic blasts and granted him invulnerability and limited flight.

STARMAN IV
FIRST APPEARANCE Adventure Comics #467 (January 1980)
STATUS Hero (deceased) *REAL NAME* Prince Gavyn
OCCUPATION Adventurer *BASE* Throneworld
HEIGHT 6ft 2in *WEIGHT* 180 lbs *EYES* Blue *HAIR* Blond
SPECIAL POWERS/ABILITIES Could absorb energy and redirect it as heat or energy bolts.

STARMAN V
FIRST APPEARANCE Starman (1st series) #1 (October 1980)
STATUS Hero (deceased) *REAL NAME* William Payton
OCCUPATION Adventurer *BASE* Tucson, Arizona
HEIGHT 6ft 1in *WEIGHT* 180 lbs *EYES* Brown *HAIR* Brown
SPECIAL POWERS/ABILITIES Could emit heat and light; had the power of flight, and could alter his physical form.

STARMAN VI
FIRST APPEARANCE Starman (1st series) #26 (September 1990)
STATUS Hero (deceased) *REAL NAME* David Knight
OCCUPATION Adventurer *BASE* Opal City
HEIGHT 5ft 11in *WEIGHT* 170 lbs *EYES* Brown *HAIR* Brown
SPECIAL POWERS/ABILITIES While possessing the cosmic rod, David could fly and direct energy bolts, although he was never especially adept at it.

THE LEGEND OF THE STARMAN, harnessing the stars for the greater good of humanity, stretches from the dawn of the atomic age through the millennia. It begins with wealthy amateur astronomer Ted Knight, who in 1939, created the Gravity Rod, which enabled him to augment or negate gravity. Crafting a super-hero costume, he took flight as Starman.

STARMAN I
Knight's heroic career led to his protecting not only his beloved Opal City, but all of the U.S. through his work with the Justice Society of America and the All-Star Squadron. He battled the Mist I again and again, creating an enmity that would last for decades. Knight, who was haunted by his role in the creation of the atomic bomb, resigned from the JSA after helping them beat the dimensional conqueror known as Stalker. Soon after this, he suffered the first of a series of nervous breakdowns and bouts of depression, which led him to temporarily give up his heroic career.

OPAL CITY CHAMPIONS
Dr. Mid-Nite took over Knight's role, becoming Starman II, and watching over Opal City. Then a time-lost David Knight (who would be Starman VI) arrived in town and was groomed by Dr. Mid-Nite to become his "secret weapon." Eventually David returned to his own time in the future and Ted Knight resumed his Starman mantle.
Ted met Adele Doris Drew at a fundraiser, and the two fell in love, married, and had two sons, David and Jack. During those years, Ted, sporting an upgraded device called the Cosmic Rod, often came out of retirement, fighting villains with such heroes as Black Canary I and Wildcat I.

CANARY KISS
When Starman took to the skies, he began an affair with the first Black Canary.

STARMAN II *Opal City guardian.*

STARMAN III
Unknown to Ted Knight, the blue-skinned Mikaal Tomas escaped from his fellow race of invading aliens from Talok III. Tomas began adventuring as Starman III while Ted raised his children. Within a year, Mikaal Tomas killed the other surviving member of his race in ritual combat, then disappeared from sight for years. After his rescue from virtual imprisonment, Mikaal joined Starman VI for several adventures before going his own way once more.

STARMAN IV AND V
Out in the distant universe, Prince Gavyn became known as Starman IV, protector of his empire. He served his people well, sacrificing his life during the Crisis (*see Great Battles, pp. 168-7*). Reduced to pure energy, Gavyn was directed toward Earth. Teenage hitchhiker Will Payton was struck by Gavyn's lifeforce, gaining extraordinary powers. At this time, Starman I was away in Limbo with the JSA, battling demons to protect the Earth. So, to his sister Jayne's delight, Payton became Starman V. Will struggled with being both a hero and a teenager, and learned the ropes from established heroes such as Batman and the Atom. Eventually he lost his life battling the villain Eclipso.

WILL PAYTON
Teenager who died a hero's death as Starman V.

STARMAN VII
FIRST APPEARANCE Zero Hour #1 (September 1994)
STATUS Hero REAL NAME Jack Knight
OCCUPATION Antique dealer; adventurer BASE Opal City
HEIGHT 6 ft 1in WEIGHT 165 lbs EYES Blue HAIR Black
SPECIAL POWERS/ABILITIES Trained in jujitsu, and uses the Cosmic
Rod to fly or to project energy bolts, levitate objects or create
force fields.

STARMAN VIII
FIRST APPEARANCE Starman (2nd series) #79 (July 2001)
See STAR BOY
SPECIAL POWERS/ABILITIES This native of Xanthu can control mass
and fly.

STARMAN 1,000,000
FIRST APPEARANCE JLA #23 (November 1998)
STATUS Hero REAL NAME Farris Knight
OCCUPATION Adventurer BASE Uranus
HEIGHT 6ft 4in WEIGHT 265 lbs EYES Blue HAIR Brown
SPECIAL POWERS/ABILITIES Uses a revamped version of the gravity
rod, enabling him to fly, alter gravimetric forces and fight with
fierce determination.

STARMAN VII

Starman I, now retired, declared his son David
his successor. David's run as Starman VI was
cut short when he was gunned down by
the Mist. David's brother, Jack Knight, then
found the family legacy thrust upon him
and reluctantly became Starman VII. While
visiting a circus, Jack discovered and rescued
Mikaal Tomas, Starman III, from captivity
as a sideshow attraction. Meanwhile, Nash,
the Mist's unstable daughter, vowed revenge
after Jack killed her brother. As Mist II, she
captured Jack and seduced him while he
was only partially conscious. A year later,
Jack was stunned to learn that Nash had
given birth to his son, Kyle Theo Knight.

STARMAN & SON The relationship between
Ted and his sons was never an easy one but
it grew warmer with time.

TO THE STARS AND BACK

Accompanied by Mikaal, Jack voyaged into space to determine
the fate of Starman V, the brother of his girlfriend Sadie
Falk (who was actually Jayne Marie Payton). Jack
journeyed to Throneworld, now which was ruled by a
cruel, despotic regime. Jack found Will and learned
of his amazing connection with Throneworld's
Prince Gavyn. The three Starmen, along with
political prisoners such
as Fastbak and the
Omega Men's Tigorr
then freed Throneworld
from tyranny. Will
Payton/Gavyn declined
an invitation to return
to Earth and Jack and
Mikaal set off homeward.
After various adventures,
they returned to Opal City, which was soon threatened with
nuclear holocaust by the Mist.

SADIE When Jayne Payton's brother,
Starman V, died, she turned to the latest
Starman for help but fell in love instead.

FOLLOWING DAD For a brief
time, Jack served with the
JSA, his father's old team.

While they had been away, Ted Knight, Starman I, had been
diagnosed with terminal cancer, contracted while battling Doctor
Phosphorus. Despite the disease, Ted used an advanced cosmic rod to
transport the Mist I's bomb safely into space. Ted and the Mist died in
the explosion, and the super-hero community mourned his passing. Jack
Knight, briefly served with the JSA before opting to retire to raise his
son. He gave his cosmic rod to Star-Spangled Kid, who renamed herself
Stargirl in honor of the legacy. RG

STARMAN VIII

Jack Knight's grandson is said to have been the
first villainous Starman. In the 23rd century,
Tommy Tomorrow II became the latest
incarnation of Starman. By the 822nd century,
the heritage of Starman had been abandoned for
at least three millennia until revived by Farris
Knight's great-grandfather, who discovered his
lineage and resurrected the heroic mantle of
Starman. Farris Knight, during the 853rd
century, was a member of Justice Legion
A and wielder of the gravity rod who
resided in his space citadel in Uranus's
orbit. He betrayed his team until
meeting the Starman line's progenitor,
Ted Knight, then mended his ways,
sacrificing himself to defeat Solaris.

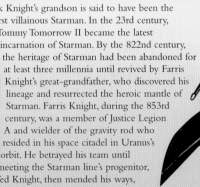

KEY STORYLINES
• STARMAN: SINS OF THE FATHER (TPB, 1996):
Jack Knight reluctantly becomes the latest Starman
and learns about the rich family legacy—complete
with adversaries.
• STARMAN: STARS MY DESTINATION (TPB, 2004):
Jack and Mikaal find Prince Gavyn and Will Payton,
but also get involved in inter-galactic conflicts with
consequences today and tomorrow.
• THE BRAVE AND THE BOLD #61–62 (AUGUST–NOVEMBER
1965): Starman I and Black Canary I share
adventures against old foes the Sportsmaster and
Huntress I.

STEAMROLLER

FIRST APPEARANCE GREEN LANTERN (2nd series) #176 (May 1984)
STATUS Villain **REAL NAME** Unknown
OCCUPATION Member of Demolition Team **BASE** Mobile
HEIGHT 5ft 11in **WEIGHT** 205 lbs
EYES Blue **HAIR** Black
SPECIAL POWERS/ABILITIES Drives a steamroller capable of leveling buildings.

Though his real name is unknown, the code name Steamroller is all one needs to know about this member of the Demolition Team. Formerly a stunt-motorcyclist operating out of Chicago, Steamroller now drives a miniature, high-powered steamroller with enough muscle to knock down any structure and flatten the pieces.

Steamroller joined the Demolition Team in hopes of becoming a high-priced mercenary, and with his new comrades—Rosie, Hardhat, Jackhammer, and Scoopshovel—tore up the Los Angeles branch of Ferris Aircraft on behalf of a congressmen nursing a grudge. Steamroller's gleeful rampage came to an end courtesy of the Predator, who later turned out to be an alternate personality belonging to Star Sapphire Carol Ferris.

After the Cyborg Superman, aided by Mongul destroyed Coast City, the Demolition Team decided to stamp out threats to the Earth and targeted a German nuclear plant. After a defeat by the Blood Pack, Steamroller and his teammates lost badly to an army of OMAC units prior to the Infinite Crisis. **DW**

STEEL I

FIRST APPEARANCE STEEL (1st series) #1 (March 1978)
STATUS Hero (deceased) **REAL NAME** Henry (Hank) Heywood I
OCCUPATION Crime fighter **BASE** Mobile
HEIGHT 6ft **WEIGHT** 378 lbs **EYES** Blue **HAIR** Blond
SPECIAL POWERS/ABILITIES Nearly indestructible due to steel construction and bioretardant skin; possesses enhanced strength and speed.

Hank Heywood nearly died when an explosion shredded his body. Rebuilt from the skeleton up, Heywood received artificial lungs, steel tubing instead of bones, metal plating on his skull, micro-motors to power his joints, and tough, bioretardant skin. As "Steel the Indestructible Man," he battled the Nazis during World War II, received the name Commander Steel from President Roosevelt, and joined the All-Star Squadron.

After the war, Steel retired from heroics and earned a fortune as a Detroit-based industrialist. His son died in Vietnam, but Commander Steel gave his grandson the same treatments he had received and turned Hank Heywood III into a new Steel. After Aquaman reformed the Justice League of America, Commander Steel offered his Detroit bunker as an HQ if Aquaman accepted his grandson as a member. Years later, Steel died battling the villain Eclipso. **DW**

STEEL II

FIRST APPEARANCE JUSTICE LEAGUE OF AMERICA (1st series) ANNUAL #2 **STATUS** Hero **REAL NAME** Henry "Hank" Heywood III
OCCUPATION Troubleshooter **BASE** Detroit
HEIGHT 5ft 11in **WEIGHT** 379 lbs **EYES** Blue **HAIR** Red
SPECIAL POWERS/ABILITIES Superhuman strength, speed, and agility; enhanced hearing; infrared vision.

Grandson of Henry Heywood, the 1940s champion Commander Steel (*see* Steel I), Hank Heywood III endured a series of painful operations to become a modern-day Steel. His bones were replaced with titanium. Micro-motors and servomechanisms enhanced his musculature. Subdermal plastisteel mesh lining a fibroplast skin made him nearly invulnerable, and cybernetic implants augmented his visual and auditory senses. After a long recovery, as his body adjusted to bio-chemical treatments and implants, the new Steel joined the Justice League of America. He was granted membership in exchange for the League's use of a Detroit-based headquarters, the Bunker, donated by the elder Heywood, a wealthy industrialist. Steel II was mortally wounded by an android creation of the League's foe Professor Ivo. Heywood died months later when Despero destroyed his life-support systems. **SB**

HEAVY METAL METTLE
Steel II was forged by the same process that saved his grandfather and molded him into the cyborg known as Commander Steel during World War II.

S

STEEL III

THE MAN OF IRON

IN THE 'HOOD *John Henry Irons loved to work with the kids in his Washington D.C. neighborhood.*

FIRST APPEARANCE ADVENTURES OF SUPERMAN #500 (June 1993)
STATUS Hero **REAL NAME** John Henry Irons
OCCUPATION Inventor, adventurer **BASE** Metropolis
HEIGHT 6ft 7in **WEIGHT** 210 lbs **EYES** Brown **HAIR** None
SPECIAL POWERS/ABILITIES A scientific genius with amazing manufacturing skills and a brave fighter with little formal training. Specially designed armor confers protection in battle and enables him to fly. His main weapon is a remote controlled hammer.

JOHN HENRY IRONS is a fighter forged from the same mold as Superman. When the Man of Tomorrow saved Irons from a fatal fall off a Metropolis skyscraper, he challenged the construction worker to make his life count for something. A former weapons engineer for the ruthless AmerTek company, Irons longed to atone for the deaths his designs caused. He chose the way of the hero as the armored champion Steel.

THE IRON MAN

John Irons grew up, surrounded by a loving family, in a poor section of Washington D.C. He entered college as a physics major and quickly rose to the top of his class. Realizing his potential as an engineer, AmerTek hired Irons and he designed the BG-80 assault rifle, also known as the "Toastmaster," as well as a flying armor prototype. Disillusioned by the misuse of his inventions, Irons faked his death and moved to Metropolis. After Superman died at Doomsday's hands, he was one of four men to briefly claim the Man of Steel's mantle. Irons and the resurrected Superman become close friends. John continued to adventure as Steel, aided by his plucky niece Natasha (*see* Irons, Natasha). Eventually, John opened Steelworks, an industrial design concern. He also worked with the Justice League of America.

During the Imperiex War (*see* Great Battles, pp.362–3), Steel suffered mortal wounds while releasing Doomsday from the JLA Watchtower to battle the cosmic conqueror. At the same time, Superman was unable to turn away the New Gods' Black Racer, who ushered dead souls into the afterlife. This time, however, the Racer delivered Irons to Apokolips, where the crafty Darkseid restored his life. Steel fought during the Infinite Crisis, but soon had a falling-out with his niece over her desire to take the "easy road" to superheroics. A resentful Natasha joined Lex Luthor's (*see* Luthor, Lex) Everyman Project and received superpowers. Irons, meanwhile, became infected by Luthor's mutagens, which temporarily transformed his body into living metal. Ultimately, Steel and Natasha realized the truth of Luthor's villainy and united to bring down the Everyman Project. **RG**

GREAT DEFENDER *Steel and his mighty hammer protected Washington, New Jersey and New York during his brief career.*

FINAL FIRES *Irons forges his last suit of battle armor.*

METAL WORK *John developed his various battlesuits in his lab.*

LIFE-SAVER *The Aegis, a piece of an Imperiex Probe, sustained John's life in the latter days of the Imperiex War.*

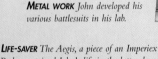

KEY STORYLINES
• *STEEL #1 (FEBRUARY 1994):* John Henry Irons moves back to Washington, D.C. and discovers that crime has ruined his once-friendly neighborhood.
• *STEEL #41–43 (AUGUST–OCTOBER 1997):* Steel has to handle his niece Natasha, political intrigue at his hospital, Skorpio, and romance all at the same time.
• *SUPERMAN VS. DARKSEID: APOKOLIPS NOW! (2003):* Superman braves Apokolips's worst forces to retrieve Steel's soul and return him to life.

MELTING POINT FOR STEEL? *Natasha, John Henry's niece, shields her eyes from the terrible explosion that claimed John's life.*

INFINITE CRISIS

The Crisis on Infinite Earths collapsed an endless number of parallel universes into a single, unified reality. But this blended existence could not contain its contradictions. With the interference of a madman, the multiverse was born again.

IDENTITY CRISIS

Fractures within the Justice League of America came to light with the stunning murder of Sue Dibny, wife of Elongated Man Ralph Dibny. Suspicion initially pointed to Doctor Light, who had horrifically assaulted Sue during the early years of the JLA. After Light's attack, a majority of League members had agreed to mind-wipe and reprogram him with Zatanna's magic – then had mind-wiped Batman when he discovered their actions.

The JLA had continued to use Zatanna's brainwashing to keep their secret identities hidden, leading to a betrayal of the trust that kept the team functioning. Yet Sue Dibny's murderer turned out to not be Doctor Light. The Atom's ex-wife Jean Loring had killed Sue, and embarked on a campaign against other people important to the League (a plan that resulted in the death of Robin's father) as part of an insane scheme to win back the Atom's affections.

Loring's incarceration in Arkham Asylum drove her further into madness, making her an easy target to become the newest host for Eclipso.

GRIEFSTRICKEN *Sue Dibny's death signaled a grim change in the super-hero community.*

BRAINWASHING *Zatanna's act of mind-wiping Doctor Light caused League members to start keeping secrets.*

LOSS *Robin's father and Captain Boomerang killed one another, leaving Robin an orphan.*

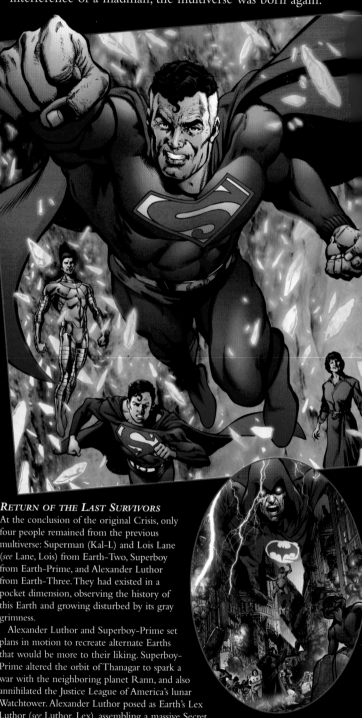

RETURN OF THE LAST SURVIVORS

At the conclusion of the original Crisis, only four people remained from the previous multiverse: Superman (Kal-L) and Lois Lane (*see* Lane, Lois) from Earth-Two, Superboy from Earth-Prime, and Alexander Luthor from Earth-Three. They had existed in a pocket dimension, observing the history of this Earth and growing disturbed by its gray grimness.

Alexander Luthor and Superboy-Prime set plans in motion to recreate alternate Earths that would be more to their liking. Superboy-Prime altered the orbit of Thanagar to spark a war with the neighboring planet Rann, and also annihilated the Justice League of America's lunar Watchtower. Alexander Luthor posed as Earth's Lex Luthor (*see* Luthor, Lex), assembling a massive Secret Society of Super Villains. Meanwhile, the rampaging forces of Eclipso and the Spectre overturned the realm of magic, while the intelligent satellite Brother Eye—created by Batman—pursued its own agenda by transforming humans into unstoppable OMACs.

SPECTRE'S SINS *The destruction of the Rock of Eternity loosed the Seven Deadly Sins on Gotham.*

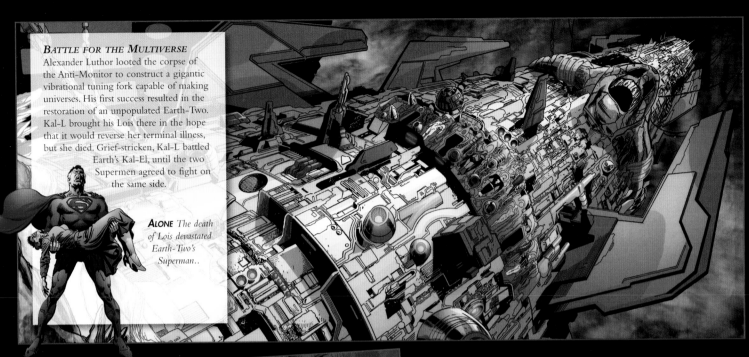

BATTLE FOR THE MULTIVERSE

Alexander Luthor looted the corpse of the Anti-Monitor to construct a gigantic vibrational tuning fork capable of making universes. His first success resulted in the restoration of an unpopulated Earth-Two. Kal-L brought his Lois there in the hope that it would reverse her terminal illness, but she died. Grief-stricken, Kal-L battled Earth's Kal-El, until the two Supermen agreed to fight on the same side.

ALONE *The death of Lois devastated Earth-Two's Superman..*

ALL-OUT ASSAULT

Superboy-Prime lashed out at Conner Kent, the Superboy whom he believed had taken his place. Superboy-Prime badly beat Conner and killed Pantha, before the Flashes (*see* Flash) hurled him into an alternate dimension. He returned even stronger, wearing an armored suit that fed him energizing yellow sun radiation.

Superboy-Prime lashed out at Conner Kent, the Superboy whom he believed had taken his place. Superboy-Prime badly beat Conner and killed Pantha, before the Flashes (*see* Flash) hurled him into an alternate dimension. He returned even stronger, wearing an armored suit that fed him energizing yellow sun radiation.

A rematch between Conner Kent and Superboy-Prime resulted in the destruction of Alexander Luthor's tuning fork, but at the cost of Conner's life. With the destruction of Alexander's machine the various universes he had created merged into a single reality, but this "New Earth" had subtle changes in its timeline.

In a last-ditch effort to crush his foes, Alexander ordered the villains of the Secret Society to take up arms against Earth's heroes, with Metropolis as their battleground. Superboy-Prime chose this moment to fly toward the planet Oa at near-light speed, hoping the collision would destroy this universe and trigger its rebirth. Superman and the Superman of Earth-Two intercepted him, steering Superboy-Prime through the heart of a red sun that sapped the powers of all three combatants. On the intelligent planet Mogo, Kal-L perished in the effort to stop his younger doppelganger.

THE NEW REALITY

The Green Lantern Corps took custody of Superboy-Prime, imprisoning him inside a miniature red sun. Alexander Luthor met his end on Earth, when the Joker took revenge for not receiving an invitation to join the Secret Society.

At the time, no one realized that Alexander Luthor had partially succeeded in his plan. He had created 52 parallel universes, identical and existing on separate vibrational planes. It would be another year before the existence of the new multiverse become known. **DW**

SUPERBOY-PRIME
Unstoppable relic of the old multiverse, he shrugged off attacks from powerful heroes.

LAST LAUGH *The Joker, left out of the action, took great pleasure in executing Alexander Luthor.*

STRANGE, ADAM

CHAMPION OF RANN

FIRST APPEARANCE SHOWCASE #17 (December 1958)
STATUS Hero   **REAL NAME** Adam Strange
OCCUPATION Adventurer   **BASE** The planet Rann
HEIGHT 6ft   **WEIGHT** 175 lbs   **EYES** Blue   **HAIR** Blond
SPECIAL POWERS/ABILITIES Adam is a brilliant strategist and expert flyer. He can teleport across space using a Rannian machine; also travels using a jet pack; wears a special suit fitted with oxygen tanks to survive in the airless vacuum of space; main weapon is a ray gun.

ARCHAEOLOGIST ADAM STRANGE was unexpectedly transported 25 trillion miles across space to the planet Rann. There, he met the scientist Sardath, who explained that his Zeta beam had been intended purely as a communications tool but had turned out to be a teleportation device instead. Over time, Adam adapted so well to this new world that he became the planet's protector, using his wits and the native technology to overcome alien invasions, rogue monsters and the occasional Tornado Tyrant.

ZETA BEAM LOVE

Adam fell in love with Sardath's beautiful daughter Alanna, but their romance was regularly interrupted, for whenever the Zeta beam radiation wore off, Adam was yanked back to Earth. To return to Rann, Adam had to calculate the next time and location the Zeta Beam would strike. It was some time before Adam learned Rann's secret: Rannian men were all sterile and Adam had been brought to Rann to father a child with Alanna and perpetuate the race!

During his exploits on Rann, Adam was aided by the Justice League of America and many other heroes. Adam was finally drained of the toxic radiation that prevented him from making long-term stays on Rann. His romance with Alanna continued, and the JLA attended their wedding. Finally drained of the energy that kept him on Rann, Adam returned to Earth.

Later, using a "Mega-Zeta Beam," Adam was permanently teleported to Rann. His happiness was shattered when Alanna died giving birth to their daughter Aleea. Sardath went mad, rocketing the city of Ranagar into space in a protective sphere. Seemingly deranged himself, Adam brought the JLA to Rann and commanded them "to restore the planet to its former glory."

In fact, Adam's actions were a ruse to outwit the En'Tarans. This race of telepathic conquerors, who sought the Zeta Beam technology for their own dark purposes, revived Alanna from her deathlike state. Adam, Alanna and Aleea were happily reunited.

Adam Strange returned to action with the Omega Men during an adventure that transported Rann into the same star system as Thanagar, sparking the Rann-Thanagar War. Strange lost his eyesight in the Infinite Crisis and spent a year stranded in space with Animal Man and Starfire, fighting the armies of Lady Styx. Returned home, he found himself replaced as Rann's champion. **RG**

BEAMED UP *The Zeta Beam conveys Adam from Earth to Alanna.*

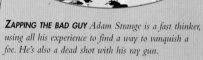

FADE OUT *After a time, the Zeta effect wears off and Adam is returned to Earth.*

LEARNING DEVICE *Sardath, who developed the Zeta Beam, also found a quick way to teach Adam his language.*

CIRCLE OF FIRE *Green Lightning, a Green Lantern from the future, rescues Adam from peril on planet Rann.*

ZAPPING THE BAD GUY *Adam Strange is a fast thinker, using all his experience to find a way to vanquish a foe. He's also a dead shot with his ray gun.*

KEY STORYLINES

• **ADAM STRANGE: MAN OF TWO WORLDS (1990):** Adam seemingly loses Rann, Alanna and his daughter in a cosmic conflict.
• **JUSTICE LEAGUE OF AMERICA #120–121 (JULY–AUGUST 1975):** Adam and Alanna finally get married, but not without considerable difficulty.
• **MYSTERY IN SPACE #68 (JUNE 1961):** Adam's first encounter with the deadly Dust Devils.
• **SHOWCASE #17 (NOVEMBER–DECEMBER 1958):** Adam first rides the Zeta Beam to discover Rann.

STEPPENWOLF

FIRST APPEARANCE NEW GODS (1st series) #7
STATUS Villain (deceased) *REAL NAME* Steppenwolf
OCCUPATION Military commander *BASE* Apokolips
HEIGHT 6ft *WEIGHT* 203 lbs *EYES* Red *HAIR* Black
SPECIAL POWERS/ABILITIES Dog cavalry commander; "cable snare" device fires lethal energy beams and entraps opponents; wields an electro-axe and is an expert swordsman.

The uncle of DARKSEID, ruler of Apokolips, Steppenwolf was the commander of Apokolips's military during the reign of Heggra, Darkseid's mother. Hoping to incite a war between Apokolips and its sister world, New Genesis, Darkseid suggested that Steppenwolf go and hunt the inhabitants there for "sport."

When Steppenwolf murdered the wife of Izaya the Inheritor, the New Genesis leader, and Darkseid pretended to kill Highfather himself, a bloody war between the two worlds began.

During a pitched battle on the plains of New Genesis, Steppenwolf was caught off guard and killed by the vengeful Izaya, whom he believed dead. Steppenwolf was later resurrected by the advanced technology of Apokolips. After menacing menaced Bart Allen (the fourth Flash), Steppenwolf lost his life during the Death of the New Gods event. **PJ**

STOMPA

FIRST APPEARANCE MISTER MIRACLE 1st series #6 (February 1972)
STATUS Villain *REAL NAME* Unknown
OCCUPATION Female Fury *BASE* Apokolips
HEIGHT 5ft 8in *WEIGHT* 330 lbs *EYES* Unknown *HAIR* Unknown
SPECIAL POWERS/ABILITIES Ruthless enforcer; heavy matter boots can pulverize even the densest material.

Reared on distant Apokolips and personally trained for terror by the vile Granny Goodness, Stompa is a member of the much-feared Female Furies, an elite squad of women warriors belonging to Darkseid's Special Powers Force. As her name implies, Stompa uses her considerable bulk to great advantage when crushing the enemies of Darkseid beneath her boot heels. Possessing considerable muscle mass, she is stronger than a Parademon and just as mean.

Recently, Stompa adopted a new costume that accentuates her feminine qualities slightly more than her previous unisex uniform. She was among the Furies dispatched to Earth by Darkseid to capture Kara Zor-El, Superman's Kryptonian cousin, so that the dreaded lord of Apokolips could mold the young Supergirl to do his bidding. As expected, this mission brought Stompa and the Female Furies into direct conflict with the Earth's finest heroes, particularly Superman and Batman, as two worlds struggled for the soul of the young Kryptonian girl. **SB**

STRANGE, ADAM *SEE OPPOSITE PAGE*

STRANGE, PROFESSOR HUGO

FIRST APPEARANCE DETECTIVE COMICS #36 (February 1940)
STATUS Villain *REAL NAME* Hugo Strange
OCCUPATION Psychiatrist; criminal *BASE* Gotham City
HEIGHT 5ft 10in *WEIGHT* 170 lbs
EYES Gray *HAIR* None (black beard)
SPECIAL POWERS/ABILITIES Brilliant deductive mind and extensive knowledge of psychology.

Professor Hugo Strange is one of the only people to have deduced Batman's secret identity. Early in the caped crusader's career, Professor Strange became a media celebrity by appearing on talk shows and providing his "expert opinion" regarding the costumed vigilante's psychological makeup. Soon appointed a special consultant to Gotham City's Vigilante Task Force, Strange's obsession with the Batman gradually unhinged his mind even as it allowed him to piece together disparate clues linking Batman to Bruce Wayne.

Strange has used his knowledge of Batman's greatest secret to torment the Dark Knight, though Strange's waxing and waning levels of insanity sometimes make him unaware of his proprietary knowledge. Bruce Wayne recently underwent self-hypnosis to temporarily forget that he was the Batman, confounding Strange and allowing Nightwing and Robin to defeat the professor. Hugo Strange has also brewed mind-altering drugs that have turned Gotham's thugs into vicious killers. Although his sporadic knowledge of Bruce Wayne's costumed identity would prove invaluable to Batman's enemies, Hugo Strange has remained at arm's length from the Dark Knight's Rogues Gallery. Strange prefers to work alone. He remains a dangerous foe, and the day when his mind finally snaps will be a grim day for the citizens of Gotham. **DW**

MASKED MANIA *Hugo Strange has allowed his entire reality to revolve around Batman. His brain is still his greatest asset, despite his bouts of psychosis.*

STRATA

FIRST APPEARANCE INVASION #2 (Summer 1989)
STATUS Hero *REAL NAME* Strata
OCCUPATION Interstellar operative *BASE* The planet Cairn
HEIGHT 7ft 2in *WEIGHT* 803 lbs *EYES* White *HAIR* None
SPECIAL POWERS/ABILITIES Superstrength; invulnerability; extremely long-lived.

Strata is from the planet Dryad, whose inhabitants are sentient, rock-like humanoids made of silicon. As a youngster, Strata was captured by aliens seeing to conquer the universe. With several other prisoners, Strata escaped with the help of Vril Dox. Strata and the others then helped Dox form an interstellar police force, L.E.G.I.O.N.

The L.E.G.I.O.N. was attacked by alien psychopath Lobo, who shredded Strata's rock-like epidermis, revealing crystalline skin beneath. It was only then that Strata realized she was female! Strata served as chief training officer of L.E.G.I.O.N and married fellow member Garv.

When the L.E.G.I.O.N. and its forces were transformed into a fascist organization by Vril Dox's son, Lyrl, Strata was separated from Garv and worked with the R.E.B.E.L.S. to end Lyrl's threat. Captain Comet reformed L.E.G.I.O.N. and Strata and Garv returned to its ranks. Strata later joined InterC.E.P.T., an organization specializing in interdimensional border control. **PJ**

STRIKER Z

FIRST APPEARANCE JLA #61 (February 2002)
STATUS Hero *REAL NAME* Danny Tsang *OCCUPATION* Super hero
BASE San Francisco *HEIGHT* 5ft 10in *WEIGHT* 175 lbs
EYES Black *HAIR* Black *SPECIAL POWERS/ABILITIES* biologically-created energy powers his "flight jacket", a visor with built-in sensor arrays, sonic generators, shock cannons and other useful devices.

While working as a stuntman in the Hong Kong movie industry, Danny Tsang developed superpowers after an on-set accident when he fell into an experimental fuel-cell medium. Danny's body became a living battery capable of fueling various high-tech devices designed by Danny's pal, Charlie Lau, a former S.T.A.R. Labs engineer and special-effects expert. Danny traveled to the U.S hoping that his flashy powers would make him a Hollywood star. Dubbed Striker Z by his talent agent, Danny instead found work with the Power Company, a superpowered law firm. After he joined the Power Company, Striker Z received several offers to star in television commercials.

While he enjoys being a costumed champion, Striker Z remains uncertain whether he's in the hero game for the fame and fortune, or for more altruistic motives. **SB**

SUICIDE SQUAD

First appearance THE BRAVE AND THE BOLD (1st series) #25 (Sept. 1959) **Status** Covert agents **Base** Mobile; formerly Belle Reve prison, La. **Notable members** Air Wave II (as Maser); Amanda Waller; Arsenal (as Speedy); Atom II; Atom III; Batman; Big Barda; Big Sir; Black Adam; Black Orchid II; Blackstarr; Blockbuster I; Bronze Tiger; Cameron Chase; Captain Boomerang; Captain Cold; Catalyst; Chronos I; Clock King, Doctor Light I, Enchantress, Killer Frost, King Shark, Major Disaster, Manhunter III, Nemesis, Parasite, Penguin, Plastique, Punch and Jewelee, Vixen, Shade.

The Squad has since been revived multiple times, once under the orders of President Lex Luthor (see Luthor, lex) during the Imperiex War, and again under the leadership of Sergeant Rock. Amanda Waller assembled a new Suicide Squad following the Infinite Crisis, setting her team against BLACK ADAM and later using Squad operatives to capture dozens of super-villains for exile on the distant planet Salvation. **PJ**

THE FIRST SQUAD
1) Jess Bright
2) Rick Flag, Sr.
3) Karin Grace
4) Dr. Hugh Evans

ELITE FORCE

During the 1950s, the Suicide Squad, became an elite force assigned to covert missions abroad. After Rick Flag's wife died in a car accident, Flag himself perished in a suicide mission against the German War Wheel. Their son, Richard Flag Jr., under the eye of General J.E.B. Stuart, grew up to became an Air Force colonel and the leader of a revamped Suicide Squad. Along with Karin Grace, Jess Bright, and Hugh Evans, Flag's Squad handled numerous threats to national security. After the tragic deaths of Bright and Evans on a mission in Cambodia, Karin Grace had a mental breakdown, and the Squad was disbanded.

Decades later congressional aide Amanda Waller created a new Suicide Squad, many of whom were superhuman criminals. In exchange for a pardon and a fee, the criminals agreed to undertake one mission. Rick Flag, Jr. was recruited to be the Squad's field commander.

By maintaining a core group, the Suicide Squad undertook a number of missions, but several operatives died along the way, including Grace and Flag himself. After the terrorist KOBRA unhinged the U.S. intelligence community in one of his attempts at world domination, and Waller was sent to prison for contempt of Congress, the Squad was disbanded.

WORKING UNDER THE AUSPICES of Task Force X, a secret U.S. government agency, the Suicide Squad is a unit of paramilitary and meta-human operatives first assembled during World War II. Under the command of Captain Richard Flag, Sr., this "Suicide Squadron," comprised soldiers who chose service with the Squad in lieu of a court martial. The squad's assignments were considered suicide missions—hence its name!

OUR WORLDS
SGT. ROCK'S SQUAD
1) Sgt. Rock
2) Modem
3) Deadshot
4) Blackstarr
5) Bulldozer

INFINITE CRISIS SQUAD
1) Cap. Boomerang II
2) The Persuader
3) Count Vertigo
4) Atom Smasher
5) Plastique
6) Electrocutioner

KEY STORYLINES
• BRAVE AND THE BOLD #25 (SEPTEMBER 1959): Rick Flag gathers together his covert team for the U.S. government, forming the first ever Suicide Squad.
• LEGENDS #1 (NOVEMBER 1986): A new Suicide Squad, comprised of super-villains, takes down the titanic Brimstone as Darkseid destroys Earth's legends!
• SUICIDE SQUAD (1ST SERIES) #17–18 (SEPTEMBER–OCTOBER 1988): The Suicide Squad prevents the Jihad terrorist group from destroying New York City!

SWAMP THING

THE TOXIC AVENGER

FIRST APPEARANCE HOUSE OF SECRETS #92 (July 1971)
STATUS Hero   **REAL NAME** Alec Holland
OCCUPATION Plant elemental   **BASE** Houma, Louisiana
HEIGHT Variable   **WEIGHT** Variable   **EYES** Red   **HAIR** None
SPECIAL POWERS/ABILITIES Earth's plant elemental can manifest itself wherever there is organic life and can sense anything that affects said life; superstrong, with amazing regenerative powers; can change size and shape; can travel back through time.

GAIA, THE EARTH SPIRIT, has always had Elemental avatars to look after the planet and its living inhabitants. The greatest among them is the plant elemental known as Swamp Thing, who protects the planet at the risk of eliminating all human life. Several individuals have been given the role of plant elemental. The most recent is Alec Holland, who fell into a Louisiana swamp polluted with chemicals, which turned him into Swamp Thing.

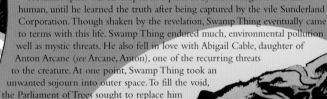

UNDER GLASS *General Sunderland studies Swamp Thing's body, trying to establish dominance.*

AVATARS OF THE GREEN

The Green was established as the Earth cooled and Yggdrasil was created. Yggdrasil gained sentience, and the Parliament of Trees grew in a sacred South American grove. Other elemental forces created their own parliaments soon after, including Water, Air, Fire, and Stone. Over time, each elemental caused a human to become its avatar. Each avatar lives until circumstances demand a changing of the guard. In the 20th Century this occurred with great rapidity, from Alex Olsen in 1905 to German pilot Albert Hollerer in 1942, to 1953's Aaron Hayley, to Alan Hallman, to the current Alec Holland.

Holland's spirit was enveloped in a plant body that thought it was still human, until he learned the truth after being captured by the vile Sunderland Corporation. Though shaken by the revelation, Swamp Thing eventually came to terms with much. Swamp Thing endured much, environmental pollution as well as mystic threats. He also fell in love with Abigail Cable, daughter of Anton Arcane (*see* Arcane, Anton), one of the recurring threats to the creature. At one point, Swamp Thing took an unwanted sojourn into outer space. To fill the void, the Parliament of Trees sought to replace him with his child, dubbed Sprout and ultimately named Tefé (a child conceived with more than a little help from John Constantine).

Upon his return, Swamp Thing endured a series of trials that had him master each neighboring Parliament until he gained total control over the world's elements. The Word I intervened and stopped Swamp Thing from being corrupted by his own absolute power. Now representing the Earth as a whole, Swamp Thing took his place in the Parliament of Worlds.

Tefe grew to adulthood, trying to find her way, rebelling against Abby's love. Swamp Thing, stripped of Holland's human consciousness, sought to destroy all life, starting with Tefe. Constantine restored Holland to the elemental and the new unified being is establishing his place in the world anew. **RG**

BEAUTY AND THE BEAST
Swamp monsters have been drawn to attractive women through the years.

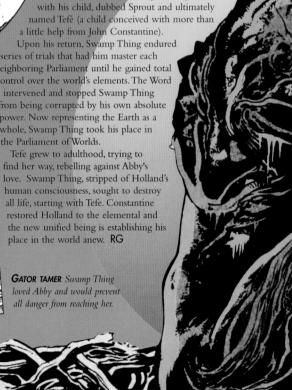

GATOR TAMER *Swamp Thing loved Abby and would prevent all danger from reaching her.*

KEY STORYLINES

• *SWAMP THING: DARK GENESIS (TPB, 1991):* The original storyline of the Swamp Thing and Abby.
• *SWAMP THING (2ND SERIES) #61 (JUNE 1987):* In "All Flesh is Grass," while exiled in space, he encounters Green Lantern Medphyl's homeworld.
• *SAGA OF THE SWAMP THING #34 (MARCH 1985):* Abby eats a tuber and experiences life from Swamp Thing's perspective.
• *SWAMP THING #21 (FEBRUARY 1984):* Swamp Thing learns he is not Alec Holland but a plant elemental.
• *HOUSE OF SECRETS #92 (JULY 1971):* The first ever Swamp Thing story.

SUPERBOY

THE TEEN OF STEEL

FIRST APPEARANCE ADVENTURES OF SUPERMAN #500 (June 1993)
STATUS Hero **REAL NAMES** Kon-El; Conner Kent
OCCUPATION Student, adventurer **BASE** Smallville; San Francisco
HEIGHT 5ft 7in **WEIGHT** 150 lbs **EYES** Blue **HAIR** Black
SPECIAL POWERS/ABILITIES Superboy has "tactile telekinesis" which mimics superstrength and flight and other Kryptonian abilities; can disassemble objects by touching them.

A clone of Superman created by the Cadmus Project, the world's most advanced genetic research facility, Superboy is a custom-made copy of the Man of Steel. In fact, Superboy was one of many such clones engineered by Cadmus for the purpose of replacing Superman, using DNA samples taken from the Kryptonian champion after his battle with Doomsday. Superboy, however, was the only clone to survive.

CLONED Created with Super DNA, Kon-El was gestated inside a laboratory!

TEST TUBE HERO Superboy emerges from his cloning tube at Project Cadmus, the spitting image of Superman at 16!

CREATING A SUPER HERO

The Cadmus scientists stabilized Superboy's gene code by grafting Superman's alien DNA on to a human DNA strand. The clone was then transformed through a rapid-aging process, becoming a 16-year-old boy in weeks. The teenage duplicate was rescued from his confines at Cadmus by the Newsboy Legion, who had learned that Superboy's "creator," the unscrupulous Doctor Paul Westfield, had planned to use the young clone's power for his own ends. Altering his costume, the headstrong Superboy then revealed himself to the world. Superboy soon became a close ally of Superman, but moved to Hawaii, hoping the distance from Metropolis might better help him attain an identity separate from his genetic "father."

There he began dating Tana Moon, a journalist who moved to Hawaii after helping Superboy make a splash at television station W.G.B.S. as the "Metropolis Kid." After his body started to deteriorate from a clone plague, Superboy's DNA became "frozen" at his 16-year old age. Superman gave the young clone the Kryptonian name "Kon-El". Soon after, Superboy had a brief affair with Knockout; Tana Moon broke up with him and moved away.

BOY OF STEEL Superboy lived in Honolulu for some time, finding enemies in the Scavenger, King Shark (above), and Black Zero, and both friend and foe in Knockout, one of the Female Furies.

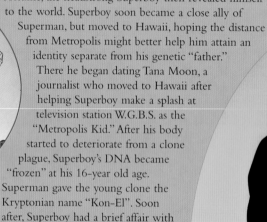

SUPER SECRET Robin helped Superboy deduce the secret from the young clones past—the source of his human DNA—a secret the Boy Wonder was sworn to conceal.

A GRIM DISCOVERY

Superboy returned to Metropolis as Project Cadmus' special agent and also helped found Young Justice. Superboy was then kidnapped by the Agenda, a clandestine organization of cloners, and was replaced for months by an evil duplicate named Match. Superboy eventually escaped the Agenda, but not before, Tana Moon was killed by the Agenda's leader Amanda Spence, Paul Westfield's cyborg daughter. Superboy was then adopted by Superman's parents, Jonathan and Martha Kent, and enrolled in Smallville High School as Conner Kent, Clark Kent's young cousin. After Young Justice's dissolution, Superboy joined the Teen Titans. He then learned that his human strand of DNA was Lex Luthor's (see Luthor, Lex), a horrifying secret he initially shared only with his teammate Robin.

FRIENDLY FIRE *Forced to fight Superboy after Lex Luthor turned him against the Teen Titans, Wonder Girl used her lasso to overwhelm her friend.*

LEX'S LEGACY

Superboy's self-identity suffered when he learned that his human DNA came, not from Project Cadmus director Paul Westfield, as he had believed, but from Lex Luthor. Consumed by thoughts that he might become a villain, Superboy found himself vulnerable to a deeply-buried brain-control trigger planted by Lex himself. No longer in control of his mind, Superboy shaved his head to resemble Lex and turned on his friends in the Teen Titans, injuring both Robin and Wonder Girl before struggling back to sanity. The experience left him deeply shaken, prompting a leave of absence from the Titans and a period of seclusion in Smallville.

INFINITE CRISIS

The universe-shaking events of the Infinite Crisis brought Superboy face-to-face with his twisted namesake Superboy-Prime. While in seclusion in an alternate universe, Superboy-Prime had grown enraged at the sight of an Earth that he deemed unworthy and an "impostor" Superboy who had taken his place. Superboy-Prime escaped exile and confronted Superboy in Smallville, beating him to the brink of death. The Teen Titans helped restore Conner's health with a Luthor-designed genetic cure, but the Crisis raged on. Prior to the final battle, Superboy and Wonder Girl shared one last, intimate night together.

Superboy, Wonder Girl, and Nightwing charged into battle to sabotage Alexander Luthor's world-birthing tuning fork. When Superboy-Prime arrived to protect the device, he and Conner clashed in a furious rematch. Ultimately, Conner sacrificed his life to destroy Alexander Luthor's machine.

FINAL MOMENTS *Just before his death, Superboy shared a night with Wonder Girl.*

SACRIFICE *Beaten once, Superboy would not let Superboy-Prime win again.*

FALLEN *The world's greatest heroes mourned Superboy's death.*

IN MEMORIAM *A statue outside Titans Tower commemorates the fallen hero.*

NOT FORGOTTEN

Conner's death became one of the most tragic of the Infinite Crisis. In memorial, Superboy received twin statues—one in Metropolis and a second outside San Francisco's Titans Tower. His presence lingered in the minds of many, especially Wonder Girl. During the subsequent year, she allied herself with a "resurrection cult" based on Kryptonian theology in the faint hope that their rituals could bring Conner back from the dead. The cult was discredited at the same time that Wonder Girl stopped dwelling on Conner's death, and she has since started a tentative romance with Robin. Superboy's presence is reflected in the face of his clone, Match, who recently reappeared as a member of Deathstroke's villainous "Titans East." **RG/DW**

KEY STORYLINES
- *ADVENTURES OF SUPERMAN #500 (JUNE 1993):* Superboy and three others begin the Reign of the Supermen after Doomsday nearly killed the Man of Steel!
- *SUPERBOY (3RD SERIES) #74 (MARCH 2000):* Tana Moon, Superboy's girlfriend, dies at the hands of the villainous Agenda!
- *TEEN TITANS (3RD SERIES) #1 (AUGUST 2003):* After joining the latest incarnation of the Teen Titans, Superboy discovers that he shares Lex Luthor's DNA!

SUPERGIRL

THE MAID OF MIGHT

FIRST APPEARANCE ACTION COMICS #252 (May 1959)
STATUS Hero **REAL NAME** Kara Zor-El
OCCUPATION Adventurer **BASE** Metropolis
HEIGHT 5ft 5in **WEIGHT** 135 lbs **EYES** Blue **HAIR** Blonde
SPECIAL POWERS/ABILITIES Under the Sun's solar radiation, Supergirl's kryptonian physique absorbs energy and can fly, has superstrength, superspeed, invulnerability, acute hearing, and a range of vision including emitting X-rays and heat.

LUTHOR'S TOY
Matrix is comforted by Lex Luthor, unwittingly becoming a tool in his megalomaniac schemes.

COUNTLESS PARALLEL UNIVERSES existed prior to the catastrophic Crisis on Infinite Earths. In one such pocket universe, Superman was not the sole survivor of Krypton. That world's Superboy, however, died in the 30th century while saving that universe's Legion of Super-Heroes. Three Kryptonian criminals managed to survive as well, and found their way to Earth. No one powerful enough was left to stop them. That world's Lex Luthor (*see* Luthor, Lex), a noble scientist, created a lifeform from protomatter, using genetic material supplied by Lana Lang, hoping it could help defeat the deadly trio.

WITHOUT SUPERMAN
Supergirl selflessly used her powers to protect one and all.

THE MATRIX

This shape-changing being was dispatched to a parallel world, hoping Superman could help. The Man of Steel answered the call to arms and was forced to kill the three Kryptonians to save the world, but not before the lifeform, known as Matrix, was reduced to an amorphous mass. Superman brought Matrix to his world and there it recuperated on the Kent family farm. Out of respect for its savior, Matrix took on a feminine form and used her more limited superpowers to become Supergirl. When Superman exiled himself to space to atone for having killed for the first time, Supergirl took on his peace-keeping role. She naïvely fell under Lex Luthor's thrall for a while, until she saw him for the manipulative despot that he was. She then saved the life of Linda Danvers in the town of Leesburg, V.A., by merging her life essence with Linda's. This created an entirely new being with different abilities, such as more limited shape-changing, psychokinetic skills, and increased strength and endurance. In time, Linda/Supergirl/Matrix discovered the violent and haunted life Linda had led and sought to redeem her existence. During her encounters with the demon Buzz and other supernatural entities, she discovered she was a reborn being known as an Earth-Angel, one of three on Earth. After several weird adventures, Linda met up with a Supergirl from yet another parallel timeline. This Supergirl was Superman's cousin from Krypton, a more innocent heroine who needed to die in order to keep the fabric of time from fraying. Linda also gave up her angelic abilities and left Leesburg hoping to lead a "normal" life.

TWO BECOME ONE
Supergirl and Linda Danvers confront cosmic forces to restore balance to reality.

KARA ZOR-EL

Following an alteration in time by the Futuresmiths, a teen named Cir-El arrived in Metropolis, claiming to be the daughter of Clark Kent and Lois Lane (*see* Lane, Lois). She was gradually accepted by Superman until the Futuresmith's plans were undone to preserve the timeline; Cir-El then vanished. These changes to the timestream had unexpected results, such as the arrival of an asteroid from Krypton. The asteroid broke up as it entered Earth's atmosphere but a spacecraft managed to splash down in the ocean. Within the damaged craft was a young teenager, Kara Zor-El, from Superman's homeworld. It was finally agreed that Kara would stay in the U.S., in Superman's care.

NEW ARRIVAL *A rocket arrives on Earth and a suspicious Batman doubts its occupant's claims of Kryptonian birth.*

KEY STORYLINES

• **SUPERMAN/BATMAN #8–13 (MAY–OCTOBER 2004):** Kara arrives on Earth, adored by Superman, suspected by Batman, trained by the Amazons, and coveted by Darkseid, tyrannical ruler of Apokolips.
• **SUPERGIRL: MANY HAPPY RETURNS (2003):** Supergirl meets her pre-Crisis self and realizes she must sacrifice everything to maintain the cosmic balance.
• **SUPERGIRL #1 (3RD SERIES) (FEBRUARY 1994):** Troubled teenager Linda Danvers is rescued by Matrix and becomes an Earth Angel.
• **SUPERGIRL (3RD SERIES) #1–4 (FEBRUARY–MAY 1994):** Matrix learns about life and love as Supergirl, under the sway of Lex Luthor's charismatic personality.

WARRIOR TRAINING *On the island of Themyscira, Supergirl learned combat under the finest Amazon swordmasters.*

RETURN OF THE ORIGINAL

The arrival of the space pod at the bottom of Gotham harbor heralded the arrival of a new Kryptonian, soon revealed as Kal-El's cousin. Unlike previous post-Crisis incarnations of Supergirl, this Kara Zor-El had lived on Krypton until her mid-teens then departed for Earth on orders from her parents Zor-El and Allura. Her mission: To search for Kal-El, who had been sent to Earth as a baby. A malfunction along the way had trapped her in stasis for decades. With Kal-El now grown to adulthood as Superman, the planet's foremost hero, Kara no longer had an official role to play. Batman's suspicion didn't help. The Dark Knight found the presence of a superpowered teenager a potential threat to public safety, and his hostility drove a wedge between himself and an overprotective Superman. Kara underwent warrior training with the Amazons of Themyscira to learn to control her powers. Despite these preparations, Batman's fears proved accurate when Darkseid kidnapped Kara and brainwashed her into becoming the leader of his elite Female Furies. Superman helped Kara break Darkseid's hold, encouraging her to take up the identity of Supergirl upon her return from Apokolips.

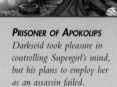

PRISONER OF APOKOLIPS *Darkseid took pleasure in controlling Supergirl's mind, but his plans to employ her as an assassin failed.*

RISE OF A HERO

Though welcomed by the superhuman community, Kara harbored doubts about her ability to live up to the name. Her self-identity suffered a literal fracture when Lex Luthor used black kryptonite to split Kara into two individuals, one good and one evil. Supergirl overcame her sinister self and recommitted herself to the fight for truth, battling bravely during the Infinite Crisis.

EVIL TWIN *Lex Luthor split Supergirl into good and evil halves, each fighting to control her spirit.*

ONCE AND FUTURE HERO

A time warp transported Supergirl one thousand years into the future, where she became a member of the Legion of Super Heroes. The Legionnaires, who revered the champions of the 21st century, gave Supergirl a place of honor within their organization, even electing her Legion president despite amnesia brought about by the time transference.

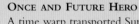

DOMINATION *Supergirl helped the Legion of Super-Heroes overrun the Dominator homeworld.*

BACK TO EARTH

After months in the future, Supergirl returned to present-day Metropolis, filling in for a powerless Superman. She also served for a brief stint with the Outsiders, and struck up a close friendship with Captain Boomerang II. RG/DW

BOOMER *Supergirl and Captain Boomerang II have enjoyed a flirtatious friendship..*

AMAZONS ATTACK

Now living on her own, Supergirl fought alongside Green Lantern Hal Jordan and the Challengers of the Unknown to end the threat of the Luck Lords, and aided the Amazons when Queen Hippolyta's warriors invaded Washington DC—even forcing the crash-landing of Air Force One. Most recently, Supergirl accepted an invitation to become a member of the Teen Titans.

SUPERMAN

THE MAN OF STEEL

FIRST APPEARANCE ACTION COMICS #1 (June 1938)
STATUS Hero REAL NAME Kal-El; Clark Joseph Kent (adoptive name)
OCCUPATION Super hero; (as Clark Kent) journalist BASE Metropolis
HEIGHT 6ft 3in WEIGHT 235 lbs EYES Blue HAIR Black
SPECIAL POWERS/ABILITIES Kal-El's powers were latent until his teenage
years. His kryptonian physiology absorbs immense energy from
Earth's yellow sun, enabling him to fly at incredible speeds, and
endowing him with superstrength, invulnerability (his only weaknesses
are green kryptonite radiation and magic), ultra-acute hearing,
freezing breath, immense lung capacity and a range of vision
including X-ray vision (he can see through anything except lead) and
heat vision.

SUPERMAN, THE LAST SON OF KRYPTON, represents the very best in humanity. His native world of Krypton, a giant planet orbiting a dying red sun, was doomed by the radioactive elements at its core and exploded many years ago, but not before scientist Jor-El and his wife Lara rocketed their son to safety, hoping against hope that his spacecraft would find him a new home in the vast reaches of the universe. Their gamble paid off in ways that have enormously benefited humanity.

FIRST ISSUE The Man of Steel first flexed his muscles on the cover of Action Comics #1.

THE SOLE SURVIVOR

The scientist Jor-El knew that Krypton, his world, was doomed. Irresistible forces gathering at the planet's core would soon tear it apart. Desperate to save his pregnant wife Lara, Jor-El salvaged a test rocket and retrofitted it with a life-support system. The system could only support a single person, but Jor-El calculated that Lara and her unborn baby would be able to survive the journey. The premature arrival of Lara's baby threw this plan into disarray.

Jor-El and Lara made the desperate decision to place the newborn infant, whom they named Kal-El, in the rocket and send him out into space, alone. Moments after the rocket left Krypton's atmosphere, the planet exploded. And the child that would one day grow to be Superman commenced his perilous voyage to a new home—Earth.

SMALLVILLE DAYS

Kal-El's ship traveled countless light-years until it crashed in a remote field near Smallville, Kansas, where it and its infant cargo were found by farmers Jonathan and Martha Kent. Raising him as their own, the kind-hearted Kents named the boy Clark Joseph and watched in amazement as, little by little, his unique abilities began to manifest themselves. Clark's body proved to be a veritable solar battery. He absorbed the sun's energy, which gave him incredible strength, invulnerability, heightened senses, and the ability to fly. Fearing that various governments or factions would claim Clark as their own, the Kents encouraged the boy to act as "normal" as possible and to keep his powers a secret. After graduating from high school, Clark left the little town of Smallville to travel the world, eager to find some purpose for his amazing abilities as he searched for a suitably heroic role in life.

AFRICAN ADVENTURE Before Clark Kent made his name in Metropolis, he traveled the world on a personal journey of discovery. Eager to try out his growing superpowers, he headed for some of the worlds troublespots, helping to resolve a bloody intertribal conflict in Africa.

SUPERMAN'S COSTUME

In time, however, Clark realized that he'd made a mistake by ignoring his alien heritage in favor of his human upbringing. Once he acknowledged that there was a place in this world not only for Clark Kent but for Kal-El, Clark used materials from his spacecraft to create a costume signifying and reflecting his Kryptonian roots—one he could wear openly whenever he wasn't disguising himself as a mild-mannered journalist.

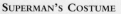

LIFESAVER!
Superman's first costumed adventure saw him saving Jimmy Olsen and Lois Lane from certain death.

LOIS LANE *As time went by, Clark Kent became a celebrated reporter and fell in love with Lois. She got over her crush on the Man of Steel, realizing what a good catch Clark was. Marriage soon beckoned.*

THE MILD-MANNERED REPORTER

Sporting horn-rimmed spectacles and wearing oversized clothes to disguise his physique, Clark Kent came to Metropolis and was interviewed by *Daily Planet* editor Perry White for a reporter post. Clark worked with young photographer Jimmy Olsen and star reporter Lois Lane. It was she who, glimpsing the Kryptonian crest on the costume of the city's amazing flying man, first called him "Superman." Clark began his dual life as a journalist and crime fighter.

THE BEGINNING OF A NEW AGE

Superman's arrival signaled a new era for costumed heroes. As more and more appeared around the world, so did super-powered villains, ranging from the alien Brainiac to the crazed Toyman. Superman's exploits inspired millions, so the world was stunned when the behemoth Doomsday killed him in battle. Fortunately, Superman was returned to life by Kryptonian technology. He has since allowed a handful of heroes—Superboy, Supergirl and Steel—to share the S-shield that is a symbol from his homeworld.

AN EVERLASTING INSPIRATION

Superman has had to contend with scheme after malicious scheme to discredit or destroy him. Virtually all of them have been engineered by Lex Luthor, first through his LexCorp business and then as U.S. President.

Alone and with the Justice League of America, Superman has become a symbol for truth and justice across the world. In the 31st century, the legacy of Superman led many people to become adherents of a secular belief called "The Spirit of the Last Son," which sees the Man of Steel as a model for mature, altruistic living.

KEY STORYLINES
- *SUPERMAN #75 (JANUARY 1993):* Superman dies defeating Doomsday, an alien genetic experiment designed to be the ultimate killing machine in the "The Death of Superman!"
- *ACTION COMICS #689 (SEPTEMBER 1993):* The Man of Steel returns from the dead.
- *SUPERMAN #171 (AUGUST 2001):* Superman begins a tumultuous defence of Earth and the Universe against the might of Imperiex as the Our Worlds at War storyline commences.
- *SUPERMAN BIRTHRIGHT #1 (SEPTEMBER 2003):* Superman's origins from his escape from Krypton to him becoming the world-renowned Man of Steel is thoroughly redefined and expanded.

SUPERMAN

LOSS OF CONTROL

Outside forces began to eat away at Superman's legendary self-discipline in the weeks leading up to the Infinite Crisis. The rogue spirit Eclipso seized its most powerful host to date by taking command of Superman's body, but Captain Marvel helped drive out the vile influence. At around the same time, Checkmate kingpin Maxwell Lord used his telepathic powers to override Superman's mental faculties. Using the Man of Steel as his puppet, Lord unleashed chaos within the Justice League of America until Wonder Woman snapped Lord's neck.

BLIND RAGE *Under Maxwell Lord's control, Superman became a threat to his teammates in the Justice League and the entire world.*

SUPER-BRAWL *Maddened by grief after the death of his Lois Lane, the original Superman from Earth-Two lashed out at his counterpart.*

INFINITE CRISIS

Despite the rescue, Superman disapproved of Wonder Woman's lethal solution. The incident soured their relationship and helped contribute to the dissolution of the Justice League. But the universe soon needed its heroes more than ever. Alexander Luthor and Superboy-Prime, two survivors of the multiverse who had existed before the Crisis on Infinite Earths, hatched a plot to birth a new multiverse in line with their twisted ambitions. Superman soon found himself face to face with Kal-L, another multiverse exile and the original Superman from the wartime Golden Age. Kal-L believed that restoring his homeworld, Earth-Two, could prevent his Lois Lane from dying. His obsession brought him into conflict with Superman, but the two shared a heroic bond that could not be eclipsed. They soon teamed against Doomsday and Alexander Luthor's army of super-villains. In the end, it took the power of two Supermen to end the threat of Superboy-Prime. Superman and Kal-L stripped the powers of their younger doppelganger by flying him through the heart of a red sun. On the surface of the living planet Mogo, the two beat Superboy-Prime into submission, though Kal-L lost his life in the effort.

DOOMSDAY *The power of two Supermen proved enough to stop this invulnerable killer.*

AMONG THE *timeline-ripples triggered by the Infinite Crisis was the reinstatement of Clark Kent's teenaged adventures with the 30th century's Legion of Super Heroes.*

GROUNDED

The trip through the red sun left Superman powerless as well, and for a time it seemed as if he would never regain his abilities. For a year following the Infinite Crisis, Superman lived as a normal human, learning to see the world again through the eyes of Clark Kent. He rededicated himself to his reporting career at the Daily Planet and his marriage to Lois Lane. But just as he grew accustomed to his new lifestyle, Superman found his powers returning—first his ability to leap tall buildings in a single bound, then his invulnerability and flight. The ramp up in power coincided with increased activity from his rogues' gallery, including the Toyman, Metallo, and an all-new Kryptonite Man. Lex Luthor reinstated his position as Superman's arch-enemy when he retrieved a long-buried Kryptonian battleship and made war against Metropolis for choosing Superman as its champion instead of himself. The battle brought the Man of Steel back before a grateful and celebratory public.

To mark his return, Superman used a Kryptonian sunstone crystal to grow a new Fortress of Solitude in the Arctic, replacing his most recent (and rarely used) Fortress in the Peruvian rainforest.

METROPOLIS PERIL *Upon regaining his powers, Superman faced fresh threats to his adopted city.*

SAFE HAVEN *Superman's new Fortress of Solitude is located in the Arctic.*

CHRISTOPHER KENT

In a mirror of the circumstances that had brought Superman to Earth, a pod arrived in Metropolis carrying a Kryptonian boy. Superman befriended the child and rescued him from government custody, convincing officials that the young Kryptonian's needs would be better served by acclimation into Earth society. Clark Kent and Lois Lane became the boy's guardians and named him Christopher Kent. With a red-sun radiating wristwatch to keep his powers in check, Christopher tried to fit in among his schoolmates. It soon became apparent that Christopher was the son of Ursa and General Zod, conceived during the criminals' sentence in the Phantom Zone. Christopher helped foil Zod's invasion of Earth after a massive Phantom Zone jailbreak, recommitting himself to his adoptive parents.

KNEEL BEFORE ZOD *General Zod's Phantom Zone breakout was more than just a way to take revenge on Superman – it left the Earth vulnerable for Zod's takeover.*

FURTHER ADVENTURES

Superman's role as humanity's protector came into question when ARION, LORD OF ATLANTIS, traveled to modern-day Metropolis from the year 1659 to bring about Superman's retirement—lest his visions of a planetary apocalypse come true. Despite Arion's claim that humanity had become too dependent on Superman, the Man of Steel chose to remain in his current role.

Superman met his friends in the Legion of Super-Heroes once more during the Lightning Saga, when the future champions traveled backward through time to bring back Wally West, the third Flash. Bizarro proved to be a perennial pain by kidnapping Pa Kent and taking him to a cube-shaped Bizarro World. And Superman found another link to his past in Karsta Wor-Ul, the "third Kryptonian" living on Earth (after himself and Supergirl). Superman listened to her tales of ancient Krypton and helped her battle a squad of alien marauders. RG/DW

FELLOW SURVIVOR *Karsta Wor-Ul had been on the run for decades, fleeing from alien bounty hunters. Her pursuers caught up to her on Earth.*

SUPERMAN-PRIME

Superman-Prime, formerly known as Superboy-Prime, is the last survivor of the now-vanished multiverse dimension called Earth-Prime. Together with Alexander Luthor, he initiated the Infinite Crisis, then escaped from a jail cell built by the Guardians of the Universe and became a member of the Sinestro Corps. Immune to kryptonite and capable of destroying entire planets, Superman-Prime is more powerful than his namesake and one of the most dangerous beings in existence.

UNLIMITED POWER *Superman-Prime has destroyed entire planets in fits of rage.*

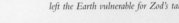

T.O. MORROW

FIRST APPEARANCE FLASH (1st series) #143 (March 1964)
STATUS Villain **REAL NAME** Thomas Oscar Morrow
OCCUPATION Criminal scientist **BASE** Mobile
HEIGHT 5ft 10in **WEIGHT** 191 lbs **EYES** Blue **HAIR** Gray
SPECIAL POWERS/ABILITIES Brilliant intellect; possesses technology that can see into or retrieve objects from the future.

Thomas Oscar Morrow studied cybernetics and computers at Harvard, where, as one might expect from a man named T.O. Morrow, he became obsessed with the future. Inventing a viewscreen that allowed him to witness events that would occur in 100 years' time, Morrow copied the designs he saw and became known as a brilliant roboticist. He also developed a "fourth dimensional grappler" that could pluck actual objects from the future. Undoubtedly, Morrow's greatest creation is the android Red Tornado, who rebelled against his creator and joined the Justice Society of America.

At one point, T.O. Morrow briefly split into two beings, including the big-headed Future Man. Later, he witnessed distressing future events and sank into a deep depression, though he has since shaken off his melancholy.

In a team-up with Professor Ivo, Morrow developed the android Tomorrow Woman as a sleeper agent whose only purpose was to infiltrate the Justice League of America. When Tomorrow Woman developed a conscience and sacrificed her life to save her teammates, Morrow was delighted—in his eyes, such humanlike behavior was evidence of his programming genius. **DW**

TAKION

FIRST APPEARANCE TAKION #1 (June 1996)
STATUS Hero **REAL NAME** Joshua Sanders
OCCUPATION Leader of the New Gods **BASE** New Genesis
HEIGHT 6ft 2in **WEIGHT** Variable **EYES** Red **HAIR** None
SPECIAL POWERS/ABILITIES A being of limitless power who can manipulate matter and energy in all its forms.

Blind since birth, Joshua Sanders had the most profound epiphany when Highfather of New Genesis stripped him of his corporeal shell. Transformed into the living embodiment of the Source, Sanders merged with the light of the universe and became a conduit between the life-stuff of creation and the New Gods empowered by it. Sanders became Takion, omniscient and omnipotent avatar of the Source. Since Highfather's death, Takion leads the New Gods and helps them protect the peaceful planet of New Genesis from the unending threat of its neighbor Apokolips. As Takion, the formerly sightless Sanders briefly enjoyed seeing the Forever People's Beautiful Dreamer in both a literal and romantic sense. **SB**

TANGLED HEARTS
Batman and Talia share a complex history and relationship, including a marriage that he has never acknowledged!

TALIA

FIRST APPEARANCE DETECTIVE COMICS #411 (May 1971)
STATUS Villain's daughter **REAL NAME** Talia Head **OCCUPATION** Former C.E.O., LexCorp **BASE** Metropolis **HEIGHT** 5ft 8in **WEIGHT** 141 lbs **EYES** Brown
HAIR Brown **SPECIAL POWERS/ABILITIES** Beautiful and brilliant, with a ruthless streak, and a superb head for business; also trained in the use of modern-day weaponry and an expert hand-to-hand combatant.

The daughter of eco-terrorist Rā's al Ghūl, the Demon's Head, Talia was raised by him and trained in seclusion. Rā's realized that sooner or later the Lazarus Pit on which he depended for his immortality would lose its power. He wanted a suitable heir for his empire and a mate for his daughter. Rā's masterminded the kidnapping of Batman's partner Robin, as well as his own daughter, in order to determine the Dark Knight's worth. Batman successfully passed the test but, despite being strongly attracted to Talia, turned down the notion of marriage. Batman then became a thorn in the eco-terrorist's side. Talia was torn between two men she loved and, not wishing to be a pawn, left to make her way in the world. She soon made a favorable impression in Metropolis business circles. When Lex Luthor (*see* Luthor, Lex) was elected U.S. President, he persuaded Talia to become C.E.O. of LexCorp.

She sealed the deal by turning over all of Rā's' plans and financial data to Luthor. Talia ran LexCorp as coldly and efficiently as Luthor, enduring encounters with Superman and Batman.

Recently, a mysterious woman named Nyssa befriended Talia then kidnapped and tortured her, revealing herself to be Talia's half-sister. Talia was loyal to Rā's, but Nyssa hated their father and longed to destroy him. She killed Talia repeatedly, resurrecting her time and again in the Lazarus Pit. Brainwashed by this terrible ordeal, Talia was unleashed by Nyssa against Rā's al Ghūl. She killed him, and has not been seen since. **RG**

NOT MAN ENOUGH *Talia shows Bruce Wayne that she packs a mean right.*

TEMPEST

FIRST APPEARANCE ADVENTURE COMICS #269 (February 1960)
STATUS Hero **REAL NAME** Garth **OCCUPATION** Ambassador; sorcerer
BASE Poseidonis, Atlantis **HEIGHT** 5ft 10in **WEIGHT** 235 lbs
EYES Purple **HAIR** Black **SPECIAL POWERS/ABILITIES** Amphibious;
swims at speeds of 97.76 knots (85 mph); superstrength; high
resistance to deep sea pressures; projection of powerful optic force
blasts; manipulation of water currents; creation of whirlpools; can
boil or freeze water; mystic powers include postcognition, telepathy,
dimensional travel, and astral projection; partially colorblind.

ABANDONED AT BIRTH by the superstitious Atlanteans,
Garth survived alone in the ocean depths for years until
he was discovered by AQUAMAN. Adopted by the Sea King
and called Aqualad, Garth was the least powerful member
of the TEEN TITANS, until he realized his potential for
wizardry and became
the powerful mage
Tempest!

UNLUCKY EYES
Garth's heritage is of the Idylists,
a group of Atlantean pacifists who
established the colony of Shayeris in
the Hidden Valley. When Garth's father,
King Thar, assembled weapons to destroy
his brother Zath's invading armies, his palace
guards mistakenly believed he was going insane,
and murdered him. Thar's pregnant wife Berra was exiled to Atlantis,
where she gave birth to Garth. Believing his purple eyes to be a bad omen,
the Atlanteans seized the infant and left him to die, abandoned to the sea.
Thanks to the sorcerer Atlan, Garth survived and grew up to cross paths
with Aquaman, who adopted him as his ward. After Aquaman joined
the JLA, and following formal schooling in Scotland, Aqualad became a
founding member of the Teen Titans. He fell in love with Aquagirl, who
tragically died during the Crisis (see Great Battles, pp. 186-7).
Sometime later, Garth's uncle Zath, now the necromancer Slizzath,
returned to conquer Atlantis. Under the tutelage of Atlan, the father of
Aquaman, Aqualad acquired a host of magical abilities, refined his own
powers, and became the mage Tempest. Garbed in
the flag of his people, Tempest defeated his uncle and
saved the undersea realms. Soon after, he became
an Atlantean ambassador. Tempest soon found new
love with Dolphin—who, awkwardly, was seeing
Aquaman at the time—and the two were married.
In time they bore a son, whom they named Cerdian.
During the Imperiex War, Tempest used his powers
as a wizard to protect Atlantis, but accidentally
sent the city thousands of years back in time
to the Obsidian Age. Tempest survived
the Spectre's destruction of Atlantis,
and disappeared for nearly a year.
When he finally reemerged,
he had lost his memory,
his magic, and his ability
to breathe underwater.
Tempest briefly teamed
with the new Aquaman,
Arthur Joseph Curry,
and later regained his
powers. DW

AQUALAD Garth
earned his stripes
against enemies that
were vexing, but
rarely lethal.

TULA The love of
Garth's life succumbed
to the monster Chemo
during the great
Crisis.

WATER WIZARD
Tempest
can summon
whirlpools, freeze
rivers, and bend
water to his will
through magic.

WEDDING Surrounded by the
Titans and other super heroes,
Tempest married Dolphin.

KEY STORYLINES
• *TEMPEST #1-4 (NOVEMBER 1997–FEBRUARY
1997):* Aqualad no more! Garth assumes his
new name and new identity as Tempest while
fighting his villainous uncle with the power of
Atlantean sorcery.
• *WONDER WOMAN #178 (OCTOBER 2001):*
Tempest joins with Darkseid and Wonder
Woman to help save the universe from
Imperiex, Destroyer of Worlds, accidentally
sending Atlantis back in time.
• *AQUAMAN #63 (JANUARY 2000):* Dolphin
gives birth to Tempest's son Cerdian, a child
who may become a future Aquaman for a
future generation.

PEERS Like Nightwing
and Arsenal, Tempest has
shed the label of "super-
hero sidekick" and now
stands on an equal footing
with Aquaman.

Teen Titans

Adolescent Avengers

First appearance (Teen Titans I) BRAVE AND THE BOLD #54 (July 1964); (New Teen Titans) DC COMICS PRESENTS #26 (December 1980); (Teen Titans II) TEEN TITANS (2nd series) #1 (October 1996); (current team) TEEN TITANS (3rd series) #1 (July 2003)
Status Hero team **Base** Titans Tower, San Francisco Bay
Current members and powers
Robin III Team leader; skill martial artist and tactician.
Wonder Girl II Superstrength, flight.
Kid Devil Enhanced strength, can breathe fire.
Ravager Skilled martial artist and assassin, augmented abilities.
Miss Martian Super strength, flight, shapeshifting, invisibility, intangibility, telepathy.
Supergirl Super strength, super speed, invulnerability, flight, heat vision, X-ray vision.

ALMOST A DECADE AGO, teen heroes Robin I (Nightwing), Kid Flash I (Flash III) and Aqualad (Tempest) brought an end to the reign of Mister Twister, a deranged weather-controlling villain. Soon after, Wonder Girl I and Speedy (Arsenal) joined the three teenagers and the quintet stopped a mind-controlled Justice League of America from committing a crime spree. Calling themselves the Teen Titans, the young sidekicks fought criminals like Doctor Light I and the Antithesis before parting ways for college and to further their budding careers.

IT'S A TWISTER! The weather-controlling Mister Twister attacks the first Teen Titans team.

THE NEW TEEN TITANS
Years later, Robin, Kid Flash, Wonder Girl and Changeling (Beast Boy) and new heroes Starfire and Cyborg were united by Raven as the New Teen Titans to thwart the demon Trigon, Raven's father, from invading the Earth. After defeating Trigon, the Titans quickly ran afoul of the villainous forces of Deathstroke the Terminator, the Fearsome Five, the Society of Sin, and Brother Blood.

DEMON SEED Trigon has frequently tried to conquer Earth, using Raven as a pawn.

Meanwhile, the Titans accepted an enigmatic young girl named Terra into their ranks. Unbeknownst to the Titans, however, Terra was a spy for Deathstroke, sent to infiltrate their ranks and learn their secrets. The insane Terra then helped Deathstroke capture the Titans and turn them over to the H.I.V.E. before killing herself. During this time, Kid Flash retired, Robin became Nightwing, and Deathstroke's son Jericho joined the team.

SOCIOPATHIC SPY Infiltrating the Titans for Deathstroke, Tara Markov helped capture her teammates and turn them over to the H.I.V.E.

COMINGS AND GOINGS
When the Anti-Monitor invaded Earth, Dove (Hawk and Dove), Aquagirl, and new Titan KOLE died during the ensuing Crisis (see Great Battles, pp. 186–7). Starfire left the planet for an arranged marriage and the original Titans reformed under Wonder Girl's unsteady leadership. After an epic battle with Brother Blood, the return of Starfire and Raven, newly purged of her father Trigon's evil, and Wonder Girl's transformation into Troia, the Teen Titans took the more adult name the New Titans.

THE TEEN TITANS II
A second group of Teen Titans were genetic experiments created by the evil alien H'San Nattall empire. Managed by billionaire Mister Jupiter, and led by the Atom II, who had been reduced in age by Extant, these half-human/half-alien Titans faced villains like Dark Nemesis and Haze before splitting up.

THE TITANS HUNT
Jericho, whose body been contaminated by souls corrupted by the evil of Trigon, ordered the villainous Wildebeest Society to hunt the Titans one by one. After killing Golden Eagle, severely injuring Aqualad and Cyborg, and destroying Titans Tower, Jericho was finally stopped when his father Deathstroke killed him. Programmed assassins for Extant, the Team Titans arrived from an alternate timeline. And Cyborg became the alien robot Cyberion. After several membership changes, the Titans teamed to stop an alien invasion and the spread of Trigon's progeny. The New Titans then disbanded.

180

TITANS REBORN

When Cyberion returned to Earth and threatened the planet, the Titans reunited and saved their former friend. The original Titans, all adults, decided to reform the Titans to train younger heroes. The team stayed together for some time, fighting criminals like Cheshire, Deathstroke, and the Hangmen.

The Titans briefly recruited a group of youngsters from an orphanage in the D.E.O., until one of them died. Later, after a rogue Superman Robot murdered Troia and Lilith, the daughter of Mister Jupiter, this incarnation of the team disbanded.

CONTINUING THE FIGHT

After the Infinite Crisis, Robin helped assemble a new team including Kid Devil, Ravager, and Miss Martian. The team, which has lost both Superboy and Kid Flash, recently spawned an east-coast spin-off as well as the birth of their villainous opposite team, the Terror Titans.

THE CURRENT LINEUP 1) *Wonder Girl II* **2)** *Raven*
3) *Miss Martian* **4)** *Cyborg* **5)** *Robin* **6)** *Ravager*
7) *Kid Devil* **8)** *Jericho*

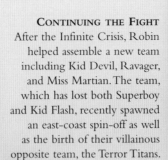

NEW MEMBERS, OLD ENEMIES

But the members of Young Justice, honoring the legacy of the Titans, reestablished the team, based in San Francisco. The latest wave of Teen Titans includes Superboy, Robin II, Beast Boy, Cyborg, and Starfire, and Wonder Girl II. Raven, her soul housed in a new body, joined the teen heroes, and Deathstroke, possessed by the spirit of his son Jericho, returned to attack them, as did Brother Blood. PJ

RAVEN'S BLOOD Brother Blood has long craved Raven's magic powers, and was responsible for restoring the half-breed demon's human body, lost in battle with Trigon.

KEY STORYLINES
• *TEEN TITANS (1ST SERIES) #53 (FEBRUARY 1970):* The final issue of the series reveals the secret origin of the Teen Titans.
• *NEW TEEN TITANS (THE JUDAS CONTRACT TPB) (2003):* The Titans are betrayed by their first recruit, the psychopath Terra.
• *NEW TEEN TITANS (2ND SERIES) #1-5 (AUGUST 1984– FEBRUARY 1985):* The demon Trigon takes over the planet, and only the Titans can stop him.
• *TEEN TITANS (3RD SERIES) #1 (JULY 2003):* The latest incarnation of the Titans is born, based in San Francisco.

TRIGGER TWINS

FIRST APPEARANCE ALL-STAR WESTERN #58 (May 1951)
STATUS Heroes (deceased)   **REAL NAMES** Walter and Wayne Trigger
OCCUPATION Sheriff   **BASE** Rocky City
HEIGHT: (both) 6ft   **WEIGHT** (both) 160 lbs
EYES (both) Blue   **HAIR** (both) Reddish blond
SPECIAL POWERS/ABILITIES Skilled marksmen and horsemen, more than capable hand-to-hand combatants.

The original Trigger Twins, Walt and Wayne Trigger, kept law and order in Rocky City during the 1870s. Walt's (greatly exaggerated) Civil War exploits earned him the position of Rocky City's sheriff. Wayne, who had been the true hero in most of Walt's tales, agreed to assume the identity of sheriff whenever danger threatened the town. The Trigger Twins became a legend of the Old West.

The modern-day Trigger Twins, Tom and Tad Trigger, are believed to be descendants of the original western heroes. They wear cowboy clothing, but unlike Walt and Wayne, the current Trigger Twins are criminals. They have battled most of Gotham's defenders, including Robin, and are now in Blackgate prison. During Gotham's year as a No Man's Land, the Trigger Twins worked with fellow inmates Lock-Up and the KGBeast to keep order at Blackgate, after the guards abandoned the facility. **DW**

TRICKSTER II

FIRST APPEARANCE THE FLASH (2nd series) #183 (April 2002)
STATUS Villain   **REAL NAME** Axel Walker
OCCUPATION Professional criminal   **BASE** Keystone City
HEIGHT 5ft 7in   **WEIGHT** 150 lbs   **EYES** Blue   **HAIR** Brown
SPECIAL POWERS/ABILITIES A variety of technological gadgets allow him to cause mayhem; he is still mastering their use and has no great athletic skill.

The first villain to be known as the Trickster was James Jesse, the stage name of Giovanni Giuseppe, a trapeze artist with a fear of heights who invented a pair of "air walker shoes" that allowed him to perform stunts safely. Eventually he turned to crime, employing numerous ridiculous gadgets, before turning F.B.I. informant and retiring.

The villain Blacksmith wanted someone with similar skills in her new gang. She selected wayward teenager Axel Walker, giving him a complete set of equipment, upgraded and more technologically sophisticated versions of the Trickster's tools. Axel was sent to attack Wally West, the Flash III as a test. He acquitted himself well. Being a modern day teen, Axel lives for the rush and thrill of danger, apparently not entirely clear on the distinction between real life and the fantasy realms depicted in his beloved video games. **RG**

NEW KID ON THE BLOCK *Young Axel Walker loves being part of the Flash's Rogues Gallery, even though he has nothing in common with his villainous peers.*

TRIGON

FIRST APPEARANCE NEW TEEN TITANS (1st series) #4 (February 1981)
STATUS Villain   **REAL NAME** Trigon; also known in other dimensions as Skath and Ddrez
OCCUPATION Demon lord; conqueror   **BASE** Another dimensional plane
HEIGHT Variable   **WEIGHT** Variable   **EYES** Red   **HAIR** Red
SPECIAL POWERS/ABILITIES Nearly immeasurable demonic powers; has drained the souls of millions of worlds and reshaped planets; can change size, fire destructive energy blasts, teleport, control demons, and transmute elements, such as stone into water.

The personification of evil, Trigon was a demon lord who destroyed his homeworld by the age of six. Slaying billions of souls in his own dimension, Trigon eventually sired a child by the woman Arella. Their child was Raven, a powerful mystic, who rejected her father's evil and was raised in Azarath, a pacifist community nestled in another dimension.

Trigon tried to breach the barriers between his dimension and Earth's but was stopped by sorcerers from Azarath. Finally tearing through the interdimensional wall, Trigon attacked Earth. Horrified, his daughter Raven, now a teenager, agreed to rule by his side if he spared the planet. But Raven realized her father would not honor the bargain and hurried to Earth, gathering a group of teenage heroes to stop Trigon's invasion. These heroes were the New Teen Titans, and together they drove Trigon into a distant nether universe that Arella agreed to guard for eternity. As time passed, Raven began to succumb to her father's evil. Trigon murdered a billion beings in his dimension and stole their energy. He once again invaded Earth's dimension, turning Earth into a wasteland. But the Titans were able to help the souls of Azarath channel all their power into Trigon, seemingly destroying the demon.

Purged of her father's evil, Raven's body was nonetheless taken over by the soul of one of her slain siblings. However, her soul was placed in Starfire's body, and the Titans were able to destroy the rest of Trigon's progeny, ending his threat, they believed, forever. **PJ**

BACK FROM THE DEAD *The demon Trigon has taken over the Earth twice, but each time he has been defeated by the Teen Titans. Brother Blood recently took Raven as his bride, resurrecting Trigon once again, who attacked the Titans from his watery grave.*

TWO-FACE

SCHIZOID CRIMINAL MASTERMIND

FIRST APPEARANCE DETECTIVE COMICS #66 (August 1942)
STATUS Villain   *REAL NAME* Harvey Dent
OCCUPATION Former D.A.; professional criminal   *BASE* Gotham City
HEIGHT 6ft   *WEIGHT* 182 lbs   *EYES* Blue   *HAIR* Brown
SPECIAL POWERS/ABILITIES A criminal genius, whose crimes reveal an obsession with duality and the number two. An average combatant, but capable of savage violence.

HARVEY DENT IS A MAN DIVIDED. Childhood abuse fractured Dent's psyche right down the middle, leaving the respected Gotham City District Attorney subconsciously sublimating a darker and more violent persona as an adult. This duality was mirrored by Dent's good luck charm, a "two-headed" silver dollar. Once Batman's ally in justice, Dent's evil side reared its ugly head when, amid a packed courtroom, gangster Vincent Maroni hurled acid in the D.A.'s handsome face!

THE DARK SIDE

As the left side of Dent's face dissolved, so did the psychic wall keeping his dark persona in check. With good and evil wrestling for control, Dent scarred one side of his lucky coin. It became the final arbiter for his new persona, Two-Face, whose every act would be decided by the flip of a coin. If the unmarked side came up, he would show mercy; if the scarred side came up he would do evil. Dent abandoned his wife Gilda Grace, who had hoped plastic surgery would restore her husband's face and help his mind heal. Gilda married Doctor Paul Janus and they became the parents of twins, children conceived utilizing Harvey Dent's frozen sperm.

DEFINING MOMENT Gangster Boss Moroni hurls acid in Harvey Dent's face, scarring him both physically and psychologically.

Believing that justice is arbitrary, Two-Face holds practitioners of the law in particular contempt. As judge, jury and executioner, he has murdered his own court-appointed attorneys and carried out lethal litigation against scores of Gotham's legal eagles.

During Gotham's year-long experience as a lawless No Mans Land, Dent turned prosecutor once more, "indicting" Commissioner Gordon for his law-breaking alliance—with Two-Face! Dent's cross-examination of his own alter ego led to a temporary mental brainstorm and an acquittal for Gordon. During that time, detective Renee Montoya was Two-Face's prisoner for five months, and she glimpsed a kinder, gentler Dent. He professed love for her, but felt betrayed when he learned she was a lesbian.

After surgeon Tommy Elliot (Hush) repaired his face, Dent reformed and earned Batman's trust, even becoming Gotham's guardian during the Dark Knight's absence following the Infinite Crisis. Yet his insanity caused Dent to re-scar his appearance, making him Two-Face once more.
RG

FICKLE FATE Every key decision Two-Face makes is decided by his two-sided coin, one side of which is scarred, and one side of which is unblemished.

KEY STORYLINES

• *BATMAN: FACES (1995):* An examination into the tortured, often violent relationship between Batman, Two-Face, and Commissioner Gordon.
• *BATMAN ANNUAL #14 (1990):* A look at how difficult it is for Two-Face to function, whose face never fits in either the normal world or Gotham City's underworld.
• *SECRET ORIGINS SPECIAL (1989):* A deep look at how Harvey Dent changed from successful District Attorney to psychopathic madman.

UBERMENSCH

FIRST APPEARANCE YOUNG ALL-STARS #1 (June 1987)
STATUS Villain (deceased) **REAL NAME** Unknown
OCCUPATION Nazi hero **BASE** Mobile
HEIGHT 6ft 3in **WEIGHT** 225 lbs **EYES** Blue **HAIR** None
SPECIAL POWERS/ABILITIES Ubermensch was capable of leaping tall buildings in a single bound, but squandered his enhanced gifts in the service of evil; possessed superstrength and superspeed; his skin was invulnerable to bullets.

UBERMENSCH ÜBER ALLES! *Hitler's follicly-challenged muscleman leads out Axis Amerika, the Third Reich's favorite team of super-villainous bully boys.*

Ubermensch was the epitome of Adolf Hitler's ideal of racial purity, selected by Nazi scientists to undergo painful treatments that transformed him into the ultimate Aryan super hero. He possessed remarkable strength and speed, and his skin was tough enough to shrug off the bullets of small-arms fire.

As World War II unfolded, Ubermensch became the head of Axis Amerika, leading Gudra, Sea Wolf, Usil, Die Grosshorn Eule, Die Fledermaus, and Kamikaze against the American heroes of the All-Star Squadron and its youthful spin-off, the Young All-Stars. Ubermensch's fate at the end of the war is still unrecorded.

Recently, an American claimed the notorious name of Ubermensch as a member of a revived incarnation of Axis America. The man, called Shepherd was the leader of the religious commune Safe Haven and persuaded the world that the Justice League of America had destroyed the commune and killed 1,000 innocent people! This accusation was soon exposed as a blatant lie, and Shepherd, revealed as the ideologue Ubermensch II, met defeat at the hands of the JLA. **DW**

ULTRA BOY

FIRST APPEARANCE SUPERBOY #98 (July 1962)
STATUS Hero **REAL NAME** Jo Nah
OCCUPATION Legionnaire **BASE** 30th-century Earth
HEIGHT 5ft 8in **WEIGHT** 155 lbs **EYES** Brown **HAIR** Brown
SPECIAL POWERS/ABILITIES Vast superstrength, speed, invulnerability, flight and vision powers, but can only use one power at a time.

Multiple versions of Ultra Boy exist in different timelines, but in nearly all of them he is Jo Nah of the planet Rimbor. Jo was on a scavenging mission in outer space when a giant space creature swallowed his ship. By eating some of the creature's flesh, Jo gained various superpowers. He used them to escape Rimbor and joined Leland McCauley's Workforce as Ultra Boy. Ultra Boy later joined the Legion of Super-Heroes, the 31st century's premier superteam, and fell in love with teammate Apparition. He eventually married her when the two were trapped in the past.

After the Blight attacked the Earth, Ultra Boy was hurled into another dimension. Although he managed to return to his wife, their marriage remains on shaky ground. Their son, Cub Wazzo-Nah, appears to have inherited meta-human powers from both his parents, although the extent of his abilities has yet to be revealed. **PJ**

ULTRA-HUMANITE

FIRST APPEARANCE ACTION COMICS #13 (June 1939)
STATUS Villain (deceased) **REAL NAME** Unknown
OCCUPATION Criminal scientist **BASE** Mobile
HEIGHT Varied **WEIGHT** Varied **EYES** Varied **HAIR** Varied
SPECIAL POWERS/ABILITIES A brilliant inventor, the Ultra-Humanite's greatest achievement was the process he devised to transplant his brain into different bodies, human or otherwise.

The Ultra-Humanite was one of the Justice Society of America's most terrible foes, responsible for the deaths of the Crimson Avenger I and Johnny Thunder among many atrocities. Originally a criminal scientist active during the 1940s, the Ultra-Humanite escaped death by transplanting his brain into other bodies, including film star Dolores Winters, a giant ant, and finally a genetically mutated albino ape. He continued his assaults upon the JSA, as well as the team's superpowered progeny in Infinity Inc., and also led the Secret Society of Super-Villains. Shaving his gorilla body, an even more terrifying Ultra-Humanite utilized resources usurped from the Council. Recently, the villain gave up his primate shell and hid his brain while taking mental control of the aged Johnny Thunder. The Ultra-Humanite recently returned to his albino gorilla appearance, and united with Per Degaton and Despero to alter the timestream. Booster Gold and Rip Hunter (have vowed to take them down. **SB**

ULTRA, THE MULTI-ALIEN

FIRST APPEARANCE MYSTERY IN SPACE #103 (November 1965)
STATUS Hero **REAL NAME** Ace Arn
OCCUPATION Adventurer **BASE** Mobile
HEIGHT 5ft 10in (as Arn); 6ft 2in (as Ultra) **WEIGHT** 157 lbs (as Arn); 163 lbs (as Ultra) **EYES** Blue (as Arn); Black (as Ultra); **HAIR** Brown (as Arn); Half bald, half green, later half bald, half white (as Ultra)
SPECIAL POWERS/ABILITIES Each quarter of Arn's body possesses a unique property such as magnetism, increased strength, cohesive energy and the power of flight.

In the late 21st century, Captain Ace Arn's spacecraft accidentally crashed into an asteroid in another solar system. The rock turned out to be the secret hideout for interstellar criminal Zobra. Arn learned the four planet solar system was artificially created with one member from each race—Ulla, Laroo, Trago, and Raaga—serving Zobra. Zobra accidentally killed himself with a poisonous gas and a free-for-all began among his underlings. When they arrived at the asteroid and found Arn there, they all fired their unique duplication weapons simultaneously. As a result, Arn was transformed into a four-segmented composite alien, representing each alien race. Granted phenomenal new powers, Arn subdued the aliens, repaired his craft and returned to Earth. He gave up piloting to fight crime as Ultra, but is haunted by regret for the loss of his humanity and his girlfriend from his previous life, Bonnie. **RG**

UNCLE SAM

FIRST APPEARANCE NATIONAL COMICS #1 (July 1940)
STATUS Hero **REAL NAME** Unknown **OCCUPATION** Patriotic spirit
BASE The United States **HEIGHT** 6ft 3in **WEIGHT** 210 lbs
EYES Blue **HAIR** White **SPECIAL POWERS/ABILITIES** Superstrength,
invulnerability; can change size; powers are proportionate to
the country's faith in the ideals of freedom and liberty.

OUT OF ACTION *Black Adam took out Uncle Sam during the Infinite Crisis, but couldn't kill the Spirit of Liberty.*

Several hundred years ago, soon after the formation of the United States, Benjamin Franklin and other Founding Fathers used a mystic ritual to create the American Talisman. The Talisman would embody the very spirit of the U.S., and materialize by magically binding itself to a nationalistic citizen. During World War II, the spirit linked itself to a man named Samuel and became the star-spangled superpatriot Uncle Sam.

Uncle Sam joined the All-Star Squadron and later formed an auxiliary unit called the Freedom Fighters. After World War II, the American talisman was destroyed and Uncle Sam's energies waned. An evil group called the National Interest tried to recreate the shattered Talisman, but the Spectre defeated the Interest as well as the American Scream, the insane personification of American culture. The Talisman was reassembled, and Uncle Sam became the Patriot, defending the U.S., most notably during the Imperiex War (*see* Great Battles, pp. 186-7). The spirit then reclaimed the title Uncle Sam.

During the Infinite Crisis, the Freedom Fighters lost a brutal fight with the members of the villainous Society. Believed killed, Uncle Sam returned to defeat the sinister Father Time and his S.H.A.D.E. agents by uniting a new team of Freedom Fighters under his banner. Uncle Sam's team is largely made up of new heroes carrying on old legacies including Firebrand, Doll Man, the Human Bomb, Phantom Lady, and the Red Bee. **PJ**

FOR FREEDOM *Uncle Sam returned to assemble a new group of Freedom Fighters, needed to defend individual liberties from the authoritarian Father Time and the agents of S.H.A.D.E.*

INSPIRATION
During the great Crisis, Uncle Sam led members of the JLA and the Titans into battle against the Anti-Monitor.

UNKNOWN SOLDIER

FIRST APPEARANCE STAR-SPANGLED WAR STORIES #151 (July 1970) **STATUS** Hero **REAL NAME** Unrevealed
OCCUPATION Secret agent **BASE** Washington, D.C.
HEIGHT 5ft 9in **WEIGHT** 155 lbs **EYES** Blue **HAIR** Blond
SPECIAL POWERS/ABILITIES Weapons and explosives expert;
expert combatant; master of disguise and impersonation.

The man who became known in U.S. intelligence as the Unknown Soldier enlisted with his older brother Harry in World War II. Harry died saving his sibling from a Japanese grenade, which left the young soldier's face horribly disfigured. He continued as an undercover agent, disguising his ruined face to resemble anyone and then infiltrating behind enemy lines The Unknown Soldier's daring exploits earned the ennity of Adolf Hitler, who frequently pitted a Nazi operative known as the Black Knight against him.

Later, as the war was ending, the Unknown Soldier infiltrated Hitler's Berlin bunker, where he facilitated the Führer's suicide. Many believed the Soldier had died saving a child from an explosion on the streets of war-torn Berlin. In reality, he continued to serve U.S. interests throughout other wars and various clandestine conflicts in the decades to follow as the U.S. military's preferred cleanup man, a man with neither a face nor a name. **SB**

GREAT BATTLES

Why are there super heroes? Perhaps the cosmic presence that governs the universe created so many meta-humans in the 20th century in preparation for the creation-shaking threats soon to follow. Without the JLA, the JSA, and other champions of freedom, the Earth and all of reality would long since have ceased to exist!

THE APPELLAXIAN CONTEST

Seven champions came from a distant star to slug it out on an Earth battlefield and determine which of the seven was fit to rule the Appellaxian empire. Assuming "battle forms" of glass, fire, rock, mercury, wood, ice, and a giant golden bird, the seven met swift defeat thanks to the embryonic Justice League of America—Aquaman, Green Lantern, the Flash, Martian Manhunter, and Black Canary. An eighth Appellaxian went unnoticed. He called seven thousand of his planet's top shock troops for a full-scale alien invasion.

GIANT STEPS
All of Earth's heroes united to defeat the Appellaxian horde, ultimately sending them back to their own planet through a mystical wormhole. The conflict is still remembered as the JLA's baptism of fire

THE IMPERIEX WAR

The cosmic tyrant Imperiex hungered to reignite the universe in a new Big Bang, wiping out all that had gone before. Superman led a galaxy-wide coalition of champions to oppose his cataclysmic scheming. The Imperiex War—a period sometimes referred to as "Our Worlds at War"—was inevitable if the universe was to be saved. Earth's defenders included an unlikely alliance of Darkseid and U.S. President Lex Luthor (*see* Luthor, Lex), whose combined forces provided the necessary edge when the computerized monster Brainiac 13 entered the fight on the side of evil. Among the war's many casualties were most of the population of Topeka, Kansas as well as Hippolyta—Princess Diana's mother and the Golden Age Wonder Woman.

DESTROYED BY FIRE
Topeka is set ablaze during the Imperiex War.

WELCOME TO TOPEKA, KS POPULATION 0

HAVEN *Orbiting 'Paradocs' sheltered those wounded in the shocking conflict, including some of the greatest heroes the Earth has ever seen.*

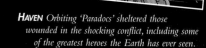

THE MAGEDDON WAR

Those who lived through it called it World War III. When the ancient doomsday device Mageddon slipped its moorings outside space-time and approached Earth, its aggressive energies caused the planet to erupt in a fury of violence. Angels from Heaven helped calm the leaders of nations, while Wonder Woman spearheaded an effort to turn ordinary citizens into temporary super heroes. In the end Superman switched off the Mageddon warhead, ensuring Earth's survival—until the next extraterrestrial threat.

Loss *Though Superman secured a victory, the young hero Aztek perished in his efforts to halt the advance of the warbringer.*

THE CRISIS ON INFINITE EARTHS

The most significant event ever to shake the universe is the one that almost no one can remember. In an earlier reality, creation was ordered into a "multiverse" with multiple parallel Earths—an Earth-2 for the Justice Society and an Earth-S for the Captain Marvel family, alongside an infinite number of others. The omnipotent Anti-Monitor began destroying all parallel universes, and his heroic mirror-image the Monitor gathered heroes from all realities and timeframes to fight him.

In order to save what was left, the Monitor merged five Earth-histories into one and the universe was reborn as if it had always been that way. Thus, while modern heroes remember a battle called the Crisis, they have no memory of a multiverse. Some heroes who died in the Crisis (such as the Barry Allen Flash) still perished in the rebooted version of the event, while others (such as the pre-Crisis version of Supergirl) had their deaths—and entire histories—retroactively wiped from existence. Among the characters who can remember bits of pre-Crisis reality are the Psycho Pirate, the Linear Men, and presumably some of God's agents, such as the Phantom Stranger and the Spectre.

ZERO HOUR

Essentially a Crisis aftershock, the history-altering Zero Hour united the villainous Extant with the delusional hero Parallax, who wanted to remake the universe and remove all pain and loss. A team of super heroes followed Parallax back to the dawn of time and prevented his larger plan, though reality was still reborn in a slightly modified form. Zero Hour's [...] were felt in the 30th century, where the [...]

VENTRILOQUIST & SCARFACE

FIRST APPEARANCE DETECTIVE COMICS #583 (February 1988)
STATUS Villain (deceased)   **REAL NAME** Arnold Wesker
OCCUPATION Gang boss; assassin   **BASE** Gotham City
HEIGHT 5ft 7in   **WEIGHT** 142 lbs   **EYES** Blue   **HAIR** Gray
SPECIAL POWERS/ABILITIES Out of shape and a poor ventriloquist (he speaks "b's as "g's); however his shattered psyche harbors dark passions, which find murderous outlet through his dummy, Scarface.

Arnold Wesker was orphaned as a child and repressed his feelings so deeply that he developed a multiple personality disorder. As an adult, he let those angry feelings out and killed a man, landing him in Gotham's Blackgate Penitentiary.

PUPPET MASTER

His cellmate, Donnegan, showed him a ventriloquist's dummy he had carved from the wood of Blackgate's Gallows Tree. Perhaps the wood was cursed, for Wesker was irresistibly drawn to the doll, and killed Donnegan for it. The psychopathic personality of Scarface emerged, speaking through the dummy.

Wesker and Scarface became major players in Gotham's underworld. When stopped by Batman, Wesker's defense was that he was an innocent dupe of the Scarface persona. When Gotham was devastated by an earthquake, Wesker created a new puppet, the Quakemaster, and tried to extort $100,000,000 from the city. Following the Infinite Crisis, Wesker died in a Gotham gang takeover. His successor is Sugar, a gangster's moll who now puppets Scarface as the Ventriloquist II. She appears to be in love with the dummy. RG

LOOK WHO'S TALKING Arnold Wesker couldn't get arrested as a ventriloquist, but when hiding behind his gangster mannequin Scarface—made from cursed wood—he becomes a real Public Enemy.

REBORN Scarface tells his rivals that he didn't die, he just 'moved to a softer lap.'

SHOT DEAD When Arnold Vesker lost his life, Scarface "died" as well. It took a new Ventriloquist to resurrect the wooden mob boss.

LAST BREATH Before he expired, Arnold Vesker left clues at his murder scene that would lead Batman and Robin to his killer.

KEY STORYLINES
• *DETECTIVE COMICS #583 (FEBRUARY 1988)* The Ventriloquist debuts, his gimmick and insanity making him a perfect fit in Gotham's bizarre criminal underworld.
• *DETECTIVE COMICS #818 (JUNE 2006)* Vesker is killed by an assassin working for mob boss, the Great White Shark.
• *DETECTIVE COMICS #843-844 (JUNE-JULY 2008)* The new Ventriloquist meets Bruce Wayne, and both realize they know one another socially outside of Gotham's world of heroes and villains.

VILLAINS UNITED

FIRST APPEARANCE VILLAINS UNITED #1 (July 2005)
STATUS Villain Team **BASE** Mobile
FOUNDER MEMBERS AND POWERS
Doctor Psycho: Telepathy and mind-control.
Talia Head: Brilliant tactician and combatant.
Deathstroke: Superior hand-to-hand fighter and weapons expert.
Black Adam: Flight, super-strength, super-speed, near-invulnerability.
The Calculator: Genius at information retrieval.

The latest incarnation of the Secret Society of Super-Villains, known informally as Villains United, took shape prior to the Infinite Crisis. Alexander Luthor, last survivor of a destroyed Earth, assumed the identity of Lex Luthor (*see* Luthor, Lex) to bring together the largest assemblage of criminals ever seen. Hundreds of villains joined the new Society, lured by promises of riches or coerced by outright threats. A six-member cabal—Luthor, Doctor Psycho, Talia, Deathstroke, Black Adam, and the Calculator—coordinated the Society's activities.

AN OFFER YOU CAN'T REFUSE *Of all the villains in the DCU, only six refused to join Luthor's team. The Secret Six (as they would come to be known) were tortured by the most sadistic mind on the planet, the Crime Doctor.*

THE CAGED BIRD SINGS *Trying to discover the identity of Mockingbird, the Crime Doctor locked the Secret Six in a small cell, where they would listen to the screams of their teammates as they are "questioned."*

FREEDOM AND INJUSTICE FOR ALL *Lockup provides valuable information to the Society for their plan to simultaneously release all prisoners from all prisons, worldwide.*

THE CURRENT LINEUP, *Left to right, Talia, Black Adam, Lex Luthor, Deathstroke, Dr. Psycho, and the Calculator.*

A WORTHY ADVERSARY

The real Lex Luthor struck back at his duplicate by posing as the unseen Mockingbird and handpicking his own villainous team: Deadshot, Cat-Man, Scandal, Rag Doll II, Cheshire, and Parademon. This group made up the new Secret Six. The Society's actions, including a plot to erase the memories of the planet's super heroes in retaliation for the Justice League of America's own mind-wipes (performed by Zatanna), met swift ends due to sabotage by the Secret Six. Alexander Luthor responded by kidnapping and torturing his rivals, and later activated his traitor, Cheshire.

Finally the Society executed a massive strike on the Secret Six's headquarters. Society member Knockout revealed herself as a mole and assisted in the Six's escape, while Parademon sacrificed himself in order to obliterate a band of attackers. Vandal Savage brought an end to the conflict, convincing Alexander Luthor to refrain from any actions that might harm his daughter, Scandal.

The Society's biggest moment came in the Battle of Metropolis at the climax of the Infinite Crisis. The Calculator orchestrated a global jailbreak, swelling the Society's ranks even further, and Doctor Psycho and Warp retrieved their ultimate weapon, the monstrous Doomsday. The army of villains marched on Metropolis and its waiting superheroic defenders, and the fight claimed casualties on both sides. The Society disbanded after the Crisis, but Lex Luthor recently assembled a similar group, the Injustice League Unlimited.

STRENGTH IN NUMBERS *With the help of his inside man, Deathstroke leads the attack on Mockingbird's headquarters.*

KEY STORYLINES
• *VILLAINS UNITED #1–6 (JULY–DECEMBER 2005):*
The series charts the rise of the society against the superheroic community, culminating in the Battle of Metropolis.

189

WONDER WOMAN

THE AMAZING AMAZON

FIRST APPEARANCE ALL-STAR COMICS #8 (Winter 1941)
STATUS Hero **REAL NAME** Diana
OCCUPATION Ambassador of peace; adventurer
BASE New York City; Themyscira
HEIGHT 6ft **WEIGHT** 165 lbs **EYES** Blue **HAIR** Black
SPECIAL POWERS/ABILITIES Blessed with the gifts of the Olympian Gods, Wonder Woman is one of the strongest beings on the planet; she can fly at sublight speed; while not invulnerable, she is highly resistant to bodily harm; she can psychically communicate with animals; she is an expert at all forms of classical armed and unarmed combat; a master of the sword, ax, and bow and arrow; a skilled tactician and diplomat; her arsenal includes a magic lasso that forces anyone within its confines to tell the absolute truth; her bracelets can deflect bullets.

WISE AS ATHENA, stronger than Heracles, swift as Hermes and beautiful as Aphrodite, Wonder Woman is Princess Diana, champion of Themyscira, the home of the immortal Amazons. Sculpted from clay by her mother, Queen Hippolyta, and brought to life by the Olympian Gods, Diana secretly entered a contest to find the worthiest Amazon and emerged as the victor. Given the task of ending the war god Ares's made scheme to destroy the planet, Diana stepped forth from her idyllic existence into the chaotic world of Man as one of Earth's greatest defenders, Wonder Woman, the Amazing Amazon!

REBIRTH The Amazon warrior emerges from seclusion on Paradise Island to thwart Nazi tyranny.

SCULPTED FROM CLAY
The reincarnated soul of a woman who had died 30,000 years ago, Hippolyta longed for the child she had carried centuries before. An oracle told her to sculpt a baby from clay; the gods themselves then gave the child life. The only child ever born on Themyscira, the infant was named Diana, after aviator Diana Trevor, who once crashed on Themyscira and died a hero defending the island. Princess Diana was raised by a nation of 3,000 teachers and sisters, always under the watchful eye of her overprotective mother.

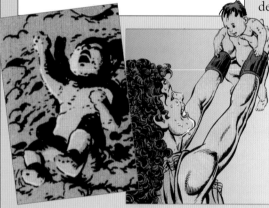

THE AMAZONS AND THEIR ISLAND
Created 3,000 years ago by five goddesses of Olympus, the Amazons are a race of warrior women charged with the responsibility of promoting the peaceful ways of Gaea, the earth spirit. After Heracles and his men ransacked the Amazons' home of Themyscira, the Amazons, by decree of the goddesses, were led to a remote island paradise, where they were granted immortality and the task of guarding Doom's Doorway, the portal to Pandora's Box, behind which a host of monsters were imprisoned.

Rebuilding their great city-state of Themyscira, the Amazons lived in idyllic solitude for millennia, until a pilot from beyond their shores named Diana Trevor arrived on Paradise Island, changing their fate forever.

DIANA TREVOR A pilot for the Women's Auxiliary Ferrying Squadron, Diana Rockwell Trevor pierced the mystic barrier between our world and Themyscira. Crash-landing on the island, the startled pilot used her weapons to force Cottus, a creature that had escaped from Doom's Doorway, back to the underworld. Diana gave her life to save the Amazon nation.

THE CONTEST
The goddesses ordered the Amazons to send for their greatest warrior to thwart ARES's mad schemes. Forbidden by Hippolyta to enter the Contest, Diana disguised herself and became Themyscira's champion. Garbed in a uniform decorated with symbols honoring Diana Trevor, Diana was rewarded with a magic lasso and silver bracelets. Soon after, Steve Trevor, Diana Trevor's son and an unwitting pawn of Ares, crash-landed on Themyscira. Diana was charged with taking him back to Patriarch's World, the mortal world of humankind, as part of her sacred mission.

THE MADNESS OF ARES
After battling Ares' monstrous sons upon her arrival in Patriarch's World, Diana, Steve, and several allies were mystically transported to a commandeered military base in Colorado where Wonder Woman stopped Ares from launching his nuclear arsenal and ended his insane threat. Diana then embarked on a worldwide tour promoting peace and Amazon ideals. Living with Julia and Vanessa Kapatelis in their Boston brownstone, Wonder Woman garnered a formidable Rogues Gallery which included the Cheetah, Silver Swan, Doctor Psycho, and the sorceress Circe, who most resented Diana's pleas for peace and harmony.

THE DEATH OF DIANA

Forseeing the death of her daughter in a mystic vision, Hippolyta called for a new contest, and used the sorceress Magala to manipulate its outcome. Diana was forced to forsake her mantle and title and a rival Amazon, Artemis, became the new Wonder Woman. But after Artemis's death at the hands of the White Magician, Diana reclaimed her role as Wonder Woman. Tragically, the spell that Magala cast on Diana was still in place when the devilish Neron attacked, and the hellspawn killed the Amazon princess with a blast of demonfire.

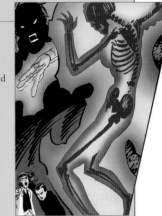

THE REBIRTH OF DIANA

Diana was resurrected on Olympus as the Goddess of Truth. Meanwhile, the Amazons tried Hippolyta for her trickery and decreed that, as penance, she would have to take up her daughter's mantle and mission as Wonder Woman.
So Hippolyta journeyed back in time to World War II and joined the Justice Society of America for a time. After Hippolyta's return to the present, Diana returned to the mortal plane, and once again became Wonder Woman.

KEY STORYLINES

• *Wonder Woman (2nd series) #1-6 (Feb.–July 1987):* Introducing Wonder Woman's modern history and mission as an ambassador of peace.

• *Wonder Woman: The Contest (TPB, 1995):* After Hippolyta manipulates a new challenge, Artemis becomes the new Wonder Woman!

• *Wonder Woman (2nd series) #196-200 (Nov. 2003–Mar. 2004):* Diana publishes her book as the Silver Swan attacks.

OUR WORLDS AT WAR

Soon after, Diana and Hippolyta abolished the monarchy of Themyscira to end a deadly civil war that had consumed Paradise Island. Then, during the Imperiex War (*see* Great Battles, pp. 186-7), Diana was severely injured by alien probes, and Hippolyta sacrificed herself to save the universe. Diana then led a united Amazon nation against the forces of Imperiex and Brainiac 13, but not before Themyscira was destroyed. With the blessings of the gods and the spirit of her mother Hippolyta, Diana and the Amazons created a new, even more miraculous Themyscira (*see* Amazing Bases, pp.72-3) to be their home.

PRINCESS, AMBASSADOR, AND AUTHOR

Forsaking her royal title after the dissolution of the Themysciran monarchy, Wonder Woman proudly wears the robes of Amazon ambassador, not only to the United Nations but to societies across the universe. After several years living, working and fighting for peace beyond the shores of Paradise Island, Diana wrote a controversial book recording her observations, thereby adding authorship to her long list of credits. Born a princess on an island of immortal women created by the gods themselves, Wonder Woman has become one of Earth's finest warriors and a legend across half the galaxy. To many her nature is paradoxical, but to Diana, her mission is clear: to promote the ways of peace, love, and equality while staunchly defending the innocent from the forces of evil as a premiere member of Earth's greatest heroes, the Justice League of America. **PJ**

WORLD TOUR
Diana promotes her book, Reflections.

GODLY TRICKERY
Ares, now the God of Conflict, has assumed a handsome, cunning guise, confounding the Amazing Amazon.

WONDER WOMAN

EXECUTION *Believing that Maxwell Lord would only kill again if spared, Wonder Woman chose the warrior's way and killed her foe. The act polarized her colleagues and public opinion.*

SACRIFICE

During the lead-up to the Infinite Crisis, Wonder Woman was forced to kill. Maxwell Lord, leader of Checkmate, had used his mental powers to take control of Superman. With one of the most powerful beings on the planet as his puppet, Maxwell Lord would be unstoppable – and he admitted that only death would force him to relent. Convinced she had no choice, Wonder Woman snapped Lord's neck. The incident eroded the trust between Wonder Woman, Superman, and Batman, which would lead to the dissolution of the Justice League of America. To make matters worse, the Brother Eye OMAC satellite beamed surveillance footage of the execution to a shocked public. The Infinite Crisis soon overtook the need for self-reflection. Brother Eye used its OMAC agents to invade the Amazon island of Themyscira, causing the Amazons to roll out their ultimate weapon—the purple death ray. Wonder Woman found a less violent solution when she convinced the goddess Athena to transport Themyscira out of harm's way. Diana's heroism helped repair the relationship between the three Justice League founders, but all agreed to some take time away from superheroics to improve themselves.

PARADISE LOST *With Themyscira invaded by androids during the Infinite Crisis, Wonder Woman fought for her homeworld.*

SUPERWEAPON *The Amazonian purple death ray cut through the OMAC units threatening Themyscira.*

DIANA PRINCE *Flanked by Nemesis, Wonder Woman shows off her government disguise.*

ONE YEAR LATER

Over the following year, Wonder Woman assumed the name of Diana Prince. Obtaining a job with the U.S. government's Department of Metahuman Affairs, she altered her look with glasses and an all-white field uniform. Paired with Tom Tresser on her first assignment, Diana helped rescue Donna Troy who had since taken up the identity of Wonder Woman. After defeating a team of familiar faces including the Cheetah, GIGANTA, and Doctor Psycho, Diana decided to resume her role as Wonder Woman and maintain a secret identity within the Department of Metahuman Affairs. Wonder Woman's return to heroics included organizing an all-new Justice League of America, and clearing up outstanding issues related to her killing of Maxwell Lord. Although the World Court had dropped all murder charges, Wonder Woman still needed to defend herself before a U.S. federal grand jury. A convincing legal defense provided by Kate Spencer allowed her to move on with a clear conscience.

ROGUES GALLERY *Brought together to menace the replacement Wonder Woman Donna Troy, this gang of killers is all too eager to face the genuine article.*

AMAZONS ATTACK

The Amazons returned with a vengeance. In a seemingly inexplicable attack on Washington D.C., Amazon warriors marched on the Capitol building while edifices from the Lincoln Memorial to the Washington Monument crumbled when assaulted by catapults and mythological monsters. Queen Hippolyta stood at the head of the invasion. Recently resurrected by the sorceress Circe, Hippolyta acted both irrational and bloodthirsty, with her decisions serving Circe's master plan. Elsewhere, the Amazonian splinter group of the Bana-Mighdall destroyed a California Air Force base and set fire to a swath of the Kansas breadbasket. At first Wonder Woman could not be found, having been taken into custody by Sarge Steel and the Department of Metahuman Affairs so the government could obtain the secrets of the purple death ray. By the time Sarge Steel was revealed as a shapeshifting impostor, the invasion had kicked into high gear. Diana's attempts to reason with her mother proved fruitless; still under Circe's influence, Hippolyta insisted on the United States' unconditional surrender. Anti-Amazon sentiment reached a fever pitch. The U.S. President authorized the forcible internment of women who had suspected Amazon ties, including Helena Sandsmark, mother of Wonder Girl. While the Teen Titans tried to obtain the prisoners' freedom, Wonder Girl and Supergirl tried to force the President's hand by attacking Air Force One. With the situation escalating out of control, Wonder Woman traveled to Themiscyra and met an Athena seemingly maddened by battle lust. Disturbed by the encounter, Diana returned to Washington and a full-scale battle between the Amazons and the U.S. military. Batman weakened Circe long enough to loosen her hold over Hippolyta, who finally accepted the truth of Diana's words and called off the invasion. An angry Athena appeared, restoring the island of Themiscyra to Earth but banishing most of the Amazons to live the rest of their lives as mortals. No one present realized that the goddess they believed to be Athena was an illusion projected by Granny Goodness of Apokolips. PJ/DW

HIPPOLYTA'S RETURN *Resurrected by Circe's magic, Wonder Woman's mother launched a scorched-earth attack on Washington DC and turned a deaf ear to her daughter's pleas.*

GROUNDED *A variety of tactics, from bombings to mystical energy screens, prevented the U.S. military's counterattack.*

APOKOLIPTIC *Disguised as the goddess Athena, Granny Goodness manipulated the Amazons.*

MONSTERS OF MYTH *The Amazon invasion force included the most battle-hardened warriors that have ever lived, in addition to cyclopses, hydras, and other creatures from Greek legend.*

NEW CHALLENGES

Due to Circe's magic, Diana could now wield her powers only in her role as Wonder Woman; as Diana Prince, she possessed the same weaknesses as any human. Still partnered with Nemesis in the Department of Metahuman Affairs, she has continued her fight against enemies to her people such as Captain Nazi, and recently welcomed a troop of intelligent gorillas to share her apartment.

BACK IN ACTION *Wonder Woman has continued the fight despite the loss of her powers while in her mortal form. Captain Nazi's troops could not hold Themyscira when Diana struck back*

APE ASSISTANCE *Diana won the loyalty of gorilla soldiers by defeating them in combat.*

XER0

First appearance XER0 #1 (May 1997)
Status Hero   **Real name** Coltrane "Trane" Walker
Occupation Closer; professional basketball player   **Base** National City
Height 6ft 7in   **Weight** 218 lbs   **Eyes** Brown (blue as Xer0)
Hair Black (blonde as Xer0)
Special powers/abilities Can speed up any object's molecular structure to walk on water or through walls; Deadeye laser; Deadlok adhesive.

African-American athlete Trane Walker was famous as the power forward for the National City Vipers. He was also Coltrane Walker, a clandestine government agency assassin who preserved his secret identity by disguising himself as a blonde-haired and blue-eyed Caucasian covert operative. Walker died on his very first mission, but was resurrected via an experimental X-enzyme that restored him to physical health, but also left him emotionally empty. Thus, he became both the perfect killer and the perfect basketball player, blunt and remorseless in getting either job done, but especially as the "closer" Xer0. Unfortunately, Walker perished again during a test set up by his superior, Frank Decker, to measure Xer0's abilities. Walker's second resurrection left him brain damaged. Whether or not Walker was left to die in peace, or if his agency will seek some way to return him to his role as Xer0, remains to be seen. **SB**

XS

First appearance LEGIONNAIRES #0 (October 1994)
Status Hero   **Real name** Jenni Ognats
Occupation Legionnaire   **Base** Earth
Height 5ft 6in   **Weight** 135 lbs   **Eyes** Amber   **Hair** Brown
Special powers/abilities Can run at supersonic speed while projecting a protective aura around her body.

Dawn Allen, daughter of the Flash II (Barry Allen), and Jeven Ognats married and had a child, Jenni, on the planet Aarok. As a teenager, Jenni found that she could tap into the Speed Force (*see Flash*). When she had fully mastered her hereditary speed powers, Jenni was invited to join the Legion of Super-Heroes at the dawn of the 31st century. On a mission back in time, at the end of the 20th century, Jenni first encountered Superboy and her cousin Bart, then known as Impulse . For a time, she was trapped in the 20th century and worked alongside her ancestors as they battled the villainous Savitar.

Jenni was then thrust into the 100th Century for a while, before being shunted to the end of time known as Vanishing Point. Thanks to the intervention of the Time Trapper, who lives there, Jenni finally managed to return to her proper time period. **RG**

EMPOWERED Like all Legionnaires, Xs is able to fly at great speed, thanks to her Legion Flight Ring.

YOUNG ALL-STARS

First appearance Young All-Stars #1 (June 1987)
Status Hero team (disbanded)   **Base** The Perisphere, New York City
Members and Powers
Dyna-Mite Can generate explosive blasts.
Flying Fox Shaman that can generate forcebolts, and cast spells; flight with fur cape and cowl.
Fury Superstrength; can summon the spirit of the Fury Tisiphone.
Iron Munro Superstrength, invulnerability.
Neptune Perkins Amphibious; can swim at superspeed.
Tsunami Can generate tidal waves.

The Young-All Stars were a briefly-lived teen-age division of the All-Star Squadron, the U.S.'s greatest assemblage of World War II heroes. The Young All-Stars were created by President F. D. Roosevelt in April, 1942, after the young heroes helped the All-Star Squadron defeat the Nazi superteam Axis Amerika.

Initially assigned to fund-raising events and morale boosters like celebrity baseball games, the Young All-Stars began their crime-fighting careers battling villains such as the despotic Per Degaton, Deathbolt, and the Ultra-Humanite when the villains infiltrated the government's mysterious Project M organization. The Young All-Stars also thwarted a gang of Nazi occultists, who had invaded an alien colony in Antarctica hoping to steal its secrets, and stopped the robotic Mekanique's plot to take over the future. The team's most frequent enemies, however were the wartime version of Axis Amerika. Fighting alongside the Allies or by themselves, the Young All-Stars battled Axis Amerika, led by Ubermensch, no less than three times within weeks of their inception.

When team member Iron Munro set out to find his missing father, Hugo Danner, he learned that Danner had used a special serum to create the Sons of the Dawn, a group of mutated human experiments. After Munro defeated Danner and the Sons in June of 1942, Liberty Belle put an end to the probationary mascot status of the Young All-Stars and made them full-fledged members of the All-Star Squadron. **PJ**

WAR-TIME TEENS The Young All-Stars did more than sell war bonds; they fought Nazi supercriminals and stopped the robot Mekanique from destroying the future by changing the past!

TREND SETTERS The first superpowered teen team, the Young All-Stars eventually became fully-fledged Squadron members. They were: 1) Dan the Dyna-Mite 2) Fury I 3) Iron Munro 4) Tsunami 5) Neptune Perkins 6) Flying Fox 7) Tigress.

YOUNG HEROES IN LOVE

FIRST APPEARANCE YOUNG HEROES IN LOVE #1 (June 1997)
STATUS Heroes (sexually active) **BASE** A very cool warehouse loft
MEMBERS AND POWERS
Bonfire (Annie Fletcher) Pyrokinetic with control over fire;
Frostbite (real name unrevealed) Generates extreme cold;
Hard Drive (Jeremy Horton) Possesses telepathy and telekinesis;
Junior (Benjamin Newton) Brilliant scientist only four inches
tall; **Monstergirl (Rita Lopez)** Transforms into a monster; **Off-
Ramp (George Sloan)** Teleporter **Thunderhead (Scott Tucker)**
Superstrength; limited invulnerability; **Zip Kid (Stacey Taglia)** Flies;
shrinks; fires pink energy bolts.

THE YOUNG HEROES IN LOVE *Raging hormones and wistful
longings are just par for the course for this super-team:*
1) *Hard Drive* **2)** *Thunderhead* **3)** *Zip Kid* **4)** *Off-Ramp*
5) *Monstergirl* **6)** *Frostbite* **7)** *Junior.*

The Young Heroes are just that, young and relatively
inexperienced super heroes brought together by the
telepathic Jeremy Horton (Hard-Drive) and his lover
Rita Lopez (Monstergirl) to form their own titanic team.
However, most of the Young Heroes did not know until
much later that Hard Drive had secretly used his powers
to coerce each member into joining to achieve his own
self-aggrandizing ends. He was summarily booted out by
his teammates when they learned the truth.

When not struggling with internal strife from several
intersecting love triangles, the Young Heroes distinguished
themselves in battle with such monsters as Totenjager the
Relentless, the Beast Grundomu, and Kalibak the Cruel.
When last seen, the Young Heroes were attending the
inaugural ball of Jeremy Horton, who had used his powers
to influence and win the Connecticut gubernatorial
election. The Young Heroes are presumably still active,
though it is just as likely that those thorny romantic
entanglements may have finally torn the team asunder. **SB**

YOUNG JUSTICE

FIRST APPEARANCE YOUNG JUSTICE: THE SECRET (April 1998)
STATUS Hero team **BASE** The Secret Sanctuary
ORIGINAL MEMBERS AND POWERS
Superboy Superstrength, flight, tactile telekinesis.
Robin III (Tim Drake) Athlete, Boy Wonder
Impulse Superspeedster.
Empress Amazing athlete.
Wonder Girl Flight, superstrength, bravado
The Secret Ephemeral wraith.

Superboy, Robin III and Impulse helped rescue a
mysterious girl called the Secret from custody by
the U.S. government-backed D.E.O. The teens
united as Young Justice and begin operating
out of the Justice League of America's
abandoned Secret Sanctuary. The boys
were soon joined by Arrowette, Wonder
Girl and the Secret. The team was given
the stamp of approval by the JLA, and
Red Tornado became Young Justice's mentor.

Klarion the Witch Boy cast a spell that
transformed the adult heroes into children
while having the reverse effect on the members
of Young Justice. The process was ultimately
reversed for all but Lobo, who took on the
name Slo-Bo. Young Justice journeyed to
Australia where they fought a team of villains
representing the rogue state Zandia. The
mysterious Empress joined the
team after Young Justice learned
that she was Anita, daughter of
government ally Donald Fite.
After a devastating mission to
Apokolips, Snapper Carr came
aboard as a senior member, succeeding
Red Tornado as team mentor. The Ray II also
joined Young Justice at that time.

After Baron Agua Sin Gaaz murdered Empress'
father, Young Justice led a squad of heroes in an all-out
war on his Zandian fortress. Corrupted by Darkseid,
the Secret then went on a rampage until Robin
managed to break through to her. Darkseid
punished the young warder by restoring
her humanity. He also banished Slo-Bo to
the 853rd Century, condemning him to
an eternity as a statue. A mysterious blue
cyborg-girl named Indigo did serious damage
to the Titans and Young Justice and unleashed
a defective Superman Robot which killed Teen
Titan Lilith and Troia. In a state of shock, both
teams disbanded. **RG**

TRAGIC CONCLUSION *In their final
mission, the team was devastated
when they were manhandled by
Indigo and a Superman robot and
were unable to save Troia's life.*

YOUNG WARRIORS
*Regardless of
threat, Young
Justice enters
every fray with
gusto and more
than a little
recklessness.*

YOUNG JUSTICE
1) *Superboy* **2)** *Secret*
3) *Robin III* **4)** *Wonder Girl II*
5) *Empress* **6)** *Impulse.*

RAEPPA YLLAGICAM SDRIB! Whether conjuring or teleporting, Zatanna says all of her spells backwards!

MAGIC MAN Occultist John Constantine—Zatanna's lover in college—often knocks on the sorceress's door when he needs a magical hand, or a bird, or a plane ticket…

ZATANNA

FIRST APPEARANCE HAWKMAN (1st series) #4 (November 1964)
STATUS Hero   REAL NAME Zatanna Zatara
OCCUPATION Stage magician; adventurer
BASE San Francisco
HEIGHT 5ft 7in   WEIGHT 137 lbs   EYES Blue   HAIR Black
SPECIAL POWERS/ABILITIES Genetically imbued with the ability to manipulate magic; sorcery includes elemental manipulation, transmutation, and teleportation; she says her spells backwards as an aid to concentration.

Zatanna is the daughter of Golden Age adventurer John Zatara and his wife Sindella, a member of the mystic tribe of sorcerers called the Hidden Ones, or Homo magi. Zatanna inherited her mother's ability to manipulate magic and her father's penchant for heroism. When Sindella faked her own death and returned to the Hidden Ones' sanctum in Turkey, she left her daughter to John Zatara's care.

Zatara traveled the world with his daughter and taught her to harness her magical abilities. Zatanna was later raised by strangers, however, when a curse by the witch Allura prevented Zatanna from seeing her father, leaving the young girl in a constant, fruitless search for her natural parents.

Zatanna discovered her father's diary and created a stage persona for herself. The young magician's quest to find her father led her into a brief affair with the occultist John Constantine (see Great Team-Ups, pp. 132–133). Later, with the help of the Justice League of America, Zatanna was able to lift Allura's curse and reunite with her father and, soon after, her mother. Tragically, Sindella died rescuing her daughter from the city of Homo Magi.

Zatanna's history with the JLA came back to haunt her when it became known that she had used her magic to mind-wipe many of the League's enemies, earning the mistrust of Batman, Catwoman, and others. She has since done her best to make amends. Zatanna also served with an unofficial grouping of the Seven Soldiers of Victory, helping her teammates stop an invasion by the far-future Sheeda. **PJ/DW**

ZAURIEL

FIRST APPEARANCE JLA #6 (June 1997)
STATUS Hero   REAL NAME Zauriel
OCCUPATION Adventurer   BASE The Aerie, high above Los Angeles
HEIGHT 6ft 1in   WEIGHT 180 lbs   EYES Purple and red   HAIR Silver
SPECIAL POWERS/ABILITIES Now a mortal, Zauriel retains his wings, granting him flight, but his angelic abilities, such as a sonic cry, have been reduced or removed. He can still speak to animals.

A Guardian-Angel of Heaven's Eagle-Host, Zauriel left heaven pursued by forces loyal to renegade King-Angel Asmodel. Falling to Earth, Zauriel found kindred spirits in the Justice League of America and Asmodel was routed. Zauriel kept his wings and remained on Earth. When Mageddon threatened all life, Zauriel sacrificed himself so others might live. His spirit pleaded humanity's cause in Heaven. As Mageddon neared Earth, Zauriel convinced the angels of the Pax Dei to fight for Heaven and Earth. Zauriel eventually left the JLA. After deciding that Blue Devil needed to perform penance to offset his infernal deals, Zauriel took Blue Devil's place with the Shadowpact. **RG**

ZUGGERNAUT

FIRST APPEARANCE FIRESTORM, THE NUCLEAR MAN #69 (March 1988)
STATUS Hero   REAL NAME Matvei Rodor
OCCUPATION (Rodor) black marketeer; (Zuggernaut) inapplicable
BASE Moscow, Russian Federation
HEIGHT (Rodor) 5ft 9in; (Zuggernaut) 7ft   WEIGHT (Rodor) 170 lbs; (Zuggernaut) 250 lbs   EYES (Rodor) Blue; (Zuggernaut) Red
HAIR (Rodor) Brown; (Zuggernaut) None
SPECIAL POWERS/ABILITIES Superhuman strength; leaping ability; resistance to physical injury; generation of explosive energy from its mouth and a jewel in its forehead.

The extraterrestrial creature known as the Zuggernaut crash-landed on Earth in Russia, near the dacha of black marketer Matvei Rodor. Merging its monstrous alien body with Rodor's human desires, the Zuggernaut found its way to Moscow and tried to kill one of Rodor's enemies, a prosecutor named Soliony. The Zuggernaut was driven off by the American hero FIRESTORM and resumed its human shape as Rodor.

Later, after returning once more to kill Soliony, the Zuggernaut was thwarted by Firestorm and the young superteam, SOYUZ. Firestorm used the Zuggernaut's own explosive energies against it, mortally wounding Rodor's body and causing the alien to flee. Its current whereabouts are unknown. **PJ**

ZATARA

FIRST APPEARANCE ACTION COMICS #1 (June 1938)
STATUS Hero   REAL NAME Giovanni "John" Zatara
OCCUPATION Stage magician; adventurer   BASE Washington, D.C.
HEIGHT 5ft 11in   WEIGHT 170 lbs   EYES Blue   HAIR Gray
SPECIAL POWERS/ABILITIES Limitless magic enabled by speaking his spells backward; merely an average fighter, who preferred sleight-of-hand over hand-to-hand combat.

John Zatara was a stage magician at age nineteen. However, when he read the lost journals of Leonardo da Vinci, his reputed ancestor, he discovered the true secrets of sorcery. By uttering his spells backwards, he could perform real magic! As his fame grew, Zatara also became a crime fighter, serving with the All-Star Squadron during World War II.

While traveling in Turkey, Zatara met and married the enigmatic Sindella. Sindella gave birth to Zatara's daughter, Zatanna, and seemingly died not long after. While raising Zatanna alone, Zatara battled Allura, an evil elemental who cursed father and daughter with a spell prohibiting either from seeing the other lest both be struck dead. It took Zatara years to lift the curse and be reunited with his daughter.

Zatara retired from the stage and super heroics, but answered the call to action when a primordial shadow creature from Earth's prehistory threatened to tear both Heaven and Earth asunder. Alongside warlock John Constantine, Zatanna, and a circle of several other sorcerers, Zatara engaged in a séance to help the SWAMP THING battle the creature. When the creature attempted to destroy Zatanna, Zatara cast a spell to save her from its staggering power. He died in Zatanna's place, the ancient darkness causing the master magician to spontaneously combust, incinerating him before the eyes of all in attendance. **SB**

ZOOM

PSYCHOTIC SPEEDSTER

FIRST APPEARANCE FLASH SECRET FILES #3 (November 2001)
STATUS Hero **REAL NAME** Hunter Zolomon
OCCUPATION Super-villain **BASE** Keystone City
HEIGHT 6ft 1in **WEIGHT** 181 lbs **EYES** Brown **HAIR** Brown
SPECIAL POWERS/ABILITIES Ability to travel at superspeed due a limited control of time. Zoom has essentially shifted himself to a 'faster' timeline, allowing him to surpass even the feats of speed evidenced by the current Flash, Wally West.

HEIR TO THE SINISTER LEGACY of Professor Zoom the Reverse-Flash, Hunter Zolomon was one of Flash III's closest friends before a series of tragedies ruined his life. Hunter came from a nightmarish family. His father was a serial killer, a fact that Hunter only learned when police gunned down his father for the murder of his mother. Zolomon joined the F.B.I. and found love with a fellow agent named Ashley, whom he later married. Once again, his world imploded when a shootout with a criminal called the Clown left him with a shattered kneecap and brought about the death of Ashley's father. She divorced him soon after and the F.B.I. eventually fired him.

REVERSE-FLASH Zolomon follows the bad example of Eobard Thawne, the original Prof. Zoom.

STRANGLEHOLD In his psychosis, Zoom believes that he can make the Flash a better hero by forcing him to deal with tragedy.

BAD LUCK AND TROUBLE

Desperate for even the pretense of stability, Zolomon wound up in Keystone City where he became a profiler of meta-human activities for the police department. He befriended the current Flash, Wally West, but his position with the K.C.P.D. made him a target for super-villains. An assault on Keystone by Gorilla Grodd left Zolomon with a broken back.

Now a paraplegic, Zolomon felt his only recourse was to beg the Flash to use the Cosmic Treadmill from the Flash Museum to travel back in time and prevent the calamities that had led to this point. Although sympathetic to his friend's plight, the Flash refused to alter time. Zolomon decided to do it himself. The resulting explosion of the Cosmic Treadmill shifted him onto a different frame of relative time, allowing him to move at superspeed by controlling time's passage. With new powers and threadbare sanity, Zolomon decided to teach the Flash a lesson about tragedy. He donned a costume similar to the one worn by the deceased Reverse-Flash and christened himself Zoom. Zoom attacked Wally West's family, causing Wally's wife Linda (see Park, Linda) to miscarry twins. Wally battled the mad monster at superspeed, ringing the globe before trapping Zoom in a repeating window of time, where he was forced to witness his disastrous shootout with the Clown again and again.

In the aftermath, Wally wished that he could protect his family by having everyone forget his secret identity—a request granted by the Spectre. **DW**

TRAGIC EFFECTS Zoom's vicious attack on Linda Park caused her to miscarry twin babies.

LUNACY Zoom is now stuck in a time loop, which should only unravel his sanity even further.

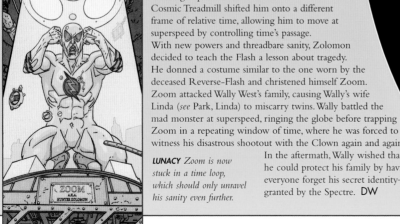

KEY STORYLINES

- **FLASH SECRET FILES #3 (NOVEMBER 2001):** Hunter Zolomon makes his first appearance in these pages, which barely hint at his villainous future.
- **THE FLASH: BLITZ (TPB, 2004):** This trade paperback, reprinting Flash issues #192-200, is the definitive collection of the Zoom saga. By the time this series had finished its run, the status quo had been upended and Wally West had embarked on a new, controversial direction.

STRANGE TIMES AND PLACES

IN ELSEWORLDS, heroes and villains are taken from their usual, familiar settings and thrust into alternate worlds, divergent timelines, or parallel realities. Some are strange forgotten times that have existed or histories that might have been. Others are places that can't, couldn't, or *shouldn't* exist. Origins begin at divergent points and the outcomes of major crises may vary dramatically. And in all these imaginary stories made real, it all begins with the question, "What if…?"

WONDER WOMAN: AMAZONIA
In another reality, Diana is stolen away from paradise by Steve Trevor and the Royal Air Marines of the 19th-century British Empire. Forced to marry the vile Trevor, Diana becomes the star of a London show, reenacting tales of heroic women immortalized in the Bible. She shows herself to be a true heroine, freeing oppressed women all over the Empire, from the terrible reign of King Jack Planters, alias Jack the Ripper!

KINGDOM COME
This futuristic, apocalyptic tale begins in the Kansas wheat fields. A battle between the Justice Battalion and the villain Parasite results in Captain Atom's death and his nuclear energies lay waste to America's heartland. As a disillusioned Superman retreats into seclusion, a new generation of meta-humans—the uncontrollable sons and daughters of the world's greatest super heroes—inherits the Earth. Unfortunately, without Superman and his contemporaries to guide them, these super-menaces might well herald Armageddon. As witnessed by a holy man and his spiritual guide, the Spectre, Superman must embrace his role as leader and unite the divided super-heroes lest his adopted world be torn asunder. The fate of all mankind is in the balance.

THE DARK KNIGHT RETURNS
Batman has retired, leaving Gotham in need of a hero as the Mutants, a nihilistic street gang, threaten to overrun the city. When Harvey Dent returns to his old criminal ways as the deranged Two-Face, the Dark Knight returns, with a new Robin—teenager Carrie Kelly—flying at his side. Desperate times call for desperate measures, and a darker Caped Crusader takes back Gotham City street by street, battling the Joker one last time. In "Crime Alley," Batman makes his final stand against his enemies, the Last Son of Krypton chief among them, as man and Superman decide the Dark Knight's destiny.

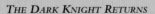

GRIEF-STRICKEN
On the devastated Kansas plains, Superman tends the graves of the victims of an accidental atomic holocaust.

LAST SON OF EARTH
Rocketed to distant Krypton from the dying planet Earth, baby Clark Kent is adopted by the scientist Jor-El and renamed Kal-El. Clad in a cumbersome exoskeleton to counter Krypton's oppressive gravity, Kal-El's discovery of a dead Green Lantern's power ring frees him to walk unfettered upon Kryptonian soil before journeying to the planet of his birth in search of his origins. There, amid the ragtag survivors of the blasted world, Clark meets the love of his life, Lois Lane (right), and his greatest foe, Lex Luthor!

BLOODSTORM

In a Gotham City where vampires rule the underworld, Batman is a bloodsucking monster who hunts those like him! Sating his own bloodlust to cleanse Gotham, Batman finds his undead foes united by the Clown Prince of Crime. Batman's only ally is doomed were-Catwoman Selina Kyle. One-by-one, Batman slays his immortal foes and bathes Gotham in red rain until only one is left. In the end, the Dark Knight knows that the killing might begin anew if a single vampire remains. Commissioner Gordon and Alfred (see Pennyworth, Alfred) have little choice but to drive a stake through the heart of Batman, bringing him the peace he has long sought.

SUPERMAN: RED SON

What if Kal-El of Krypton had landed on an agricultural collective in the Soviet Union rather than a farm in Kansas? Earth's greatest hero would fight for truth, justice, and the *Russian* way of a life as the Soviets' most powerful secret weapon! What follows is an arms race of unparalleled intensity as the U.S. commissions its greatest scientist, the brilliant Lex Luthor (see Luthor, Lex), to tilt the balance of power in America's favor. The world stands on the brink of annihilation as Superman assumes leadership of the Soviet Union, bidding to unite the planet under Communism.

THE BIG RED With a hammer and sickle emblazoned on his chest, Superman is a propaganda tool of the Stalinist regime. But the Man of Steel cares only for helping his fellow man, regardless of politics or nationality.

SECRET WEAPONS The U.S.'s elite troops are the Green Lantern Marine Corps, led by Hal Jordan.

JLA: THE NAIL

Imagine a world without the Man of Steel. On an Earth resembling the DC Universe in every way—with all its requisite heroes and villains save one—for want of a nail Superman was lost. When infant Kal-El's rocket plummeted to Earth, Jonathan and Martha Kent missed their fateful rendezvous with the Last Son of Krypton because of a flat tire… all for want of a nail. Instead, Kal-El was adopted by an Amish family and never ventured forth from his rural backwater to become a hero. That is, until an evil regime outlawed all meta-humans and tried to drive the planet's heroes into imprisonment or extinction. The plains of Kansas become the scene of the final battle between a power-mad Jimmy Olsen (see Olsen, Jimmy) and what remains of the world's greatest super heroes.

DOUBLE HIT Batman battles the Joker—given staggering power by Jimmy Olsen—and Olsen finally meets his match when Kal-El of Krypton saves humanity (right)!

AT EARTH'S END

Welcome to the Earth after disaster! It is one year since a bearded and remarkably long-lived Superman helped the young humans Kamandi, Saphira, Sleeper Zom, and the cyborg Ben Boxer to defeat the maniacal Mother Machine, cause of Earth's second apocalypse. When Boxer targets Gotham City for destruction, Superman flies to Batman's old stomping ground armed to the teeth to aid a band of youths and free the remains of Bruce Wayne, alias Batman, from the DNA Dictators!

199

INDEX

ACKNOWLEDGMENTS

SCOTT BEATTY would like to thank his editors Chris Cerasi, Alastair Dougall, and Laura Gilbert for their enduring patience. Thanks also to fellow writers Bob Greenberger, Phil Jimenez, and Dan Wallace for always watching my back. Additional gratitude goes to Ed Brubaker, Joey Cavalieri, Chuck Dixon, Devin Grayson, Scott McCullar, Jerry Ordway, Greg Rucka, Gail Simone, and Michael Wright for helping to ply the choppy waters of comic book continuity. Finally, special thanks to Jennifer Myskowski, my first and best reader, and Wilbur, a dog's dog and source of endless distraction.

BOB GREENBERGER would like to thank John Wells (first and foremost, much of this book wouldn't be this good without him).

PHIL JIMENEZ would like to thank the writers and artists who created the DC Universe with their talent and imagination; few places feel so much like home. I'd also like to thank Chris Cerasi for the hot fruit, the Diablo Dogs, and the grape sodie; Alastair Dougall for actually reading my hundreds of e-mails, even the ones about Tempest; and as ever, George Pérez, for without his influence on my work I'd never have had a career. And finally, a nod to Neal Pozner, a decade after his death, for so much, to Jack Mahan, for taking care of me for so long, and to Joe Hosking, for just about everything.

DAN WALLACE would like to thank DC Comics' Chris Cerasi for his unceasing cheer and for bringing him on board to play in the biff-bam-sockiest fictional universe ever created; his co-writers Phil Jimenez, Scott Beatty, and Bob Greenberger for producing such great work and for supplying arcane bits of DC lore; DK's Alastair Dougall and Laura Gilbert for always coming through at the eleventh hour; Kelly, Andrew, Grant, and Emma for their love and support; Detroit's own Time Travelers Comics and Books for their back-issue bins, and Jerry Siegel and Joe Shuster for birthing a genre. Thanks also to the Absorbascon, Again With the Comics, AICN, Alert Nerd, Beaucoup Kevin, Blockade Boy, Bully, the Comic Treadmill, the ISB, Dave's Long Box, Doomkopf, Living Between Wednesdays, Polite Dissent, Progressive Ruin, Second Printing, and the rest of the comics blogging community.

DORLING KINDERSLEY WOULD LIKE TO THANK THE FOLLOWING AT DC COMICS:
Emily Ryan Lerner, Bob Joy, John Morgan, Andrea Shochet, Marc Bolling, Chris Cerasi, Paul Levitz, Steve Korté, Georg Brewer, Allan Asherman, Triss Stein, Roger Bonas, Anton Kawasaki, Ivan Cohen, Kilian Plunkett, Patrick Gleason, Christian Alamy, Carla Johnson, Demetri Detsaridis, and Richard Callender. And of course Scott Beatty, Bob Greenberger, Phil Jimenez, and Dan Wallace.

DORLING KINDERSLEY WOULD ALSO LIKE TO THANK THE FOLLOWING:
Nick Avery, Dan Bunyan, Lisa Crowe and Sandra Perry for additional design assistance.
Julia March and Kate Simkins for editorial assistance,
and Ann Barrett for the index.

ARTIST ACKNOWLEDGMENTS

Contains material previously published in *The DC Comics Encyclopedia*, which contains illustrations from the following artists:

Dusty Abell, Jerry Acerno, David Acuña, Arthur Adams, Neal Adams, Dan Adkins, Charlie Adlard, Kalman Adrasofsky, Ian Akin, Christian Alamy, Gerry Alanguilan, Oclair Albert, Jeff Albrecht, Alfredo Alcala, Alcatena, Michael Allred, Bob Almond, Marlo Alquiza, Sal Amandola, Brent Anderson, Murphy Anderson, Ross Andru, Jim Aparo, Jason Armstrong, Tom Artis, Stan Asch, Derec Aucoin, Terry Austin, Brandon Badeaux, Mark Badger, Bernard Baily, Michael Bair, Kyle Baker, Jim Balent, Darryl Banks, Matt Banning, Carlo Barberi, Dell Barras, Mike Barreiro, Eduardo Barreto, Al Barrionuevo, Sy Barry, Hilary Barta, Chris Batista, Eric Battle, John Beatty, Terry Beatty, C.C. Beck, Howard Bender, Scott Benefield, Ed Benes, Mariah Benes, Joe Benitez, Joe Bennett, Ramon Bernado, D. Bruce Berry, Simone Bianchi, Jack Binder, J.J. Birch, Steve Bird, Simon Bisley, Stephen Bissette, Bit, Fernando Blanco, Greg Blocks, Bret Blevins, Will Blyberg, Jon Bogdanove, Brian Bolland, Philip Bond, Richard Bonk, Wayne Boring, John Bolton, Ron Boyd, Belardin Brabo, Craig Brasfield, Ken Branch, Brett Breeding, Ryan Breeding, Jeff Brennan, Norm Breyfogle, Mark Bright, June Brightman, Pat Broderick, Greg Brooks, Joe Brozowski, Mark Buckingham, Rich Buckler, Danny Bulanadi, Rick Burchett, Ray Burnley, Sal Buscema, Buzz, Mitch Byrd, John Byrne, Ralph Cabrera, Jim Calafiore, Talent Caldwell, Robert Campanella, Marc Campos, W.C. Carani, Nick Cardy, Sergio Cariello, Richard Case, John Cassaday, Anthony Castrillo, John Cebollero, Dennis Calero, Joe Certa, Gary Chaloner, Keith Champagne, Travis Charest, Howard Chaykin, Michael Chen, Jim Cheung, Cliff Chiang, Tom Chiu, Ian Churchill, Matthew Clark, Mike Clark, Andy Clarke, Dave Cockrum, Olivier Coipel, Gene Colan, Jack Cole, Simon Coleby, Hector Collazo, Vince Colletta, Bill Collins, Mike Collins, Ernie Colon, Amanda Conner, Kevin Conrad, Darwyn Cooke, Pete Costanza, Denys Cowan, Dennis Cramer, Reed Crandall, Saleen Crawford, Steve Crespo, Jake Crippen, Chriss Cross, Charles Cuidera, Paris Cullins, Rodolfo Damaggio, Antonio Daniel, Alan Davis, Dan Davis, Ed Davis, Shane Davis, Francisco Rodriguez De La Fuente, Sam De La Rosa, Mike DeCarlo, Nelson DeCastro, Randy DeBurke, Nuzio DeFilippis, Adam Dekraker, Jose Delbo, John Dell, Luciana del Negro, Jesse Delperdang, J.M. DeMatteis, Mike Deodato, Jr., Tom Derenick, Stephen DeStefano, Tony Dezuniga, Dick Dillin, Steve Dillon, Steve Ditko, Rachel Dodson, Terry Dodson, Colleen Doran, Evan Dorkin, Les Dorscheid, Alberto Dose, Bob Downs, Mike Dringenberg, Armando Durruthy, Jan Duursema, Bob Dvorak, Kieron Dwyer, Joshua Dysart, Dale Eaglesham, Scot Eaton, Marty Egeland, Lee Elias, Chris Eliopulos, Randy Emberlin, Steve Epting, Steve Erwin, Mike Esposito, Ric Estrada, George Evans, Rich Faber, Mark Farmer, Wayne Faucher, Duncan Fegredo, Tom Feister, Jim Fern, Pascual Ferry, John Fischetti, Creig Flessel, John Floyd, John Ford, John Forte, Tom Fowler, Ramona Fradon, Gary Frank, Frank Frazetta, Fred Fredericks, George Freeman, Ron Frenz, Richard Friend, James Fry, Anderson Gabrych, Kerry Gammill, German Garcia, José Luis García-Lopéz, Ron Garney, Brian Garvey, Roy Garvey, Alé Garza, Gabrynch Garza, Carlos Garzon, Stefano Gaudiano, Drew Geraci, Frank Giacoia, Vince Giarrano, Dave Gibbons, Joe Giella, Keith Giffen, Michael T. Gilbert, Craig Gilmore, Dick Giordano, Sam Glanzman, Jonathan Glapion, Patrick Gleason, Frank Gomez, Fernando Gonzales, Jason Gorder, Al Gordon, Chris Gordon, Sam Grainger, Jerry Grandinetti, Mick Gray, Dan Green, Sid Greene, Mike Grell, Tom Grindberg, Peter Gross, Tom Grummett, Fred Guardineer, Renato Guedes, Butch Guice, Yvel Guichet, Paul Guinan, Mike Gustovich, Matt Haley, Craig Hamilton, Cully Hamner, Scott Hampton, Scott Hanna, Ed Hannigan, Norwood Steven Harris, Ron Harris, Tony Harris, Irwin Hasen, Fred Haynes, Doug Hazlewood, Russ Heath, Don Heck, Marc Hempel, Andrew Hennessy, Phil Hester, Everett E. Hibbard, Bryan Hitch, Rick Hoberg, James Hodgkins, Josh Hood, Ken Hooper, Dave Hoover, Alex Horley, Richard Howell, Tan Eng Huat, Mike Huddleston, Adam Hughes, Dave Hunt, Jamal Igle, Stuart Immonen, Carmine Infantino, Frazer Irving, Geoff Isherwood, Chris Ivy, Jack Jadson, Dennis Janke, Klaus Janson, Dennis Jensen, Oscar Jimenez, Phil Jimenez, Geoff Johns, Dave Johnson, Drew Johnson, Staz Johnson, Arvell Jones, Casey Jones, J.G. Jones, Kelley Jones, Malcolm Jones III, Arnie Jorgensen, Ruy José, Dan Jurgens, Justiano, Barbara Kaalberg, John Kalisz, Michael Kaluta, Bob Kane, Gil Kane, Kano, Rafael Kayanan, Stan Kaye, Dale Keown, Karl Kerschl, Karl Kesel, Kinsun, Jack Kirby, Leonard Kirk, Barry Kitson, Scott Kolins, Don Kramer, Peter Krause, Ray Kryssing, Andy Kubert, Joe Kubert, Andy Kuhn, Alan Kupperberg, Harry Lampert, Greg Land, Justin Land, Andy Lanning, David Lapham, Serge LaPointe, Michael Lark, Greg Larocque, Bud Larosa, Salvador Larroca, Erik Larsen, Ken Lashley, Bob Layton, Rob Lea, Jim Lee, Norman Lee, Paul Lee, Alex Lei, Steve Leialoha, Rob Leigh, Jay Leisten, Rick Leonardi, Bob Lewis, Mark Lewis, Steve Lieber, Rob Liefeld, Steve Lightle, Mark Lipka, Victor Llamas, Loh Kin Sun, Don Lomax, Alvaro Lopez, David Lopez, Aaron Lopresti, John Lowe, Greg Luzniak, Tom Lyle, Mike Machlan, Dev Madan, Kevin Maguire, Rick Magyar, Larry Mahlstedt, Doug Mahnke, Alex Maleev, Tom Mandrake, Mike Manley, Lou Manna, Pablo Marcos, Bill Marimon, Cindy Martin, Cynthia Martin, Gary Martin, Marcos Martin, Shawn Martinbrough, Kenny Martinez, Roy Allan Martinez, Marco Marz, José Marzan, Jr., Nathan Massengill, William Messner–Loebs, Rick Mays, Trevor McCarthy, Tom McCraw, John McCrea, Scott McDaniel, Luke McDonnell, Todd McFarlane, Ed McGuinness, Dave McKean, Mark McKenna, Mike McKone, Frank McLaughlin, Bob McLeod, Shawn McManus, Leonardo Manco, Marcus Marz, Lan Medina, Paco Medina, Linda Medley, Carlos Meglia, David Meikis, Adriana Melo, Jaime Mendoza, Jesus Merino, J.D. Mettler, Pop Mhan, Grant Miehm, Mike Mignola, Danny Miki, Al Milgrom, Frank Miller, Mike S. Miller, Steve Mitchell, Lee Moder, Sheldon Moldoff, Shawn Moll, Steve Montano, Jim Mooney, Jerome Moore, Marcio Morais, Mark Morales, Rags Morales, Ruben Moreira, Gray Morrow, Win Mortimer, Jeffrey Moy, Phil Moy, Brian Murray, Todd Nauck, Paul Neary, Rudy Nebres, Mark Nelson, Denis Neville, Dustin Nguyen, Tom Nguyen, Art Nichols, Troy Nixey, Cary Nord, Graham Nolan, Irv Novick, Kevin Nowlan, Todd Nauck, John Nyberg, Bob Oksner, Patrick Oliffe, Ariel Olivetti, Jerry Ordway, Joe Orlando, Richard Pace, Carlos Pacheco, Mark Pajarillo, Tom Palmer, Jimmy Palmiotti, Peter Palmiotti, Dan Panosian, George Papp, Yanick Paquette, Francisco Paronzini, Ande Parks, Mike Parobeck, Sean Parsons, Fernando Pasarin, James Pascoe, Bruce Patterson, Chuck Patten, Jason Pearson, Paul Pelletier, Mark Pennington, Andrew Pepoy, George Pérez, Mike Perkins, Frank Perry, Harry G. Peter, Bob Petrecca, Joe Phillips, Wendy Pini, Al Plastino, Kilian Plunkett, Keith Pollard, Adam Pollina, Francis Portela, Howard Porter, Howie Post, Eric Powell, Joe Prado, Miguelanxo Prado, Mark Propst, Javier Pulido, Jack Purcell, Joe Quesada, Frank Quitely, Mac Raboy, Pablo Raimondi, Elton Ramalho, Humberto Ramos, Rodney Ramos, Ron Randall, Tom Raney, Rich Rankin, Norm Rapmund, Ivan Reis, Cliff Richards, Roy Richardson, Robin Riggs, Eduardo Risso, Paul Rivoche, Trina Robbins, Clem Robins, Andrew Robinson, Jerry Robinson, Roger Robinson, Denis Rodier, Anibal Rodriguez, Danny Rodriguez, Jasen Rodriguez, Rodin Rodriguez, Marshall Rogers, Prentis Rollins, T.G. Rollins, William Rosado, Alex Ross, Dave Ross, Luke Ross, Duncan Rouleau, Craig Rousseau, George Roussos, Stephane Roux, Jim Royal, Mike Royer, Josef Rubinstein, Steve Rude, P. Craig Russell, Vince Russell, Paul Ryan, Bernard Sachs, Stephen Sadowski, Jesus Saiz, Tim Sale, Javier Saltares, Chris Samnee, Jose Sanchez, Medina Sanchez, Clement Sauve, Jr., Alex Saviuk, Kurt Schaffenberger, Mitch Schauer, Christie Scheele, Damion Scott, Nicola Scott, Trevor Scott, Bart Sears, Mike Sekowsky, Mike Sellers, Val Semeiks, Eric Shanower, Hal Sharp, Howard Sherman, Howard M. Shum, Joe Shuster, Jon Sibal, Bill Sienkiewicz, , Dave Simons, Tom Simmons, Walter Simonson, Howard Simpson, Alex Sinclair, Paulo Siqueira, Louis Small, Jr., Andy Smith, Bob Smith, Cam Smith, Dietrich Smith, Jeff Smith, Todd Smith, Peter Snejbjerg, Ray Snyder, Ryan Sook, Aaron Sowd, Dan Spiegle, Chris Sprouse, Claude St. Aubin, John Stanisci, Joe Staton, Jim Starlin, Arne Starr, Rick Stasi, John Statema, Joe Staton, Ken Steacy, Brian Stelfreeze, Dave Stevens, Cameron Stewart, Roger Stewart, John Stokes, Karl Story, Larry Stroman, Lary Stucker, Rob Stull, Tom Sutton, Curt Swan, Bryan Talbot, Romeo Tanghal, Christopher Taylor, Ty Templeton, Greg Theakston, Art Thibert, Frank Thorne, Alex Toth, John Totleben, Tim Truman, Chaz Truog, Dwayne Turner, Michael Turner, George Tuska, Angel Unzueta, Juan Valasco, Ethan Van Sciver, Rick Veitch, Sal Velluto, Charles Vess, Al Vey, Carlos Villagran, Ricardo Villagran, José Villarrubia, Dexter Vines, Juan Vlasco, Trevor Von Eeden, Wade Von Grawbadger, Matt Wagner, Brad Walker, Kev Walker, Chip Wallace, Bill Wray, Lee Weeks, Alan Weiss, Kevin J. West, Chris Weston, Doug Wheatley, Mark Wheatley, Glenn Whitmore, Bob Wiacek, Mike Wieringo, Anthony Williams, J. H. Williams III, Scott Williams, Bill Willingham, Phil Winslade, Chuck Wojtkiewicz, Walden Wong, Pete Woods, John Workman, Moe Worthman, Chris Wozniak, Bill Wray, Jason Wright, Berni Wrightson, Tom Yeates, Steve Yeowell, Leinil Francis Yu.